I0820047

PRESERVING THE LEGACY

PRESERVING THE LEGACY

CREATING THE NATIONAL WWII MUSEUM

GORDON H. “NICK” MUELLER

Foreword by TOM BROKAW

LOUISIANA STATE UNIVERSITY PRESS
BATON ROUGE

Published by Louisiana State University Press
lsupress.org

Manufactured in the United States of America
First printing

Designer: Barbara Neely Bourgoyne
Typeface: Calluna
Printer and binder: Sheridan Books

Jacket image: American assault troops in a landing craft off the northern coast of France on June 6, 1944. Courtesy U.S. Army Center of Military History.

Frontispiece: "From the crest of Mount Suribachi, the Stars and Stripes waves in triumph over Iwo Jima after US Marines fought their way inch by inch up its steep lava-encrusted slopes," February 1945. Records of the US Coast Guard, Record Group 26, National Archives and Records Administration.

Cataloging-in-Publication Data are available from the Library of Congress.
ISBN 978-0-8071-8449-3 (cloth: alk. paper) — ISBN 978-0-8071-8483-7 (pdf) — ISBN 978-0-8071-8482-0 (epub)

in memory

of

STEPHEN E. AMBROSE

★

1936–2002

CONTENTS

FOREWORD

THIS IS A STORY of two friends, historians, who had an enlightened view of what America deserved in its postwar years.

In the late 1980s, Stephen Ambrose, PhD, was already a well-known historian, the author of highly regarded books about World War II and American presidents. His comrade and fellow historian at the University of New Orleans was Gordon H. "Nick" Mueller, PhD.

At the end of many a workday, they would pour drinks and talk about "what next?" For historians of their generation, the answer was easy: World War II. The greatest war in the history of mankind. More than 65 million died in the brutal conflict, fought on land, in the air and at sea, and around the globe, including Asia, Europe, North and South America, and on little-known atolls in the Pacific.

Together, Ambrose and Mueller decided that America needed a defining history of World War II and that New Orleans would be the perfect spot for it. Not only was it a major tourist destination, it was also the home of the Higgins boat, the innovative landing craft that changed the whole strategy of amphibious warfare in World War II.

These landing craft, designed by New Orleans boatbuilder Andrew Jackson Higgins, made it possible to carry 36 combat infantrymen ashore against enemy-defended beaches. The Higgins boats were key to the D-Day invasion of Normandy in 1944 and were especially effective in the Pacific, with its polka-dot array of small islands fortified by the Japanese Imperial forces.

The two friends got some early seed money from Congress, and, with the help of local organizers who found space in the New Orleans warehouse district, they began to plan a permanent tribute to WWII veterans from all the branches—including the sailors, soldiers, airmen, and Marines who fought on land, in the air, and at sea, as well as the nurses and doctors who cared for the wounded and the factory workers who supported them on the home front.

Mueller and Ambrose were super visionaries, overseeing a tribute to the memory of the generation that fought the epic battles for the survival of democracy against global fascism in the mid-twentieth century.

The Museum and its exhibits began to take shape with very generous help from the state of Louisiana and leadership of local New Orleans business interests, who transformed a rundown warehouse district into a magnificent new neighborhood that became a mecca for tourists. The Grand Opening of the National D-Day Museum on June 6, 2000, was a spectacular multiday event for the ages. For those of us in on the beginning, it was a dazzling start. We did not realize it was a prelude.

An amazing array of WWII equipment was on display, including fighter planes suspended from the ceiling. In another section featuring live entertainment, the Museum's version of the Andrews Sisters—dressed in WWII wardrobes—belted out songs from that era. The event was filled with prominent New Orleans business families, local and national celebrities, and leaders of federal, state, and city governments, including Secretary of Defense William Cohen. Hollywood was there, too, including Director Steven Spielberg, hot off his *Saving Private Ryan* movie about D-Day, and Tom Hanks, the movie's star. We all spoke, but on this occasion, the real attractions were the WWII veterans and Medal of Honor recipients in attendance.

The star was a WWII veteran, Hal Baumgarten of the 29th Infantry Division, who was grievously wounded on D-Day. At the gala dinner the night before the grand opening, Baumgarten described how he was hit shortly after crawling ashore on Omaha Beach. From his face-down position, he could see a German sniper on the upper ridge of the landing site, zeroing in on arriving Americans. From his prone position, Hal took aim at the German sniper and killed him with one shot. He then made it to a higher ridge and signaled for American help. He was picked up and taken to a rescue boat, where he made a vow: when the war was over, he would go to medical school and spend his life saving lives, not taking them. After he finished his harrowing account, the room was dead quiet. I whispered to Hanks, "Well, we're just the supporting cast today." This was a special moment for the American Spirit and foretold a bright future for the new attraction in New Orleans.

The D-Day Museum was off to a memorable start. Mueller and Ambrose had turned afternoon drinks ten years earlier into a fabulous, permanent tribute to the Greatest Generation, and this was just the beginning. They continued to expand the Museum, and before long it occupied three city blocks. With a big push from these two friends, it was soon designated by Congress as The National WWII Museum in New Orleans.

Unfortunately, Ambrose died before his dream could be fully realized. His funeral in 2002 became a touching salute to his vision, with a large crowd of VIPs flying in for the ceremony, including George McGovern, the former South Dakota senator and presidential candidate, who as a B-24 Liberator bomber pilot during World War II saved his crew by skillfully crashing landing the plane.

Mueller and the Museum team moved forward with a stunning expansion plan, but it nearly died at creation when devastating Hurricane Katrina nearly destroyed much of the city of New Orleans in 2005. Mueller and his courageous board led an amazing recovery and opened the Museum's first pavilion, a testimony to persistence and survival. As he told the board after the hurricane, "It's not as bad as D-Day, no one is shooting at us, so let's get this Museum built."

Soon, the Museum became a favorite New Orleans destination, unrivaled in America for its unique message, its mind-blowing array of WWII artifacts—including submarines, fighter planes, and machine gun displays—and riveting eyewitness accounts amid immersive media. Prominent New Orleans businessmen, national donors, and trustees, with exceptional leadership from the governor and state legislature all stepped up and took the Museum to impressive new levels of wartime experiences that lifted it to one of the top three museums in America. Quite a feat.

I know of no other history museum of such scale and importance to have been initiated and sustained by the private sector, much less by two historians. All such museums in the world are funded by national governments, with the stories of World War II told through the lens of their official public narratives. Not so in New Orleans; Mueller gathered top WWII historians to help shape the exhibits, and he and his team developed special programs featuring WWII veterans, notable national citizens, and great American writers and historians, among them David McCullough.

New Orleans, known for the French Quarter, Mardi Gras, and dancing in the streets, is now the home for this salute to the heroism and sacrifice, the triumph and conquest, and the pride and legacy of the WWII generation. As Nick tells the unlikely story of this remarkable Museum's creation, historians led the way, just as the Rangers who scaled the cliffs at Pointe du Hoc on D-Day.

Two historians sitting together, sharing drinks one lazy afternoon in New Orleans, made an enduring contribution to history and pride, sacrifice, and courage of America at her best.

—**TOM BROKAW**

PREFACE

HISTORY, LIKE ART, is concerned with the performance of factual content. The best history museums tell stories visually; in addition to historical records, they rely on art and design to move the audience to the heart of the historical experience, to make it personal, meaningful, and authentic. The National World War II Museum—and this book—aspire to the highest levels of that performance.

Preserving the Legacy—part memoir, part narrative history—relies on primary and secondary historical sources, among them the Museum's institutional records, WWII oral histories, government documents, newspaper articles, images, and artifacts. The story, naturally, is viewed through the lens of my memory. I recount some private events and conversations for which there is no historical record other than my memory. Those moments were often the ones most critical to building The National WWII Museum and remain seared in my memory. To incorporate the memories of others, I interviewed many people who were on this journey, including key board members, major donors, and government leaders who protected the integrity of our exhibits and historical accounts. These interviews and historical records helped shape the collective memory of the Museum's creation as well as its historical narrative and America's memory of the war. This approach, I hope, breathes life into the story while adhering to high standards of scholarship. It enabled me to produce the fullest account I can of the creation of The National WWII Museum, including the American experience of the war and the enduring legacy that changed America and the world.

PRESERVING THE LEGACY

1

THE IDEA

There at the Creation

IT WAS AN unusually warm evening in late fall 1989 when Stephen Ambrose and I got together for drinks, our weekly routine, to brainstorm new trips or professional plans. This day was different. Steve had a determined look in his eyes as he poured me a glass of cheap sherry. It was the same drink every time. “Sit down Nick. I have an idea you will like.” I had a feeling that this idea was going to be important. We had schemed up many ideas this way in the past, and we had a record of doing exciting things together—both on and off campus. Regardless, I was not ready for what Steve said next: “We’re going to build a small D-Day Museum.”

We would build this Museum in New Orleans, he informed me, on land where the university planned to develop a Research Park, a project I oversaw as Vice Chancellor. Steve had been working for years on a book about D-Day, and he had collected hundreds of firsthand accounts from veterans, along with artifacts they had given him connected to their personal stories. “These artifacts are golden,” he told me. “I don’t know how to take care of them. So, I need a small museum.” These invaluable veterans’ eyewitness accounts needed to be preserved in a place where future generations could hear them, Steve insisted.

No museum in the United States honored the men who fought and died on D-Day, he complained. “Congress is never going to build a D-Day Museum or a World War II Museum in Washington, DC,” he said. “I know, because I’ve tried everything to convince friends in Congress that they should build a museum to honor them, save their stories, and their deeds before they all die. They keep telling me, 'Great idea, Steve, it should happen but never will.' So, I say, screw 'em, we'll build it right here in New Orleans."

Steve was on a roll and would not let me interrupt. He brought up a story about one of his favorite historical figures from D-Day, Brig. Gen. Theodore Roosevelt Jr., the eldest son of the president, who served as the bold assistant commander of the 4th Infantry Division at Normandy. "Just like General Teddy Roosevelt said on Utah Beach on D-Day when he discovered his troops had landed in the wrong place, 'We'll start the war from right here.'"[1] Steve said this with such emphasis that he almost looked like Roosevelt himself on the beach.

The research for his D-Day history was complete, Steve told me, and he was ready to start writing. The book would be published in five years, in time for the fiftieth anniversary of D-Day on June 6, 1994. We needed the Museum finished by then, too, he said.

By now, I could not hold back. "Steve, that's the best damn idea you've ever had," I said. "I'm in. Let's do it!"

My enthusiasm encouraged Steve to amp up the passion of his argument. We knew that American popular memory held D-Day as arguably the most decisive battle of World War II. We considered it the pivot point of the twentieth century in the struggle of the forces of democracy, which before World War II appeared weak and mired in deep depression, against the rising threat of fascist and communist dictatorships. Steve's research at Normandy deepened his understanding of what an extraordinary military operation D-Day was as had his interviews with veterans and his tours with them retracing their steps. There was no question about the importance of telling the D-Day story in a national museum—or why the two of us should do it.

Our conversation shifted quickly to less obvious reasons for building the Museum in New Orleans instead of the nation's capital. Steve already envisioned how the Museum could work in tandem with the university's Eisenhower Center for Leadership Studies, one of our collaborative projects, created six years earlier. The center supported research into World War II, including Steve's interviews with veterans, but was housed in a cramped spare classroom. The center, Steve declared, "Needs a home, and what better place for the center than within a D-Day Museum located in the Research Park property that fronts Lake Pontchartrain?" Steve added, "It's university land, you're in charge of it, and it's free."

That land, Steve reminded me, was more than just a convenient spot to house a museum. New Orleans was home to the Higgins boats, the famous landing craft used by the D-Day invasion forces. Andrew Higgins, a local boatbuilder, used the beach at the Lake Pontchartrain property to test the design of a landing craft with a bow that lowered to offload troops. Satisfied with the results, Higgins put 30,000 men and women to work in seven manufacturing plants in New Orleans to build over 20,000 landing craft. Andrew Higgins, Eisenhower once told Steve, "Is the man who won the war for us."[2]

The landing beach on the property was a historic site, Steve pointed out. "Higgins is the most forgotten hero on the WWII Home Front," he said, with not a street or school in the country named after him. "So, we will recognize him for his achievements, as well as the men who stormed the beaches of Normandy in his boats on D-Day."

This was the launch of the National D-Day Museum. By the third glass of sherry, our enthusiasm knew no bounds. We immediately began to discuss the next steps, which meant, of course, raising money. But first there were questions: How big would the Museum need to be, how much would it cost, and where would we get the funds? Steve's initial gambit was to propose a very modest Museum with exhibits and offices for the Eisenhower Center. "It shouldn't cost more than a million dollars, and we can open on the 50th anniversary of D-Day on June 6, 1994, to coincide with the publication of my book," he said. I countered quickly. "Steve, you are so naïve about these things; it's going to cost at least 4 million."

"Impossible, we could never raise that kind of money," Steve replied.

Obviously, neither one of us had any idea what we were doing. We knew nothing about building a museum. We did not even know what we did not know, which in our case was a lot. What we did know was that this was a big idea and, despite our naivete, we felt confident we could overcome the challenges before us. Even my seemingly high estimate of $4 million was not too daunting.

Steve was among the first to realize that public interest in World War II was growing as the aging veterans began sharing memories about the war. Until the mid-1980s, many veterans did not want to talk about the war at all. They wanted to forget it and loathed speaking about their wartime experiences to their wives, kids, or even fellow veterans. They wanted to put the war behind them and did not clamor for any recognition, much less a museum.

After frequently speaking with veterans on his D-Day tours, as well as for the oral histories he collected, Steve knew that they had meaningful stories to tell. He knew this history from the top down because he had written numerous books on World War II, including *Supreme Commander: War Years of General Dwight Eisenhower.* Steve had been the associate editor of the 21-volume collection of books called *The Papers of Dwight David Eisenhower,* and he published a two-volume biography on Eisenhower's life as a soldier, general, and president. Now, he had the oral histories of the citizen soldiers to add authenticity and weight to justify the need for a repository for their personal accounts.

Steve had always admired *The Longest Day,* Cornelius Ryan's classic history of D-Day, written in 1961. His epiphany on the need for a new account came in 1983, when he led a D-Day tour and was stunned by the growing number of WWII veterans and their sons and daughters who were traveling to Normandy. The following year, on June 6, 1984, Steve was emotionally and intellectually moved by President Ronald Reagan's stirring speech at Pointe du Hoc before the assembled Rangers of the 2nd Ranger Battalion, who scaled those cliffs on D-Day.

Steve was hooked. From 1983 onward, he believed that the 50th anniversary was going to be huge, and he wanted to write the best seller for the occasion. He sensed, perhaps before anyone, that D-Day and World War II were going to gain mainstream attention in the next decade, that the 50th anniversary in Normandy was going to be a major international event, and that there would be a wave of popularity focused on citizen soldiers. He wanted and needed my help.

When Steve returned from his 1983 D-Day tour, I was three years into service as a University Dean. He asked if I could find space for an office, funding for staff, and a few graduate students to transcribe the oral histories of D-Day veterans he assembled over the next six years. I told him we had no funds, but I helped him raise enough to convert a classroom in my college into offices, where I proposed we establish the Eisenhower Center for Leadership Studies. From this research and program center, he could apply for grants and private funding to support recordings and transcriptions for his oral history collection.

We also envisioned that the center would host a series of major conferences and programs on D-Day and World War II. I proposed that Steve invite top WWII historians for a kick-off event in the coming year to raise funds to support the center and other WWII programs. Over the next six years, we succeeded beyond our expectations, and, by the time of our 1989 conversation in Steve's backyard, we both knew he was sitting on a gold mine of firsthand testimonies of those who fought on D-Day.

By early 1990 we were off and running. Despite our innocent beginnings, the combination of our friendship, mutual trust, and the curated collection of oral histories were enough to convince us that Steve's dream had a chance to become a reality. We also knew the idea to build a National D-Day Museum in the UNO Research Park was ambitious, even for us. As a renowned military historian and a biographer of President Richard Nixon as well as Eisenhower, Steve Ambrose already had a huge national reputation among historians and many history enthusiasts who loved his books. He was in growing demand around the country as a popular speaker and commanded high honoraria.

Since the early 1980s, Steve also developed a following among wealthy participants on his "D-Day to the Rhine" tours to Normandy. These included corporate executives, many of whom joined his advisory board and made small donations to the Eisenhower Center. This base of support gave Steve and me a false confidence that corporate America would rally to support a D-Day Museum. Moreover, Steve was a regular on the evening news with NBC News anchor Tom Brokaw, he made WWII documentaries with the BBC, and he often boasted of his years of collecting eyewitness accounts from the guys on the beaches, in the planes, and on the ships during Operation Overlord. At the University of New Orleans, Stephen Ambrose was the highest-ranking and highest-paid faculty member and was a Boyd Professor in the Louisiana State University System, a title only awarded to two members of the UNO faculty. As word of the proposed Museum spread, Steve's reputation gave the idea important credibility at UNO, in New Orleans, and in the state of Louisiana. The city's connection to Higgins and the D-Day story was a good selling point. Of course, this was just the beginning. I knew that learning how to design, build, operate, and raise money for a museum would be no easy task.

What assets did I bring to the table? First, Steve looked to me for leadership skills and my ability to get things done within a university bureaucracy. On campus, as Professor of European History, I had a reputation as a higher education entrepreneur, the designated "startup guy" for any new university project that needed to be developed on a self-supporting basis with little more than a green light and some meager seed money. UNO was the second-largest public university in the state, but in its 32nd year was still regarded as a stepchild to Louisiana State University in Baton Rouge. General fund money was hard to come by in those days, despite a rapid expansion of buildings and dramatic student growth.

As a young Assistant Professor in 1973, I launched a six-week International Summer School that transported 25 faculty and 180 students to Munich, Germany. After a few years, we moved to a permanent home and partnership with the University of Innsbruck in Austria. From the start, it was the largest summer school abroad offered by any American university.

UNO rewarded me for my efforts in 1980 by appointing me as founding Dean of a new Metropolitan College to extend the boundaries of university offerings, credit and noncredit, to serve nontraditional students and new young audiences at remote locations and times in New Orleans and overseas. The college grew rapidly, and I learned much about management, fundraising, conferences, and especially how to market on a shoestring to new learners. I established several other institutes and off-campus centers, including the university's first distance-learning courses. All these programs and outreach initiatives supported themselves, created significant income streams to UNO, and helped the programs that Steve and I launched through my college.

In 1985, I was promoted to Vice Chancellor for Extension, and the success of my entrepreneurial ventures led UNO Chancellor Gregory O'Brien to appoint me in 1989 to execute his vision for a new Research and Technology Park adjacent to campus on Lake Pontchartrain. It was soon after that unexpected assignment in fall 1989 when Steve plied me with drinks and his "eureka" idea to build the D-Day Museum together.

Despite our inexperience in designing and building a history museum, we did not see any obstacles we could not surmount, and we never doubted we would succeed. There was some urgency, however, given our self-imposed four-year goal to open the Museum on the 50th anniversary of D-Day. In that window of time, we had to raise the money, assemble the core historical assets of oral histories, find selected artifacts, design the exhibits, construct a building, and figure out how to operate a museum once we opened. What could go wrong? Just about everything.

2

PUTTING STRUCTURE ON THE IDEA

THAT WAS IT. We had no money, no feasibility study, no demand, and no dedicated staff. We had no design concepts for a museum beyond telling the story of D-Day. To make achieving our idea even more difficult, Steve and I needed to squeeze the Museum project around the margins of our full-time jobs.

For my part, I was consumed with finding money for the master plan and infrastructure for UNO's Research Park. I was getting a crash course in capital development—including real estate development, marketing, and securing federal and local grants—all challenges that had to be mastered if we were to succeed. Very few in the city believed in the viability of the Research Park. But I knew the fledgling park had to succeed for the D-Day Museum to have a chance. Steve was deep into writing his D-Day book, as well as teaching, giving talks around the country, and leading tours to Normandy. He was also organizing conferences and seminars for the Eisenhower Center, using his advisory board as a think tank for our Museum plans. It was becoming clear we had grossly underestimated the amount of time creating a museum from scratch would take—a mistake we would make repeatedly over the years.

As we entered the spring of 1990, we began to survey people we knew locally and nationally for advice. With Ambrose's reputation, everyone we asked quickly understood our concept. Steve captured the imagination of small groups of business leaders who told us it was a splendid idea. But no one rushed up to donate significant amounts of money to the project. I suspect many of them were too polite or too starstruck by Steve to tell us what they really thought—that these two delusional historians could never pull this off. Thankfully, UNO Chancellor O'Brien was an ardent champion of using the Research Park site for the Museum and encouraged us to forge ahead. University support was vital, since locking in the land was a critical first step that would reassure prospective donors and government officials. We also received strong support from UNO colleagues and staff. Steve was ably assisted by the Eisenhower Center Associate Director Guenter Bischof, a recent PhD in history from Harvard and an expert on postwar diplomacy. Guenter was a godsend in keeping the train on the tracks and helping us with research and initial planning for the project. My Associate Vice Chancellor, Norma Grace, a superb university executive with an MA in urban planning, had real-world experience in real estate that would be of vital help in developing a Research Park.

The next major issue was to secure the land for the park. Chancellor O'Brien negotiated to purchase the property from the Orleans Parish Levee District. The district proposed a lease/purchase arrangement that was barely workable in the short-term. The contractual terms were sufficient to secure a legal right to broker the land, but it would not guarantee title to those who built on the land. We knew that clear title to the land was essential for the success of the park and our promise to build a Museum there. We suspected the district wanted to keep the land for residential development. "Louisiana-style" politics were at play, and the Chancellor was greeted with skepticism from members of the Louisiana legislature and local agencies in the community.

O'Brien got the best deal he could, a long-term, 60-year lease that was sufficient to secure sites for the Museum and for UNO's first research enterprise, the Center for Energy Resource Management. Getting future title for those two projects was not certain, but O'Brien secured the necessary legal authority to proceed. He gave me the task of finding the millions of dollars needed for the park infrastructure and to purchase the property outright eventually. This would take time and complicated our planning for the Museum, but we had a beachhead. My strategy was to seek funds for the land purchase from Louisiana Gov. Buddy Roemer and go to the US Department of Commerce for the infrastructure. A good friend from the Research Park Association, Will Ginsberg, who had connections in Washington, DC, and later became Assistant Secretary for Economic Development in the Department of Commerce, offered to assist with matching funds for the roads and utilities. Meanwhile, with the long-term lease in hand, O'Brien could claim a preliminary victory and work the media with the message that millions in economic development were at risk until the ownership issue was resolved.

We also needed to dig deeper into the market feasibility and scope of the Museum. Beyond the dozen or so New Orleans corporate executives we had already consulted, Steve turned to trusted friends from his alma mater, the University of Wisconsin, who were mostly successful and wealthy business leaders. We called them the "Wisconsin Mafia," and they flew in every three or four months for a meeting of the Eisenhower Center Advisory Board.[1]

It quickly became clear that we needed a professional feasibility study to ascertain whether the idea for a National D-Day Museum was even viable, but we had no money for such a study. We could not find anyone to donate the $50,000 to $100,000 needed for the study.

Then came a lucky break. In early February 1990, Steve received a call from Dan Cremins, an employee of Peter Kalikow, a wealthy New York businessman. Cremins invited Steve to New York City to spend a day with Kalikow to describe what the war in the Pacific was like for young soldiers. Kalikow had never asked his father about his experiences in the war, explained his assistant. Kalikow offered to pay all travel expenses for Steve and his wife, Moira, for a weekend in New York City, including a limousine for sightseeing and a luxury suite at the Ritz Carlton. Steve declined twice. He was busy writing a book and had no time to waste on a weekend in New York City talking to a businessman about the war. "I have had many requests over the years from sons and daughters who failed to ask their dad, 'What happened to you in the war?'" Steve told Cremins. "It's sad. And I wish I could speak with them all, but no."

When Kalikow threw a $2,000 honorarium into the pot, Steve relented. Few paid that high an honorarium in those days. But Steve had one further condition; he told Cremins: "At the end of the day of our discussion, I would like to ask Mr. Kalikow for a contribution for a project I am working on here in New Orleans," Steve explained. Kalikow agreed, and Steve and Moira went. At the end of the day, Kalikow asked Steve to tell him about the project in New Orleans. "I summoned up my courage and asked Kalikow if he could donate the $50,000 we needed to conduct a feasibility study to build a National D-Day Museum in New Orleans," Steve reported to me by phone after his meeting. "Peter asked me a few questions, thought it an interesting idea, and without further ado wrote out the check for $50,000 on the spot!" I could not resist chiding Steve a bit for not asking for $100,000. "Can't you be happy we got this?" he retorted.

Indeed, we were both elated. The Kalikow gift was critical to our path forward, and it was completely unexpected, as would happen so many times during the evolution of the D-Day Museum. One can be passionate and convinced of the desired outcomes for all the right reasons, but the final direction often occurs by happenstance, a fork in the road that one could not foresee. The Kalikow gift was modest, but it made all the difference. The road opened a little wider.

As soon as Steve returned, we decided to use the funds to pay for travel and honoraria for the directors of selected presidential libraries to come to New Orleans for a workshop to discuss whether a National D-Day Museum, devoted to "one day in history," was both worthwhile and feasible. Steve invited Harry Middleton, Director of the Johnson Library and Museum; Tim Walsh, Director of the Hoover Library and Museum; and Richard Norton Smith, a distinguished historian and Director of the Eisenhower Library and Museum.[2] All three agreed and gathered with us on the weekend of March 10–11, 1990, for a workshop at the Eisenhower Center.

Their experience and knowledge poured down like rain in the desert for us novices to the history museum business. The directors gave us much needed professional advice on all the critical elements of building a museum: the mission, story, design, scope, funding, and our chances of success. They suggested design firms that might bid on the project and curators from their museums who could consult with us. Once we selected a design firm, they said, we could work out the space requirements, cost estimates, and concept sketches needed to put together a presentation brochure for a capital campaign.

Steve and I were still under the delusion that we were talking about a $4 million project to build a Museum that would provide a permanent home for the Eisenhower Center and its oral history collections and that UNO alone could contribute to the operating costs of this research and education center. The directors knew better and suggested the costs would be at least three or four times more than we expected. They focused on one overriding question: Where would money for the initial capital investment come from? From the private sector? The federal government? The state of Louisiana? The city of New Orleans? The directors told us that the answer to that question would frame our case for the scope of the project and the funding needed.

The biggest takeaway drummed into our heads was that the D-Day Museum had absolutely no chance unless we first secured federal support, whether through legislation, a grant, or a capital outlay earmark. Steve and I had naively believed some wealthy donor would materialize to make a major gift that would in turn stimulate a matching grant from Congress. The directors made it clear it would have to be the other way around. Their sobering conclusion was that the private sector would be hard-pressed to donate major funds to a museum conceived by a couple of creative historians—the free land, Ambrose's reputation, our oral histories, and a worthy cause notwithstanding.

Like it or not, they told us, a congressional appropriation providing a significant capital construction grant was our only path forward. A federal grant would not only provide instant credibility to the Museum's national mission, but it would also spur the private sector and the state government to support the project. They believed that with secured funding from Congress, we had a fighting chance to succeed. The workshop gave us our marching orders and destination: Washington, DC.

Before going to Congress, Steve and I had much to prepare. We needed a concept paper that would flesh out the scope of the project and make our case. We had to define the Museum's mission, describe the education and exhibit design elements that would tell the D-Day story, and explain the significance the Museum would have for the nation. We would also have to answer the question everyone had: "Why New Orleans?"

FORMING THE D-DAY STORY FROM BONDS OF FRIENDSHIP AND HISTORY

We went to work. Steve and I spent many evenings discussing how to define the exhibit and concept elements. By this time, Steve was well into the early chapters of his D-Day book, and, as was frequently the case, we also talked about his approach to writing the story. Our discussions on the narrative arc of his book synced with our need to settle on the core story in the exhibit design for the Museum.

We settled on several obvious and common themes for his manuscript and for the Museum. First, there should be a focus on the eyewitness accounts from citizen soldiers, drawn from the recorded oral histories, to illuminate the drama and violence of the battle. Second, we wanted to focus on the strategic planning for Operation Overlord, which consumed Eisenhower and his staff and played such a critical role on D-Day. Third, we wanted to concentrate on the American experience but not ignore the Allies, while also including enough on the Axis to understand Hitler's ambitious strategy to defend against an Allied invasion along 3,000 miles of European coastline. Finally, we agreed a key story should be the crucial role Andrew Higgins and his amphibious landing craft played in the invasion.

Debating the significance and storyline for D-Day was an ongoing conversation between us. Our friendship and intellectual camaraderie made it much easier and helped both projects. Steve and I were used to challenging each other on a variety of historical subjects on our travels together, whether camping in the Rockies, sailing in the Bahamas, or traipsing through Europe.

We now had the challenge to turn our scope of ideas into a story that would bring D-Day to life in a public history Museum. We had to carefully refine and vet our ideas, whether big or small, and examine the collected memories of veterans for authenticity. The story needed to be well framed and accessible to a larger public audience. Fortunately, this was during the same period that Steve was moving away from heavily footnoted, scholarly books published by university presses; he was drawn more to writing popular history for lovers of great history—enthusiasts, we called them—the same audience the Museum would seek as visitors. His writings fit naturally with our vision for how the Museum should tell the story.

Steve Ambrose was an unabashed admirer of the citizen soldiers of World War II. He frequently shared his memories of being a ten-year-old boy in his hometown of Whitewater, Wisconsin, and seeing WWII veterans welcomed back as heroes and defenders of democracy. To Steve, they were giants protecting America against evil forces seeking empires and world domination. His own father was a veteran of the war, serving as a Navy doctor on the island of Espiritu Santu in the Southwestern Pacific, and had returned home even though others had fought and died for the Allied victory. Steve never forgot those early impressions when he became a serious historian. World War II was the "Good War," and he wanted to tell the story of the citizen soldiers from that perspective.

It was often my job—along with Moira and his children—to caution Steve against hyperbole by going too far with what we called "Ambrosia." We argued, he listened, and he usually toned down his narrative when putting words to paper or while approving a story for the D-Day Museum exhibits. Steve never changed his belief in the American Spirit and that we were on the side of the angels in World War II. America wanted to hear this story, and he was going to tell it. It would form the backbone of the narrative story for the National D-Day Museum. Using my doctoral training in Western European history, my role was to help enlarge the story as an epic war, a watershed event unlike anything that had happened since the Battle of Hastings in 1066 or the Battle of Marathon in 490 BC.

Steve and I approached the narrative for the Museum from different perspectives. I was only five years old when the war ended, too young to have the same impressions Steve did of returning veterans. One of the most profound and formative experiences of my life came in 1953, at the age of 14, when my dad took the family on a visit to his native Germany, and I saw the horrific destruction of Hamburg, Wuppertal, Cologne, and Munich, cities still in ruin. Such experiences, coupled with my study of European history and my father's influence, predisposed me to believe that American freedom and democracy had been at stake in World War II.

From our different starting points in life, Steve and I agreed as historians on the major goals for America's role in World War II. What had been ultimately at stake, we believed, was a fight for civilization itself. Our goal now was to place the climactic battle of D-Day in the context of this historic American struggle for the survival of our freedom and democracy. We would frame this larger story through the eyewitness accounts of the battle that testified to the courage and values of the citizen soldiers who survived—and of those who did not make it back.

Our personal and intellectual bonds helped to shape our common vision for the story we would tell in the National D-Day Museum . . . if we could ever manage to build it.

3

D-DAY

Making the Case for the Day That Changed History

THE ENTHUSIASM STEVE and I felt from what we learned from the Presidential Library Directors carried over into the next meeting of the Eisenhower Center Advisory Board, convened just ten days later, on March 20, 1990. It was a watershed meeting, and it felt like an official launch of the project.

Steve took the reins with clear-eyed purpose, reporting on the strong encouragement and productive ideas we received from the Library Directors. He presented a draft report on the case for the National D-Day Museum, a concept piece that began with a retelling of his meeting with Eisenhower in the late 1960s, when the former Supreme Commander first told Steve that Andrew Higgins was "the man who won the war for us."[1]

Steve reviewed the purpose and themes of the D-Day Museum. The "core idea is to build a museum that tells the biography of a day—June 6, 1944—a day that changed history," he said. "The lesson that the Museum will teach is what the American people and American democracy can accomplish when everyone pulls together. Teamwork was Dwight Eisenhower's favorite word; it was teamwork at home and abroad that made D-Day a success."[2]

To dramatize his emphasis on the citizen soldier, Steve recounted the personal testimonies of veterans who served on D-Day, including the story of Allen Stephens of Alexandria, Virginia, who was a bomber pilot on the day of the invasion. Looking down on the English Channel enroute to his target at first light, Stephens later told Ambrose, he saw the "mightiest armada ever assembled, some 6,000 ships, and around him . . . nearly 5,000 aircraft; . . . the first wave of infantry hitting the beaches . . . and 'a surging sense of seeing the greatest show ever staged.'"[3]

That, Ambrose told the board, is "exactly what it was. It was a bigger undertaking than building the Interstate Highway system, or the Empire State Building or the pyramids. On one day, some 175,000 men crossed the English Channel, coming from staging points as far as 100 miles away, to converge on Normandy, to establish a beachhead, . . . and start the process of destroying the Wehrmacht and liberating France and Europe."[4]

Steve identified target audiences for the Museum. Veterans and their families would come from near and far to visit, he told the board, and as time passed their sons, daughters, and grandchildren would come. He also predicted the Museum would draw schoolchildren from the New Orleans community and farther afield.

Mindful of the need for attractions beyond exhibits, Steve said the Museum would also include spaces for the Eisenhower Center, archives and research, a gift shop, administrative offices, circulation areas, parking, and other amenities found in most museums. We planned to designate space for temporary exhibits to lure repeat visitors, who would be needed to sustain the Museum. He also envisioned earphones for patrons to listen to eyewitness testimonies, whether a paratrooper from the 101st Airborne Division, describing his experiences, or a member of the 29th Infantry Division, telling how he hit Omaha Beach and got up the cliff. These features would draw the visitor directly into the experience of the soldiers, sailors, and airmen who took part in the climactic battle.

Turning to the schematics for the exhibits, Steve returned to what we had learned from the Presidential Library Directors. Simple is best, they told us. Focus on the stories we absolutely had to tell and make sure that visitors left the Museum with two or three vivid impressions. Steve then outlined the core exhibits a museum professional would design for the Museum:

1. The Higgins Boat Yard and the bigger picture of how Americans across the land contributed to D-Day and the war effort on the home front.
2. The Anglo-American deception schemes preceding D-Day to fool the Germans on the date and place of the landings.

3. The Army Rangers at Pointe du Hoc and the 82nd and 101st Airborne story in and around St. Mere Eglise.
4. The 1st and 29th Infantry Divisions landing at Omaha and 4th Infantry Division at Utah.
5. The Army Air Force, Navy, and Coast Guard allied invasion forces.
6. Ike's dramatic decision to postpone the invasion on June 5 and then to "go" on June 6.

Steve concluded his report by telling board members that he did not think of the Museum as a memorial to General Dwight Eisenhower, but rather a Museum that "intends to honor the men and women of D-Day, not the brass."[5]

This was Steve's call to action. He and I both believed the next year would be decisive, but we were still primarily volunteer members of an advisory board, and we had consuming university responsibilities. To move forward, we knew we needed a major fundraising effort from the Eisenhower Center board and a significant grant from the federal government. Neither of these appeared promising in late spring and summer of 1990.

In the meantime, we did what we could to keep some semblance of activity to keep the idea for a Museum alive. Steve and Associate Director Guenter Bischof promoted awareness of D-Day with programs and new publications, including a newsletter called *The Crusade* and a small book collection of Eisenhower quotations, to raise funds. Steve inaugurated a lecture series that celebrated the centenary of Eisenhower's birth in 1990, featuring preeminent historians such as Forrest Pogue. A spring 1991 conference on World War II in the Pacific brought in more well-known historians, including Ronald Spector and John Keegan, as well as veterans of the Pacific War. We held a symposium on author James Bacque's allegations that Eisenhower and the US Army deliberately starved around a million German POWs after the war.

This was the beginning of a tradition of using the future Museum platform as a forum to discuss and debate the most controversial documents and historical interpretations of both Allied and Axis roles in World War II. As intended, these events demonstrated the credibility and popularity of the programming and research arm of the Eisenhower Center and the D-Day Museum. We found receptive audiences to these more public airings of historical knowledge of World War II.

But even as the programming and fundraising continued, we faced a growing controversy over the Research Park site. UNO still hoped to convert its long-term lease for the property to an outright purchase, but negotiations with the Orleans Levee District were bogged down over an inflated purchase price driven by local politics. Some leading Eisenhower Center board members began to question the Research Park site and suggested options closer to the city's thriving tourism attractions. The American Standard Building, which was less than a mile from the UNO campus, was proposed. Another idea was to put the Museum on a WWII aircraft carrier, the USS *Cabot,* recently located on the Mississippi riverfront as part of the planned New Orleans "Riverfront 2000" project. Steve and I, backed by Chancellor O'Brien, continued to press for the Research Park.

Projections for the scope and cost of the Museum were rising, but without an architect and exhibit designer, they were purely speculative. Our figures ranged from the $5 to $8 million estimated by the Presidential Library Directors to a much higher figure of $25 million dollars that came from Steve's discussion with architects of the Nixon Museum Library.[6] Given the anemic results on the fundraising front, Steve and I often mused about returning to my initial modest guesstimate of $4 million for a small museum. But there was no going back. As more supporters came on board, the concept and costs inevitably continued to grow. I quickly learned that such projects never get smaller.

Building on the central theme and concept as outlined by Steve's presentation in March 1990, some board members wanted to expand the idea to include all the Pacific amphibious landings. I tentatively suggested for the first time that we might want to consider doing all of World War II.[7] Despite these flirtations, Steve and I always came back to the original mission to concentrate on D-Day. Most directors agreed, including a prominent board member, Arthur Q. Davis, the famed architect and a Pacific War veteran. Davis believed this focus allowed for a highly dramatic conception, and that it would be less costly and more manageable.

The board, led ably by Chairman Ollie Brown Jr., of Freeport-McMoRan, a prominent mining company with a location in New Orleans, was patient and not overly discouraged about the pace of things. Brown kept the board motivated and helped persuade members of the need to succeed in local fundraising efforts before national donors would come on board.

By spring of 1991, we sorely needed money for staff. We used some of funds left from our modest donations to contract a few fundraising consultants, while our Eisenhower Center advisors began to identify national and regional donor prospects, including several prominent business leaders who were also WWII veterans. We got a lift in April from a grant by the state of Louisiana for $115,000.[8]

The board leadership and fundraising consultants agreed that Ambrose should be the principal salesman for a campaign appealing to patriotism and emotional connections to World War II. Meanwhile, Steve was approaching major national figures to serve on an honorary board, while Guenter Bischof helped sustain momentum through conferences and a book series with LSU Press entitled the *Eisenhower Center Studies of War and Peace,* which made use of the center's oral history collection and provided an important revenue stream. Ambrose's reputation drew helpful press coverage as well. Bruce Alpert of the *Times-Picayune* wrote an in-depth story on the scale and scope of Steve's plan for a D-Day Museum to portray the magnitude of the invasion and the Higgins connection to New Orleans.[9]

We claimed some progress, but we were still searching for a funding breakthrough. Steve and I worried that confidence and support from the board and our few donors would wane if some noteworthy progress did not happen. It was time to make a serious effort to target Congress for federal funds, as the Presidential Library Directors had recommended. Steve arranged for a meeting in Washington, DC, to make our case to our Louisiana congressman, Rep. Bob Livingston, a member of the powerful House Appropriations Subcommittee on Defense.

The story of that meeting, recounted by Steve many times over the years, is part of our Museum's lore. Steve met with Livingston at his Capitol Hill office in late March. Steve presented his vision for a National D-Day Museum in New Orleans, describing how it would tell the story of Andrew Higgins and his boats in securing victory for the Allies, and the historic ties to the Research Park land on Lake Pontchartrain. Steve told him about our urgent need for a capital grant paired with matching funds from the private sector and said we had the full support of UNO and many New Orleans business leaders.

At the end of Steve's pitch, Livingston's response was immediate. "I've heard a lot of crazy requests come to me in this office, and this is the best idea I've ever heard," he told Steve. "We will get you the money."[10] Steve was stunned to hear an immediate "yes" after so many disappointments over private fundraising attempts. He was not at all prepared for Livingston's next question: "How much do you need?" Put on the spot, Steve blurted out the only number he could recall: "$4 million!"

"You've got it!" Livingston replied. He promised to earmark it in the current Department of Defense capital outlay appropriation. Steve was on cloud nine and rushed to call me. I was elated, but as usual I chided Steve a bit. "Why didn't you ask for more, and where did you get that number?" Steve gave me a terse reply: "I got it from you, 18 months ago when we first discussed the idea."

"Geeze, Steve, that was over drinks and was just a wild guesstimate," I said, reminding him that we had talked about costs of as much as $25 million in recent board meetings. He rightly hit back at me for my lack of appreciation for the great news, and we both laughed. Indeed, news of the Livingston appropriation was the breakthrough we desperately needed. The promise of $4 million was a huge motivator for the Eisenhower Center Advisory Board, the university, and prospective donors.

Shortly after the meeting, Livingston called to tell us that because of recent scandals in financial aid and misuses of overhead research funds at several major universities, congressional leaders had decreed that no funds beyond what were already appropriated could go to any university that year. Livingston said we should immediately establish an independent 501(c)(3) nonprofit corporation unaffiliated with the university with a new Board of Directors that could be named as the recipient of the federal funds. We notified the Eisenhower Center Advisory Board of the dramatic news and began to implement the requested legal changes in late spring.[11]

There is nothing like a large swag of money to focus the hearts and minds of an institution. The news of the $4 million grant gave us credibility and grabbed headlines, including a big story in the *Times-Picayune* on June 8, 1991, which called the funding "a major boost" and reported that UNO officials said the Museum "had the potential to become a major tourist attraction."[12]

More good news quickly followed. After several years of lobbying in Baton Rouge by UNO, Gov. Buddy Roemer secured passage of a bill in the spring state legislative session to grant the university $5 million to purchase the lakefront property outright from the Orleans Levee District, replacing the onerous long-term lease agreement.[13] The state appropriation also provided $2 million for infrastructure, including roads, parking, and utilities as a match for a $2 million economic development grant from US Department of Commerce.[14] Will Ginsberg, now Deputy Secretary of Commerce, assured me a federal grant was available, pending the required match from the state. The title to the property for the Museum was now clearly in UNO's hands, and the infrastructure funds were assured. The state and federal money meant our meager private funds of less than $100,000 had suddenly mushroomed to $13 million in assets, a shot of adrenaline for everyone involved with the project.[15] We needed that boost, as our recent successes created pressing demands in the fall of 1991 that needed to be quickly addressed by UNO and the Eisenhower Center Advisory Board. The need to create a new nonprofit corporation meant major shifts in the organization and membership of the board. Decisions and bid processes were needed to contract professional architects, designers, fundraisers, and marketing consultants.

Ollie Brown, who had chaired the Eisenhower Center Advisory Board for the last three years, resigned that fall and passed the gavel to Arthur Q. Davis. While facing the new governance mandate for a separate Museum board, Davis resolved to keep the UNO Eisenhower Center Advisory Board intact, with its fundraising focused on research and education. This allowed the Eisenhower Center to become more connected to UNO, while still serving as the education research arm of the future D-Day Museum. It was understood that the Eisenhower Center office and personnel at UNO would eventually be located in the D-Day Museum and integrated into the Museum's mission. The Eisenhower Center Advisory Board would remain separate from the new National D-Day Museum Board, which would include 23 directors and an executive committee to act on behalf of the board between meetings.

Separating the two boards was complicated but not unusual in the creation of nonprofit institutions with ambitious goals. While the Museum's origins were clearly grounded within the University of New Orleans, there were unavoidable conflicting interests between the fundraising efforts of the university and the business leaders on the Eisenhower Center Advisory Board. In addition to fundraising, there were issues of divided loyalties between Directors who served on both boards, including Ambrose, O'Brien, and me. We quickly learned that the two boards had to operate at arm's length to avoid conflicts.

Meanwhile, there was a flurry of activity in the late fall of 1991, including Eisenhower Center programs featuring well-known WWII veterans and special appearances by John Eisenhower, Viscount David Montgomery, and Manfred Rommel, all sons of prominent WWII Commanders, giving the fledgling Museum extraordinary publicity.[16]

Our immediate focus, however, was on the final passage of the federal legislation awarding us the $4 million promised by Representative Livingston. On November 26, 1991, the Department of Defense Appropriations Act, 1992 was passed, with these glorious words in print: *"Provided further... the funds appropriated herein, $4,000,000 shall be made available only for a grant to the National D-Day Museum Foundation"*[17] This was a momentous time for the Museum. As required by the legislation, we moved immediately to create a new corporation. On December 2, 1991, the state of Louisiana formally incorporated the National D-Day Museum Foundation, Inc. as a tax-exempt 501(c)(3) nonprofit institution. In drafting the bylaws and articles, we took the opportunity to incorporate an expanded vision of the Museum's purposes:

- Preserve and maintain research and oral histories in its exhibits.
- Educate through personal accounts, artifacts, photos, and experiential exhibits of the invasion.
- Expand awareness through outreach to schools locally and nationwide.
- Present national and international perspectives of D-Day and World War II.
- Provide public access to educational resources and events surrounding the D-Day invasion and its implications for the understanding of American history and durability of American values.
- Pay tribute to American civilian patriotism, resourcefulness and effort that contributed to victory, and
- Provide insight into international wartime cooperation and leadership which exemplified values and served as a model for today's world and future generations.[18]

These goals, supported by all board members, were considerably broader than our original mission statement, which had focused primarily on the content and themes for the D-Day exhibits and broad educational goals. The added goals of outreach, public access, patriotic tributes, insights into values found in wartime leadership, and seeking to become an aspirational model for future generations gave us new responsibilities.

We created the new D-Day Foundation Board on December 12, 1991, another major milestone in the creation of the National D-Day Museum. It had been almost two years since the afternoon epiphany when Steve and I embraced the embryonic idea to build a modest D-Day Museum. Now, everyone knew that our world had changed; the two historians were not just dreamers after all.

The spirit in the room during the first meeting was electrifying. Steve and I were ecstatic. We felt this was the turning point we needed to increase the funding, organization, and planning. It may sound trite, but success fuels optimism, faith, and commitment. The appropriations, the Congressional stamp of approval that came with it, and the creation of the new National D-Day Museum Foundation gave us reinvigorated confidence and a sense of independence. We would succeed or fail on our own. The University of New Orleans was no longer the backstop; the National D-Day Museum Foundation was in charge of its own destiny.

We set about the business that day of electing the new board leaders, choosing as chairman our WWII veteran, Arthur Q. Davis, who transitioned from the same position on the Eisenhower Center Advisory Board.[19] From UNO, Steve, Chancellor O'Brien, and I became Ex-Officio Directors of the new board. From the community, we added most of the business leaders from the Eisenhower Center Advisory Board, including Lee Schlesinger, Alden McDonald, and several trusted friends of Ambrose from his University of Wisconsin days, including Mary Mohs, Don Hoffman, and Dick Holtz.

George Wills, our fundraising consultant, presented a plan to appeal to donors that emphasized teamwork akin to the American Spirit of World War II. He proposed a two-for-one challenge campaign to leverage the $4 million federal grant into $8 million raised from the private sector for a total of $12 million.

The good news kept coming on that December day. Department of Defense organizers agreed to include the Museum in the events planned for the 50th anniversary D-Day commemoration in Normandy on June 6, 1994. The Eisenhower Center acquired a Higgins Landing Craft Vehicle Personnel (LCVP) with the help of a WWII veteran, Coast Guard Ensign Marvin Perret, who served as the Coxswain of an LCVP on D-Day.[20] Steve asked Trinity Marine, a Louisiana company, to refurbish it in time for a full-scale reenactment and assault on Pontchartrain Beach, planned for the next D-Day anniversary, June 6, 1992, which would feature flyovers of WWII aircraft and troops spilling out of the LCVP as it hit the beach. Steve also reported that Simon & Schuster would publish his latest book, *Band of Brothers,* on June 6, 1992. He planned to invite Captain Dick Winters and other surviving veterans from Easy Company, who were featured in the book, to a publisher's party that would raise awareness and funds for the Museum.[21]

Ideas flew right and left throughout that exciting meeting. We believed we had an abundance of assets—a compelling mission, a new board, the right people, a Higgins boat, donated land—and all of this combined with the growing fame and credibility of national best-selling historian Stephen Ambrose.

For that brief shining moment, we had no doubts. We had persevered and gained a toehold on the future. Yet the road ahead was much longer than we could ever imagine. We rocketed out of that December meeting but coming years would reveal we lacked the fuel to propel us to our goal.

We had significant capital funds from the federal grant, but we still had financial challenges on the operating side, and not all board members thought we could afford a full time Director and CEO. This was a big mistake, in my opinion. Steve and I were still fully engaged with our university responsibilities, and the Museum's progress remained dependent upon a volunteer board. We faced various monetary challenges, most glaringly fundraising and the supervision of a construction budget. The Chairman held the title of CEO, but that was a legal formality. Pressing forward without a full-time and salaried Executive Director or CEO is a common error in nonprofit start-ups, a big one in our case. We would encounter many ups and downs, missed deadlines, and a few internal controversies.

Steve and I began to understand that the Museum project would not be a straight line. For every bit of good news, there would be setbacks and detours, with many hills and near-death valleys to cross. Steve and I could both appreciate the observation of Prime Minister Winston Churchill after the second battle of El Alamein in 1942, when he declared that this was "the end of the beginning."[22] Perhaps it was good that we could not see what lay ahead.

4

GROWING PAINS

Bringing the Story to Life

Really? What, were we crazy? We all knew it was a risk, but when you have something that you believe in, you've got to take a little risk.

—LEE SCHLESINGER,
Chairman and CEO, National D-Day Museum

WITH THE RECEIPT of $4 million dollars in federal support, we all understood that the project had gained new momentum that required much larger commitments of time and money from everyone involved, especially Steve and me. We both felt the stakes and spirits were higher than ever. But we still had considerable naivete and slightly different expectations about the challenges ahead. Steve thought we were going to be shooting the rapids; I had a stronger sense it was going to be a tough paddle upstream.

I saw strong currents and headwinds from every direction. Together with our brand-new board, we had to find new professionals who knew the Museum business and who could help us develop a plan to raise the funds needed to build and operate a successful museum and education center—skills that none of us possessed. Most of all, we knew we had to raise a lot of money to complement the federal funds, which could only be used for capital development and construction purposes.

Steve was counting on my organizational experience with nonprofits to assist the new board. I enlisted the aid of some of my senior staff from the Research Park, including Norma Grace, who at that time was UNO's Associate Vice Chancellor for Technology and Economic Development. Steve drew upon the Eisenhower Center staff to help with fundraising and developing programs to bring publicity and support. But given everyone's other UNO responsibilities, we were in desperate need of professional help.

From a broader institutional perspective, the major responsibilities for the project shifted from the university to the leadership of the National D-Day Museum Board and Chairman Arthur Q. Davis. Arthur's leadership at the board's first meeting focused our attention on the urgent need for professionals to turn our concept ideas for the Museum exhibits into reality based on the scope of our mission, vision, and budget. And it was from Arthur that Steve and I first heard the name Jack Masey.

Masey, head of the New York exhibit design firm Metaform, was one of the top museum exhibit designers in America.[1] He had created exciting attractions with Arthur for the New Orleans World's Fair of 1984, and he was the lead designer of the Ellis Island National Museum of Immigration, which had opened in 1990. Masey was a WWII veteran himself, having served in Europe in the mysterious 603rd Camouflage Engineers, or "Ghost Army," in France, which specialized in deceiving German forces in the final year of the war. This unit used visual, sonic, and radio techniques to manipulate and confuse Hitler's armies. They used several modes of deception, but most often used decoys made from inflated pneumatic tubes and painted fabric to fool the Wehrmacht into thinking the Allies were more powerful than they were.[2] Masey's role in World War II and his exhibit design experience gave him a unique advantage in understanding and executing our vision. We were convinced that he was the only man for the job.

We got Masey under contract immediately, and he quickly proved to be an extraordinary addition to the Museum team. We all fell in love with his big personality, sense of drama and excitement, and his confidence in bringing our conceptual ideas for the Museum exhibits to life. He was a force of nature. When we met him, his creative approach to the drama of D-Day was breathtaking. But we also knew that we could not progress with Masey or with architects who would design a building until we had more funding. We also needed a stronger Board of Directors that could stand on its own legs independent of the university.

Turning over the "ownership" of the Museum idea was bittersweet for UNO, but we all embraced the transfer immediately. We had no choice, given the terms of the federal grant. We now had foster parents who would take over all legal, fiduciary, and development responsibilities. The new board assumed full responsibility for hefty fundraising, marketing, design, and construction efforts that required professionals. They would be able to help us clarify our plans and meet our ambitious goals for a national Museum. We also had to learn to collaborate in order to preserve our core D-Day educational mission while coming to grips with a board that had to tackle the goals related to the development of a business plan for the Museum. Steve and I undertook the responsibility of preserving the connection to the original idea and vision of the D-Day Museum. Although our new board was fine with the mission of the Museum, many were uncomfortable with the location and the ties to the university, despite the allegiance that Steve, O'Brien, and I had to the Research Park. The board certainly understood the special education and research partnership that came with Steve and the Eisenhower Center, but it soon became apparent that we were going to have difficulties in sorting out this new relationship.

Arthur Davis and the carryover members of the Eisenhower Center Advisory Board began the board recruitment process with some modest success. Every nonprofit board has struggles in filling out its ranks, but even with our assets and Steve's star power, this proved more difficult than we expected. Arthur's successor as chairman, Lee Schlesinger, took the reins of the board in the fall of 1992 and brought fresh commitment, energy, and business acumen to every task and challenge we faced.

Lee Schlesinger was previously Vice Chair of the Eisenhower Center Advisory Board, and he came to the leadership of the D-Day Museum project as owner and CEO of one of the top real estate development firms in New Orleans. Stephen Ambrose was the reason he joined the Eisenhower Center Advisory Board. He had attended a lecture by Steve at UNO one evening in the late 1980s. "I . . . found him fascinating to listen to," Lee recalled years later. "Just fabulous in the way he could weave a historical narrative that was second to none!" After the lecture, Steve invited Lee to visit the Eisenhower Center, and a few days later he did. "To my astonishment, he's got thousands of interviews of people involved and soldiers from World War II . . . he had collected," Lee said. "All of a sudden it dawned on me; this is something pretty special."[3]

Lee succeeded Arthur Davis at a critical time. We did not know him well except for his reputation as a successful business leader, but we could see his passion and aggressive approach to the Museum. Additionally, as a real estate developer, Lee saw that we had a cultural project that lacked a defined scope and business plan and that we could benefit from his financial expertise. Lee was just as confident in his development abilities as Steve and I were confident in our knowledge of the significance of the D-Day story. So Lee was an even better match than we initially realized.

The serendipitous story of how Lee became one of the first leaders of the board was the sort of thing that would be repeated many times and is key to understanding how the D-Day Museum was born and survived many crises in years ahead. We continually seemed to find good fortune from unlikely places and people at critical junctures. In later years, when I asked Lee why he took on this venture, he professed some initial skepticism to Steve's idea, but he was impressed by Steve's passion and historical interest in the Higgins landing craft. Lee came under the spell of Ambrose and was sold, but he never lost sight of the development challenges we faced. Despite some differences with him on some major issues, neither Steve nor I doubted Lee's business abilities or his desire to do what he thought was best for the project.

From the outset, the Museum nonprofit corporation lacked the operating funds to make up for the in-kind support the university previously provided. Lee's office only had one part-time secretary who was paid out of the Museum's budget to support routine record keeping and communications of the Chairman. Much of our federal funding went toward contracts with high-quality consultants for exhibit design, film production, museum expertise, and architectural planning.

During 1992 and 1993, Lee led the charge to raise money and recruit new board members who could bring fresh energy, advice, and pledges of private contributions. This was the board's immediate priority, while we negotiated with the exhibitors, filmmakers, architects, and fundraisers. Four new members stood out in those years: Robert Howson, CEO of McDermott International and Chairman of the Business Council of New Orleans; John Kelly, President of Textron Marine Systems, whose firm was building the latest generation of landing craft for the Navy and Marines; Theodore (Ted) Solomon, President and CEO of Gulf States Theaters, Inc., and a WWII veteran; and Frank Walk, President and CEO of the Walk-Haydel Engineering firm, who as a young officer had served as a beachmaster on Omaha Beach on D-Day. These four contributed their leadership and credibility, and each became important future donors. Others accepted our invitation, and all came with enthusiasm, but little in the way of donations we desperately needed to expand operational support.

Board recruitment was tough, as top prospects were in great demand by other nonprofits. Some were skeptical about the D-Day Museum—the idea, the location, and whether funds needed to make it successful could be raised. Many "just thought we had no chance and didn't want to be on this leaky vessel, knowing it had a good chance of never seeing the light of day," Lee recalled.[4] The slow pace of donations and our problems recruiting for the board came as an unwelcome surprise to us.

Lee was on the front lines and quickly learned we had a marketing problem. There was no great demand for the Museum, no matter how important we believed our mission to be. It was going to be "a real selling job," Lee recalled. "We were getting a lot of doors closed in our face with just the idea."[5] Steve and I recognized Lee was right. We had to sell the D-Day Museum. From the moment Steve first broached the Museum idea with me, I knew he would never have time to commit himself completely to the project. Steve rightly expected that I and others would manage the organizational leadership and fundraising. This is where our close friendship came into play. We talked candidly about Steve's other priorities, and I never questioned the time he needed for his own work or leisure. Steve never wavered from his leadership role and was a major asset in approaching donors. He was the Museum's "historian-in-chief," always exuding confidence that we were onto an idea that would capture the public's imagination.

Stephen Ambrose had both star power and charisma. He was arguably the preeminent presidential and military historian in America. He held donors and audiences spellbound talking about the importance of D-Day and the Museum. We built the campaign and board recruitment around his celebrity status as a best-selling WWII author, popular speaker, and media personality, a frequent guest on *Meet the Press* and all the major TV networks. He was loved by members of Congress (especially the WWII veterans) and by military, government, and business leaders. National journalists, such as Tom Brokaw, Cokie Roberts, and David Gergen, were close friends. His professional acquaintances included President Bill Clinton, statesmen such as Henry Kissinger, Warren Christopher, Richard Holbrooke, and military leaders such as Colin Powell and Wesley Clark.

Steve was always ready to make an appeal to groups for support. Nevertheless, all of us, including Steve, conflated his celebrity status with his ability to raise private funds for the Museum. Board and donor prospects would often take our meeting requests just to meet with Steve Ambrose. It took years before Steve and I realized how often our fundraising meetings ended with comments along these lines: "You have a great cause, but that's not a priority of mine or my corporation," followed by the suggestion that we "go see 'so and so' who could surely be of more help." Steve always preferred the Lewis and Clark trail to the fundraising trail. He never became comfortable asking a private donor for a contribution. Asking for money was hard for me too, especially for the amounts we needed in the early years, but I gradually got used to it.

The amount of money we needed kept rising. While we negotiated with Jack Masey for the exhibit design in the latter part of 1992, Brokaw suggested that we hire Charles Guggenheim, the Academy Award-winning documentarian and filmmaker, to produce a dramatic film on D-Day as one of the central attractions of the new Museum.

We loved the idea, and in the fall of 1992 we completed initial contracts with both Masey and Guggenheim to design the exhibits and produce the film for the Museum. Masey's fee was a staggering $8 million, and the initial contract for Guggenheim was $800,000 for a forty-minute film.[6] These sums seemed astronomical. The nearly $9 million total was more than twice what we had in the bank from Congress, and at the time we had just raised a little under $300,000 privately. Regardless, Lee persuaded the board that we had to move forward. It was a gutsy move and perhaps borderline reckless. Lee reflected on his decision years later: "Really? What? Were we crazy? We all knew it was a risk, but when you have something, you believe in . . . you got to take a little risk."[7]

It was indeed a big risk, but signing the contracts was the right thing to do. We needed Lee's entrepreneurial ability and spirit in that moment. This was critical to sustaining our momentum and committing the board to an ambitious campaign goal. We now had to stop talking and start designing the exhibits and the building that would house them. We had to do this with only the vaguest notions of a capital budget and virtually no business plan to get us there. It was a stretch. We could have gone broke.

CROSSING THE RUBICON

Our funding strategy was threefold. First, recruit major business leaders to serve on the board and make contributions. Second, seek more state and private funding beyond what we could expect board members to raise, including targeting defense industries that had profited from manufacturing contracts during World War II. Third, create an honorary board to give us national recognition and contacts. Additionally, I proposed our new funding plan include preliminary estimates for the cost to design, construct, and sustain the Museum. We had learned that donors expected more realistic figures. The $12 million funding goal the board set was little more than an educated guess. We divided the budget into three parts: $4 million for the exhibits, $4 million for the brick-and-mortar building, and $4 million for an endowment to contribute additional revenues for operations and pay a visiting professor in military history. The Museum would also include the Eisenhower Center with research and conference facilities and a library. We had urgent decisions to make on the Museum's size and scope before an architect could design the building around Masey's exhibit plans. We agreed to begin a juried competition to select an architectural firm in the summer of 1993. Arthur Davis, our previous chairman and a renowned architect, would head the jury, which included me, the Dean of Tulane School of Architecture, and several other architects and directors.

We climbed way out on a limb to keep up with our mushrooming expenditure commitments. In addition to the Masey and Guggenheim agreements, we also signed a contract for $8,000 a month for our fundraiser, George Wills, to help us find new contributors and national prospects for the board. We further charged him to find a museum professional to evaluate our mission as well as our strengths and weaknesses and to then develop a realistic capital campaign and business plan for the Museum.

Wills and Ambrose had some early success in securing pledges of $100,000 each from the Forbes Corporation and Norfolk Southern Railroad, plus some lesser gifts in the $10,000 to $20,000 range.[8] It was nothing spectacular, but any news on the fundraising front was good news. Around this time, Ambrose brought in former CIA Director William Colby, who had served as a Jedburgh operator with the OSS during World War II (Operation Jedbergh was a top-secret spying effort behind enemy lines), to head up a new honorary board. The honorary board also included Steve Forbes, whose father, Malcolm Forbes, served in World War II, Sen. Chuck Hagel of Nebraska, a Vietnam War veteran, and Viscount David Montgomery, the son of Gen. Bernard Montgomery. We thought that was quite a list of luminaries and a great way to start the year.

As we gathered a bit of steam continuing into 1993, we recruited some new board members from among top business and professional leaders in the community who added substance to the Museum effort, including Howard Gaines, President of First National Bank of Commerce; Bob Howson, Chairman and CEO of McDermott, one of the world's leading energy services industries with business roots in World War II; and John Cordaro, President of New Orleans Public Service. We also added Fred Baldwin from McDermott; prominent lawyer Jack Weiss; businessman Bob Tucker; and former UNO Chancellor Dr. Homer Hitt. We also made progress on exhibit planning. Steve took Masey and Guggenheim to Normandy in the fall of 1992, where they traversed the invasion and battle sites and absorbed Steve's stories about the courage of the citizen soldiers who had fought and died there. Back in New Orleans, Jack Masey reported to the board that he had formed a conceptual outline of the story and was ready to begin working with an architect to design the exhibit.

Yet, huge controversies were brewing on the board. Just as we began to look for an architect, there were growing questions among board members over the location of the Museum at UNO's Research Park. The very feasibility of the Museum and a funding strategy were still murky. There were also issues about the board's relationship to UNO on the operational side. It was becoming clear that the goal of opening the Museum on June 6, 1994, was not achievable. There could be no coherent plan until these issues were resolved. I feared we could lose momentum if the board could not come to an agreement on the site and these other big decisions. Fortunately, Wills responded to our SOS at just the right moment, introducing Lee Schlesinger to Ann Allston Boyce of Boyce-Mansfield, a museum consultant from Baltimore. Lee engaged her immediately in early 1993, and he could not have made a better choice. Ann parachuted into our Museum project with an outstanding résumé of executive nonprofit experience and professional credentials in capital campaigns and strategic planning for museums in Baltimore and the Washington, DC, area.

Since Ann reported to Lee, I knew she might not affirm planning decisions we made before the new board took over the project. Nevertheless, I was glad to have Ann identify the strengths and weaknesses of our board, make recommendations on our mission, fundraising, and location, and provide her expert view of our feasibility. She did all that and more. By the time she arrived, we had already reluctantly agreed to push back the Museum's opening date by one year to June 6, 1995. Ann moved quickly to conduct in-depth interviews with thirteen board members, including Lee, Steve, and me. She pushed all of us hard on our assessment of the project, willingness to contribute, and estimates of probability of success.

Her report to the board on April 14, 1993, was like taking a cold shower. From the moment Ann began her presentation, we realized how much we had needed the advice of a knowledgeable museum professional. For the next forty-five minutes, you could hear a pin drop. Ann was diplomatic, smart, articulate, and gracious—but also blunt. She asked us to think hard about our priorities on controversial issues, such as funding and location. Based on our answers, she could outline alternative futures for the Museum.

Ann reflected on the power of the Museum's mission, to tell the story of a single day in World War II—a unique but risky idea that she thought could help the Museum attract audiences. She understood that our vision was a monumental and emotional story that could also be educational and entertaining. She offered high praise for Masey and Guggenheim and gave accolades for the commitment Steve and the board had shown to the Museum. The $4 million federal grant was a major plus, she said, adding that the Eisenhower Center's oral history collection and staff gave us a tremendous research and education foundation rarely found among start-up museums.

Just as we began to feel proud of our accomplishments, Ann put the hammer down. She told us that no one she interviewed thought raising money would be easy, nor did anyone believe that New Orleans could support a Museum of national focus. Moreover, given the increased emphasis in those days on funding needs for human services, social issues, education, and health care, many donors would not see a history museum as a priority. We also lacked donor research, a business plan, or an eye-catching exhibit brochure we could show to donors. She ventured that our capital campaign goal would need to be upgraded from $12 million to at least $30 million.[9] She concluded her opening remarks by apologizing for bringing such "discouraging news," but she estimated it would take at least four to five years to complete the Museum, with June 1997—not 1995—being a realistic goal.[10]

The entire board looked to be in a state of shock after Ann's opening remarks. I certainly was. Before I could pick myself up off the floor, Ann dove into a deeper analysis of other issues based on her interviews with thirteen directors. The board, she noted, had two distinct groups: those associated with UNO, and those who represented the community at large. There were serious differences between them regarding the Museum's relationship to the university, its educational scope, and the designated location in UNO's Research Park.

The group of directors aligned with UNO tended to view the Museum as a UNO "academic project" along the lines of what Steve and I had originally conceived, namely, a "legacy for Steve's research interest in World War II and as an outgrowth of the Eisenhower Center," Ann noted. Ironically, she added, it was the grant itself that showed the Museum could be "planned on a grander scale than previously imagined."[11]

The community-oriented group had misgivings on several levels. They were concerned about the viability of the Museum's lakefront Research Park location instead of downtown, where a larger Museum could become a prime visitor attraction that would sustain operations over the long term. They were also concerned that the Eisenhower Center's scholarly needs and fundraising efforts could conflict with other university fundraising priorities in New Orleans. Ann reported that the Research Park site had a primary focus that was more "university-related" than on numbers of visitors. She also noted that the prominent business leaders and community donors we wanted to engage were more interested in a D-Day Museum as a tourist attraction. While Ann reported these community leaders were open to the idea of the Museum being on Lake Pontchartrain, they strongly favored a downtown location that might enable a national focus.

Ann was brilliant. She gave us tough love and laid out hard choices by highlighting the major issues of mission and fundraising that were inextricably linked to the choice of the Museum's location. She addressed problems that we were not willing to face, providing a professional analysis of the pros and cons that the board had been wrestling with, mostly behind closed doors. I was aware of the discussions about location, and I understood why the directors who favored a downtown site could not confide in me. I was President of the Research Park and was pursuing the location that Steve, Chancellor O'Brien, and I believed to be the least expensive option, with free land and UNO's institutional resources as backup. I had a vested interest in the location, a big decision that directly affected my university duties as well as my commitments to the chancellor and Steve. I also understood how a downtown site would benefit the long-term operating success of the Museum, so I wondered what Ann would propose to resolve two very different options.

With artful diplomacy and candor, Ann began by suggesting the competing visions were not as incompatible as they seemed. On the one hand, the university group would not "object to having a museum which has national profile that can attract significant visitors,"[12] she noted. On the other hand, the community group "would not object to having a serious educational component of the museum." Merging the two visions could have great value, she said. She then posed the strategic decision the board had to make: did we want to be an education and research endeavor that happened to have a museum or did we want to be a museum that happened to have an education and research center as a supporting function? Ann posed the crucial decision directly to us, saying how we as a board answered that question would determine the scope of our location, our mission, and our fundraising strategy.

I remember thinking, "Wow, she made the choice so clear that the board will eventually decide to move the Museum downtown." After learning from Ann that we could not open before 1997 or before reaching the $30 million goal, we decided not to vote on a location just yet. There was no urgency to decide since there was no alternative site we could afford downtown. The board agreed to move forward for the time being as if the Museum would be in the Research Park; the plans could always be modified if we found a way to buy property in downtown New Orleans.

Ann Allston Boyce brought about a major shift in our thinking about the Museum, including the location, the scope, the timeline, the capital costs, the national focus, and the hard realities of our fundraising prospects. Like it or not, Steve and I realized she was closer to right than we were. Most importantly, she energized us with a new direction and concrete goals to take us through 1994. Ann said we needed constituency research to confirm visitation estimates, and she proposed a national direct-mail campaign to acquire members and donors. Before the meeting ended, Steve appointed a task force to answer the questions she had raised about the site and to define the relationship between the university and the Museum.

Later in the year, she proposed a new goal for the board to raise at least $12 million in pledges by May 1994, culminating in a grandiose public event on the beach in front of the proposed Museum site.[13] The event would feature our biggest D-Day invasion reenactment yet, along with a USO dance and the announcement of our capital campaign to build the National D-Day Museum by 1997. The event would also celebrate the publication of Steve's much anticipated book, *D-Day June 6, 1944: The Climactic Battle of World War II.* Ann persuaded the board that this would provide a wave of national publicity on the eve of the D-Day 50th anniversary, and she convinced us to spend $317,000 to organize and execute the event.[14]

Our fundraising campaign would kick off around a specific theme: "Teamwork USA: Key to D-Day and the Future." Defense industries that had supplied the WWII mobilization would be invited and honored for their role. We hired the firm Odell, Roper, & Simms, Inc., to identify potential contributors. We planned to premiere the Guggenheim film on the same evening as a USO dance in a downtown hotel. We also intended to unveil our exhibit and architectural plans for the Museum. We needed to make a final decision on the Museum's location, Ann said, as well as hire a firm for a national marketing campaign to bolster the event and fundraising.

Ann submitted her final report at the August 1993 board meeting in a 31-page business plan that served as our blueprint for executing the initiatives she proposed. Her blueprint included a capital campaign strategy, building planning, collections and archives, and operations.[15] Ann Allston Boyce had identified the tough decisions we needed to make. With that roadmap, we began to feel like the D-Day Museum was coming out of the incubator and had a chance at life.

5

THE TASTE OF VICTORY TURNS SOUR, 1994–1998

BY MID-1993, ALL efforts shifted to the immediate goal of hosting the National D-Day Museum dedication and national celebration in May 1994. Despite internal concerns about the location, we knew the 50th anniversary of D-Day was a big opportunity to ride a wave of national and international media coverage. Simply put, our plan was to insert the Museum into the center of the national media attention tied to the release of Steve's D-Day book and the D-Day anniversary.

In preparation, Ann Boyce planned the event execution and charged Jack Masey to complete the concept design for the Museum exhibits. After a competitive search led by Chairman Arthur Davis, we contracted the noted local architect firm of Eskew-Filson to design the building that would accommodate the D-Day exhibits.

We threw everything into the anniversary events. Steve led a tour of more than 500 D-Day veterans, historians, donors, and board members to London and then sailed on a chartered ship to Normandy for five days of international commemorations. Steve was under contract with NBC to serve as its official D-Day historian for the commemoration. He joined panel discussions to speak about the battle and its meaning in history with Tom Brokaw. It was a great opportunity to drum up support for the Museum before a national television audience. Taken together, these events would put us over the top, or so we thought.

Yet, there were still significant issues that remained unresolved as the anniversary approached. Perhaps the biggest was the Museum's location, whether at the Research Park or downtown. Since we had nowhere near the funds needed to build in either location, we still had no choice but to proceed for now with the Research Park plan. It was the only site we could guarantee to donors or to state and federal legislators who controlled funding that we had secured. To make the Research Park more appealing to board members who questioned the location, in December 1993 Chancellor O'Brien increased the size of the site offered by the university from 2 to 3.15 acres, at no added cost. He also offered another two acres of usable land on the beach side of the levee for outdoor exhibits, as well as four more acres for the Museum entrance and added parking on the UNO campus. This represented over nine acres, plus overflow parking across the street on the main campus. It was a generous offer, and, with no other options in view, we hoped that this would resolve the location debate.

Steve was growing impatient with the politics of the controversy and wanted to move forward with the Research Park site, despite the dissenting voices. He wanted to get on with the exhibit and building designs, and to focus on plans for the anniversary events. As head of the park, I wanted the matter settled as well. Steve and I both felt that it was time for a big push in the year ahead without the distraction of the location issue. We thought any public uncertainty about the location was a deal killer. The Chancellor added more help in his letter by further committing the UNO Eisenhower Center to continuing collaboration in support of the Museum's education and research mission, both before and after its eventual opening.

At the board meeting in December 1993, Steve pushed hard to end the controversy by offering a motion to officially approve the UNO Research and Technology Park site as critical to the success of the Museum. However, a majority of the board was not convinced, voting to table Steve's motion. They argued for time to hire a firm to analyze downtown versus the Research Park in terms of their potential sustainability as a tourist attraction.[1]

The motion made no mention of the relative weight of the education and research objectives, which Ann Boyce had recommended being assessed, in comparison to the Museum's competing opportunity for tourists and visitors. While Steve and I were exasperated by another delay, we agreed not to press the issue so we could concentrate on the immediate priorities for the 50th anniversary. We desperately needed a conceptual design for a building and exhibits for the lakefront site by that date regardless of whether we changed locations later. We agreed that the exhibits could always be shifted to another location—if we ever got to that point.

On the fundraising front, we had new causes for optimism. The Chairman-elect, Bob Howson, established a well-thought-out campaign to approach local business leaders to raise $1 million by May 1994, and he already had pledges of $300,000 toward that goal. We figured $1 million dollars was the critical base of local contributions needed to establish credibility with national foundations and private donors. The board also agreed to hire the Harrison Price Company, a national attraction economist firm, to perform a marketing study to assess the scope and size of the future Museum. Apart from lending credibility to our national fundraising campaign, Lee Schlesinger and other board members hoped the study would reveal new data that would help decide the issue in favor of a downtown location.

For the moment, we had no choice but to assume that Research Park was the site. We plunged ahead with our commitments to spend millions of federal funds in the next year for exhibit and building design for the historic lakefront site. Everyone on both sides of the location issue agreed we could not hold a groundbreaking and major national fundraiser without three things: first, a firm site for the Museum; second, a completed concept plan for a physical Museum with actual exhibit renderings; and, third, the Guggenheim documentary film ready for premiere and a national broadcast. By May 1994, we were four years into planning and promoting the mission of the Museum. It was three years since we had obtained our $4 million federal grant, and two years since forming the National D-Day Museum Board. We had to demonstrate substantial progress and prove to the world that we knew what we were doing. We had to capture the national media spotlight from May through June, when all eyes would be fixed on D-Day's 50th anniversary. We had to make clear the connection between our proposed Museum and the historic importance of D-Day. Perhaps, most of all, we had to convince Americans that the National D-Day Museum should be built in New Orleans.

THE 50TH ANNIVERSARY OF D-DAY: THE MUSEUM SURGE OF 1994

As we hoped, there was a drumbeat of publicity in the weeks before our big events in New Orleans that built local excitement. "It will be a love song to democracy," Ambrose told the *Daily Advertiser* of Lafayette, Louisiana. The article also included Jack Masey's descriptions of the planned exhibits. "This Museum will have something for everybody," he told the paper. "We will make it very experiential for all visitors with state-of-the-art technology designed to make people feel what it might have been like to land on Utah beach on June 6, 1944."[2]

On May 21, 1994, a crowd of 1,500 packed the Orpheum Theater to view the premiere of the Guggenheim film *D-Day Remembered,* which was narrated by Pulitzer Prize–winning historian David McCullough.[3] Guggenheim's film absorbed the historical interpretation of Steve Ambrose along with the Museum's mission, and he merged both with his own artistic sensibilities. The film delivered the story with power and emotion, and the audience responded with a standing ovation.

The entire evening was spectacular. US Rep. Lindy Boggs of Louisiana was in attendance, along with board members, UNO leadership, donors, friends, and several government dignitaries. The audience enjoyed a banquet in the Roosevelt Hotel with inspiring remarks by Steve, Lee Schlesinger, Masey, and Guggenheim.[4] Spirits and optimism ran high as Masey publicly revealed the new exhibit designs and conceptual architecture treatments for the first time, describing how the Museum would bring the D-Day story to life.

To highlight the appeal of the Museum to younger audiences, Masey described the experiential simulations, a full-scale reconstruction of a German bunker, interactive maps, data on costs in lives, personal accounts of veterans who fought on D-Day, and a giant video wall, which displayed the scale and scope of the invasion. Of course, there would be archives and space for the UNO Eisenhower Center to curate exhibits and support WWII research and education programs. The presentation was quite breathtaking. The "good war" messaging in the exhibits was vintage Ambrose. Steve announced that the Museum would now cost $30 million—a figure that was little more than a guesstimate—and was scheduled to open in early 1997.[5] Amid all the excitement and drama of the moment, nobody seemed to notice or care that the completion was postponed by another year.

A far bigger media boost came in mid-May with the publication and reviews of Steve's *D-Day* book: it became a blockbuster best seller. Here was the core story written authentically by America's most popular military historian at the time. Steve's book struck a chord with readers by zeroing in on the drama and personal stories of the Americans who fought at Normandy. "The literature they read as youngsters was antiwar, cynical, portraying patriots as suckers, slackers as heroes," Steve wrote in the prologue, foreshadowing themes of the future Museum. "None of them wanted to be part of another war. They wanted to be throwing baseballs, not hand grenades, shooting .22s at rabbits, not M-1s at other young men. But when the test came, when freedom had to be fought for or abandoned, they fought. They were soldiers of democracy. They were the men of D-Day."[6]

The popularity of his book also helped make the case for a national Museum that would honor the veterans of D-Day, save their stories, and share their accounts for all future generations. No amount of paid advertising could replicate what reviewers were saying. In a laudatory review headlined "Telling it like it Was," Raleigh Trevelyan wrote in the *New York Times* that Ambrose's "descriptions of individual ordeals on the bloody beach of Omaha make this book outstanding."[7]

When Steve talked about the Museum to admiring journalists, I could scarcely find a doubter among them. Steve was a star. No one asked him in those days if we had the funds to build it or where the money was coming from. He had them all "drinking the Kool-Aid," which was just fine with those of us promoting the Museum to donors and government leaders. We were riding the wave of Ambrose and the D-Day publicity.

To expand on the lift, the UNO Eisenhower Center also hosted a multiday, world-class D-Day symposium in May, featuring Normandy veterans and dozens of WWII historians. This event highlighted the ultimate educational mission of the Museum, and it showcased the center's oral history collection, which would be housed in the future Museum.

The highlights were many, but particularly remarkable was a panel featuring two former enemy commanders involved in a pivotal D-Day episode. British Major John Howard led the midnight glider raid across the English Channel to capture the key Pegasus Bridge. German Colonel Hans von Luck's planned counterattack against the amphibious landing failed because the captured bridge blocked his 21st Panzer Division tanks from reaching the beaches. Von Luck and Howard brought laughter and tears to the audience, which had a rare chance to hear these two opponents speak about their key missions. These were men of D-Day lore, and everyone in their presence was thrilled. The stories and personal accounts told that day were only a preview of those being saved for the exhibits in the National D-Day Museum.

The Museum's groundbreaking events exceeded expectations and became the first celebratory milestone, much to my and Steve's relief. It was just the beginning. As the 50th anniversary ceremonies in Normandy neared, the White House invited Steve to brief President Clinton, Secretary of State Warren Christopher, and communications adviser David Gergen about Operation Overlord in preparation for the President's remarks in Normandy.[8]

Steve and I flew to England in late May for the Museum's long-planned anniversary Normandy tour, packed with donors, D-Day veterans, and friends of the Museum. The tour had been organized and marketed by Peter McLean, President of Student Services International, and the longtime developer of Steve's top-level "D-Day to the Rhine" tours. Steve had led these tours since 1980 with veterans as well as military and government leaders, primarily from the United States, United Kingdom, and France. McLean assembled amazing insider stories at war sites as settings for Steve's mesmerizing talks and interviews with veterans.

Based on Steve's conviction that the 50th anniversary was going to be a major milestone, we had booked speakers and engaged veterans years in advance. We understood WWII veterans were at that time in their 70s and 80s and that Americans of all ages increasingly appreciated what was owed to those 16 million men who fought and, in some cases, died for the peace, strength, and prosperity that we had enjoyed since the end of the war.

The Department of Defense had prepared for the 50th anniversary for several years. World leaders, including President Clinton, Queen Elizabeth of England, British Prime Minister John Major, and French President Francois Mitterrand, would be in attendance, as well as heads of state from Canada, Australia, Norway, Luxembourg, and top military brass from many NATO nations.

Knowing there would be no vacant rooms within 100 miles of Normandy beach, Peter chartered a ship, the *Black Prince,* to accommodate our 500-plus tour-goers. We planned to sail across the English Channel from Portsmouth to Caen in Normandy, and the ship would serve as our hotel for five days during the events. We secured busses and top guides to make sure we had access to the key battle sites, events, ceremonies, and even arranged for French resistance fighters to tell their stories alongside American veterans.

Steve's visits to the beaches of Normandy over the years had inspired him to write his book, create the Eisenhower Center, and, ultimately, gave him the vision to build a National D-Day Museum. Everyone on the tour was moved by the visit, but few could grasp how fulfilling that moment was for me and Steve. We had not built a Museum yet, but we had come a long way in the last four years. We were convinced that our major supporters would feel the power and emotion of the American Cemetery at Colleville-sur-Mer above Omaha Beach and that they, and those yet unknown to us, would soon join our campaign. Steve and I designed the 1994 D-Day tour to build support and awareness of the historic mission for the National D-Day Museum and to generate the national publicity we needed. We felt this would be our moment to put the project on the fast track.

Our group arrived in London on May 27 and enjoyed a whirlwind schedule that included tours of the Churchill War Rooms, the Imperial War Museums, a US Embassy event that featured Bob and Dolores Hope, and an intimate evening with Churchill's youngest daughter, Lady Mary Soames. We then traveled to Portsmouth and visited the Southwick House Map Room where Eisenhower met with his commanders in the early morning hours of June 5 and made the fateful decision to launch the invasion of Normandy the next day.[9] Finally, we sponsored a USO dance near the Portsmouth Harbor, where the D-Day veterans in our group showed they could still swing with the best of them. On the evening of June 1, 1994, our 500 eager tour members boarded the *Black Prince* for the overnight channel crossing to Caen.

As our ship approached the Normandy coastline at 5 a.m. the next morning, we asked the captain to throttle back the engines and cruise as close to shore as possible. We glided at four knots along Utah Beach, Pointe du Hoc, and Omaha Beach in the overcast early morning. The only element missing was the rough weather that greeted the Allied invasion forces on June 6, 1944. As dawn arose from the mist, Steve spoke from the bridge over the ship's loudspeaker to passengers gathered on the upper deck and others in their cabins. He asked the veterans to recount their memories of storming the beaches that morning 50 years earlier. Their stories were riveting.

Frank Walk, a US Army captain with the 6th Engineer Special Brigade Group, spoke first, describing the moments he left the mothership for a Higgins boat and sailed through withering fire to reach Omaha Beach amid total confusion. Upon landing, he replaced a beach master, who was suffering from shell shock. The memories Frank and others shared with us over the next few hours were astonishing. A hush fell over the gathered passengers, who listened in awe as one veteran after another told their harrowing stories that morning. It was quite an emotional way to approach Normandy for the 50th anniversary.

Once at anchor in the Caen harbor, busses took our tour participants to all the landing sites at Omaha and Utah beaches, the villages where paratroopers landed, and the site of the 2nd Ranger Battalion's daring climb up the cliffs of Pointe du Hoc to capture the heavily fortified German defenders. Steve spoke on Omaha Beach, and the veterans recounted their personal memories of the first 24 hours of that day. We also visited the Bayeux Museum, which holds the Bayeux Tapestry. This incredible artifact, created in the eleventh century, chronicles another epic battle—William the Conqueror's successful invasion of England in 1066, a story embroidered in fabric for posterity. We hoped that our Museum would help people remember D-Day in the same way a millennium from now.

The 50th anniversary was the largest, most well-attended, and most well-publicized D-Day commemoration to date. More than 100,000 people, many of them veterans, attended the ceremony at the Normandy American Cemetery and Memorial above Omaha Beach.[10] Visitors paid their respects to fallen comrades at the cemetery gravesites and traversed the trails down the bluffs to the beaches below. An imposing fleet of naval vessels from the former Allied nations was anchored offshore. "On these beaches, forces of freedom turned the tide of the 20th century," Clinton declared in his stirring remarks at the ceremony.[11]

Standing there, I was overwhelmed by our task to do justice to that day in history 50 years before. I reflected on my afternoon drinks with Steve when we first embraced his idea to build a small Museum. The project gained traction and increased in scope and significance since we began in 1990. As a European historian, I understood D-Day's importance as the turning point of the war, but, in that moment in 1994, the Museum project became more personal and daunting to me. Though I had been to Normandy several times before, I now began to grasp more fully the enormous responsibility and challenge before us.

Re-creating all the drama and tragedies that took place on those beaches, or in the planes and ships sent to do battle, was impossible. But somehow, the Museum had to find innovative ways to immerse visitors in these stories. The exhibits, media, artifacts, and personal stories had to help them see and feel what it was like to be in battle. We had to accomplish this in a Museum some 5,000 miles from the scene of the battle. We needed to surface moments when the fear, courage, motivation, and sacrifice of those who fought at Normandy would touch the hearts and minds of visitors. We would have to show visitors a battle that was at once horrific but also necessary, as the war had to be won at all costs. Our galleries had to be historically authentic, depicting the good and the bad. Most importantly, the future Museum would have to create a transformative, emotional, and meaningful experience for all visitors, young and old alike, long after all WWII veterans had passed from the scene.

I suddenly felt very humbled, even though I was not leading the charge for the Museum. Steve and the board were in the lead, but he and I began this together, and we knew each other well enough to know we had to finish it together. He did his part on a big stage. I needed to do more, and I began to realize how much I still had to learn about creating a museum. Steve and I were still novices and more anxious than ever to bring professional museum leadership on board as soon as possible. In the meantime, I was ever more grateful for the genius of Jack Masey, whose creative exhibit designs provided professional expertise and began to give shape to what the National D-Day Museum could be.

June 6, 1994, turned out to be a banner day for the Museum in so many ways. The experience of that day brought us new friends and loyal supporters on the tour who connected to our mission through their shared experience of the unfolding events.[12] Even more important for the Museum was Steve's role as the featured D-Day historian on the NBC stage all day on June 6, along with Tom Brokaw, Katie Couric, and Bryant Gumbel. They sat perched above the bluffs overlooking Omaha Beach; the weather was perfect. Brokaw and Steve carried on conversations with each other as well as veterans and guests. They provided commentary and insights about the battle, the near disaster mid-morning on Omaha beach, the stories of valor, and the meaning of D-Day in history. Both Tom and Steve were deeply moved by the thousands of D-Day veterans, families, widows, and war orphans, who streamed past the NBC stage from the cemetery to the beaches below.

Standing on the NBC broadcast platform, Brokaw spoke emotionally to Steve about these proud veterans and mused off-camera that they might be America's "greatest generation." Steve quickly challenged Tom: "That's a great idea for a book, and if you don't write it, I will." Thus was born the idea that inspired Brokaw's best-selling book by that title.

Throughout the day, Tom gave Steve ample air time to describe the significance of the D-Day Museum project in New Orleans before an audience of millions. We could never have purchased such publicity. Tom had learned of our Museum project from Steve several years earlier, and he was an ardent advocate from the start. Tom and Steve's relationship grew into a close friendship over the years. Brokaw was our greatest champion with a national profile, keeping the D-Day Museum project in the forefront of news whenever the memory and history of D-Day and World War II were relevant.

I stood on the side of the NBC stage for much of that day, listening to the televised discussions and thought how fortunate we were. As America's most trusted news anchor for many years, Tom brought credibility and visibility that made us appear viable, even though we were still a long distance from the goal line. Brokaw and the 50th anniversary of D-Day 1994 in Normandy will always hold a special place in my memory.

NEXT STEPS

We were buoyed by the events, and the future looked bright. We began to understand how big the Museum might become. The stakes were rising, the project scope was expanding, and the funding goals were growing dramatically. On the governance side, Bob Howson was unable to assume his full responsibilities as Chairman because of business demands at McDermott International, so Steve temporarily took on those duties, while Greg O'Brien stepped in as President and Vice Chairman.

We had belatedly learned about a big gap in our Museum planning: the lack of artifacts to support our exhibits. Aside from the Steve's oral histories and a few artifacts donated by veterans along with them, we had no real collection plan and had not thought much about any future archival holdings until Jack Masey pointed out it was imperative for a history museum to have a core collection of artifacts to support the exhibits. Up to that point, Steve and I assumed we would never be able to raise enough operating funds or afford space to become a major collecting museum. Collecting and preserving artifacts was very expensive, and we knew that. The board never envisioned a need for artifacts in our planning, either. Our conceptual plans included space for a modest core collection of selected D-Day artifacts to support the exhibits—and, at most, one curator, but that was it. We learned from other museums that collecting required more space, buildings, people, and money, all of which constituted a black hole that we could not afford. We never expected having operating funds like a Smithsonian Museum, but we knew we needed artifacts to support our exhibits.

That issue suddenly found a solution in 1993 when we learned that the town of St. Lô in Normandy planned to close its museum and sell all its holdings gathered from the battlefields of Normandy. We struck gold. St. Lô was a key objective during the Allied breakout from the Normandy beaches. Its museum contained more than 100,000 artifacts, large and small. Acquisition of the collection would provide a stamp of authenticity for our Museum and avoid years of searching. The collection included cars, motorcycles, weapons, artillery, uniforms, and other artifacts left by Americans, Germans, and even French resistance fighters.

Steve and I were ecstatic; the board immediately gave the green light for board member Fred Baldwin to fly to Normandy, secure an inventory, and negotiate a price. Fred, an astute corporate attorney, was in the middle of everything in those years thanks to his boss, Bob Howson. After some wrangling, Fred signed an option to acquire most of the collection for approximately $300,000. Howson announced that McDermott would underwrite the entire purchase price. We were stunned and grateful. The purchase was the largest single corporate gift that we had received to date.

Despite the great news, we quickly needed to return to the controversial location issue. In June 1994, we received the results of Harrison Price's marketing study. Bill Stevenson, a representative from the Harrison Price Company, reported that to succeed in New Orleans, we had to be oriented toward tourists. His analysis estimated that a downtown location would attract 400,000 to 500,000 visitors a year compared to 200,000 to 300,000 at the lakefront. The report sparked renewed debate among the board. Steve made another strong argument for keeping the lakefront location because of its historic connection to D-Day and the strength of the Eisenhower Center. We had just seen during the 50th anniversary how much the Center's educational programs and events contributed to credibility and publicity for the Museum. Steve argued that the lakefront would appeal to audiences from both higher education and tourists. "We can have the museum where, it seems to me, it best fits with all of its many purposes," while losing the Eisenhower Center and UNO connection to the museum would limit broader audiences.[13]

Arthur Davis, Greg O'Brien, and others backed Steve, and said our decision should be driven by our mission. "Is the museum to be a popular tourist attraction or a place where you go to learn lessons, and grow?" O'Brien asked.[14] The board remained divided on the issue and once again no decision was made.

Aside from the location, many outstanding questions about the scope of the Museum persisted. The main question was how big should it become? Our growing success brought increased pressure to expand the scope of the Museum and its exhibits to include the Navy and the Marines in the Pacific War. After all, Higgins boats were used during most of the Pacific amphibious assaults as part of the island-hopping strategy. They were also used during amphibious assaults in North Africa and the Mediterranean. Some thought a broader scope would make the Museum more appealing and expand our donor base beyond those focused on Normandy.

The debates continued into the fall. At the October 1994 meeting, John Kelly warned that expanding the scope would alienate the Museum from its original rationale and could have an adverse impact on the efforts to obtain federal funding. Others suggested that a change in scope might positively affect private funding. While we made no decision then, Steve presented a draft of a new, broader mission statement at the next meeting on November 16, 1994. He suggested a phase 1 to focus on the Normandy D-Day as planned and a phase 2 to focus on amphibious operations in other theaters, as well as perhaps a phase 3 to cover the home front and air war.[15]

Over the coming months, Steve and I further developed this new mission statement, which he submitted to the board on March 21, 1995.

> The National D-Day Museum will tell the story of American amphibious operations around the world in World War II, highlighting June 6, 1944, the day of the Normandy invasion, along with the invasions in the Mediterranean and Pacific Theaters that ensured the preservation of democracy. The Museum stands as America's tribute to the men and women who made these invasions possible, presenting their stories to an international audience, preserving material for future research and scholarship, and inspiring us and future generations to apply lessons learned from the most

complicated military operations ever staged—primarily teamwork and the value of democracy to solving problems in our society.[16]

We recognized that our revised mission moved us toward a larger project. Steve and I also had the growing realization that this expanded mission further tipped the scales to a downtown location to reach more visitors. We sensed that the board gravitated toward the downtown location, even as exhibit designs moved forward and as negotiations were underway for the Eskew-Filson architectural firm to build the Museum in the Research Park site per the approved Master Plan.

Fundraising remained a big issue. Aside from McDermott International's donation for the St. Lô collection, there was no significant movement on the private fundraising side. We raised a paltry $8,000 in private donations in 1994 and expected another $20,000 in future donations.[17] At least we had good news on the public side of fundraising. As a result of all the positive national publicity, board member Fred Baldwin and I helped secure a $3.2 million grant from the Louisiana state legislature, but it would not be available until we had enough other funds to build the future Museum. Still, on top of the $4 million from Congress, we thought having major federal and state grants would motivate donors and foundations to help close the gap, even though we could not yet define the size of that gap without more precise cost estimates. We were clearly nowhere close to the funds needed for a completed project, which most estimates put at beyond $30 million. Our current plan was to build the lakefront Museum on donated land for a barebones budget of $9 million.

The St. Lô collection arrived in August 1995, and Greg O'Brien arranged for it to be stored in a climate-controlled American Standard storage facility near the Research Park. Receiving the collection was a huge step forward, but it underscored a huge problem: we still had no Museum to display artifacts. The incoming collection necessitated the need to hire Karen Reisch, who was our lone administrative assistant. She tackled a myriad of tasks, including keeping tabs on our budget, fundraising figures, and facilitating every facet of Museum correspondence.

Necessity is the mother of invention. Rumblings from board members in favor of a downtown site grew and eventually filtered to Steve and me outside of board meetings during the summer of 1995. We were aware that the hunt for a new location was quietly underway by key members on the board.

We had a new board member, John Kushner, an avid collector of personal military artifacts and one of the top commercial realtors in New Orleans. At a board meeting on November 29, 1995, Kushner made the dramatic announcement that an empty warehouse known as the Gallagher building was for sale for an asking price of just over $1 million. It was located at 945 Magazine Street near Lee Circle, an area known as the Warehouse District.

The three-year controversy over the location ended immediately. Once there was an affordable option downtown as an alternative to the lakefront site, there was no longer a debate. It was a watershed moment in the survival of the Museum. The building committee quickly went to work pursuing the purchase. The committee, chaired by influential developer Jerome Goldman, included Arthur Davis, John Kushner, and Fred Baldwin. Preliminary estimates were that the 40,000 square-foot warehouse could be renovated to meet standards for the Museum and at a cost we could raise money for in stages.

In a single stroke, the board made the most important decision in its short history by changing course on the Museum's location. Kushner was the visionary who found the building and made it happen. The decision shaped the Museum's future as a tourist attraction in ways that we could not imagine at the time. Everyone was on board, including Steve, Chancellor O'Brien, Arthur Davis, and me. The downtown site was almost a slum, and the warehouse needed major rehab, but the choice was made.

Coincidentally, we had a very consequential motivator, the realization that the last $1 million of the initial $4 million federal grant from 1992 was going to revert to the Department of Defense if we did not spend it before September 1997. Someone happened to notice the grant condition in the fine print.[18] This was a rude awakening. I suppose we once knew of the five-year time limit but had forgotten over the years. The imminent forfeiture of a million dollars sent hearts racing and focused the minds of everyone on the board.

The warehouse site still had unknown challenges of construction, cost, and the desirability of the location. However, these issues appeared minor compared to the uncertainties of building a smaller museum from the ground up at the lakefront at a much higher project cost than renovating a warehouse in a relatively abandoned part of the city. New construction in the Research Park would have been more costly, particularly since our architectural firm, Eskew-Filson, recently requested a higher fee than we could afford. Renovating a warehouse was the more practical option by far.

We believed the warehouse site downtown gave us a viable path to get close to the $9 million we thought we needed to finish and open the Museum. The board thought the promise of $3.2 million in state funds was firm enough and could be used to rehab the old warehouse.

The new site was certainly not a tourist hot spot. The Warehouse District was a sketchy area with a myriad of decrepit and abandoned warehouses alongside a few new art galleries, a couple of decent restaurants, and several condo conversions. The nearby Confederate War Museum was languishing and was about to close, we heard.

The entire Warehouse District was as large as the bustling French Quarter, but a little bit up the river in the Central Business District. Property values and economic activity had worsened rapidly with the advent of container shipping in the mid-20th century in the nearby port area. The container system bypassed the need for warehouse storage for goods coming off ships. Businesses either moved out or went broke. The Gallagher warehouse was in the worst area, on the far end of the district. By 1995, the site was a far cry from a tourist destination. Developers had begun converting a few warehouses along the Mississippi River into apartments, but most of the district was rundown. Regardless, we saw the promise of the site. The Gallagher building was only three blocks from the New Orleans Convention Center, the largest driver of tourism in the city. Local real estate agents predicted a robust development of the entire Warehouse District in the coming decade. The visionary developers and real estate brokers on the board concurred with these rosy projections and encouraged us to take advantage of the dirt-cheap real estate prices in the district.

The location had other advantages. The warehouse was four stories tall and built like a fortress, with walls two feet thick. It was a 19th-century brewery; hence the thick concrete walls and floors needed to bear the weight of heavy vats and distilling equipment. The warehouse withstood many hurricanes and was above the flood plain. The entire structure exuded strength and permanence, ideal for telling the story of D-Day. In addition to the main building, there was also an attached shedlike structure that served as a loading dock, which some envisioned as a possible entrance area. The entire building was complicated. Upon inspection, we discovered there were structural quirks, ancient wiring, and possible termite damage. The building urgently needed a new roof and required replastering, painting, air conditioning, and demolition of some interior walls and floors. Luckily, these issues could be resolved by good architects and contractors, and we could use the earmarked state funds to pay for the repairs and renovations. Jack Masey thought the warehouse was perfect for exhibits and very similar to the historic structure used to house the exhibits he designed for the Ellis Island Museum of Immigration.

The stars aligned, it seemed. For the first time since we formed the D-Day Museum Foundation in 1992, all the directors were in unanimous agreement that this downtown location was the solution, and we moved fast. At the board meeting February 14, 1996, John Kushner reported that we could purchase the warehouse for $725,000, all-cash. Later, in April, he proposed we purchase two other adjacent properties that were available from another owner, one at 923 Magazine Street and the other at 527 Howard Avenue, for an additional $330,000. John suggested the Howard Avenue lot might be used for outside exhibits and entrance. The two-story brick building at 923 Magazine Street was in good shape, with space that could serve as offices for the Museum and Eisenhower Center.[19]

The Building Committee pushed forward with the due diligence, inspections, and financing options through the summer of 1996. The board engaged a new architect, Lyons and Hudson, to work with Masey and his Metaform company to produce detailed plans for the building's exhibit spaces and to generate more realistic estimates of the renovation and exhibit costs.

At the same time, we needed final assurance that the state appropriation was available for the new project site. This was the key piece for our purchase, even though we knew it would not be available for spending until summer or fall. The bill, now reduced to $2.5 million, cleared the state legislature in 1996, but the Museum could not spend the money until we proved we had the balance of nonstate funds to complete the building renovations. We were short by at least $3 million, but our board leaders convinced state officials that we would have the necessary funds from new federal and private commitments in the coming years, and key legislators assured us that our progress was encouraging. Though our figures were not yet concrete, the reputation of Steve Ambrose and our board leaders sufficed.

On April 26, 1996, the board approved the purchase of the three properties for $1,055,000 with the remaining funds from the 1992 federal grant. By the November 26, 1996, meeting, we were the owners of all three properties. We knew that we still had to find $3 million more in private dollars to meet our matching commitment to the state, but we were confident that we would succeed. The taste of victory was getting sweeter.

During this same period, Steve and I were making major personal and professional decisions that affected our positions at the University of New Orleans and would mean that we could not devote as much time to the Museum. Steve and I were both leaving our UNO posts in different ways for different reasons. Steve retired from the university and as Eisenhower Center Director in May 1995, after hiring a young rising star, Dr. Douglas Brinkley, to replace him. Brinkley was a presidential historian with a growing reputation, publications, ambition, and entrepreneurial instincts that Steve thought would help the Museum. Steve was making a good living as an author, busy with research, and nearing publication of several new books, and in growing demand as a celebrity historian and public speaker. He had published four books since 1989, culminating in his bestseller, *D-Day* in 1994. His book, *Undaunted Courage,* about the Lewis and Clark expedition was coming out in 1996, and he was deep into research and writing of *Citizen Soldiers,* the sequel to *D-Day,* due for publication in 1997.

In the spring of 1996, Steve asked the board to allow him to step down as Acting Chairman. He suggested as his replacement a new board member, retired Marine Maj. Gen. James Livingston, a Medal of Honor recipient for his valorous service in Vietnam. The board accepted Steve's resignation and recommendation with appreciation.[20] Steve pledged to continue to help raise money for the Museum and to remain as a board member to see it through to the end. I knew from our personal conversations and plans, however, that the Museum would not get as much time from him in the coming years. In addition to his forthcoming books, his speaking schedule was keeping him busy. He was also spending half the year in his Montana home. Livingston was a popular choice. He had recently retired as the Commander of the Marine Forces Reserves Headquarters in New Orleans and was the Vice President of Canizaro Enterprises, the top commercial real estate developer in New Orleans.[21]

As for me, I needed a break from an intense 20 years in my various leadership roles as Director, Dean, Vice Chancellor, and President of the Research Park. These were exciting years in my higher education career—I had played significant roles in starting UNO's study abroad programs in Austria and elsewhere, establishing the Metropolitan College and our satellite university centers, creating two new degree programs, funding the Research and

Technology Park, and leading UNO's downtown Business/Higher Education Council. While I relished these opportunities and was proud of my reputation as a higher education entrepreneur, the pressures were unrelenting and exhausting. I was ready to turn the page and return to teaching history. Steve also encouraged me to return to the classroom. Doing so would allow me more time to write and to take up some ventures we wanted to pursue together. One idea Steve had was that I help him manage Ambrose-Tubbs, Inc., the family company he established in 1993 to oversee his many publication enterprises.

After seven years as head of the Research and Technology Park, I felt my job getting it launched was finished, albeit without the National D-Day Museum. This was a good time for me to step aside and turn the park over to my Associate Vice Chancellor, Norma Grace, who deserved much of the credit for what we had achieved. In late 1996, Chancellor O'Brien approved my request for a sabbatical beginning in 1997, with the plan to return to my department as Professor of European History from 1998 to 2002, when I would retire from UNO.

Our professional and retirement plans, however, did not alter our deep commitment to complete the Museum. Both of us were well into the design development of Jack Masey's exhibits, which now had to be reconfigured from the Research Park site for the downtown warehouse space. Since the board approved the expanded mission statement that included new exhibits for *D-Day Invasions in the Pacific,* we also began conceptualizing how that story should be told. Steve and General Livingston flew to Washington in the spring of 1997 for meetings with Louisiana Rep. Bob Livingston, Sen. Mary Landrieu of Louisiana, and Sen. Ted Stevens of Alaska to seek an appropriation for the Museum for the Pacific exhibit. We knew that a Pacific exhibit would grab the interest of Stevens, an Army Air Corps pilot in the China-Burma-India Campaign. Bob Livingston, Chairman of the House Appropriations Committee, gave Steve and the General strong encouragement for an appropriation in the 1997 legislative session. If approved, we could spend the funds for the design and planning of the Pacific Theater galleries. It was good news but offered no immediate funding to build the Normandy D-Day exhibits. While board leadership transitioned away from UNO with the move downtown, the university remained deeply involved. Steve and I continued to serve as volunteers on the board, while Brinkley, the new Eisenhower Center Director, was added as one of the three ex-officio UNO members of the board, along with Chancellor O'Brien, who pledged the university's continuing support of the Museum's research and education mission. Getting the Museum open and staying open with operating funds was another matter; no one was thinking about that yet.

Heading into early 1997, General Livingston reduced the size of the Executive Committee to the major players who drove the Museum project. Steve retired and I went on sabbatical, so we stepped down from the committee. Other members were rotated off in favor of Livingston appointees, but we felt he had the right to pick his key players. Livingston whittled the Executive Committee down to the following: Greg O'Brien, Vice Chairman and President, Jerry Goldman, head of the Building Committee, Tom Snedeker, Treasurer, Bill Detweiler, Secretary, Fred Baldwin, Robert Howson, and John Kushner. Steve, of course, remained the historian-in chief and was regularly consulted on major decisions and strategies.

Soon after came a blockbuster development at the January 28, 1997, board meeting, when Livingston recommended hiring retired Col. Howard Lovingood as the Museum's first Executive Director. Lovingood was not on our radar in previous discussions about filling this important role. He served over 40 years in the Marine Corps and worked directly under Livingston while on his last active duty in New Orleans. Livingston said Lovingood's strong ties to the veteran community would help accelerate our desperately needed private fundraising. Though Lovingood had no experience with museums, fundraising, or nonprofit management, Livingston expressed great confidence in him, and the board approved his appointment.[22] Steve and I had some misgivings, as we felt the candidates we had recommended to the board were head and shoulders more qualified. Nevertheless, this was a long overdue step. We all knew Lovingood had to prove himself, but at least someone could now take over the expanding operational duties from UNO and our volunteer board members.

While it might seem crazy, we made another big commitment only two months earlier to spend our last capital funds for a project that was not in our critical path for the warehouse construction. Livingston reported that Pat Taylor, the owner of Taylor Energy Company in New Orleans, had called from London with word that Sotheby's planned to auction a British Spitfire, with the pilot's log documenting that the plane flew over the beaches on D-Day. Livingston presented this as a rare opportunity to acquire a unique and authentic D-Day aircraft. Taylor offered to pay for the plane's restoration if we would pay the auction and shipping price of approximately $120,000.

Livingston said funds left in our federal grant were available for the Spitfire, and the board approved the deal.[23] The Spitfire generated excitement, and I was one of those who supported the decision for that reason. I do not recall if everyone knew that it was the very last of the $4 million federal grant when we were scraping for money everywhere for the warehouse reconstruction. The subtraction of any capital funds for the Museum construction meant we had to divert scarce operating funds from fundraising to keep the contractors working. Buying the Spitfire may not have been prudent, given our dire financial straits, another indicator of how creating our Museum often involved a string of ad-hoc decisions.

Those dire straits became clearer at that same meeting, when we heard shocking financial news from our new Board Member and Treasurer, Tom Snedeker. After close examination of our financial records, he reported that we had to raise an additional $3.5 million in private funds to open the Museum, even if we received the state appropriation of $2.5 million in June.[24] Without any more private money, we would run out of cash in six months. His report brought everyone back down to Earth in a hurry. Our sense of urgency became more acute with the latest building and exhibit construction estimates. The warehouse renovation overseen by Lyons and Hudson would cost around $2.5 million and Masey's exhibits another $2.5 million, making a preliminary total of $5 million. This did not even count other planned expenditures such as administrative offices and ground floor temporary exhibit space. These additions, if approved, would increase the Lyons and Hudson contract to $3.35 million.[25] Opening a national Museum without offices for staff, planned special exhibit space, or space for the Museum store and food service was difficult to imagine. The $3.5 million shortfall projected by the Treasurer was most likely going to be considerably more with all costs included.

These were hard numbers to digest. After buying the warehouse a couple months earlier, hiring an Executive Director, buying the Spitfire, and needing $136,000 for the end-of-the-year operations, anyone could see we were in a cash-flow crisis. Some board members felt disillusioned as the goalposts for completion moved further and further away. Members of the business community had growing skepticism about the project and that hurt our fundraising. Hoping to pump up the board's sagging morale, Steve volunteered to accelerate his pledge and contribute $100,000 immediately.[26] Even so, it was a bleak outlook for the spring of 1997.

Livingston told the *Times-Picayune* in May 1997 that a scaled-back Museum at the warehouse site could be built for around $11 million, considerably less than the earlier estimates for as much as $30 million at the Research Park site.[27] His spin was optimistic, but it also publicly displayed our widely fluctuating cost estimates, with the implicit suggestion that we were spitballing our numbers and did not have a handle on our finances.

In June 1997, I began my year-long sabbatical, during which time I was to become Director of UNO's new Center Austria. I knew things looked problematic for the Museum, and I was going to be less involved. Steve and I met constantly during that time, and we were determined not to give up. We knew there were good funding prospects on the horizon from both state and federal sources. We hoped Livingston and Lovingood would ramp up the contributions, especially among private donors. Unfortunately, every promising development for public funding was met with setbacks on the private side. In June 1997, Livingston recommended a new fundraising goal in the neighborhood of $5 million to $8 million, a seemingly unattainable target that greatly deflated board members and caused some to question whether the Museum was even viable.[28]

I convinced Steve and Moira to join me on a sailing trip to the British Virgin Islands in the fall of 1997 to relax together and discuss other ventures we hoped to pursue beyond our Museum commitments. We also talked about how we could help the Museum dig out of its financial hole. Steve was frustrated with the poor fundraising results that were now affecting him personally. He was irked at the purchase of the Spitfire and the hiring of Lovingood. These expenses had exhausted our operational funds, which meant Steve had to write personal checks to cover our secretary's salary. This was on top of his additional contribution totaling over $200,000 by 1997.[29] The ocean sailing and gorgeous weather made our problems seem distant and solvable, so, as was our habit, we began to talk about solutions more than problems. After all, we had a building and enough state funds to begin construction.

Still, the realities back in New Orleans were inescapable. The lack of funding heavily taxed our Chairman and volunteer board. Board members felt pressure to give money, and the volunteer work of fundraising became harder. Board meetings rarely had more than half the Directors in attendance, and some members resigned. Many began to sense that the complexity of the operation required someone with more experience in museum management than Lovingood.

Reconstruction and repairs of the warehouse had been underway since the summer of 1997. Steve and I received informal hints from Jack Masey in late fall that his last contractual price of $2.5 million for the D-Day exhibits was likely to increase, but we kept this news to ourselves. Since I was no longer on the Executive Committee, insider information only came to me from Steve, at intermittent board meetings I attended, or from disgruntled board members. My focus was on preparing lectures and research for my return to teaching in the fall of 1998. Little did I know that my life was about to change.

Something was up. The first sign was word in early January 1998 that I was back on the Executive Committee, along with notice of a meeting in a week at 943 Magazine, the Eisenhower Center location. I will never forget the day of that meeting. It was a beautiful yet cold New Orleans winter day. The skies were blue, but a passing cold front brought the chill factor into the twenties. I had forgotten my overcoat, so I hustled to get to the porch and inside the warmth of the Museum offices. As I approached from the street, I saw General Livingston, Chancellor O'Brien, and Steve chatting on the front porch as if it were 70 degrees. I remember being puzzled. Steve was smoking a cigarette, as he would frequently do outside, but that did not explain why Livingston and O'Brien were there with him.

"This is weird," I thought to myself as I tried to rush past them. Livingston grabbed my arm. "Nick, stop for a minute, we need to ask you something," he said. I stopped, wondering what could be so important. "Nick, my term as Chairman is up in September, and we need to get my successor in place soon," the General said. "We want you to be the Museum's next chairman."

I was stunned. I gave Steve a look of surprise. We had just talked a few months earlier on our sailing trip about our other big plans, and Steve never mentioned this possibility. Steve shook my hand before I could digest the proposition. "Nick, you helped me get into this; we've been in it together from the start, and I need you to help us get the Museum to the finish line," he said in a serious tone. "You are the only one who can do it. We think this is the most important thing you can do for the next few years."

They all knew that I planned to resume my full-time teaching job that fall, including teaching two courses a semester in the history department and leading Center Austria programs. To my surprise, O'Brien, my UNO boss, was in on this hijacking. "You know more than anyone that the project needs experienced executive leadership," O'Brien said, adding that he would adjust my duties to allow me to dedicate three-quarters of my time to getting the Museum open. "What does that mean?" I asked. "You will only have to teach one course per semester instead of two," the Chancellor replied. Well, that did not sound like a 75 percent reduction of my UNO duties. I told them I was flattered but quite overwhelmed. This was a radically different career direction than what I planned for the last two years. Livingston wanted to inform several members of the Executive Committee waiting inside, but I said I was in no way ready to make a commitment of that magnitude. Livingston agreed, saying there was no immediate rush and that I could take a few months to decide.[30] Meanwhile, he would bring me up to speed on the current Museum situation and arrange meetings with Tom Snedeker, Bill Detweiler, and other members of the Executive Committee. This was a stunning turn of events. In football lingo, it felt like a Hail Mary pass. I suspected that in the Museum's desperate situation, they had no other play, as they could not find any other board member to take on the heavy load of Chairman with all the financial, fundraising, and construction challenges before us.

Later that evening, Steve defended his sudden change of heart. What further swayed him, apart from our close friendship and mutual trust was my decades of senior leadership at UNO and successful record of startups. He said he did not tell me beforehand because he thought I would say no without Livingston and O'Brien with him for reinforcement. He was probably right. Still, I was blindsided and peeved he had not warned me.

Since the proposition was a major change in my career plans, I took five months to decide. While I was committed to staying on the board and helping Steve all I could, taking the position would be a huge commitment, as our Board Chairman was also CEO. That looked like 30 to 40 hours a week on operations, exhibit design, and fundraising alone, with the Chair's responsibility for the governance of the board on top of that. Chancellor O'Brien's offer was a generous one for the Museum, but I would still need to spend at least 15 to 20 hours a week for my history courses and Center Austria. It would be intense.

This was a real fork in the road for me, personally and professionally. I was 58 and envisioned only four more years of teaching before retiring from UNO. After retirement, I planned to pursue opportunities with Steve on various history enterprises, with some travel and sailing thrown in as well. I was still young enough to pursue other journeys while enjoying some important lifestyle changes in retirement.

Nevertheless, I moved forward that spring with the inclination to take the position as Chairman, provided the board could meet some conditions: I asked to head a strategic planning committee to address our personnel needs and get a handle on our financial picture. I especially needed documentation of our fundraising status and outlook. With full-blown construction underway, I asked O'Brien and Livingston to bring in engineering, development, and fundraising leadership from UNO to help meet professional challenges. Both agreed and I took some time from my sabbatical to dig into Museum operations.

Once I started looking into details, several concerning developments came to light. I immediately began working with Snedeker to get a better picture of our financials, and they were more dire than I initially suspected. Jack Masey wanted an additional $1 million, increasing the Metaform contract fee to $3.5 million.[31] The board was surprised and very upset with this news, as it completely offset the $1 million Forbes gift.[32] Steve again became frustrated with the financials after he was asked to make another cash call to pay staff salaries. At the April board meeting, Livingston announced his intention to resign as Chairman in September. While he made no announcement that I was invited to stand for election, there was an informal indication that a successor had been identified. Some of the Executive Committee already knew I had been asked. I figured if a few knew, everyone knew. A few weeks after this meeting, Lovingood submitted his resignation, effective in May.

Steve and I met in late May in Montana to weigh the pros and cons of my accepting the Chairman position. At the same time, Steve received a letter from General Livingston, with a copy to me, informing us of nearly $150,000 in unpaid construction bills. "The Museum's funds are at rock bottom again, a situation which has occurred repeatedly throughout the history of this project," he wrote. "It is a monumental job trying to keep heads above water on a daily basis!" He also suggested recommending me to the board for Chairman before August 1, 1998.

Livingston's candid letter described the tough situation I would face if I agreed to become Chairman and CEO. The drumbeat of both good and discouraging financial news at the recent board meetings did not bode well, and, despite some good progress, the overall picture was not a rosy one. We hung by a thread. The press knew it. Steve knew it. I knew it. We had been in similar situations before, but in late May 1998, the Museum faced steepening financial challenges with rising construction costs and many unknowns. I leaned toward accepting, but this was not a slam-dunk decision. Steve understood the stakes and did not push me too hard. He made it clear that if I said no, he was ready to pursue our other ventures together. If I accepted, he had full confidence that I could do the job, raise the funds, and get the Museum open. He also promised to do everything he could to help and promised he would remain committed to me and to the Museum until it was done. While I was confident I could do the job, it was very important for me to hear from Steve that he was not going to disappear.

Though Steve had been retired for a couple years, I could see that the demands on him were growing, pushing him to the limits of his time and health. *Citizen Soldiers* had just been published, and several more books were due to be published in the next couple of years. Steve and his book *Undaunted Courage* were featured prominently in the Ken Burns documentary *Lewis & Clark: The Journey of the Corps of Discovery,* which aired on national public television in 1997. He was in constant demand for major speaking engagements, and he donated his speaking fees to the Museum on numerous occasions. He was stretched thin. If I decided not to accept the Chairman position, I could help him manage his ever-growing family company. He had personal reasons for me to say no, but in the end Steve said the biggest relief to his time would be for me to take on the Museum so he would have less to worry about on that front. With me as chairman, Steve felt sure I would make sure his efforts on behalf of the Museum would be for maximum efficiency, made when and where he needed it most. He made a special point to assure me that he would be available to meet with major donors to help close the biggest gifts. He just could not keep responding to the incessant cash calls to pay salaries or deal with the constant crises. Bottom line, Steve said he would continue to be available to me anytime that I needed him by phone or in person. If I accepted, he could look to his son Hugh and daughters Stephenie and Grace to assist him with Ambrose-Tubbs, Inc. He was fine with either decision but said he hoped I would lead the Museum and get it open.

Steve had one final card up his sleeve to persuade me to take the Museum job. I knew he had been working with Steven Spielberg on his D-Day movie, *Saving Private Ryan,* starring Tom Hanks and Matt Damon. Steve saw a private screening a few months earlier and was an unabashed fan of the movie. He called it "the best film on World War II ever made." He promised Spielberg he would do everything in his power to promote the film around the country without reimbursement. In exchange, Ambrose had a couple of requests for the famous director. He asked Spielberg to support the National D-Day Museum publicly, make a significant donation, and promise that both he and Tom Hanks would attend the grand opening on June 6, 2000. Not only did Spielberg and Hanks agree, but Spielberg invited Steve and me along with our spouses to Los Angeles to attend the premiere and private reception for *Saving Private Ryan* in July.[33] This new alliance with Spielberg was dramatic and wonderful news. Steve knew how to close a deal. He gave me that crooked smile. "Think this star power can get us over the top?" he asked. We laughed and delighted in this good fortune.

That was pretty much it. I left Montana knowing my decision was made, even though I still had mixed emotions. Being chairman was a two-year commitment, but I guessed it could be longer if the Museum was not finished. This was a decision where one door opened, but others closed. I might never have the chance to pursue my other dreams. As I flew home, I thought back to June 6, 1994, when I was so overwhelmed with the D-Day commemoration in the Normandy cemetery and the burden of the Museum mission. I remembered on that day I knew I had to do more for the Museum, and now I would. When I got home, I told Livingston my decision: I would accept the position as the next Chairman and CEO of the National D-Day Museum.

An emergency Executive Committee meeting was immediately called on June 5, 1998, to prepare the board leadership. Chancellor O'Brien, presiding in the absence of Livingston, announced that I agreed to become Chairman. In addition to reducing my teaching load, O'Brien volunteered the services of university leadership and technical staff to help fill in the expertise the Museum needed to overcome our financial challenges. Pat Gibbs, Vice Chancellor for Business Affairs at UNO, deployed engineering staff to help oversee our construction, while a newly elected board member, Liz Williams, the President and CEO of the UNO Foundation, assisted our Treasurer with Museum accounting for fundraising and grants. No one could be more grateful than I was for this enormous support at a crucial time in our history. From our beginning in 1990 until now, the University of New Orleans played a vital role in the survival and success of the National D-Day Museum.[34] Greg O'Brien's leadership support was always there.

During that June meeting, Steve spoke by phone from Montana to report on the upcoming *Saving Private Ryan* premiere in Los Angeles with two screenings in New Orleans the day after, as well as Spielberg's commitment to promote the Museum, including in upcoming stories in the *New Yorker* and *Newsweek.*[35] To top it off, Spielberg pledged a $250,000 donation.[36]

I also announced that we were ready to make hires for two key staff jobs, including C. J. Roberts, a highly recommended young professional from the George C. Marshall Foundation, for the job of Deputy Director/Chief Administrative Officer. In addition, thanks to groundwork by Lovingood and board member Herschel Abbott, we received a grant from the Baptist Community Ministries to hire a Curator and Education Director. The board was excited by this rapid movement. It gave all of us a boost of confidence in our future direction. We were starting to act like an emerging Museum.

The planets aligned once more, just as they did in June of 1994. The buzz in the local media picked up rapidly as we headed off to Los Angeles for the premiere of *Saving Private Ryan,* which was everything Spielberg had promised. The focus was on the veterans and the film, of course, but the National D-Day Museum had time in the spotlight. Spielberg even greeted the guests before the screening with a five-minute speech in which he lavished praise on Stephen Ambrose, paid tribute to the D-Day veterans in our midst, and made a tremendous pitch for support of the long overdue National D-Day Museum.[37] I wondered how we could possibly fail with champions like Spielberg and Hanks. As Brokaw had four years before, they gave us national stature and credibility that money could not buy.

We returned home to General Livingston's final board meeting as Chairman, on August 3, 1998, one month prior to my formal election in September. In his farewell remarks, Livingston thanked Steve Ambrose profusely "for his leadership, enthusiasm and financial support."[38] Livingston noted some recent improvement in private gifts but added we had not received the $500,000 promised by the state and that we would need to find those funds somehow. Snedeker gave an enthusiastic report about the sudden improvement in our finances over the last six months, with a cash balance of $739,000 on hand and the highest number of private pledges in years.[39] This was our best report in several years. We all thought we could see the light at the end of the tunnel.

A *Times-Picayune* article by James Varney on August 1, 1998, recapped the ups and downs of the Museum since the much-ballyhooed optimism around the 50th anniversary of D-Day in 1994. Since then, the Museum "quickly foundered like a Higgins boat strafed by Nazi gunners," Varney wrote. But, he added, "Suddenly . . . the museum's fortunes are brightening."[40] The article cited the closing funding gap and soaring interest in D-Day in the wake of *Saving Private Ryan* and noted that Ambrose "deserves most of the credit for its resurgence."

The article reported that the $2.5 million in state money was closing the funding gap. Just a short time ago, Varney wrote, "Directors of the D-Day Museum had all but given up hope for such good fortune." Steve also took the blame for the Museum's "rocky history," saying his push for the Lake Pontchartrain site had divided the board and led many to question the wisdom of the project. "I had no idea what I was doing," Steve acknowledged. "I'm an academic and I didn't know how to deal with a board, how to even create a board or how to raise money or any of those things." Steve's mea culpa was a little overboard, but the candid story hit like a bombshell.

Then, a few days later, on August 7, 1998, *Times-Picayune* published an op-ed by Steve appealing to the New Orleans community to help meet our goal to open the Museum on June 6, 2000. Steve noted he had already personally contributed $500,000 and pledged more; he asked the community to match his gifts; he even made an appeal to the nearly 5,000 UNO students he taught over the years to pitch in. Spielberg and Hanks would be at the grand opening, along with D-Day veterans, he wrote. Then he cut to the chase: Steve promised access to receptions and VIP events for those who contributed. "This matters to me more than anything else," he concluded. "Please help me."[41] His plea was certainly an unorthodox approach to fundraising. The positive response was enough to keep the Museum surging forward with wonderful publicity and rising expectations on the part of the board and the city of New Orleans. We rode a new wave into the coming year. My own spirits rose as I prepared to step into the fray for the next two years as Chairman.

6

ROAD TO VICTORY

Getting to D-Day, June 6, 2000

IT NOW FELL on me to get the Museum to the finish line. After nine years, the Museum could no longer be called a start-up. We were on the clock, with the demands of construction, funding, marketing, and operations increasing every day. Time was running out and so were our funds. Our contractual commitments appeared to be running well ahead of our known revenues. My immediate goal was to improve the trend line of the past eight years and raise several million more dollars to get the Museum open by June 6, 2000. I did not yet know how, but I was sure that part of the answer was to instill confidence in the board, donors, and government leaders that we were going to reach the finish line this time.

I had to convince everyone, including the media, that victory was within our grasp. We needed a solid baseline and had to be honest about our past mistakes as well as our prospects. The last dollar would be easier than the first, but there could be no further missteps in our accounting, forecasting, or results. The public was well aware we missed three previous projected opening dates since 1994, and that the cost of the total project shifted often, from $12 million to $30 million, and then back to $11 million in our recent media release in May.[1]

General Livingston told me that summer that I only needed to raise another $1 million to complete the Museum and open in twenty months. As I dug deeper into the financials with Tom Snedeker and accounting whiz Liz Williams, I realized that $1 million was not nearly enough. It was a figure that included no plans for an entrance pavilion, and it would leave many critical spaces unfinished at opening. I privately estimated we would need an additional $4 million to build an entrance pavilion. We also needed a big increase in private funds to oversee operating costs of the final design and installation of exhibits, manage the building construction, hire startup staff, and execute a national marketing effort.

Clarifying the Museum's financial situation was my number one priority in the months before I became chairman in September 1998. It would not be easy. For years, our greatest challenge was our inability to raise private funds to match our state and federal grants. When I became Chairman, I commissioned Liz Williams and Tom Snedeker to crunch the numbers on our pledges to give us an idea of the amount we still needed to raise. Their results showed that we were on average raising a measly $500,000 in private funds per year. Even worse, Liz and Tom's report showed that we needed to raise about $6 million in just two years for us to reach our goals—at least half of which needed to come from private funds. I needed the board to buckle up and work as a team, harder than ever before. I needed to re-energize the Directors and delegate clear responsibilities. One of my first decisions before becoming Chairman was a plan to give the board greater ownership of the Museum mission and responsibility for its completion.

ORGANIZING FOR VICTORY

On September 9, we met in our board room at 923 Magazine Street. Those in attendance seemed excited by the changing of the guard, but the pattern of poor attendance continued, with less than half of our members present and some key Directors missing. I expected this based on board meetings in the past year, and this was part of our problem. General Livingston opened the meeting and brought us to order with my election to Chairman and CEO as the first order of business. The outgoing Chairman offered a few reflective remarks of his two-year term, with special appreciation for federal funding support received with help from Congressman Bob Livingston. He warned us about the perilous state of our finances and advised us "to not repeat the mistakes of the past."[2] He wished us well and passed the gavel to me.

After leading the board in a resolution of appreciation for the general's service and leadership, my first act as chairman was to make clear my strong commitment to complete the funding, construction, planning, and marketing in order to open the Museum on our newest and final target date, D-Day, June 6, 2000. There was no alternate plan. I was borrowing a page from Eisenhower. "We're throwing everything we have into it, and we're going to make it a success," Ike told his Allied Commanders a month before D-Day. "This operation is planned as a victory."[3] We were in our own battle. While the stakes for completing our Museum were far different from the life and death battle on D-Day, we took inspiration from the Allied forces who fought for our freedom that day. Our job was to preserve their history. Everyone understood that we were "all in" at this point.

I came with a thorough agenda, titled "Countdown to June 6, 2000," that presented tasks and objectives with milestones leading up to the date, along with two years of operating and capital campaign goals. I wanted eight committees with specific charges and deliverables, with Directors serving on at least two. Aside from the shortfall, the board learned we had an immediate need to raise $2 million by late spring 1999 just to complete our current expansion plan. I was ready to put enough pressure on the Directors to enlist their support or ask for their resignations in favor of new prospects ready to work and donate.[4]

A new energy flowed from the assembled board members. They confirmed my slate of officers and Executive Committee members, who comprised some of the heavy hitters on the board, including Boysie Bollinger, CEO of Bollinger Shipyards as First Vice Chairman, and Herschel Abbott Jr., President of BellSouth Louisiana, as Second Vice Chairman. Neither was in attendance, but in those days oftentimes if you missed a meeting, you ended up getting elected. However, both were outstanding Directors with great visibility in the business community. Chancellor O'Brien was elected as President with Steve Ambrose as At-Large member and Ex-Officio on all committees. This was a winning team, with the Chairs of all the key committees among the most dependable and committed leaders of the board.

After reviewing and accepting the daunting capital campaign goals, the board members recognized an overall goal of $4.868 million, which included unfinished spaces we previously omitted up to now, though there was still no budget for an entrance pavilion. They also approved a two-year operating budget that identified the immediate cash-flow deficit, which was projected to be between $1.7 million and $2.1 million by May 1999, just eight months away. I outlined my operating plan featuring new staffing positions, including a Deputy Director and Chief Administrative Officer, as well as Directors for Education, Development, and Collections.[5]

My plan was simple. We would launch an aggressive publicity and fundraising campaign to generate at least $2 million to erase the cash-flow deficit by next May. To do that, I committed to mobilizing the entire board, while I developed a Museum staff of ten to fifteen professionals to manage the installation of state-of-the-art exhibits at the highest standards of curation and presentation. I also pledged to seek their help to bring the mission of the Museum to life by honoring the veterans of World War II and inspiring future generations with their achievements. I concluded my opening remarks by reminding the board that "the Museum is more than a museum and [another] cultural attraction; there is only ONE National D-Day Museum, which makes the Board members stewards of a national responsibility."[6]

Before concluding the meeting, I introduced the Museum's recently hired Deputy Director and Chief Administrative Officer, C. J. Roberts, the first employee in the Museum's history with executive-level experience in museum development. C. J. would oversee the Museum operations, including completing the restoration of the warehouse, supervising the exhibit design and installation, managing the budget, and supporting the Museum's strategic planning. C. J. was a godsend, and we were fortunate to have him. We desperately needed his expertise to oversee the acquisition and restoration of our macro artifacts, including several planes, a Sherman tank, a half-track, several jeeps, and the ongoing work on our Higgins landing craft. The restorations had to be funded, accessioned into our collection, and installed along with the curating of the 100,000 St. Lô artifacts purchased four years earlier. C. J. was young, smart, and confident in his skills. His high-level museum experience allowed me to focus on my top priorities as Chairman and CEO: meeting our fundraising goals, designing a new entrance pavilion, and assuring the historical accuracy of Jack Masey's installations.

Over the summer we contracted with the Ehrhardt Group, the top-ranked public relations and communications firm in the Gulf Coast region, to initiate national publicity for the Museum. I had worked with the company's founder, Malcolm Ehrhardt, at UNO and knew he was a marketing genius. He was also a trusted friend. I wanted an opening designed to generate national media attention that would fuel visitation once the doors opened. I modeled this opening plan on the 1993 opening of the National Holocaust

Memorial Museum, which had captured the imagination of the nation in every form of media. I knew Malcolm was the one who could do it. Malcolm presented a vision for the Museum's marketing and fundraising campaign that would culminate in grandiose fashion with a massive, days-long grand opening celebration. The events would conclude with a citywide parade that crossed in front of the Museum. The parade would not only signify the long-awaited opening of the Museum but would also pay homage to D-Day veterans. The scope and creativity of Malcolm's plan energized the entire board and demonstrated why I wanted him under contract. The plan was far more ambitious and costly than a simple dedication and ribbon cutting, but we knew it would create a national buzz.

THE CATCHER POUCH

In the late nineteenth and early twentieth century, speeding trains could not stop in many rural towns to pick up the US Mail. The railroads devised a system to hang bags full of mail in a "catcher pouch," hanging from a pole along the tracks. As the train passed the station at full speed, the clerk would raise the mail catcher arm and the pouch would be snagged at 45 miles an hour. In the days after the September 9 board meeting, I felt as if I was caught in a bag that had been snagged by a speeding train—in this case the D-Day Museum moving at breakneck speed through construction, fundraising, and exhibit installations and onto the grand opening.

Our most urgent need was an entrance pavilion worthy of a national museum, which would cost a lot of money, and I needed it fast. We needed something far superior to the existing shed covering a loading dock as our major Museum entrance. About a week after the board meeting, I approached our architect, Pio Lyons, and asked if he could design a simple industrial-style rectangular structure rising 53 feet to the ceiling with an all-glass façade facing the street, something bold that would allow visitors to see planes and macro artifacts from outside the Museum. Pio dropped everything and designed a perfect structure that could be built quickly for the $3 to $4 million budget I had in mind. The striking design would allow passersby and visitors to see some of our collection from the street.

The problem, of course, was how to pay for it. My plan was to seek money from the state of Louisiana, but it was admittedly a long shot. I had not discussed this with the board yet because I did not want to raise false hopes. The entire board knew we failed to secure the $500,000 earmark in the recent state legislative session and most believed getting more than the $2.5 million appropriation that we were already spending was not likely. General Livingston warned me before stepping down that the unofficial word from Baton Rouge is "don't come back for more, they were pretty much done."

I wanted to give it a try. I took the plans to Jerry Goldman, head of the Museum's building committee, to get his take. Jerry, who worked for Higgins Industries during the war, was a businessman of big vision who carried a lot of sway on the board. He had extraordinary expertise as a naval architect, marine engineer, and inventor during the war. If Jerry was willing to support the pavilion, I hoped I would be able to get the board behind me. Jerry looked over Pio's drawings. "It's a bold plan," he said. "Go for it." That was all I needed.

I called Jackie Clarkson, our insider in the Louisiana legislature, to get an appointment with Gov. Mike Foster as soon as possible. I told her my plan. I did not want to ask the state to reinstate the $500,000 that had failed to pass in June. I had a much bigger idea in mind. I wanted to ask the governor to fund an entirely new entrance building for the Museum that could be built quickly and for under $4 million. "We don't have a minute to lose," I told her. Only the state could fund a new building within the time we had left until June 6, 2000.

Jackie soon called me to say she had set the appointment with Governor Foster for the next day. Before driving to Baton Rouge the next morning, I called Boysie, a close friend of the Governor, to ask if he could join us for the meeting. "Of course, I'll leave now," he replied. "See you there." I did not know Boysie well yet, so it was a boost of confidence to know he would drop everything to make the appointment a priority. Jackie and I drove to the Governor's office with the pavilion drawings, still hot off Pio's drafting table.

When we arrived, Boysie was already in the Governor's office, but to our surprise Mark Drennen, the Governor's Chief Administrative Officer, was there too. Mark had a reputation for cutting unnecessary capital projects, so his attendance was worrisome. Nonetheless, I plunged forward, thanking Foster for the state's past support now being put to good use in the warehouse renovations, but quickly turning to the problem at hand. The Museum was due to open in 20 months, but as things stood, we would have to use a large shed with a loading dock as our main entrance. "It would be embarrassing for the state of Louisiana and the city to open a national museum without a grand entrance pavilion," I told him.

I rolled out Pio's design plan for a dramatic entry pavilion. I told the Governor that the estimated cost would be about $3.5 million and reported the architect's assurance that the pavilion could be built in nine months if the legislature appropriated the funds by June 1999. I promised that if the state supported the building cost, we would name it the Louisiana Memorial Pavilion to recognize the state's contribution and to honor the thousands of Louisiana veterans who served in World War II.

The Governor asked Boysie what he thought. He replied that the Museum was going to be a phenomenal cultural project for the city, state, and nation. I could see Boysie's remarks made an immediate impression on the governor. Foster then asked for Drennen's opinion. I thought to myself, this is the whole ball game. To my pleasant surprise, Mark said it was a good project for the state and added that he thought Steve Ambrose was one of the great WWII historians in America. The project would considerably enhance other investments the governor had already approved for the Warehouse District, Mark added. Foster asked a few more questions and then gave his approval. We were thrilled! Getting such a quick green light was unexpected and gave us a fighting chance to succeed.

Eight years earlier Steve had called me from Washington, DC with word that we would receive our first $4 million grant from Congress. This time it was my turn to call Steve with big news. He was as stunned and exuberant as I was. "It's why I wanted you as chairman," he said.

The Governor's commitment gave me a great boost of confidence in the first weeks of my Chairmanship. The news galvanized our board and donors as nothing had in recent years. While the funds could not arrive until approved by the legislature the following June, support from the Governor and his budget officer seemed as good as gold. I was assured we could build the new entrance pavilion in nine months, in time for our grand opening. I told the board that we still needed $8 million to complete construction, but the state grant would reduce that number by nearly half. There was still a mountain of private money to raise, buildings to complete, and exhibits to install, but the state commitment was a great leap forward in October of 1998. Thinking of the Normandy D-Day landings, I felt as if we had secured a beachhead but still had lots of fighting ahead.

The board soon authorized me to sign a contract with Lyons and Hudson architects to begin serious design work for the Louisiana Memorial Pavilion. We had to move fast if we were to be ready to get construction bids out and get the pavilion built and open so soon after receiving the money. Our new board member, Councilman Jim Singleton, voiced worries about the state funds and exhorted us to remain vigilant to make certain these funds were appropriated in June—it had to be our highest priority. State Sen. Diana Bajoie said she would endorse our request, which meant a lot as the Governor expected strong support from the New Orleans delegation in the legislature.[7]

Steve provided more good news that added to the celebratory mood. His public appeal to his former students in the *Times-Picayune* generated $109,000 from 460 donors. Steve himself gave another $100,000 and reported that IBM and Phillip Morris promised significant sums to the Museum as an honorarium for speeches he had given to them. More contributions flowed from his donor tours to Normandy and on the Lewis and Clark trail. All this positive news gave us a sense we were on a rising tide that would lift all ships.

On November 5, 1998, President Clinton awarded Steve the National Humanities Medal at a White House ceremony.[8] Just two days later, Steve was in Madison, Wisconsin, speaking to a Winston Churchill club when he fell and struck his head. He was in the hospital with a serious concussion and bleeding on the brain. His family rushed to Madison with fears for his life. Thankfully, Moira called me daily with updates.

The accident came as a shock to the board and many donors, who immediately wondered what would happen if we lost our founder before the Museum's completion. We had all felt dependent on Steve and his national reputation over the past eight years. No one contemplated his death at 62. My phone rang off the hook for two days with calls from board members who wondered if we could make it without him. "What will you do without Steve?" they asked me.

"We would prevail," I said, with perhaps more confidence than I felt, and the news of the state commitment of $3.5 million eased board member worries. Steve was my closest friend in New Orleans for 27 years, so the prospect of losing him meant more to me personally than anything else. Fortunately for his family, me, and the Museum, welcome news came by the end of the week that he was recovering. Steve bounced back quickly, and, by December 7, he was at a board meeting and recovered to his usual robust self; he even hit the road fundraising within days of coming home. But Steve's fall and hospitalization were a wake-up call. We were riding on Steve's larger-than-life coattails, but were they long enough? Would they carry us into the future?

The countdown clock was ticking, and the days passed quickly as 1998 closed. I appointed General Livingston to chair the Grand Opening and Special Events Committee, which consisted of several board members, event planners, and military liaisons. We decided to meet every week until the grand opening. Bill Detweiler, Director and former National Commander of the American Legion, suggested that we seek Congressional designation as an official event of the Department of Defense, a brilliant idea that I promised to pursue with Sen. Mary Landrieu and US Rep. Bill Tauzin, Louisiana natives and staunch Museum supporters.

Meanwhile, it was imperative for the Capital Campaign Committee to have solid financial reports, indicating our position and funding needs through grand opening and beyond. This was, of course, critical for the management of the operations and ongoing construction, but it was also vital for donors, who heard conflicting stories of our financial outlook, with costs ranging widely. Our numbers going forward had to be rock solid, and our mission clear. I asked Tom Snedeker and Liz Williams to document all revenue sources and costs, past and projected. I divided the project into two phases: Phase I, from December 1998 to June 6, 2000, and Phase II, to completion of the *D-Day Invasions in the Pacific* gallery on December 7, 2001.

In keeping with the promise I made at my first meeting as Chairman, I presented the board at our meeting on November 19, 1998, with a comprehensive account of total funds raised and expended since 1992, as well as detailed documentation of all expenditures needed for Phase I and II, including operations from 1998 to 2001. These numbers also included the private funds promised to complement the new state appropriation in June 1999 and identified the remaining gap of funds still to be raised. Despite the wave of optimism generated by the Governor's commitment, I noted that Steve's recently announced pledges were not likely to arrive in time to close our current shortfall. A month after our September board meeting, our funding gap grew by at least one million dollars. We still faced a cash-flow crunch of significant proportions, which prompted a discussion of the idea that some members might have to cosign a secured bank loan of several million dollars. I was pleased everyone understood the gravity of the situation and remained committed to the goal. For the first time, the sum of all Museum project costs since inception in 1992 to the end of 2001 were realistically totaled at $20 million.[9] Though daunting, the clarity of the dollars needed and total project costs through 2001 built confidence among board members. We knew exactly what we needed, with the immediate priority to meet an estimated $2 million cash-flow challenge by June 1999. Our fiscal cliff loomed just ahead.

By any account, New Orleans was an unlikely city for a national Museum with such high aspirations. It was a small-market city with only one Fortune 500 company headquartered there. We were distant from the nation's Capital in Washington, DC. as well as from the major financial markets in New York City, Chicago, and on the West Coast. New Orleans was far off the radar of the large corporations and wealthy individuals based in such places. Texas was the main place in the region where they focused their philanthropy. We were known mostly for food, music, Mardi Gras, and architecture. The city was not known for great museums. Our plans for a 70,000-square-foot Museum were not significant when measured against nationally known museums in Washington, DC, New York, and other larger cities. Even our most optimistic projection in 1993 was that we might achieve 750,000 visitors some years after opening. We hoped we could reach those numbers, but I sometimes wondered if it was realistic when compared to similar tourist attractions. Despite our recent progress, donors could readily see that the venture was led by a couple of historians and a board with no experience starting or running a museum, and that it had taken us nine years to get close to opening.

I often worried about the doubts major donors likely had about the Museum's prospects in New Orleans. It was difficult for me to tell if the growing fascination with D-Day, World War II, Ambrose, and veteran stories necessarily translated to interest in building a museum. The Museum had to become a centerpiece of the larger story to attract funders. We needed to elevate the Museum mission into the epicenter of America's memory of D-Day and World War II. Indeed, part of the task we faced was to present the National D-Day Museum in New Orleans as the first history museum in America to tell the greater story of our role in World War II. We needed to become "the mouse that roared." We needed to convince donors and all of America that this Museum, through its extraordinary exhibits, veteran oral histories, and grassroots support, would bring to life the story of how the

United States led the Allies to victory. We won a war that not only defeated fascist empires but won peace as well. The story was worthy of commemoration and support. In some fashion, all Americans participated in the fight to preserve our way of life. Just as the famous tapestry in the tiny town of Bayeux, Normandy, tells the epic story of William the Conqueror's victory in the Battle of Hastings in 1066, the National D-Day Museum would tell the epic story of the victory of the Allies on the beaches of Normandy on June 6, 1944.

A critical part of the plan to parlay publicity into national donations was the need to secure at least a $1 million gift from a local business leader to demonstrate to national donors that our business community was all in. Putting myself in the thoughts of a big-city donor, I imagined questions I kept mostly to myself, such as: "Why should I make a seven-figure gift if no one locally had done so?"

In the early months of 1999, my focus settled on one of the wealthiest local business leaders in New Orleans, Frank Stewart Jr. Frank was a Navy veteran, entrepreneur, and Chairman of Stewart Enterprises, Inc., the nation's third-largest funeral and cemetery services corporation with cemeteries and funeral homes spread across the United States and abroad. Frank was known for his generosity, patriotism, commitment to our military, and as a prominent community leader. I learned that he was a well-read history enthusiast with a philosophical bent. The board agreed with me that we had to approach Frank. He was my top prospect, and I was running out of time. I called Frank's office and asked if he would meet with a group from the D-Day Museum, including Steve and me. We secured an appointment for May 9, 1999. The UNO Development Office conducted some research and advised me that a $500,000 gift would be an appropriate request, which was disappointing news. Steve and I knew it was not enough, but we were still gun-shy about making large requests from private donors, having been rebuffed so many times before. I was nervous; the night before the meeting, I called Malcolm Ehrhardt, one of my most trusted confidants on all matters related to the New Orleans business community, and asked him for advice about whether we should stick to the $500,000 recommendation.

"How much do you need?" Malcolm asked. I said it would take $2 million to open on schedule. "Frank is one of the wealthiest and most generous business leaders in New Orleans; tell him what you need and why," Malcolm said. "He can give $2 million as easily as $500,000." Malcolm gave me the advice and confidence I needed. I told Steve that $2 million was the number and that Frank would want to hear the request from him personally.

Steve and I, accompanied by Chancellor O'Brien and Steve's son Hugh met with Frank the next day in his office. I gave Frank a brief update on our mission, our construction progress, and our plans for a spectacular grand opening. Steve then dove into a mesmerizing description of the forthcoming D-Day exhibits and our plans to expand a year later with a new exhibit on the Pacific Theater. Of course, Steve recounted the story of Andrew Higgins and emphasized that New Orleans would be one of the stars of the opening. Steve was terrific. Since he knew about Frank's passion for the family business he operated, Steve paraphrased from his book *Citizen Soldiers,* which he often recalled in his fundraising and speeches around the country: "That spirit—we can do it . . . was the great gift of the New World to the Old World in the 20th century. America paid for that gift with the lives of some of its best young men."[10] In the same vein, Steve reflected on his many visits to the American Cemetery above Omaha Beach and described Eisenhower's thoughts about the futures that were sacrificed for so many who landed at Normandy. I do not believe Steve ever gave a better presentation to a prospective donor.

Frank was clearly moved and impressed with our project and with Steve. He said it was an honor to hear our explanation of the importance of the Museum. He asked a few hard questions about the schedule and funding. He was a little skeptical that funds from the state appropriation would be available in time to get the Louisiana Pavilion built. We answered as confidently as possible. As the meeting wound down, Steve rolled his eyes at me with the look I knew all too well; "You make the ask." I hoped Steve would ask, but I took a deep breath and jumped. "Frank, as you can appreciate, this Museum tells the national story of World War II but also represents those who didn't make it," I said. "To that extent, the D-Day Museum will be a memorial, a shrine of sorts. So, we would be especially honored with a gift or pledge of $2 million dollars, which would assure the completion of the National D-Day Museum on schedule, and, for such a generous gift, you would be recognized as the capstone donor of the Museum for helping to close the critical gap in our funding." To our great relief, Frank immediately replied, "Yes, I want to do it and think I can, but I will ask my CFO to review my commitments and feel confident I can commit to the amount if it can be pledged over four years." We were almost speechless. It was the first moment Steve and I knew for sure that we would open on time. Construction would not be delayed due to lack of funds in the next 30 days. Going forward, we still had a funding gap of several million dollars, but we had another twelve months to raise the remaining funds, an easier task with Frank's enormous gift in hand. We soon met with his VP for Finance, John McNamara, and had Frank's pledge in hand within a few weeks. We had a steep mountain to climb in the coming year, but the crest was in view and in reach. Steve and I celebrated as never before. For the moment, Stewart's pledge made the struggles and disappointments of the last nine years fade from our memories.

My attention quickly shifted to the Louisiana legislature and the $4 million appropriation, which was proceeding through the final committee approvals before the session wrapped up in early June. I remained in contact with the President of the Senate, Randy Ewing, and House Speaker Hunt Downer, who both assured me that the Governor and Delegates were firmly behind the bill. Sen. Diana Bajoie and Rep. Jackie Clarkson monitored our appropriation daily. Ron Henson, a new board member who served as Undersecretary for the Department of Economic Development provided invaluable inside help in navigating complex state processes, keeping me informed on an hourly basis as our appropriation passed from committee to committee. Boysie stayed in touch with the Governor, and other major players in the Louisiana House and Senate, to keep the bill in place in the closing days of the session, a time when earmarks were vulnerable to cuts or reductions.

The appropriation was a huge victory for the Museum, one that enabled us to tell national donors that Congress and the state of Louisiana had appropriated over $6 million each. We could also point to Frank Stewart's gift to answer questions from potential private national donors about local giving commitments. This became the basis for our future funding strategy as our needs continued to grow: our goal was to get a third from Congress, a third from the state of Louisiana, and a third from the private sector. This public-private partnership became a model for building a museum as a nonprofit corporation, not one funded principally by the state or federal government.

The next immediate task was to get the Louisiana Memorial Pavilion built in less than a year from the date of the appropriation, a challenge that some considered unlikely if not impossible, given the bidding, contracts, and permitting processes. The board had already approved our architecture and construction blueprints in the fall of 1998, which we hoped to go out for construction bids by July 1999. Unfortunately, unexpected delays in the bidding process meant we could not award the contract until early fall, putting enormous pressure on any firm to build the four-story, 17,000-square-foot pavilion in nine months.[11] Gootee Construction, Inc. a local firm, won the bid, and luckily, the company owners, Elaine and Kathy Gootee, promised to make every sacrifice to ensure that the new pavilion was ready for the grand opening. As daughters of WWII veterans, they understood the importance of the Museum's mission and vowed their company would make every sacrifice to get the Museum open. In the first meeting with Gootee Construction, Elaine said her father told her and her sister-in-law: "You go get that contract and get that building built on time." Elaine promised they would do whatever it took to comply with her father's wishes. Her letter after the award of the contract was one of the most inspiring I ever received from any contractor or subcontractor.

Despite the pressure of looming deadlines, enthusiasm grew among board members and staff as everyone got to work. Rosie the Riveter posters were everywhere. Her famous slogan "We can Do it!" became our mantra too. C. J. Roberts installed a "Countdown to D-Day Clock" in the Eisenhower Center administrative offices to countdown the remaining months, days, hours, minutes, and seconds to opening our doors on June 6, 2000.

The marketing front, guerilla marketing I called it, was active from every source, via earned media and by every grassroots measure. Malcolm Ehrhardt secured an in-kind contribution of $100,000 of advertising space from the *Times-Picayune,* which he proposed we use for ads to sell named bricks inside and outside the Museum.[12] For $100 anyone could purchase a brick that honored a WWII veteran, parent, or loved one they wanted to memorialize as part of the local and national effort to fund the Museum. These memorial bricks provided a fundamental link to World War II, and the appeal was to the common refrain of the war, "We are all in this together." The campaign worked. We sold thousands of bricks that generated capital funds from fall 1998 to 2000. We still had more fundraising to do to ease the pressing need to pay contractors beyond May 1999. Missing that deadline would mean postponement of the June 6, 2000, opening. We were focused intensely on that objective.

The physical Museum and exhibits were now fully designed for construction in two prominent buildings. First would be the grand entry, the

Louisiana Memorial Pavilion, with its 36-foot-high soaring glass windows fronting Howard Avenue, allowing views into a dramatic open space with rugged, industrial-style steel beams holding aircraft suspended from the ceiling. The space would present our replica Higgins boat in a prominent spot near the window, with other spaces reserved for tanks, jeeps, and artillery pieces. The exterior of the connected warehouse building was already painted in olive-drab green and yellow to evoke WWII color schemes. Inside, visitors would follow the "road to victory" passage of memorial bricks from the entrance into the primary exhibitions on the first floor, where the Forbes Theater would show the Guggenheim *D-Day Remembered* documentary. The Museum gift store and coffee shop would also be on the ground floor, with an open atrium inviting visitors to view the bunkerlike structure leading to the upper floors of exhibits. The second floor would start with exhibits dedicated to the home front, Pearl Harbor, and then go into the heart of Operation Overlord and the Normandy D-Day galleries on the third floor. Masey and the fabrication firm Explus, Inc., began to install the exhibits, filled with images, immersive environments, oral history stations, and the latest technologies. The final Metaform designs promised to feature the latest in museum exhibit technology and design, with nothing comparable anywhere in the United States.

We were thrilled to see the Museum coming to life after so many years of planning. We were at the crossroads of where vision met reality, with exhibits that brought history, memories, and the meaning of D-Day together in an extraordinary experience. Steve was the flag bearer, and Jack Masey was the maestro, executing the mission along themes that Steve and I approved. We had a point of view. We would help shape America's memory of D-Day and World War II as an epic crusade against the tyranny of fascism that held Europe under the yoke of Adolf Hitler and threatened global freedom and democracy. Our newly minted mission statement, approved by the board following our retreat in February, laid this out: "The National D-Day Museum celebrates the American Spirit, the teamwork, optimism, courage, and sacrifice of the men and women who won World War II and promotes the exploration and expression of these values by future generations."[13]

There it was: our north star shining on the deeply held values and themes Steve Ambrose highlighted in his many books on American history and World War II. Our mission also resonated with the highly acclaimed but often criticized theme of Tom Brokaw's affirmative ode to the Greatest Generation for what they had achieved and sacrificed. While I was a bit more reserved on this historical theme than Steve, I strongly shared his belief that the Allied victory saved America and the rest of the world from the evils of fascism and racist regimes. The Museum exhibits were telling the story, curating both memory and meaning of what America would remember about D-Day and World War II.

Keeping with the idea that every American was part of the war effort, it became clear that the Board of Directors needed more diversity in its membership. The largely white, male-dominated board was not a good reflection of our community, so for several years Steve and I pushed to recruit more women and minorities. In addition to Liz Williams and Jackie Clarkson, another strong female voice on the board was Adelaide Benjamin, a seasoned leader in the nonprofit sector. They all added leadership and fundraising support in untapped areas of the community. Prominent African American leaders from the business and government sectors joined the board around this time, notably Sen. Diana Bajoie, who would later become President Pro Tempore of the Louisiana State Legislature, City Councilman Jim Singleton, Nolan Marshall, President of a major sanitation corporation in the city, and Lenny Burns, President of a travel agency. Marshall and Burns were both WWII veterans who served with the Montfort Point Marines. Another distinguished African American veteran of the war, Col. Henry Johnson, joined after being nominated by Bajoie. In the 1990s, we added Harry Lee, the Chinese American Sheriff of Jefferson Parish, who first rose to prominence while overseeing the integration of New Orleans–area restaurants in the 1960s. We also added a few young guns to the group around this time, including Jimmy Duckworth, an active-duty Coast Guard Commander, who led our Higgins boat project, Alan Franco, a business marketing guru, and John Cordaro, President of New Orleans Public Service.

Commodore Tommie Lupo, a WWII Navy pilot who served in the Battle of the Philippine Sea, came on board in 1998 after he heard me give a fundraising talk to a local business group about our planned expansion to include exhibits on the D-Days in the Pacific. Lupo came up to me afterwards and said, "I want to help and am giving you $100,000 tomorrow." Of course, I immediately invited him to join the board.

I also continued to rely heavily on continuing support from business leaders on the board. Boysie Bollinger was a major player in the New Orleans business community and gave extraordinary support for my ambitious goals. He well understood the challenges before us. Strong leadership also came from John Kelly, recently retired President and CEO of Textron, who joined the original board in 1993, bringing continuity and enthusiasm for the amphibious doctrine initiated by Andrew Higgins that transformed America's strategy in World War II. Along with Boysie and Kelly was Herschel Abbott, a Vietnam veteran and prominent businessman, whose commitment to the Museum ran deep.

In my first year of chairmanship, the burden of responsibility was palpable. It started to lift a little as the Museum buildings and exhibits entered the final stages of construction. Operations, construction, exhibit installers, and swarms of contractors and designers were everywhere. C. J. Roberts led the day-to-day operational activities, overseeing the construction work of the several contractors with support from Gus Cantrell, UNO's Vice Chancellor of Capital Projects, and his Assistant, Jean McDuffie. We welcomed their much-needed participation in weekly contractor meetings and benefited from the professional oversight they gave us as we dealt with one new building going up and another having its interior spaces and exhibits installed in the warehouse building.

To prepare for opening and full operations in the following month, C. J. prepared a business plan for operations for July 1, 1999, to June 30, 2000, which I took to the board for approval in July. It included professional goals and objectives that prioritized everything that had to get done before the grand opening, including the ramp-up of Museum staff by May 1, 2000. Based on a new feasibility study, I predicted 200,000 visitors in year one, conservatively pegged at half of our optimistic estimates of 400,000. The plan detailed final capital and operational budgets and provided fundraising and revenue projections for the first month of paid visitation. From the feasibility study, we decided upon a top admission fee of six dollars.[14] Amazingly, this proposed admission price was the subject of heated debates during board meetings, with some concerned that it was too high, given our hopes of opening our doors to as many of students and community members as possible. I reminded board members we had no state or federal operating support and would have to operate from our revenues and business plans.

We forged ahead with the grand opening Committee's ambitious plans for D-Day 2000, which included a WWII veterans' parade, government dignitaries, and celebrities such as Brokaw, Hanks, and Spielberg. The board allocated $150,000 for the event, though some worried it was a huge sum given our meager budget for the year. Other board members thought that the budget would likely grow. I promised that such an event would draw sponsors and funds to cover the budget and that the grand opening was critical to attracting future visitors. Boysie, Herschel, and other business leaders were enthusiastic supporters.

A key to the plan was for Senator Landrieu to get a formal resolution passed by Congress declaring the grand opening to be an official event of the United States government, with language that gave Secretary of Defense William Cohen the discretion to deploy resources of the Department of Defense to support it. In addition, Malcolm, Steve, and I planned to travel to New York City with the important mission of persuading the national media that this event was going to be a historic occasion with enormous human interest. The advance commitment from the national media mostly depended on help from Brokaw, behind-the-scenes work by Malcolm Ehrhardt, and our promise to have thousands of WWII veterans present for the opening. Serious support of nationally recognized government and military leaders, diplomats, and top historians was also significant, as was the engagement of A-list celebrities like Spielberg and Hanks. We believed our years of sustained work and building relationships would help us now. Those who understood the importance of saving the history of D-Day and World War II would bring credibility to our event even if we were not in the nation's Capital.

Because Brokaw was fully committed to serve as emcee for all four days of the events, he was more than glad to help arrange the media blitz in New York with Steve, Malcolm, and me. Ambrose was raring to go. Brokaw put out the word to his NBC producers to work with Malcolm to arrange briefings on the Museum opening. Naturally, Tom wanted NBC to have the favored media position by assuring advance commitments and participation of its programs. He made it known to NBC he would anchor the evening news from New Orleans for two nights out of his stay, so the network paid attention. Tom lined up producers from NBC, MSNBC, *Today Show, Late Night,* NBC radio, and the big one, *NBC Nightly News.* Brokaw also advised Malcolm to reach out to regional NBC affiliates in the Gulf South.[15]

The big meeting day in New York to get the media coordinated arrived in late October 1999. Malcolm set up the main meeting for 10:30 a.m. with NBC producers. Brokaw was with Steve and said Malcolm and I should meet them for lunch at the Four Seasons after the briefings. As we walked to the Rockefeller Center that morning, Malcolm told me to have my A game ready. He advised that I would likely have no more than twenty minutes to hit highlights of the three-day opening events and to cover the importance of the opening coinciding with the D-Day anniversary. He said to stress the key takeaways: the historical meaning of victory on D-Day to the war and to America. He stressed that I should emphasize the scale of the veteran's parade, our Congressional designation and funding, and, of course, the headliner celebrities, including Stephen Ambrose. "Okay," I responded warily, "but all that in twenty minutes?" "Plan for that and hope for more." Malcolm said.

We got much more. There were six executive producers in the conference room, which was a great sign. I set out to give my 20-minute briefing but after 10 minutes the questions started coming, one after another. It became clear that this was not a perfunctory meeting to satisfy Brokaw. The meeting lasted an hour and a half. The producers were blown away by the scale and importance of the Museum, the grand opening plans, and the notion that it all started with an idea of two historians 10 years before. It seemed many ingredients, including the impact of *Saving Private Ryan,* Ambrose's run of best-selling books and his TV appearances, Malcolm's publicity campaign for the Museum, and the nostalgia about aging WWII veterans, had converged to create a news story with enormous substance. Malcolm felt it as well. As we walked out of the meeting, Malcolm cracked his great smile. "That was a home run. I have never been in a national media briefing at such a high level for ninety minutes," he said, "They were fully engaged." We headed for lunch at the Four Seasons to share the news with Tom and Steve.

When we arrived, Tom and Steve were seated at a large round table in the center of the restaurant. With them was a distinguished cast: former Assistant Secretary of State Richard Holbrooke; John Whitehead, the longtime head of Goldman Sachs and a former Deputy Secretary of State; Tex McCrary, a WWII Army Air Corps veteran who was one of the first Americans in Hiroshima after the atomic bombing and who went on to pioneer the modern TV talk show; and Douglas Brinkley, the Eisenhower Center Director. I was wowed, suffice it to say. After introductions, Holbrooke, Ambrose, and Brokaw jumped into their opinions on current politics and foreign policy, but Tom quickly redirected conversation to the National D-Day Museum opening in six months. "Let them tell you about what's coming and who's coming," Tom said. "It's big."[16]

Everyone immediately peppered Steve with questions, just as we had experienced with the NBC producers. They all had strong opinions on the national meaning of World War II, its legacy in the postwar years, and the importance of the Museum. It was heady stuff. Those comments had a lasting impact on me.

The longer we sat at our central table, the more a noticeable buzz in the restaurant grew, with a steady stream of admirers stopping by, drawn mostly by the celebrity status of Ambrose and Brokaw. Katie Couric, who was on set with Steve in Normandy in 1994, came running over to the table, as did several top New York business leaders, many curious about the Museum. Tom remembered the lunch well in later years and said he was surprised to see so many hard-to-impress business leaders asking, "Are those the D-Day Museum guys?" Tom told me the commotion and interest at that luncheon was the first moment that he believed our Museum idea struck a national nerve and that we were onto something big. [17]

For me, Steve, and Malcolm, the lunch was memorable beyond words. To this day, I cannot fully describe our high spirits as we walked away from the Four Seasons. Malcolm elbowed me. "Nick, we will never, ever, have a power lunch like that again in our lives," he said. We both knew he was right. We flew back to New Orleans feeling confident we would have great national news coverage for the grand opening—if we finished construction on time.

The only missing piece was getting the Department of Defense on board to provide the military elements of the event. Senator Landrieu and Representative Tauzin muscled through Congressional approval to designate the opening as a federal government event. Secretary Cohen still had the discretion to decide whether the Defense Department would support the opening. Getting Cohen's approval was not as simple as sending him the resolution with a letter request. It would take a personal visit, not easy to get, and time was running short. Landrieu and Tauzin worked to secure the appointment during the first week of January.

Landrieu told Steve and I that we had to describe the scope and importance of the event for the aging veterans, for our active military, and for the nation. We were excited and hopeful. Steve and I knew a commitment from Cohen would be a game changer, not just for the Secretary's impact on the grand opening, but for the symbolic importance his presence would have for the Museum and the memories we sought to preserve.

7

THE MARCH TO THE GRAND OPENING

To the Beaches and Beyond

I ARRIVED AT Ronald Reagan Washington National Airport around 5:45 p.m. on January 6, 2000. I was anxious. It was raining hard, and my plane was two hours late for the long-awaited 6:00 p.m. meeting with Secretary of Defense William Cohen. I had directions to enter the high-security back entrance of the Pentagon near the Secretary's office, but there was no way I could get off the plane and get to the meeting before 6:30 p.m. This was a crucial meeting. I knew Steve and Moira were already in town and would be on time for the meeting with Cohen. Steve and I had reviewed our roles, and mine was to describe the plans for the programs and events, including details of dignitaries, celebrities, government officials, and military elements of the grand opening ceremonies in June. We knew we had to be good. It was critical to secure the Secretary's support for the military parade and to instill the event with the historic significance that would come with Congressional designation and public engagement of the Department of Defense.

The Pentagon was only minutes from the airport, but as I raced for a taxi at 6:15 p.m., I knew that Steve had only the most general knowledge of the three-day grand opening events. He would soon run out of words and might be embarrassed. Fortunately, the driver knew exactly where the back entrance was, so we made it through security, and I was met and escorted a short way up the back stairs about 6:30 p.m., where I was told to enter. As I burst into Secretary Cohen's office, somewhat disheveled in my raincoat, carrying a bag and briefcase, Cohen was already seated at his desk across from Steve and Moira. To my great relief, the Secretary greeted my belated and unorganized entrance with a warm smile and welcome. I could tell he was clearly enjoying his time with Steve and Moira. I sensed that Steve was embarrassed that I was 30 minutes late. He gave me a look that said, "How could you be late for THIS meeting?" Steve relaxed with the warm greeting from Cohen, and he described my role as the Museum's Chairman and CEO, and his closest friend, and that I could provide all the details about the grand opening plans.

Before I could begin, Cohen told us that he was a great admirer of Steve and his books and referred to his favorite passage from *Citizen Soldiers,* which he often recited when visiting troops stationed in the United States and around the world. Cohen recounted Steve's words by heart: "At the core, the American citizen soldiers knew the difference between right and wrong, and they didn't want to live in a world in which wrong prevailed. So, they fought, and won, and we, all of us, living and yet to be born, must be forever profoundly grateful."[1]

It was a relief to know we had a receptive audience in Secretary Cohen. We sensed that he had a deep appreciation for our mission and our desire to make D-Day veterans front and center of our opening events. Steve said that the Secretary's participation would assure that the grand opening would be a spectacular success and a timely way to thank the veterans who never received enough appreciation from the nation when they returned home from World War II. The thousands of veterans we would invite to New Orleans in June would stand in for all of them, said Steve—those six million still alive, as well as those who had died in combat in the years since. Steve closed with assurances to Cohen: "Mr. Secretary," he said, "with DoD support, the grand opening program to honor veterans would be better, not bigger." Steve was pitch perfect.[2]

Cohen was moved. He continued to listen closely as I gave a rundown of the events, as well as the commitments of coverage from Tom Brokaw, all NBC programs, C-SPAN, and other national media outlets. I spoke of our coordination with Maj. Gen. David Mize, the Marine Forces Reserve Commander in New Orleans. Of course, the Secretary was aware of the recent Congressional resolution and appreciated the ambitious scope of the plans for the grand opening. He commended us for our careful planning of the event over the past year, which we took as a great compliment considering the source.

At the end of an hour-long discussion, Cohen pledged to attend the opening and to provide full DoD support from all service branches. He further promised he would ask General Mize to serve as the DoD liaison to coordinate and lead the military participation and to organize the parade of military vehicles and marching bands led by D-Day veterans. Steve, Moira, and I were ecstatic. This was one of the best outcomes we could have imagined. We left in a taxi to the hotel, still digesting the magnitude of Cohen's commitments, when I received a cellphone call from a very surprised and agitated Lt. Col. Mike Humm in New Orleans. He was the Public Affairs Officer assigned by General Mize to participate in our weekly Grand Opening Committee meetings. Mike was breathless, as we still were. "What in the world just happened with you and Steve in the Secretary's office this afternoon?" he asked. Mike said the Secretary had just called Mize a few minutes ago and requested the general fly up to meet with him tomorrow to discuss DoD's role in the grand opening. "Mize just called me to ask what I knew about the meeting, and I told him I knew nothing, but would call you," Humm said. "So, what's up?" I gave Humm the good news. "Boy, the military sure moves fast when they want to," Steve said after I hung up. We were on cloud nine. We got out of the taxi, went straight to the hotel bar and had a couple of stiff drinks. This time it was not cheap sherry.

The next day, Mize was in Cohen's office getting his orders. Mize was the senior active-duty military officer in New Orleans, and Cohen put him in charge of a joint task force of all the armed service branches to organize and execute the grand opening parade. "He [Cohen] wanted to help the Museum get off to a grand start so that future generations could appropriately understand and celebrate the great achievements of our WWII Veterans," Mize later told me.[3]

I delivered the great news to the Museum Executive Committee on January 11, including word that Cohen would send me a letter designating the National D-Day Museum Grand Opening as an official event of the Department of Defense. I reported that he would invite the NATO Defense Ministers, who were meeting with him in early June, to fly down with him for our opening events, and he would encourage President Clinton to attend as well.[4] Board members applauded the news. It was overwhelming enough, but I would have been even more overwhelmed had I known then what I would learn years later from General Mize: Cohen had given him the specific task of "putting on the biggest military parade in the country since World War II."[5]

Excitement was growing, but there were still anxious moments in the months ahead, with the timetable of construction being the most challenging. For the first time in our 10-year history, finding money to get through the next months or days was not our highest priority. Frank Stewart's gift, along with brick sales and other donations, brightened our financial picture sufficiently that, by the fall of 1999, the board authorized me to add another fifteen staff members. This was part of Deputy Director C. J. Roberts's business plan from the previous summer, as we needed staff to assist with the final exhibit installations and prepare for the opening and operation of the Museum. Financial pressures were never far from my concern, however. By spring 2000, shortfalls showed up again. In addition to staff, construction, and other cash pressures, the projected grand opening expenditures had snowballed from our original budget of $150,000 to $780,000. While sponsors came in fast to cover most of the costs, by May we only raised $596,000, and the board had to authorize taking out a loan of more than $200,000 to cover outstanding expenses.[6] There was no stopping now. We had to deliver on the promise for a spectacular grand opening.

The spring of 2000 found us caught up in a rising crescendo of publicity, exhibit installations, new staff hires, fundraising, around-the-clock construction, and intense planning. Though all systems ran hard inside and outside the Museum, much of my work as Chairman was nearing completion. I faced another crossroads in my life and career. My term as Chairman and CEO would end with the annual meeting in September 2000, four months after the Museum opening. At that time, the CEO role would shift from the Chairman to a President position. UNO needed to know if I would return to teaching or continue in the top Museum leadership position. I crafted a description for a prospective new President and CEO position while C. J. was developed the staffing plan for the initial Museum operation with a total of 26 employees. The President and CEO position was key to the plan.

The Museum had to be ready on the day we opened to receive what we expected would be droves of visitors. A decision about the President position had to be made by summer if I were to return to UNO fulltime. Steve and others on the board, especially Herschel Abbott and Tom Snedeker, urged me to continue. For me, Boysie's view was critical. He was Chairman-elect of the Board of Directors, so his opinion was the most important, even more than Steve's. Boysie was regarded as one of the top CEOs in the city and state. He also had more extensive experience on nonprofit boards than anyone I knew in New Orleans. He was a highly respected executive and business leader, and he understood the challenges we had overcome in the past 18 months. He also understood that he would certainly face other challenges during his two years as Chairman. We respected each other, and Boysie and I were the ones who would be working together should he and the board want me to continue.

When I met with Boysie in early 2000 to discuss this, he encouraged me to stay on as President and CEO to help the Museum get on its feet during his two-year term. "You've gotten us this far and overcome every challenge," he told me. "I think you should stay on if you can work things out with UNO, and if it's what you want to do." We already had a good working relationship, meeting several times every week for breakfast at his "office" in the dining room at La Pavilion Hotel to discuss many big decisions. Boysie gave me hands-on support as we pursued government and fundraising opportunities. He always dug into our finances until he was satisfied and kept up with the details of the various decisions cascading on me in those days. He was involved with everything from the capital campaign, strategic planning, exhibit design, board building tasks, and the exhibit construction that would continue through our Pacific Theater grand opening in 2001. A year or so before I became Chairman, he toured Normandy, visiting the beaches, the airborne landings, Pointe Du Hoc, and the American Cemetery. That trip changed everything for Boysie, who grew even more committed to the Museum. It was my good fortune to have Boysie's leadership and judgment available to me during those years when every week seemed to bring another financial crisis or sudden opportunity that required decisions that could make or break us.

He understood the issues with the university. Because of the vesting conditions of my impending retirement from UNO in 2002, the Museum would expect me to teach a reduced teaching load to allow me considerable time to devote to the Museum. While UNO contributed my time and absorbed my salary for two years, I told Boysie that going forward the Museum would have to reimburse at least 60 percent of my UNO salary if I accepted the President position. UNO could no longer contribute my salary beyond the summer of 2000. Boysie thought that was acceptable and would cost less than a new President and CEO; plus, there would be no time wasted on a search at this critical juncture. We had to come to a decision and get board consideration at the next Executive Committee meeting.

Even with Boysie's endorsement, it was not an easy decision for me. I had already postponed several personal and professional plans when I accepted the Chairmanship in 1998. I decided if the Museum wanted me to continue after my term ended, I could serve another two years as President and CEO to finish the job. I would fulfill my commitment to Steve and the board to get the Museum open and operating successfully. By 2002, I hoped and expected to pursue my delayed personal plans.

The Executive Committee met on February 28, 2000, to consider the matter. Steve, of course, supported the move, saying that I was an excellent Chairman, and he did not believe I "ever put more effort into a job than [I had] in this one."[7] Boysie added that it was important to have me as President for continuity in the programs we were developing at the time. Following that meeting, both UNO and the Museum agreed to the terms, and the matter was settled. I would continue as President and CEO the coming September.[8]

Settling the leadership question allowed me, C. J., and the board to focus on the cascading events and Museum activities currently underway. We did not need any further distractions. Local and national news about the Museum's imminent opening flooded the airwaves and print media throughout the spring of 2000. The meeting with NBC Executives the preceding October paid off. They mobilized local stations as well as scheduled coverage from the Today Show, MSNBC, and NBC Evening News. C-SPAN and advance teams of other networks showed up to prepare for live broadcasts.[9] The History Channel planned a marathon of D-Day and other World War II films in the lead-up to our opening. Spielberg produced a personal testimonial supporting the Museum as a five-minute introduction on the DVDs and videotapes of *Saving Ryan Private.*[10]

Beth Courtney, President of Louisiana Public Broadcasting and the daughter of a WWII Air Corps officer, invited Steve and me to join her in a three-hour television show broadcast live over PBS outlets throughout the state in January 2000. We had a lively three-hour discussion about the Museum, Andrew Higgins, the Museum's exhibits, and personal accounts of D-Day veterans. We also had the opportunity to talk about the excitement over the impending grand opening. The show was broadcast with an open mic, and calls flooded in. It was a big hit. As much as any other publicity, this program demonstrated that there was tremendous interest in the history of World War II across demographics, just as Steve always predicted.

The remaining uncertainty was whether we could finish construction and exhibit installation in time for the grand opening. Numerous venues and major hotels were already booked for the event. Secretary Cohen, celebrities, and government leaders from city, state, federal, and foreign nations were confirmed. With DoD help, our military partners predicted that we would have at least 10,000 D-Day and WWII veterans on hand for those four days. Momentum was building. Gootee Construction had teams running three to four shifts a day, 24/7. The countdown clock reminded us daily how little time remained. The ticking grew louder the closer we got to the deadline.

We remained publicly confident that the Museum would be ready for prime time by June 6. Our internal message also exuded the "we can do it" spirit, and for all those engaged in the final push to finish, this was more than a slogan. The contractors and Museum staff believed in our mission and each other, and everyone tackled daily problems together to ensure that we stayed on schedule. C. J. Roberts was heavily engaged with the weekly construction meetings, immersing himself deeply into the blueprints, change orders and timelines, and monitoring everything happening throughout the myriad construction sites. C. J.'s museum expertise guided Explus, the exhibit fabrication firm, as it installed exhibits filled with technology, animations, film, and artifact cases. I asked C. J. almost daily if there were any problems that threatened our timetable. Invariably he assured me that we would make itbut we were going down to the wire.

Ken Gootee said the same, so long as nothing went wrong, including bad weather. Additionally, the senior professionals involved with our board, including Arthur Davis and Gus Cantrell, visited often to participate in the construction meetings and offer independent verifications of our progress and schedule. While I trusted the positive assessments, the spectacle of the construction site did not always inspire the confidence of Museum Trustees and donors. In early April, the Louisiana Memorial Pavilion looked half-finished, with roof sections missing, steel rafters still being welded, and construction machinery everywhere. Painters and electricians worked from the ceiling to the ground floor.

In early April, the *Times-Picayune* sent reporter Betsy Mullener, who covered the Museum for several years, to visit me at the construction site. She had always given us positive reporting and was enthusiastic about our cause, but she was a top reporter whose cheerful questions always belied her unflinching pursuit of a story. I suspected she was on a mission to determine if we would really be ready for June 6. On top of that, our $2 million capstone donor, Frank Stewart, called me to request a hard hat tour and planned to inspect our progress that same day. Frank made his gift with my absolute assurances that his capital donation would get us open in time.

Betsy and Frank arrived a few hours apart, but they both were confronted by the same scene that day. The timing could not have been worse. We had one of those spring thunderstorms with rain pouring down on the metal roof, which sounded like a freight train. Aside from the noise, the pavilion was not a pretty sight. Mullener described the scene accurately in the lead story of *Times-Picayune* a few days later: "There are eight iron workers, 11 painters, 13 carpenters and six electricians. There are two Bobcats, six lifts and a 60 ton-crane. There is hammering and buzzing and spraying and drilling. And not a single exhibit in place. Still, board Chairman Nick Mueller, standing in a cavernous exhibit hall with water pouring in through the ceiling, is confident the National D-Day Museum will open on time. "This is our D-Day," he said, "this date cannot be moved. The whole world has been invited and we WILL be ready by June 6."[11]

That was my story, and I was sticking with it for Frank, who came a few hours later. Opening the Museum on June 6 looked impossible to him. As we stood together, the furious work activity appeared more like the early stages of construction, and it seemed particularly chaotic that day. The tropical downpour added to the negative impression. Nearly sixty feet above us, there was a large section of the metal roof that had not yet been connected to the original warehouse roof. As we stood in the pavilion and Frank surveyed the scene, a thunderous waterfall poured from the roof opening. I knew this was going to be tough. "Nick, you'll never make it," Frank declared. He told me he had been involved with multiple construction projects across America and abroad, and he knew from what he was looking at that we probably were three or four months from completion. I assured him that, despite what he saw, we would open on schedule. I cited daily reports from C. J. and the construction firm. Frank did not buy it. He tried again, as politely as he could. "Nick, I can tell you from my experience that you cannot finish before the opening in the next eight weeks," he said. "So, what is your plan B?" Frank was the capstone donor, and I did not want to disrespect his experience, but I politely told him I had the utmost confidence in the assessments of C. J. and Gootee. Frank did not want to argue but repeated his question with greater emphasis: "What is your back-up plan, your plan B?" All I could do was smile and say, "South America." Frank sighed and gave up. In truth, there was no alternate plan at this point. The world was indeed coming, including thousands of WWII veterans. There was no way to postpone the events or the opening. We just had to finish on schedule.

Elaine and Kathy Gootee delivered on their promise to do whatever it took to finish the job on time. In the last weeks of April as our D-day drew closer, Gootee sent more construction workers to join the subcontractors, exhibit fabricators, and others on the work site. They were from numerous companies but worked as a single team on a mission. Every worker in the building knew the deadline and what was at stake. One morning at the end of April, Steve came by my office, and I suggested he go onto the construction site to give the workers a pep talk during their lunch break. He had seen how hard they were working and said he would love to speak to them. I asked Ken Gootee to assemble the workers at noon, and Steve and I went down to the floor of the pavilion construction site to meet them. They all knew Steve was the founder and a big-name author and saw him on his occasional visits, but this was different. He thanked them for their hard work and sacrifice and told them to "think of the men of D-Day and what they had sacrificed" as they devoted their full time and energy to finish. "Years or decades from now you will be telling your children or grandchildren that you helped build the national museum that honored and paid tribute to those who fought and died for our country," he told them. The performance of the Gootee workers was magnificent, as Steve later said. "They toiled at all hours," he wrote. "They applied their skill and knowledge, their sweat and time, their hands and hearts, and they got it done."[12]

General Mize worked on organizing the military bands, marching units, and drill teams from around the country, while coordinating the arrival of naval vessels. Dignitaries from Washington, DC, and abroad were coming, along with virtually all New Orleans city and Louisiana state officials. Press inquiries poured in from across the country. The Ehrhardt Group, which was handling grand opening registration, reported some 10,000 veterans and their spouses, widows, and other family members planned to attend. Pat Denechaud of Crescent City Consultants had helped organize multiple events in different venues around the city on our behalf, and the city swelled with tourists and locals eager to participate.

Construction teams worked nonstop to finish the pavilion and exhibits in the final days and nights before opening. Beyond the physical construction, we were thrilled to see the galleries, exhibits, and media treatments come to life with immersive environments, media, riveting personal accounts, artifacts, photos, and maps that told the story with drama and engagement. In a word, it was stunning. After years of striving to achieve our vision, seeing it come to fruition was a proud moment. We were ready.

Steve and I especially welcomed the frenetic pace of national media briefings and press inquiries. The big splash of grand opening publicity generated demand for visitors to see the new Museum. My goal was to put the National D-Day Museum in the country's consciousness. Nationwide exposure was critical to future success. Without state or federal support for operational expenses, we knew we had to sustain operations with large numbers of visitors well into the months and years ahead. General Mize had his troops, bands, and service branches in position. Events of each of the four days had been organized down to the smallest detail, leading up to the ceremonies and parade on June 6. Just as in 1944, the biggest unknown for us was the same one Eisenhower faced in 1944—what would the weather be like on that morning?

GRAND OPENING EVENTS

The grand opening kicked off on June 3 with a military reenactment that stormed New Orleans City Park with WWII military vehicles. American, German, British, and French reenactors were meticulously dressed in authentic WWII fatigues, "right down to the underwear," as Steve put it.[13] Veterans and families watched as the reenactors expertly maneuvered across an open field, staging an historic battle that took place in Normandy in the days following D-Day. The morning was warm and sunny, and Steve and I spent ample time talking with reenactors and enthusiasts about WWII history.

Steve was asked what he hoped children would come to understand from the Museum. "I want them to understand that the freedoms that they enjoy, to worship as they please, to say whatever comes into their minds, to vote for whoever they want to vote for, to live where they want to live, to work on what they find to be satisfying; those freedoms were paid for," he replied. "They were paid for by the men and women of World War II, and we all owe them. And I want them to be prepared to go out and defend democracy just as their grandfathers did."[14]

After a concert featuring military bands, we held a VIP reception at the Museum followed by a USO-style show and swing dance at the Roosevelt Hotel. The 1940s style prevailed, with women in snoods and sharp-dressed men in Navy uniforms. I, too, was dressed in my finest: a bright blue pin-striped zoot suit with a red carnation in the lapel, a geometric tie complete with red, yellow, and purple shapes, and my khaki Panama hat. Steve, on the other hand, kept his dress simple but elegant, with a cream-colored tuxedo and black bow tie. The show was mostly attended by veterans and their spouses, who danced through the night like they were young again. These veterans and their families lived through the darkest moments of the twentieth century and arguably all of human history. Despite that, they spent that night celebrating themselves, their brethren, and their shared past. Watching them, I knew our mission would not only celebrate their generation, but also inspire future generations to come to the Museum.

The next day, June 4, brought even more activities. Limousines whisked Steve and I from one event to another. We started with a naval port visit along the river. WWII–era navy vessels from France and the United States lined the waterfront. We had lunch on one of those grand ships but soon had to jump to the next event. Later that day, we moved to the historic Pontalba Buildings, located alongside Jackson Square in the French Quarter, where our board and major donors held a reception for the Congressional Medal of Honor recipients. It was a lively event but took on an air of solemnity as the honorees remembered those who died in battle. "Mainly I'd like to speak for those who are not here; our fallen comrades who made it possible to have this great freedom that we have to be able to establish places like this. . . ," Medal of Honor recipient Jack Lucas said in remarks to attendees. "We have a great amount of freedom that was brought about by our fallen comrades."[15] This Museum would be for all veterans, those who fell and those who survived this monumental conflict.

Just down the street at the St. Louis Cathedral, we held a solemn memorial service to honor all those who died during all the D-Days of World War II; appropriately, it was officiated by the former Archbishop of New Orleans, Rev. Philip Hannan, who served in the 82nd Airborne Division in World War II. That evening, we held a Flags of Honor presentation in Woldenberg Park, with rarely seen battle flags, honoring each division that participated in the various amphibious D-Day assaults. Together with an elaborate color guard display, it was an impressive demonstration.

The next day, Monday, June 5, we moved forward with our symposium sponsored by the Eisenhower Center. An esteemed panel of veterans, including 101st Airborne Officer Dick Winters of Easy Company, and Len Lomell of the 2nd Ranger Battalion, spoke before a crowd of hundreds at the Hilton Hotel about their wartime experiences. Chaired by board members Douglas Brinkley and Chancellor Gregory O'Brien, the symposium featured introductory remarks by Steven Spielberg, Tom Hanks, and Tom Brokaw. We heard from dozens of veterans who told their harrowing stories of combat.

We also heard the voice of another participant who, along with her millions of compatriots, played an essential role in World War II. Marguerite Guthrie Boyd, a native of Gretna, Louisiana, told us about her time in the US Army Nurse Corps. Starting in North Ireland, she and her company followed General Patton from Normandy all the way to Paris, and she was there the day it was liberated. At the Battle of the Bulge, they tended to thousands of wounded soldiers. She and her fellow nurses flew in C-47s on dangerous expeditions from the battlefield to the hospital. They performed amputations and other care, often in bombed-out convents or other hazardous locations.[16] Her work and the work of her fellow nurses were indispensable to the war effort. Her service and its challenges took its toll on her, and she deserved acclaim, honor, and recognition for it. At the end of her remarks, Marguerite stated: "I'm so glad I was invited to be on the panel because I want the world to know that women are veterans too."[17]

Later that morning, while Ambrose and Brinkley continued with a packed house to listen to the "Conversations with Veterans," I greeted Steven Spielberg, his father Arnold, and Tom Hanks in the Museum to give them a private sneak peek of the exhibits. I am not sure what they expected, but they seemed awestruck as their eyes looked upward to the Spitfire and Avenger planes, then to the floor towards the Higgins landing craft, a half track, army jeeps, as well as a German general staff car and motorcycle, the latter two from our St. Lô collection. We then moved upstairs into the galleries, where they saw a stunning display of hundreds of model soldiers that told in one glance the story of America's unpreparedness for war. The model exhibit showed that Americans were outnumbered 20 to 1 by the

Axis powers. The display reminded visitors that, at the time of the attack on Pearl Harbor, we were up against nearly nine million combat-hardened Axis troops, compared to our combined forces of a meager 500,000.

As we entered the D-Day exhibits, Steven, Arnold, and Tom were drawn to the personal touches within the exhibits. They experienced our oral history listening stations and viewed personal artifacts, each of which carried the story of a soldier, a sailor, or an airman. We swept through the defense fortifications of Hitler's massive bunkers and beach obstacles, animated floor maps of the Allied plans and the attack routes, Ike's "Decision to Go" exhibit, Operation Overlord, and the invasion itself. We entered the exhibit of the nighttime Airborne parachute drops that began in Normandy shortly after midnight on June 6 and an immersive environmental exhibit of a crashed Waco glider. We then surveyed the animated floor maps and media of the amphibious assaults on Omaha and Utah beaches, as well as the daring Ranger attack up the cliffs of Pointe Du Hoc. Since *Saving Private Ryan* had been released just eighteen months earlier, Hanks and the Spielbergs showed great familiarity and intense interest as we explored each gallery. Steven had a special interest in the invasion galleries, as he made a major donation to support them at Ambrose's request. Steven wanted to honor the service of his father, Arnold.

We entered the Omaha Beach exhibit. Steven stopped in his tracks when we got to the famous Robert Capa photo of a soldier struggling to get to shore in the face of German machine gun fire. Jack Masey had greatly enlarged the timeless photo to maximize the impact and drama of the image for our visitors. Steven described the kinetic energy flowing from the blurriness of the Capa photo, explaining how he directed the scenes of the bloody beach landings in *Saving Private Ryan.* "The images that made me understand how I needed to tell the story visually in [*Saving*] *Private Ryan* were the nine surviving Robert Capa shots," Steven told us. "Those nine surviving shots with all the vibration and the unsteadiness, that informed every single inch of the photographic approach to *Private Ryan.* Every single frame of that movie was inspired by those shots,"[18] Spielberg said. Those photos gave him the idea to use handheld cameras at water's edge to convey the energy and chaos of those horrific scenes. I took it as high praise that the famous director approved of our effort to use the Capa photo to convey the same drama and violence he achieved in his great D-Day film.

We continued through the other battle scenes as we traversed exhibits of the hedgerows of Normandy to the defeat of the German Army. The ending image of our tour through the Normandy gallery was a large scene of the American Battle Monuments Cemetery, where the graves of some 9,387 Americans who died lie buried from that battle. Up to this point on our tour, Arnold Spielberg enjoyed every inch of the galleries. He had no idea that his son had named the gallery for him, but it was here beside the American Cemetery photo that we had placed a plaque, from his son Steven, in Arnold's honor. Arnold became quite emotional during this moment, which deeply touched Steven, Hanks, and me.

The evening brought our "Victory Celebration," a private reception and dinner that offered thanks to the dignitaries, government officials, major donors, board members, WWII veterans, celebrities, and military representatives who helped us bring the Museum to fruition. The evening was one of the most memorable events I have ever attended. An elegant reception in the Louisiana Memorial Pavilion kicked off the evening. Board members, donors, and veterans rubbed elbows with famous dignitaries in a spirited celebration that simmered with the anticipation of the events to come the next day. We began with Secretary Cohen offering a champagne toast to the Museum supporters who brought us to this moment. Next, he made a surprise presentation to Steve Ambrose, recognizing him with the Department of Defense Medal for Distinguished Public Service, the highest medal a civilian can receive from the Department of Defense. Steve, usually a man of many words, was speechless from emotion. He simply raised both hands and flashed a victory sign to the crowd. His writings on American military history, plus his visionary idea for this new Museum, led Cohen to offer this signal recognition and honor for Steve. "Walter Lippman once wrote that, 'The American past can be brought alive again only by men who tell the majestic story once more, aware that they are making history, not merely writing history,'" Cohen said in presenting the award. "Stephen Ambrose has not merely written majestic history; he has indeed made history."[19] The honor was well deserved, and I was choked with emotion for my friend and all the years leading up to this moment.

Buses then transported some 400 guests from the Museum to the Roosevelt Hotel for the gala dinner and program of appreciation for our dignitaries. Tom Brokaw, emcee for the event, alongside Secretary Cohen, and a star-studded cast of distinguished veterans of D-Day and Hollywood stars poured into the hotel along with me and Ambrose. The evening was meticulously planned, but upon our arrival to the hotel ballroom, we discovered that some tables had been commandeered by WWII veterans who heard about the event. In their audacious style, these veterans, mostly in their 70s and 80s, crashed the party and took over about ten tables that were paid for by sponsors. The surprise led to mass confusion in the seating, but I thought it was great fun. The veterans locked their arms around each table saying, "We took Normandy and Iwo Jima, and we think we can hold these tables." Some of the sponsors who paid for their reserved tables came to me in frustration and asked that I do something. "Are you kidding?" I said, "This is their show, but if you are brave enough, go ahead and try to move them." We found a solution by delaying the dinner for an hour while the hotel staff brought in more tables and enlarged the ballroom to make enough room. It was a spirited start to a celebratory evening.

The night was filled with many special moments, but perhaps the most meaningful was when Dr. Hal Baumgarten described landing in the Dog Green sector of Omaha beach with the 29th Infantry Division, 116th Infantry Regiment, a unit that lost 90 percent of its soldiers in the first moments of battle. Hal, wounded five times that day and the next, told his story in graphic detail, reciting the names of each of his comrades as they were killed next to him so "their names would never be forgotten." You could have heard a pin drop in the ballroom when he finished.

Cohen, Hanks, Spielberg, and others gave remarks and brought levity to the evening. "I'd like to congratulate all the D-Day veterans," Hanks told the audience. "It seems against impossible odds that you have successfully taken New Orleans!" The good humor mixed with celebratory comments lasted past midnight, when Brokaw finally closed the evening with the remark that "this night will always be remembered as going from the longest day to the longest dinner."

The next morning at 5 a.m. sharp, General Mize called me at home. To our dismay, the early morning was grey and misty, and Mize said weather reports indicated a chance of rain around the start of our opening ceremonies, set for 8:30 a.m. We agreed not to cancel the parade or flyovers yet, but to meet at the Louisiana Pavilion at 7:00 a.m., after the breakfast planned for the board members and dignitaries just before the official ceremony. We agreed we could decide then. If it rained, we would have to move the event inside. For months we counted on a spectacular day for our grand opening ceremonies. It would be a huge disappointment if we could not have the ceremonies and parade outside as planned.

As Steve and I arrived at the Louisiana Pavilion at 7 a.m. with our families, we were worried. Mize was there getting the latest military weather forecast. Crowds had already gathered outside for blocks as far as we could see. Governor Mike Foster, New Orleans Mayor Marc Morial, US Senators Mary Landrieu and John Breaux, board members, and distinguished speakers milled about. Senator Johnny Hainkel notified us he was on the way from Baton Rouge with 60 members of the Louisiana State Legislature in a chartered bus.

Our hopes sank when a slight drizzle began at 8:00 a.m. Mize and I conferred and decided to stick with our plan. Prepared for the worst, we handed out ponchos and other rain gear to our guests and requested they head to their reserved seats outside in front of the Museum. I wished for the luck of Eisenhower, and much like D-Day 56 years before, I got my miracle. Just before the ceremony began, the rain stopped, and the sky turned blue. It was a good omen, and the rest of the day was glorious.

The scene in front of the Museum was amazing. Aside from the dignitaries on the Museum side of Howard Avenue, there were hundreds more notables and WWII veterans lining the opposite side of the street alongside platforms for the national media and television cameras.[20] Everyone exuded excitement. As we began, the dignitaries for the ribbon cutting ceremony stepped up one by one to speak on the importance of the Museum's opening and this overdue tribute to WWII veterans. Emcee Tom Brokaw began with inspiring remarks about the Museum's journey to arrive at this historic day. Officials, including Morial, Foster, and Breaux, took the podium next. Secretary Cohen followed and remarked that "last evening we heard that Steven Spielberg was referred to as the 'Homer of our times.' Well, if Steven Spielberg is the Homer, then Stephen Ambrose must be our Thucydides."[21]

Spielberg spoke of the Museum's importance to future generations. "I really think that this [Museum] is something that our children need to frequent, that our teachers need to facilitate, from now into forever, because this is the way, this is the only way, young people are going to be able to have an appreciation of all the events that came before them that made their lives possible," he said.[22] After brief remarks from me and others, Steve Ambrose had the last word: "There are too many dignitaries here for me to say all of their names, but the real dignitaries, they're sitting right in front of me, and they're scattered all through this audience; the men and women of the Second World War and what they've done for us."[23]

With the final nod to the veterans, we cut the ribbon to open the National D-Day Museum. Steve and I celebrated a moment of triumph after ten long years, embracing each other and sharing a private look of pride and friendship that said the obvious: "We did it!"

The military parade commenced in front of the Museum at 10:00 a.m. with great fanfare, as military branches and equipment passed before the Museum's grandstands, filled with VIPs. Throngs of citizens lined the parade route to celebrate the opening and pay tribute to WWII veterans. Thanks to the support from Secretary Cohen and the efforts of General Mize, the two-hour parade exceeded all expectations. It featured marching bands from the United States, France, and England, 80 trucks that carried over a thousand veterans from the many of the amphibious invasions of World War II, and periodic flyovers from military planes and helicopters. The Ehrhardt Group circulated tens of thousands of flyers throughout downtown office building, asking employers to release their employees from 10 a.m. to noon so they could come out to the parade route in the central business district. It worked. WWII vehicles, military marching bands, and trucks filled with D-Day veterans passed along the route from the Museum to the New Orleans Sports Arena. Each of the Medal of Honor recipients, waving to the crowd like rock stars, rode in their own individual cars as the parade moved forward.

Ticker tape rained down on parade goers as the convoy rolled by the cheering crowds. We always anticipated a large crowd for the parade, but what we saw was astonishing. In the three to four visible blocks of the parade I could see from the front of the Museum, crowds were 20-feet deep on either side of the street. I wondered what it was like on the two-mile-long parade route, so I asked Mize if he had any idea of the size of the crowd. He smiled and said that his liaison with the New Orleans Police Department estimated that there were nearly 200,000 people lining the streets from the Museum along every block until the parade's end. Mize had certainly fulfilled the task given to him by Cohen five months earlier: he put on the nation's biggest military parade since World War II. We were thrilled, not only by the success and size of the parade, but by how the public expressed its appreciation to the veterans. People in the crowd smiled, waved, clapped, cheered, saluted, and many carried signs stating, "Thank you for our freedom."

Steve was proud to see the spirit of generosity, solemnity, and gratitude in the crowds. "The citizens of New Orleans, who love Mardi Gras, who love parades, who all know what to do when a float comes by who are rowdy, having a good time and drinking, were *not* rowdy," he recalled. "There was no drinking. Police were not even seen. [I] was so proud of the people of New Orleans holding up signs that said, 'Thank you.'"[24]

The crowds and bands created a thrilling atmosphere, and the tremendous flyovers included vintage aircraft, modern fighter jets, and a B-52 bomber. The convoy of trucks filled with WWII veterans was the central feature of the parade; the veterans exhilaratingly poured out their emotions of gratitude and pride. The public's support was a fitting tribute and an example of the best of the American Spirit. The symbols of American valor, patriotism, and pride of our military had not lost its power among those who came to share the occasion.

Immediately after the military parade came the Museum's final commencement event in the New Orleans Arena at the end of an extraordinary day. Here, an audience of some 10,000 listened to inspirational remarks from some of our dignitaries, as well as poignant and heartfelt words from Medal of Honor recipients and other WWII veterans. Master of ceremonies Tom Brokaw opened the ceremony and set the tone: "It lifts my spirits to look out into this crowd and know that there are other generations as well assembled here today who want to lay claim to the title 'the greatest generation' for their own age group. They've come to listen and to be inspired. Fifty-six years ago, today, at this hour, the first day of the invasion that would turn the course of the war was nearing its end."[25]

Nothing was more moving that day than the words we heard from our veteran speakers about their part of the D-Day battle and how it affected their lives. Medal of Honor recipient Len Lomell told us about the Ranger assault on Pointe du Hoc and then relayed his experience after his company was relieved after two days of fighting. With some difficulty, he told us of what he saw walking down a road to an aid station to have his wounds treated by medics that day:

> Suddenly, I found myself on that road, alone, with all of my dead brothers. . . . [They were] spread out along the edge of the road on both sides of the road, with blood, mud and dirt, dust and everything on their faces. Now, we Rangers have a brotherhood that is much stronger, in many cases,

than blood brothers. And here I never anticipated in my life that this is what I would run into or see. . . . But I tell you, that is a shocking thing to see. So many dead men; I don't really know what the real count was. It was over a few dozen of them, anyway, from our company, laying there on the side of the road. They were all my friends and we had done everything together. And planned our lives for the future. We didn't really think about dying. I think most of them were overconfident, as I was, didn't think anything would ever happen to us. But I have not been able to get that out of my mind for 56 years.[26]

Walter D. Ehlers, another Medal of Honor recipient, spoke of his brother, killed in the second wave on D-Day, with so many others: "Those men laid down their lives for our freedoms, and I'm sure they would want us to know why they did that, and it was for God and country, and for our freedom, and I thank you very much."[27] Robert Bush, a Navy Corpsman who received the Medal of Honor for his actions at Okinawa, poignantly reminded us that the days we would have such heroes with us were numbered. "It won't be long, and we too will be riding into the sunset, and that's what brings into play the tremendous amount of effort that was put forth by this community to build and open the National Museum that we have here in New Orleans."[28]

Secretary William Cohen posed and then answered a question he had been asked by various reporters: "What is the significance of this Museum?" he asked. "The short answer is that it forces us to pause and to reflect about the meaning of who we are, and what we've done, and what we're going to do tomorrow." He further declared that the "heart of this new museum [is] to capture our ideals and our values." Cohen reminded the audience of Auschwitz survivor Eli Wiesel's observation that "a museum is a place where we should feel united in memory."[29] That, Cohen concluded, is "the essence of what this museum is going to represent."

Tom Hanks captured the audience by reading a piece by the great Scripps-Howard Newspaper Correspondent Ernie Pyle, who walked the Normandy beaches a few days after D-Day.

. . . It was a lovely day for strolling along the seashore. Men were sleeping on the sand, some of them sleeping forever. Men were floating in the water, but they didn't know they were in the water, for they were dead. . . .

> The wreckage [on the beach] was vast and startling. The awful waste and destruction of war . . . has always been one of its outstanding features to those who are in it, anything and everything is expendable . . . all kinds of wrecked vehicles . . . jeeps that had burned to a dull gray. . . . But there is another, and more human litter. It extends in a thin little line, just like a high-water mark for miles along the beach. This is the strewn personal gear . . . of those who fought and died to give us our entrance into Europe. . . . [Here are] soldiers packs, a pair of socks and shoe polish, sewing kits, diaries, bibles and hand grenades . . . snapshots of families back home staring up at you from the sand. . . . [There was] writing paper and air mail envelopes. . . . The boys had intended to do a lot of writing in France. Letters that would have filled those blank, abandoned pages. The strong, swirling tides of the Normandy coastline shift the contours of the sandy beach as they move in and out. They carry soldiers' bodies out to sea, and later they return them.[30]

These words from the past brought tears to the many children, wives, and family members of those who died on those beaches.

The words of Tom Hanks and Ernie Pyle made it difficult to speak after them, but as we closed the event, I spoke to the veterans in the arena and those watching on television. "We are all standing to honor you, and to honor those left behind on the battlefield and to honor the children of deceased soldiers." I pledged that we in the audience and the Museum would never allow future generations to forget what they did in World War II "to preserve our democracy at the turning point of the twentieth century. Your history and legacy will always be preserved, as well as freedom and democracy."[31] I then gave the podium to General Livingston, who proudly read the names of the Medal of Honor recipients who were in attendance. Finally, Steve Ambrose ended the afternoon that all would remember. Steve was at his best, closing with his most passionate refrain:

> We want our children, our grandchildren, and their grandchildren, on through the 21st century, to know who it was that preserved and extended their freedom for them. In the museum, [they] will learn . . . that in the mid part of the worst century in the whole of human history, the 20th century, the United States stood tall to fight for democracy . . . that D-day is, above everything else, the story of the triumph of democracy over totalitarianism.

> . . . The museum is, in its conception, in its essence, in its spirit, a love song to democracy, and it is here in New Orleans, on Mark Twain's Mississippi River, the heart of America.[32]

With this sweeping vision, which was just as vibrant and compelling as the moment Steve first proposed the idea for a D-Day Museum to me some ten years earlier, we concluded the Grand Opening Ceremonies. We were elated, grateful, and inspired by all those who had lifted us up over the years and come to help us celebrate the result.

After days of work, we could finally relax and celebrate. We all headed to Steve's large suite atop the Roosevelt Hotel, where families and friends gathered to celebrate. Champagne bottles popped, and the mood was exuberant. Congratulatory phone calls poured in from friends who had been part of the events or witnessed them on television. My son John was with us the entire day, but my oldest son, Dave, missed the event because he was studying abroad at the University of Innsbruck in Austria. He and his friends were glued to a computer for eight hours as they streamed the events live. I did not even know that was possible. It was 2:00 a.m. in Austria, but he still wanted to call to congratulate me and Steve. Since his early teens, Dave had a ringside seat to all our ups and downs over the years, and now he saw our dreams culminate from Europe, courtesy of modern technology. It was wonderful to hear his voice and know he was able to share the excitement of the day.

The revelry in the Ambrose suite continued till late night. For one shining moment, we did not have to worry about fundraising, construction, or the crisis of the moment. One journey was over; another was about to begin. We now had a Museum to run—and hopefully many thousands of visitors to greet.

BEYOND THE OPENING: THE VISITOR AND PUBLIC EXPERIENCE

When I got to the Museum shortly after the doors opened on June 7, visitors were pouring into the entire Louisiana Memorial Pavilion to buy tickets. The line was wrapped around the Museum, down the street, and wound around two city blocks, where people waited for at least an hour to buy their tickets. Malcolm told me after the opening, "We knew we would hit a homerun with the opening, but I didn't expect to hit it out of the ballpark." The crowd size was exciting and gratifying. Steve came to watch as the galleries filled up with several generations of families walking in tight groups as they followed their WWII veteran husbands, fathers, and grandfathers around the exhibits. They listened intently as veterans pointed out maps and photos showing where they fought. Veterans told their families personal stories of their war experiences. "He has never spoken about his time in the war before," family members kept saying. It was amazing for children and grandchildren as they learned long-lost family history. Some shed tears and others laughed at the stories they heard. It was just as Steve and I hoped. Young visitors learned about a war they only knew as ancient history and suddenly became very personal. So many Museum guests asked me, "Why didn't my husband, father, or grandfather every speak about the war all these years?"

That's the same question families had been asking Steve Ambrose ever since he began recording veterans' stories for the Eisenhower Center 20 years earlier. There are many reasons given for the silence of that generation of veterans, but I came to believe that for most, their experiences were so intimate, so personally linked to their comrades, and sometimes so filled with the grief for those left behind that they could not speak of the memory to anyone who had not had their common experience, even family members. For some, it was guilt that they survived when a brother-in-arms did not make it. It was a difficult story to tell, or for anyone else to ever comprehend. So, they kept the stories inside. Some also kept silent because of depression, the aftershock of battle that we now know as PTSD. I have also concluded—after years watching veterans open up to Steve, conducting my own oral histories, and meeting veterans in great numbers—that Steve and the Museum gave these aging veterans "permission" to tell their stories to family and friends with honesty. Steve and the Museum lifted the burden from veterans by telling the larger story of their war experience. The exhibits, the embedded oral histories, and the artifacts were treated with respect and were surrounded by maps and photos that carried the story of their experiences with authenticity, emotion, and historical accuracy. The veteran did not have to convince relatives just how intense and violent their experience had been, or how great the sacrifice that was made, or how large the conflict had been. This was a difficult task for the nonhistorian veterans when they returned home from the battlefields in 1945. So many clammed up, only opening up to their buddies at reunions, which many often never bothered with until 30 or 40 years after the war. The Museum became their new home, and we were proud and pleased to help the veterans and their families fill a hole in their hearts and history.

One example of how personal stories poured out came during a visit in the early weeks after opening when an extended family from south Louisiana toured the exhibits. They were completely surprised, as I was, when they spotted a photo of their grandmother's home in Plaquemines Parish that displayed three stars hanging in her front window, stars representing each of her three sons who were fighting overseas. The photo came from the Library of Congress, and most of the family had no idea it even existed.[33] It was one of the first exhilarating moments of discovery for visitors and Museum staff alike. These moments happened every day. The war was no longer a remote memory. It was personal, present, and palpable. Visitors told me and others that they could now understand the journey of ordinary citizens who went to war. Museum guests could also feel the emotions and pain of families from the letters, photos, or remembrances of those killed in action.

During the first week after opening, I passed by one of my favorite display cases, holding a medic's web belt that belonged to Leo Scheer, a Navy Corpsman. To my great surprise, there was Leo, standing in his WWII uniform beside his web belt. He was a modest man and told me he carried the belt of first aid pouches attached throughout France and Belgium. Every time he used an individual pouch, he remembered the face of the dead soldier on Omaha Beach whose medical kit he had taken to save the lives of others. Speaking with him there beside the prized artifact was an emotional, personal, and memorable moment for both of us. Steve understood the power of these personal artifacts that carried such amazing intimate stories, and it was his gift to us all.

These stories were displayed against the tapestry of violence and death represented by other objects, large photos, and visual media that engaged the sight, hearing, and tactile senses of visitors. Weapons, uniforms, supplies, journals, and letters were all linked to accounts that drew visitors into a story. These personal features of the exhibits were the most popular. Our exhibits also had an authentic human element that added value to the stories—the veterans themselves. While we enjoyed an overflow of visitors of all ages after opening, we were blessed by an abundance of WWII veterans who came in large numbers. We gave all veterans a bold lanyard saying, "I'm a

World War II Veteran." Many vets, after touring the exhibits, stood around the entrance pavilion to greet visitors and tell their stories. We also had more than 50 World War II veterans, many who fought in D-Day battles, become permanent volunteers and docents at the Museum. They were very special to all of the staff and visitors. They served in various capacities in every part of the Museum and added authenticity that we would not have 10 or 15 years later.

Out of the 16 million American veterans who served in World War II, we were fortunate to have nearly six million WWII veterans still living at the time of our opening. Tens of thousands made a pilgrimage to visit "their Museum." We quickly became a destination, almost a shrine, for veterans who served in all aspects of the war. Local veterans came in droves, of course, but as word got out, growing numbers came from across America, usually with their families in tow. They yearned for a Museum that told the story of WWII with authenticity and meaning. Many visiting veterans who served in other theaters, including the Mediterranean, China-Burma-India, or Alaska, urged us to keep expanding the Museum to tell all the campaigns of the war; they wanted additional exhibits on the Pacific and the home front.

Veterans and families proudly showed off their charter membership cards, and many of them could be found searching for their bricks named for a loved one. They often snapped photos or made rubbings of the brick to take home, and they exuded pride that they shared a small piece of the national Museum. They felt that their membership, bricks, and stories helped to build the National D-Day Museum, and indeed they had. The immediate impact the Museum had on visitors was incredibly special to Steve and me. Under Jack Masey's guidance, we had created a museum experience that was popular, engaging, and accessible to visitors of all ages.

Will Hales, the 14-year-old son of a well-known New Orleans doctor, was one of those whom the Museum impacted from the start. Will said he wanted to volunteer to work in the Museum. His father proudly told me that Will had read all of Ambrose's 30 books, quite an accomplishment at any age, and it was true. "I can never know enough about World War II," Will later said. "This Museum understands that there's always another story to be told, and it wants to honor the common American, the person you'd never read about in any textbook."[34] That was exactly what the Museum was designed to do. This broad appeal to young and old alike drew crowds that became our best advertisement for our future success and expansion.

The news of the Museum spread like wildfire. In the first month we had 52,000 visitors, and, by January of 2001, the Museum had welcomed over 231,000—an impressive feat.[35] Everything worked according to the plans we laid in 1998. We were ahead of all our targets for visitation, membership, and revenues. As we looked back after the first few months, the board and staff knew the grand opening was everything we wanted it to be and more. Malcolm estimated that widespread media coverage of the grand opening reached over 50 million people over the four days of events.[36]

Though there was an overwhelmingly positive response to the nation's new Museum and our grand opening events, we received criticism from some media outlets that highlighted the absence of African American veterans in the parade. This led to an impression that the African American experience in World War II was omitted in the Museum and other grand opening Ceremonies. The absence was entirely unintentional, but a glaring oversight nonetheless, and deserving of criticism. However, I knew we needed to set the record straight on the unfounded charge that the African American contribution was omitted from our Museum. Later that month, I wrote an article for the *Times-Picayune* addressing these claims head-on.

Long before the Museum opened, Steve and I spent countless hours meeting with board members, designers, and staff to discuss how best to tell the D-Day story and its many facets. This included discussions on how to incorporate the African American experience into our exhibits. In my article I explained that we all agreed that this story must be told. The heart of our discussions centered on the decision to either incorporate the African American experience within the overall exhibit narrative or to highlight that experience by setting it apart. We opted for the former. I wrote: "The final decision was one that satisfied both the need to examine the unique nature of the African American experience during World War II and the desire not to segregate African American participants from the larger struggle."[37] During our exhibit design phase, I consulted on this issue with two good friends and future board members, Nolan Marshall and Lenny Burns. Both were veterans of the famed Montford Point Marines, a segregated unit of the Marine Corps in World War II. They told me emphatically that they had been segregated in the war and did not want to be segregated in this Museum; they wanted their story to be part of the narrative. Consequently, in the exhibits, visitors encountered African Americans on the home front, whites and blacks building Higgins boats together, segregated training at military bases, the Barrage Balloon Battalion over the beaches on D-Day, the Red Ball Express, and fighting in every theater of the war while fighting at home for equal rights. Our depiction of the African American experience in the war was not perfect, but I thought that through my article people would be encouraged to view our exhibits before forming an opinion on how we handled a sensitive and important topic.

Four months before the grand opening, the board had asked another African American board member, Col. Henry Johnson, to chair a task force to identify ways we could find more black veterans to contribute to our oral history collection.[38] Additionally, our education department created lesson plans and special training material for tour guides that highlighted the African American experience.[39] Still, we knew we could not be complacent on this subject going forward. In February 2001, we held a series of programs and events meant to honor our Black veterans, which we called "Double Victory: Fighting on Two Fronts—The African American Experience of World War II." We partnered with a broad coalition of educational institutions throughout New Orleans, such as the Amistad Research Center, the Center for African and African American Studies, and the UNO Eisenhower Center, to organize several days of events.[40] The Museum hosted a three-day symposium at which Black veterans told their stories, as well as a grand gala event at the Museum. These events gave us the opportunity to honor over 150 black veterans who were in attendance. Among them were Vernon Baker and Ossie Davis. Baker was among the first Black veterans to receive the Medal of Honor, which was awarded in 1997, for his service in World War II. Davis, the famed actor, director, writer, and civil rights activist, was a veteran of World War II and served as a guest speaker at the symposium. Their presence added valuable insight into the black experience in World War II.

The events culminated on Saturday, February 4, with a victory parade, which began near the D-Day Museum and ended in Congo Square. Vernon Baker rode in the jeep as Grand Marshall at the head of the parade. After 56 years, black veterans were honored and celebrated for their service. Lenny Burns rode on a two-ton military transport and was quoted by the *Times-Picayune* as saying, "Finally they're recognizing us for something we'd done."[41] Approximately 1.2 million Black men and women served in the military in World War II, and their service was crucial to victory against the Axis powers. However, when they returned home, they found a nation that denied them adequate recognition of that service. The "Double-V" events were only a small step toward understanding and honoring the contribution of black veterans. We knew that to present an honest account of WWII learning, we needed to portray the fullest version of WWII history we could, even the uncomfortable parts. We were committed to honoring all veterans, regardless of their color, ethnic group, or gender. It was imperative to include their stories and to show the diversity of the American experience during the war.

LEADERSHIP CHANGE AND PLANS FOR THE PACIFIC EXPANSION

After the grand opening, we immediately started looking to the future. As planned, I transitioned from Chairman into the role of President and CEO, while continuing to serve on the board with Steve. The official shift took place September 20, 2000, at the annual meeting, when the board elected Boysie Bollinger to assume the role as Chairman.

As I turned over the gavel to Boysie, I thanked him and the board for the support and teamwork they provided in creating such a meaningful expression of the American Spirit. I expressed my deep debt of gratitude to Steve for convincing me to accept the chairmanship in 1998, and for never giving up, even in the darkest hours. I took a brief victory lap by recounting the goals I promised to meet when becoming Chairman two years earlier: to open the National D-Day Museum on June 6, 2000, to mobilize the Board of Directors to help meet that goal, and to develop a professional staff that would bring the Museum to life and to preserve the stories of World War II.

Boysie stepped into his new role as Chairman with the high expectations and optimism that were a trademark of his leadership style. Boysie announced his immediate goals for the next 14 months would be to open the Pacific wing of the Museum in December 2001 and help me secure funding for the production of the *Price for Peace* documentary that Ambrose and Spielberg were making with James Moll as the film director.[42]

Boysie set our course to another major milestone, but this time we had a Museum to market and operate, visitors, and most of the funding already in place for the Pacific wing. All that helped, but we needed to plan another grand opening and get ready for the ambitious goals that Boysie would bring forward to the board in the coming year. We were again racing into the future to fill a new chapter in the Museum's history. Our train was still speeding along the tracks. Boysie Bollinger was the perfect Chairman to keep up our speed and stay on the rails. He was already caught in that "catcher pouch" by the speeding train, and he was now in the pouch with me. It felt good to have company.

The *D-Day Invasions in the Pacific* exhibit represented a major expansion of our original mission, which had focused only on Normandy. While it seemed a bit much to tackle so soon after opening the Museum, the board had considered it since Steve first recommended expanding our mission in 1994, and the exhibit had been planned and under design since 1998. For years, we had felt a growing push from donors and Pacific War veterans to expand our mission to cover the Asia-Pacific War. We knew expanding to the Pacific War promised another chance to gain national publicity on the 60th anniversary of Pearl Harbor. More importantly, the new galleries would broaden interest to include all the veterans of World War II, not just those in Europe, and from every service branch, especially from the Marine Corps and the Navy. There was no time to lose. December 7, 2001, was just around the corner.

We had already laid the groundwork for the designs that were in progress. In November 1999, we held a focus group meeting to begin forming ideas for the new galleries and to allow Kenneth Rendell, board member and professional collector, to begin procuring artifacts. We had a $2.1 million appropriation to fund the design and construction of the new galleries that US Rep. Bob Livingston and Sen. Ted Stevens helped us obtain in 1997, but we still needed more funds on the private side for the exhibit and Pacific D-Days film. However, it was a good feeling knowing we were not scrambling to the goal line without the funds to get there.

Jack Masey had presented his conceptual design for the Pacific galleries to the board several years earlier, going into great detail on all aspects of the new exhibits. "While the Exhibition's primary focus will be on the amphibious landings in the Pacific," Masey said, "emphasis will also be placed on the key role that American naval and air forces played in the Pacific Theater. Massive naval battles preceded the American offensives in the Central Pacific Zone, led by Admiral Nimitz, and in the South Pacific Zone, led by General MacArthur and many of the key island D-Day landings, included a major related naval battle."[43] As in the original D-Day exhibits, Masey strove to make the exhibits personally interactive through a blend of technology, personal artifacts, and documents. He also promised that he would continue to draw on the Ambrose Oral History Collection at the Eisenhower Center to maintain a personal element in the exhibits.

We wanted to make another big publicity splash to attract new visitors and keep World War II fresh in the minds of our growing public audiences. Our experience from planning the first grand opening was a big help. The Department of Defense again promised to support our events fully, and we had commitments from Tom Hanks and other celebrities to attend. Additionally, we could count on leaders from local and national government as well as military brass to participate in our grand opening. George H. W. Bush agreed to speak at the opening ceremonies, appearing not so much as a former President but as a WWII combat veteran who served as a Navy aviator on 58 missions and was the recipient of the Distinguished Flying Cross and three air medals. Bush and his wife, Barbara, were close to Steve Ambrose and great admirers of his books. Following his visit to the Museum site in 1999, Bush was extremely pleased that we succeeded in getting open and was excited about our expansion to the war in the Pacific. His advance commitment to attend the opening on December 7, 2001, was a huge boost. The opening included four days of events that played out throughout the city, beginning December 6. We held several receptions and galas, another major military parade, a naval port visit, Pacific War film festival, a USO swing dance, and a spectacular reenactment of dogfights between American fighter planes and Japanese Mitsubishi Zeroes above Lake Pontchartrain Research Park. We premiered the Museum's new Steven Spielberg and James Moll documentary, *Price for Peace: From Pearl Harbor to Nagasaki,* at the Orpheum Theater in New Orleans. The capstone event of the Pacific grand opening was a symposium with distinguished scholars on the war in the Asia-Pacific, who examined, among other things, the strong democratic partnership that America forged with Japan since 1945.

At 7:55 a.m., December 7, 2001, church bells rang out across New Orleans, recognizing the moment when Japanese forces attacked the US fleet at Pearl Harbor 60 years prior. That morning, Tom Brokaw was again our reliable master of ceremonies, hosting the NBC *Today Show* and the *Evening News* from inside the Museum with Tom Hanks. George H. W. Bush joined Brokaw and other dignitaries who spoke at our dedication ceremony in front of the Museum. The parallels between Pearl Harbor and the 9/11 attacks on the World Trade Center and the Pentagon three months prior were on the minds of many attendees and Bush addressed this issue in his remarks. "On September 11 our nation suffered another surprise attack, and today we are in a different war, but I think that the duty-honor-country still prevails. So that when we say today 'Remember Pearl Harbor,' . . . I think we as a nation all say, 'Remember September 11.'"[44]

Crowds again lined the streets for the military parade, which included WWII Veteran Joe Foss and five other Medal of Honor recipients who stole the show. Steve and I were among those who spoke at the ribbon-cutting ceremony, but it was Tom Hanks who offered some of the most compelling remarks: "The National D-Day Museum is a mirror where we see the American soul and spirit reflected back at us through exhibits and artifacts and oral histories. On permanent display here is the fortitude, which has proven indominable throughout the life of our nation, never more than through the campaigns and sacrifices of Americans at home and abroad during the Second World War when our citizens fought against tyranny and terror on two sides of the planet."[45]

With the opening of the Pacific Exhibit, we completed our final mission as the National D-Day Museum we envisioned it in the 1990s. Much had changed in the 11 turbulent years since Steve and I conceived of the idea of creating a small museum. We succeeded with a much larger location in downtown New Orleans. An even bigger idea loomed on the horizon—the vision for a new mission to expand and become The National WWII Museum. The train sped forward, and the "catcher pouch" was filling with new passengers.

8

BECOMING THE NATIONAL WWII MUSEUM

IT BEGAN WITH a phone call from Sen. Ted Stevens to Steve, five days before the grand opening of the Museum on June 6, 2000. The Senator was in New Orleans for a fundraising event but would not be able to attend the grand opening as planned due to a major schedule conflict. Since he was in town, he said he would like a preview tour of the Museum. We were thrilled to have some private time with Stevens, as he was our most ardent champion in Congress and a distinguished WWII veteran. Moreover, Ambrose had visited Stevens at his fishing camp in Alaska for several summers, and the two had become close friends.

Stevens arrived at the Museum later that day accompanied by several staff members. We greeted him in the Louisiana Memorial Pavilion and could see that he was both surprised and impressed by the size of our main entry hall. While admiring the iconic aircraft suspended from the ceiling, Stevens commented on his wartime duty as a flight navigator with the Army Air Corps in the China-Burma-India Theater, service for which he had received two Distinguished Flying Crosses. There was no one in the galleries except a gang of workers who were putting the finishing touches on some of the exhibits. He was enamored with the exhibits and how we told the story in a chronological sequence from the prewar period through the Pearl Harbor attack. After a few hours, we went to the fourth-floor offices to review his impressions. Though we could sense his deep interest from his questions to Steve during our tour, we were anxious for a full debrief, as we were counting heavily on his support to obtain more federal funds. Stevens had already helped secure our $2.1 million Department of Defense appropriation in 1997 that was earmarked for our *D-Day Invasions in the Pacific* exhibit, due to open in December 2001. We had most of the funds needed for those exhibits, but we knew the Senator wanted us to do more on the China-Burma-India Theater.

Standing outside my office, we asked for his impressions. "Let's talk in your office," he replied. He signaled to his staffers to stay outside, and we closed the door and sat down. "What you two have accomplished here in New Orleans is the best museum on World War II in America," Stevens began. "It's engaging, personal, authentic, and you tell a huge story of the D-Day invasion." Then came the kicker.

"While this is the best museum on a critical battle of World War II, you have left out my war in the Pacific Theater, and you've not covered Danny Inouye's war in the Mediterranean," he said. Inouye, the Democratic Senator from Hawaii, was the ranking member of the Senate Defense Appropriations Committee and had been awarded the Medal of Honor for his service in Italy with the Army's famed 442nd Regiment Combat Team of Japanese Americans. Stevens and Inouye were major players on the committee for 25 years, and Stevens noted the two of them agreed on nearly every major defense bill, despite coming from different parties. I thought to myself that this was a promising start for a conversation we hoped would lead to more federal funding. Then came the game-changer. "If you guys will talk to your board, figure out how to get the land to expand this Museum to cover all of World War II, I'll help," Stevens said.

Those last two words hung in the air. Neither Steve nor I expected such an ambitious, open-ended proposal. We were both satisfied that we were finally about to open the Museum after a decade of work. We were exhausted and believed we were almost done. We just needed to complete the *D-Day Invasions in the Pacific* exhibits. Before either of us could answer, Stevens reminded us that the Defense budget is "where all the money is" in Congress and added that he was confident he and Inouye would work together to appropriate the funds we needed if we agreed to pursue the idea. We only had seconds to answer. The yes or no options raced through my mind. I looked over at Steve, who rolled his eyes over to me, with a pleading look that said,

"Nick, don't say yes." But to me this felt like a one-time offer with no one in the office except the three of us. If we said no, Stevens would probably understand, but that would be it.

So, I said, "Yes," with more confidence than I felt. "We will ask the board and professionals to help us figure out the scope and costs of expanding to the entire war and see if it's feasible," I told him. Ambrose quickly understood that we had little choice but to say yes, and he added his commitment to try. That was all Senator Stevens needed to hear. We shook hands, he wished us well for the grand opening, and urged us to come visit him in Washington in the fall so he could learn about the board's commitment and appropriate the initial DoD funds to get us started.

That moment was the genesis for the idea of expanding into a WWII Museum that would cover the entirety of the war. After the Senator left my office, Steve sat down and wondered aloud if he had enough juice left in him to go beyond the opening of the *D-Day Invasions in the Pacific.* We were both overwhelmed by what just happened, and we had only the vaguest idea of how to proceed. This goal was far bigger and more ambitious than our original idea ten years earlier, but the promise of help from Stevens and Inouye was a huge motivator. We did not dwell on it long, because the coming days were entirely consumed with the grand opening.

From the moment we opened, the overwhelming public reception to the Museum put the idea back on the front burner. "You need to expand," Sen. John Breaux told Boysie that day as they watched the crowds build outside the Museum during the grand opening.[1] He suggested we would be crazy not to start purchasing the warehouses across the street. Indeed, many visitors asked for more and were already impatient for the galleries on the Pacific to open. I told Boysie about our meeting with Senator Stevens and suggested he lead the board in the effort to expand our mission to cover all of World War II. Boysie seized the opportunity immediately. He understood that it was ambitious, but with Stevens in our corner, Boysie knew we had the Senate Appropriations Committee chairman asking us to take it on. This was far different from us making asks of him or any Senator. We would have to move quickly, but we still had to be deliberate in our approach.

Our first test was to see what Stevens could secure for us in the Defense Appropriations Bill in the autumn of 2000. Nothing would happen until we had the funds to purchase the needed properties across the street but that was just the beginning. We would also need a clear vision of the exhibits and all the property needed to cover the entirety of World War II, even before a building or buildings could be designed. Defining the scope, costs, and design were what Stevens expected when he told us to "figure it out." The work was daunting, given the sheer enormity of World War II, with tens of millions of troops and civilian populations engaged in existential battles on almost every continent. This was an exponentially bigger challenge than covering a single D-Day operation. Visitors would need to understand that World War II required every human, economic, technological, material, government, and military resource of the nation to defeat the Axis forces. Covering military operations in all theaters of the war across the globe was a staggering challenge. Somehow, we had to determine how to tell that story and what it would cost.

Aside from the land for expansion, we needed professional consultants at the front end to help us with our conceptual planning, exhibit design, and architecture. Absent any public funding, we would have to design and build a Museum that would be self-sufficient from its opening day. We needed creative imagination and entrepreneurship as well as the brain power of the best museum professionals and architects in the world. Plus, we needed feasibility studies to accompany the prepared building and exhibit design. Boysie and I understood the board had to be prepared to meet all these challenges. To satisfy Senator Stevens, we needed to convey the board's commitment to the expanded mission and begin the planning, which was going to be tricky. The 42-member local board that opened the D-Day Museum would now have to accept the transition into a national board that had to approve the larger vision for a WWII Museum. The original D-Day Museum Foundation was not structured for this larger task, nor could we raise the private funds in New Orleans alone. Those were the realities.

Boysie was ready and eager to embrace the challenge, and I was too. Steve was on board but more focused on writing a new book on the Pacific War, finishing our Museum documentary film, and helping to get the remaining Pacific D-Day exhibits ready to open by the end of 2001. He was content to leave the heavy lifting on planning, government funding, and management of transition to Boysie and me. While Steve had plenty on his plate, he was always ready to join me and Boysie on trips to Washington, DC, to meet with Senators Stevens, Landrieu, and other legislators to help keep the federal funds flowing.

Boysie assumed the Chairmanship in September 2000 as I transitioned to my new role as President and CEO. While I was devoting nearly full time to the Museum, I continued teaching part time at UNO. This had been a workable arrangement for the previous two years, but the dual duties were becoming more burdensome. The new demands of leading a fully operating Museum with thousands of daily visitors were coupled with increasing time spent securing state and federal funds and managing the board to achieve Boysie's goals and mine.

I added Samuel Wegner, a museum executive in the public sector, as our new Vice President and COO, replacing C. J. Roberts, who left to become President and CEO of the National Museum of the Mighty Eighth Air Force in Pooler, Georgia. Sharon Gruber, an experienced nonprofit executive, also joined our senior staff as Vice President for Development. Our lone Curator, Paula Ussery, worked mightily to handle the avalanche of personal artifacts and memorabilia donated by veterans and families. Our new staff was small, but it was supplemented by an extraordinary group of volunteers, and they managed the new Museum with heart and commitment. They kept pace with the overflowing visitors, school groups, special-event rentals, store sales, and our own special events and programs.

Our spectacular exhibits had to be matched by the quality of people who met our visitors on the front lines and operated the Museum. Our staff and volunteers all shared the thrill of being a part of such an important endeavor. The pioneer spirit of the first years created a special comradery and an infectious "can do" attitude among our team. Everyone felt connected to doing the impossible every day. They were entrepreneurial and open, with new ideas flowing and being implemented almost daily. Everyone was excited by the great reception from our visitors, which created a buzz in the air that something remarkable was in the making. While we had not sought board approval for the WWII expansion at that point, most board members could see that the World War II "train" was on the tracks. At the Executive Committee meeting on October 31, 2000, Boysie outlined a planned expansion that would require some restructuring of the board, a revised mission, and the purchase of additional land for exhibits that would go beyond the *D-Day Invasions in the Pacific.* With DoD funds promised in 2001 and 2002, we intended to at least include exhibits and buildings on the China-Burma-India Theater and most likely the Mediterranean campaign as well. Steve chimed in to say, "We could easily become a World War II Museum," citing his desire to better cover the North African campaign.[2] The board greeted his comments with enthusiasm. While Stevens's new $2.1 million appropriation was not available to spend until the next fiscal year, the grant gave us the confidence to take the first steps toward becoming a WWII Museum.[3]

The shape of the future expansion gained clarity by the fall of 2000, when Boysie authorized board member John Kushner to start investigating the purchase of properties surrounding the Museum. Everything depended on how much property we could purchase to support the other planning efforts. That would determine everything else, including the scope of the project, exhibit concepts, the costs, and our public-private fundraising goals.

We needed a stealth approach to the land purchases, since the Museum had already drastically increased the value of the surrounding properties. Across the street from the Museum and running along Magazine Street, there were three city blocks filled with warehouses. Some were abandoned, a few had some light industrial business activity, and there were vacant lots in between. Most if not all the buildings would have to be torn down to make way for new Museum pavilions to accommodate state-of-the-art exhibits, theaters, restaurants, entertainment, group venues, and back-of-house security and storage. John Kushner approached the property owners through other realtors and third parties to keep them unaware of who was making offers to purchase. In his report to the Executive Committee on March 29, 2001, John identified three properties over 13 lots that could be bought for $2.72 million.[4] Allowing time for ongoing negotiations and due diligence periods, John said we could lock in the purchase prices in the coming year with deposits and options until we had cash on hand from Congress to close on the acts of sale—depending on the scope of the Museum and available funds.

With this encouraging news, the board authorized Boysie and me to begin advancing deposit money for realtors to quietly secure the purchases or enter lease-purchase agreements for the three properties. John's stealth negotiations were complicated, as there were multiple owners involved, and, pending more funds from Congress, there were additional properties we would need to purchase. Assurances from Senators Stevens, Inouye, and our two Louisiana Senators, Landrieu and Breaux, gave us the confidence to risk depositing money to hold the properties until we determined how much land we would need for the expansion. We figured if we did not need all the property we acquired, we could easily sell what we did not use.

Almost concurrently with the land acquisition, we began the process of restructuring our governance and mission into a new national board with an expanded mission. Boysie's first step was to ask Herschel Abbott to chair a Committee of the Future. As a corporate lawyer, he could cut to the quick on any difficult legal problem. He was the right man for the job. I relied on my higher education contacts and national trustee organization to find Maureen Robinson, an experienced strategic planning consultant who specialized in helping nonprofit organizations and museums improve or change their governance structures. She was exactly who we needed. I invited her to New Orleans in the fall of 2001 to meet with Herschel and Boysie to help organize the work of the new committee.

Our task was not going to be easy. We would have to lose some members and add national directors. By this time, we had 42 board members, composed entirely of local business leaders plus Chancellor O'Brien, Steve, and me. Together with Boysie, we assembled a few well-respected members of the board to join the committee with Maureen for a two-day retreat to hammer out the governance solutions. Boysie offered his houseboat, berthed at Grand Isle, the southernmost reaches of the Louisiana marshlands, for the retreat. We agreed to lock ourselves down there until we created a new mission statement, a new governance structure, the basic terms of new bylaws, and a transition plan for shifting from the old board to the new one with an expanded mission. We needed a truly national board to lead an effort to convert a big vision into reality—and hopefully to provide a big boost to our private fundraising campaign.

For two days we debated every aspect of the plan; it was an exhausting process carried out in hopes that it would form the foundation of our future success. The size and composition of our new board came first. Despite resistance from Maureen, who thought a smaller board was preferable, we finally agreed on a larger board of up to 50 trustees with no less than 40 percent of its members from New Orleans and the surrounding region. The rest of the board would be new trustees from across the nation. The situation was agonizing. Our new ratio requirements meant 30 seats would be reserved for national members and only 20 for local members. That meant that, of the current 42 members, 22 would see their terms ending. To ease the pain, we devised a plan to stagger the term endings of these 22 over two years, while recruiting new national members to fill their seats on the board. It was tough having to say goodbye to leaders who helped us achieve our dream. As Boysie put it, we were looking "for the next generation of leadership."[5] This change, though difficult, was critical to the future of the Museum.

There were also steep financial conditions for new trustees, local or national. All new and continuing trustees had to agree to contribute $10,000 per year to support operating costs and were expected to make a capital contribution during their first three-year term. The full board would meet only twice a year, around the anniversaries of D-Day in June and Pearl Harbor in December, but trustees would be required to attend the two-day board meetings in person. We also established strong committees that would keep trustees engaged in the essential functions of a board, and we were clear that we expected participation.[6]

We also modified the Museum mission to envision a Museum beyond the D-Days of World War II. This governance plan designed a board for trustees with deep pockets matched by a passion for preserving WWII history. It was an ambitious organizational effort. We left Grand Isle with the feeling we had accomplished what was needed.

Herschel brought the Committee of the Future recommendations to the board on May 16, 2002. The board received it while knowing that more than half of the members would lose their board seats. It was a bitter pill for many loyal board members who had stuck with us through the dog days of the 1990s and then helped get us over the finish line with two grand openings. Boysie, Herschel, and I were all impressed by the selfless actions of many who wished to remain on the board. There was no dissent on the final vote to implement the transition plan and expanded mission. It was a key moment in the Museum's history. Of the major steps to becoming the National WWII Museum, the change of governance and mission were foundational.

CSAS AND DISCOVERY HALL

Long before any talk about a major expansion, Steve and I had known what we wanted next for the Museum. To truly start the next chapter in the Museum's life, we needed to create more diverse forms of learning for the public. We envisioned a space that would serve as the intellectual core of the Museum. Not only would it house and grow the foundational oral history collection, created by Steve and the Eisenhower Center, it would also accommodate researchers, an archive, a library, and give ample space for WWII conferences, symposia, and local telecourses. Steve and I called this facility the Center for the Study of the American Spirit, or CSAS for short. As Steve had said a long time ago: "[The World War II generation's] sense of duty, of right and wrong, their teamwork and their courage embody the American Spirit. The National D-Day Museum celebrates the American Spirit. Young and old will come to learn of their proud heritage. . . . Visitors will learn not just of what we have done. They will learn of what we can do. They will learn that we are still in this together."[7] Now that we had received our new, lofty charge from the government, we were even more determined to create an institution to help us study, understand, and nourish the American Spirit.

CSAS would be the Museum's beating heart and help guide the historical legitimacy of the remainder of the exhibits. Steve and I wanted to place it right at the corner of Andrew Higgins Boulevard and Magazine Street, which would be the anchor of the expanded Museum and prime real estate. As we envisioned it, CSAS would be housed in a 32,000-square-foot building that would exponentially expand our capacity for WWII education and help mark us as an important research center, especially as an archive of personal accounts. As President and CEO, I found the idea of drawing diverse scholarly parties to the Museum was enticing. But, as a historian, the endless possibilities for WWII learning was the most thrilling prospect. We still had a long way to go in planning the details and integrating our ideas into the larger Museum expansion, but this initial idea was inspiring. Steve and I wanted to get started on it right away.

The board members always embraced the Museum's educational mission as the pillar of our exhibits and historical integrity, and they supported its construction even before we had a new master plan. We were so excited that this vision was coming to life that Steve, Boysie, and I held a press conference to announce it on October 10, 2001. As I told Betsy Mullener of the *Times-Picayune,* "It confirms our position as the premiere World War II Museum in the world."[8]

CSAS would provide us with resources for higher learning, but we also wanted to create a space for K–12 students and educators. Steve knew that dedicating spaces for education would serve as a vital link between the Museum and the larger community of public historians, enthusiasts, and educators interested in WWII history. As this idea developed, we envisioned another space adjacent to the Louisiana Memorial Pavilion to be called Discovery Hall, meant to advance our educational mission for K–12 students. Here, we could create cutting-edge resources for teachers and students. Some of our initial ideas were for classrooms, a teacher resource center, a space featuring our oral history collection, and a special exhibit space.

Beyond CSAS and Discovery Hall, our staff created new initiatives that allowed us to spread our mission to wider audiences. Our stellar education team, headed by Kenneth Hoffman, created distance-learning programs that allowed K–12 students to engage digitally with the Museum from anywhere in the world. They allowed students to have real-time, face-to-face experiences with a Museum educator, explore the Museum's exhibits, ask questions of WWII veterans, and study artifacts and other primary sources of WWII history. They set up teacher training workshops that provided classroom teaching materials and other support. They created summer camps and traveling exhibits, and they revamped our website. In less than two years, we had overhauled and sharpened our educational mission. Our commitment to education had become a hallmark of our mission and a major focus going forward.

In the fall of 2001, Senator Stevens told us that he had secured a $4.25 million Defense appropriation to jump-start the expansion.[9] This wonderful news was a defining moment in the Museum's history. Together with the opening of the *D-Day Invasions in the Pacific* exhibit on December 7, 2001, it felt as if our transformation to a National WWII Museum was being propelled by a booster rocket.

In early 2002, the various master planning efforts shifted into high gear. On January 29, 2002, the Executive Committee authorized John Kushner to exercise due diligence by expediting the goal of purchasing all the properties needed for the expansion by late 2002 or early 2003. I was also authorized to work with Arthur Davis to engage a national consulting firm to create a concept for the Master Plan. Boysie said in the same meeting that he expected the cost of the project to range between $60 to $80 million from both public and private sectors. He won approval for a capital campaign goal to raise $40 million from the private sector over the next 8 to 10 years. This came with the expectation, or at least hope, that more funds would be forthcoming from Congress and the state of Louisiana. Boysie had already told the *Times-Picayune* that the expansion might reach $50 to $60 million and include 100,000 square feet of space. "Have you ever seen a museum that wasn't trying to raise a jillion dollars?" he told the paper.[10] Boysie was our champion, and he exuded confidence in the interview as he trumpeted his faith in the Museum's expansion: "I never thought this [Museum] would be a $100 million enterprise," he said. "In fact, some days I didn't think we'd ever finish what we'd started. But I have no question now that we'll get to the end. The momentum is just phenomenal."[11]

By contrast, Steve Ambrose himself was clearly getting worried about the consultant costs and rising estimates for the expansion. At a board meeting in early 2002, Steve pressed me for a top number of what I thought the expansion might cost. I tried to dodge his question, telling him we had not really gotten into our concept planning yet. But Steve insisted that I give him my best estimate, so I reluctantly said that our architect board members guessed it might go as high as $80 million. Boysie and I have never forgotten the next moment. Steve groaned, put his head down on the boardroom table, and pounded his fist on the table. "No! No! No! We can NEVER raise that kind of money," he moaned. "Look how long it took us to raise $25 million for the D-Day Museum." Everyone was a bit shocked. But Boysie reassured Steve that he was confident we could reach $80 million with more funds coming from Congress and Louisiana. I'm sure that Steve's sudden impatience came in part from the stress over the time he would need to commit to help raise that vast sum of money. He finally yielded to Boysie's continued optimism and leadership.

Since Boysie's $40 million capital campaign goal was four times more than we had raised in private funds for the D-Day Museum over 10 years, we could all understand Steve's shock. And it was also a bit of a shock to the board members, as they were still trying to absorb the magnitude of an expansion covering three city blocks. No doubt, the news of $4.25 million from Congress was the honey that made it easier for the board to swallow.

The Executive Committee approved the contract of the Eskew Dumez Ripple architect firm to design the Sky Bridge connecting the Louisiana Memorial Pavilion to the future expansion across the street and to secure all the city permits needed for the bridge and rezoning of the future properties. We also commissioned Eskew to do the design work on CSAS and Discovery Hall, projects we needed to start immediately to elevate our education mission, even as we began our master planning. [12]

In February, the board agreed to spend $500,000 of our federal appropriation to hire museum consultants to help us conceive the scope and exhibits of a National WWII Museum. Boysie asked Davis, Kushner, and me to take the lead on the master planning process. We sent a request for proposals to several internationally recognized consultant firms. Steve was a bit reluctant to spend so much money to hire planning consultants, and it was true that this would eat into the federal allocation. Boysie and I reassured him that an experienced firm would help assure potential donors that their money would be well spent, thus encouraging them to donate. Arthur explained that a master planner would test our exhibition ideas, perform feasibility studies to determine what we could afford and support, and integrate CSAS into the overall scheme.[13] Steve had great respect for Arthur's architectural genius and appeared satisfied. Our Development Committee, chaired by Kushner, would review the proposals and help us choose the best firm.

With board approval, I negotiated a contract for $170,000 with Lord Cultural Resources, a Canadian firm and a global leader in museum strategic planning. Gail and Barry Lord, the company heads, had written the manual on master planning for museums. They were passionate about history museums and provided conceptual plans and redesigns for hundreds of cultural organizations around the world. They also worked with the Audubon Nature Institute in New Orleans, giving them insight into our local market.[14] We asked Lord to produce a final design concept plan with a financial feasibility analysis to support the estimated scope of costs for the new buildings and exhibits. They would work with me, Steve Ambrose, and a small planning charette of top WWII historians, media professionals, museum heads, and creative individuals from the entertainment industry.[15] Barry and Gail embraced the terms, and we got rolling with the first charette group meetings in spring 2002.

COMRADES TO THE END

The beginning of 2002 should have been a happy time for Steve. We had just returned from a two-week, well-deserved sailing vacation with family and friends to our old haunts in St. John in the US Virgin Islands. With the opening of the Pacific D-Days exhibits and master planning for the WWII Museum expansion underway, we were feeling pretty good about the future. Then everything went from almost perfect to the worst possible news. In January accusations of plagiarism against Steve in several of his recent books made national headlines. Accusations began in an article in the *Weekly Standard* that some passages from Steve's 2001 book, *The Wild Blue,* about American B-24 air crews in World War II, were identical to those by another author.[16] Steve promptly acknowledged the errors and apologized. The news snowballed as other journalists began competing to find other examples of missing or incomplete attribution and errors in Steve's work. Coming at the peak of his fame as a public historian, the attacks on his scholarship were devastating. He saw a lifetime of writing accomplishments and his reputation going up in smoke. "I am not out there stealing other people's writings," he told the *New York Times*.[17]

Steve desperately wanted to defend himself publicly and more vigorously, but his publisher discouraged him from doing so. He was as stressed as I've ever seen him. Steve responded by digging into his research and writing, but he needed a diversion from the drumbeat of media attacks. Steve pressed forward on a month-long trip to the Pacific to conduct research for a book and documentary on the Pacific War he was doing for the Museum and Steven Spielberg. Moira and Hugh traveled with him, leaving behind the charges of plagiarism. Steve was tackling a part of World War II he had never written about, and his family thought the trip would be good for him. Hugh told me Steve was irritable and not himself much of the time. Still, he traversed battle sites on the islands, some of the amphibious D-Day assaults, and gained a sense of the jungle fighting, as well as the vast oceans where major naval battles took place.

We all hoped it would be therapeutic, and to some extent it was. Still, after his return, I could see the stress of staying silent on the plagiarism charges ate at him. We got together at his house one weekend in April and discussed the possibility of writing an op-ed in the *Times-Picayune* to give his side of the story. I suggested defenses that would provide him some high ground against his critics in the controversy. He liked the ideas.[18] He wrote the piece and awaited publication, but we did not know that a much more arduous fight was just around the corner.

The phone call changed everything. Steve called me in my office toward the end of April. "Nick, I just got home from the Doc. Worst news. He says I have the big 'C'; lung cancer, stage four. Six months to live." Steve always got to the point quickly. My heart sank. I had been worried since Christmas about his persistent cough, but this was shocking. "Oh crap, Steve. That's horrible news," I said. "It sounds hopeless. Is it really? You got a diagnosis by your doctor in Bay St. Louis?" He said, "Yep, he's pretty good." I immediately said we had to get a second opinion. He agreed, and I was able to get him an appointment a few days later at the LSU Health Sciences Center in New Orleans, where they have a cancer center with a terrific team of oncologists.

In the days before his appointment, Steve was stoic about the diagnosis. Over the years, he always accepted that his heavy smoking since his teenage years would kill him one day. It now looked like a reality. Steve called in to our Executive Committee meeting on April 30 to tell the members how pleased he was with the Museum's success and that his involvement with it was one of his "proudest accomplishments." He then announced to the committee that he was diagnosed with lung cancer and requested privacy. Boysie extended the thoughts and prayers of all members and said we would be there to provide any assistance. Steve then disconnected from the call, leaving the committee members in a state of shock.[19]

A few days later, on May 2, Steve and Moira showed up in my office to pick me up to join them for his appointment at LSU. He wanted a second opinion and to fight the cancer as best he could. Ironically, it was the same day the *Times-Picayune* published Steve's op-ed publicly defending himself on the plagiarism charges. Steve gave a confident smile when he saw me. He felt good about fighting back on the plagiarism charges as he prepared for the biggest fight of his life. His op-ed was filled with clarity and confidence. He wrote: "I stand on the originality of my work. It is entirely my own, not taken from anyone else's work. I use the discoveries from my research into primary and secondary sources combined with my general knowledge of American history to produce a new story line, an approach to the subject that is my own." Before we left, Steve wanted to proceed with a scheduled film shoot in our Purple Heart Board Room next to my office. Steve reflected on the pride he felt in what the National D-Day Museum had achieved since its opening.

Steve, Moira, and I left for his appointment. We met with the specialist, Dr. Paul Schwarzenberger, and discovered he was born in Germany. He was a fan of Steve's books, and they both saw some irony that Steve's life was in the hands of a doctor from Germany. Then we got down to the diagnosis. Schwarzenberger reviewed new X-rays done on Steve, which gave the same stage four results as those taken in Mississippi. Without giving Steve false hopes, Schwarzenberger proposed an immediate chemotherapy treatment that might prolong his life, but there were no assurances of long-term survival. Steve smiled, shook his hand, and said "You're my doctor. When do we start?" His treatment would be in New Orleans, close to his home.

Steve started chemo immediately, but he had his own plan of action. He told me and Moira he was going to write another book in the next two months, before the side effects from chemo made it impossible. "The doc said I would have till July before I would feel too bad to write," he told me. "I've still got something to say." He went to work writing a semi-autobiographical book about his life, career, and his intellectual journey as a historian. He was going to have *his* last word and in his own voice. He wrote like a man possessed. He knew his personal memoir would be his last book, and the clock was ticking. He finished it and sent off to Simon & Schuster in July 2002. *To America: Personal Reflections of an Historian* was his final love song to America.

After his diagnosis, Steve encouraged me to press forward on the Museum's expansion plans. His reservations about the rising costs vanished as he knew it would be up to me and the board to make those decisions. Boysie had positive news at the May 16, 2002, board meeting, which was a relief at a time when we were so concerned about Steve. Boysie announced that the Smithsonian had designated our Museum as one of its affiliates. He also had encouraging word from Senator Stevens that we could expect at least $9 million from the next Congressional appropriation bill. Moreover, there was support from the state to include $15 million for the Museum in the next year's budget. In that same meeting, I formally announced I would retire from the University of New Orleans at the end of July to continue as the full-time President and CEO of the Museum and would accept the four-year contract offered by Boysie and the board.[20] With Steve's cancer prognosis, Boysie and I thought that it was important to reassure the board of my continuing commitment in the midst of our expansion plans. Of course, just as with Steve's fall and concussion a few years earlier, questions arose about the future of the Museum without Steve and whether I could lead the Museum's expansion without my best friend at my side. By that time, my performance and Boysie's confidence in my leadership over the last four years allayed any fears about me with other members of the board.

Steve's chemo treatments did not affect him much in the first three months, physically or mentally. He felt good enough in mid-July to come to the Museum to give a personal tour to Senators John Breaux and Daniel Inouye.[21] I was with him and Moira almost every week during the summer of 2002. By August and September, however, he was declining rapidly.

CHARETTE PLANNING

Nearly at the same time as Steve's diagnosis, we pressed forward with the first serious planning for our conceptual approach to World War II. We knew our expansion was going to cover the entire American experience in World

War II, but we needed to understand what that would look like. How would we organize our exhibits to tell the whole story? What campaigns, battles, or military branches would we focus on? How could our exhibits narrow the focus to cover all campaigns in a meaningful way? Would we include other attractions apart from exhibits? What was the market demand for a Museum such as this? It was a huge war. How large of a Museum could we build? There were so many questions to be answered before we even thought about breaking ground on the new properties. In May 2002, we began the charette to help us answer some of our lingering questions. The charette was chaired by Dr. Allan Millett, then the Gen. Raymond E. Mason Jr. Professor of Military History at Ohio State University. We also invited fifteen experts in their respective fields, including historians, such as Dr. Terrence M. Cole from the University of Alaska–Fairbanks, attraction specialists, such as Van Romans, Executive Director of Walt Disney Imagineering, and museum professionals, such as Marc Pachter, the Director of the Smithsonian's National Portrait Gallery, among many other esteemed participants.[22] Our team included Hugh Ambrose, John Kushner, and myself. Despite his health, Steve also participated in one day of the charrette at the end of May. Professional staff from Lord Cultural Resources led the discussions. We assembled an elite team for our concept design. Now, we needed to put its members to good use.

This three-day-long brainstorming session created the whole conceptual basis for the expansion. Ultimately, the team decided on military and combat engagements that the Museum would explore in the new exhibits, including the role of the different service branches, major battles, and the air, sea, and land wars. In addition to military campaigns, we identified the major topics we would focus on, including American volunteerism on the home front, industrial production, advances in science and technology, and the long-term legacies of World War II.

We also received insights on different approaches to interpretation and display. Lord consultants advised us on theatrical audio-visual presentations, immersive environments, interactive multimedia within exhibits, and ways to incorporate oral histories into our story. In this regard, the professionals in the charette urged us to play to the strengths that reside in our original exhibits, allowing people of the WWII generation to speak for themselves by showcasing their personal stories and oral histories within our exhibits. Keeping those veteran voices running throughout the fabric of our expansion would retain the authenticity visitors loved so much in the D-Day exhibits. With these insights from Lord and the charrette team, we began to shape a conceptual model for the future exhibits. We agreed the perspective of the American experience was primary; artifacts and photos could be used selectively to enhance the core experience, with a focus on those artifacts that helped carry a personal story.

At the broadest levels of design, the charette participants agreed that chronology and geography should illuminate the major events and military campaigns. We wanted a well-defined point of view reflected in the Museum experience: that America emerged as the hero of the Allied victory. We expected the Museum to be designated as America's official Museum for World War II, and, despite some criticism of the "good war" interpretation, we believed our exhibits would reflect an authentic public memory of the war—that America's role was necessary, justified, and decisive. Dr. Millett and other historians on the charette team concurred with this broad interpretation of America's memory of our experience in the war. This view—that Americans were fighting authoritarian regimes bent on the destruction of our freedom and democracy—was famously held by Steve and others. We wanted to design the Museum to make Americans proud of what the entire nation achieved in our existential struggle to defeat the Axis nations. These top WWII historians and museum leaders helped frame our historical content and public memory of the war from these foundational themes.

As we moved through 2002, we began to believe we were destined to create an extraordinary and important institution. Pushing forward was going to be difficult considering Steve's condition, but he continued to cheer us on and believed in us unconditionally throughout his battle with cancer. I could not have asked for a better champion.

AMERICA'S STORYTELLER

In the first week of October 2002, I visited Steve in his home in Bay St. Louis on a beautiful day with the ocean breeze blowing across us. Steve physically showed the ravages of chemotherapy. He had lost at least 60 pounds. We both knew his time was limited, maybe weeks or a month, but his spirit was undaunted. Steve, Moira, and I sat together that day, as we so often did, and reflected on our friendship and our many wonderful memories of the last 30 years. Steve spoke with great optimism of the bright futures he foresaw for Moira, his family, me, and the Museum. His big heart and generous spirit were overflowing. Steve was in the acceptance stage and showed no anxiety or fear. He told us with a big smile that all would be well, Moira would be well taken care of, and the Museum should reach for the stars. He was also pleased that Simon & Schuster would publish his book in the next few weeks.

I had another reason for my visit that day. I told Steve that I was canceling my five-day trip to Normandy scheduled for the following week with a New Orleans Trade Mission. We had planned this trip in the spring with the purpose of concluding a formal partnership with the President of the Mémorial de Caen. The museum and war memorial in Caen was France's national museum of the Allied victory on D-Day, the counterpart to our National D-Day Museum. Steve and I visited there many times and collaborated with museum staff on several levels of research and on Steve's D-Day tours since 1994. Now that our Museum was open, we were ready to formalize our collaboration in a partnership agreement between our two national museums. The signing ceremony in Caen would link the two great museums of D-Day in the presence of government and city officials from Louisiana and Normandy. Given Steve's health, I had decided to cancel. I told him his cancer had progressed too far, and that Moira only had his son Barry to help. Steve objected strenuously and said I absolutely had to go. "We have worked on this so long. You have to go," he said. "I'll be here when you get back." I agreed with a heavy heart.

A few days later, I called Steve from the plane at the New Orleans airport to check on him before leaving as we taxied to the runway. Barry answered the phone and had alarming news. Steve had gone into shock and an ambulance had taken him to the emergency room. I could not get off the plane, so I told Barry I would call Moira when we changed planes in Atlanta. I would scrub the trip and catch the next plane back to New Orleans. When I called Moira a few hours later, she was with Steve in the hospital. She told me he had two similar setbacks as result of the chemo treatment, but he was resting and that I should not cancel the trip. She thought Steve would be okay and that I should follow through with his wish to get the agreement signed. I reluctantly rejoined the New Orleans delegation for the flight to Paris. The flight was hard. I had a bad feeling and could not get Steve off my mind as we flew across the Atlantic.

We arrived in Paris and went straight to the Hotel Intercontinental. I hurried to my room to call Moira. It was uncanny. I turned on the TV first, and, as soon as the screen lit up, there was a photo of Steve Ambrose, with the announcer saying he passed away during the night, October 13, 2002. It was a horrible moment, one of deep personal loss and a heavy feeling of guilt for being in Paris and not with Steve and Moira. I called Moira immediately, and she reported that the cancer did not kill Steve. He died of renal failure several hours after I called from the Atlanta airport. This time I insisted that I was canceling my trip to Caen and coming back to New Orleans the next day. I caught the first flight home, and the delegation went on to Caen to conclude the partnership. I asked our Board Secretary, Bill Detweiler, to represent the Museum and sign on behalf of our board and to speak in memory of Stephen Ambrose and his legacy.

I arrived in New Orleans the next day to find many national news reports about Steve's death, as well as tributes to his work as a renowned historian and Museum founder. Most of his friends and family had known of his grave illness and had braced themselves for his death. That did not ease the tragic sense of loss we felt, including everyone at the Museum. Among the mourners were millions of Americans who were profoundly influenced by his books, which reminded readers of the best of our nation's history and people. One of the first to call me after I arrived back in New Orleans on October 15 was Tom Brokaw. "Nick, what are the plans for funeral services for Steve?" he asked. "I'm coming." He suggested that we organize a memorial service at the Museum that could be attended by his many friends. I told him it was a wonderful idea and would be more meaningful to his fans than the funeral services in Bay St. Louis, an hour's drive from New Orleans. Moira and the family agreed and plans for both the funeral and the memorial service got underway quickly.

The memorial service would be an opportunity to praise Steve for his contributions to public history, his crowning effort to build the Museum, and to make a statement about the survival of the Museum without him. Steve was the founder and chief historian of the Museum for over twelve years, and many believed his national stature was indispensable to its creation. I always knew that there never would have been a Museum at all without Steve, and he believed we would never have opened if he had not pushed me to be Chairman. He was my dearest friend of 30 years, and this was our common endeavor for 12 of those years.

Steve dreamed of creating a Museum that reflected his deep regard for our nation's citizen soldiers, workers on the home front, and the hardships that many endured to achieve victory and destroy fascist dictators in Germany, Italy, and Japan. He did not live to see how the Museum would grow and change throughout the years. However, in his last months, he still used his fame and his typewriter to build support for America's story and for the Museum. Steve's many friends across America, as well as those on the Museum board, drew strength and resolve to carry on the mission beyond his passing.

A few days before the memorial, Moira and the extended Ambrose family held a wake in Bay St. Louis, Mississippi, for a few invited friends, including Tom Hanks and Steven Spielberg. The wake was simple, with a few heartfelt remarks about Steve. Moira wanted to reserve most of the testimonials for Steve for the memorial service a few days later in New Orleans. After the wake, Moira invited everyone to come to their home on Beach Boulevard for drinks and a chance for close friends to share memories of their love and friendship for Steve. It was a special evening. Both Spielberg and Hanks were curious about the expansion plans for the National WWII Museum and promised me their continuing support. I had a chance to speak at length with Tom about the progress of our concept planning with Lord Cultural Resources and our charette of historians and museum professionals. He was especially interested in our ideas for an epic cinematic experience of America's journey through World War II. I told Tom that Steve and I both believed that a major cinematic attraction was vital to our future plans for the expansion. Tom agreed.

Given Tom's expertise as an actor, director, and producer of exceptional films and documentaries, I ventured to ask if he would be willing to offer me some expert advice occasionally as we progressed. Tom said, "Of course," without hesitation. Whether it was his friendship with Steve or his sincere commitment to the D-Day Museum and our plans for expansion, his offer to help was genuine and would one day be a godsend to me and to the final film we produced. Neither Tom nor Steven was able to remain for the memorial service, but their very presence signified so much about the life and contributions of Steve Ambrose.

After the small private wake and funeral in Bay St. Louis on October 16, we held Steve's memorial service in front of the Museum on October 19, 2002. Hundreds came to pay respects, including friends, military leaders, members of Congress, state representatives, trustees, UNO faculty, historians, former students, WWII veterans, as well as home front and Higgins Industries workers. All came because they were touched by Steve Ambrose through his life and career of writing, teaching, speaking, and generosity of spirit. Local and national media were there reporting on the final farewell to Stephen E. Ambrose. Boysie presided and paid tribute to Ambrose and his work.[23] The speakers included former President George H. W. Bush and former Sen. George McGovern, both distinguished World War II combat pilots and supporters of the Museum. Bush said Ambrose's works "made us proud of our courageous, hard-working, visionary forebears" and added that Steve reminded all Americans that "freedom has its cost, that honor never dies, and that greatness is a calling still beckoning us today."

The speakers helped shape a full story about the legacy of the life and contributions of Stephen Ambrose. Most spoke to his values, his rugged personality, his prodigious work ethic, his generosity, and his passion for writing of the deeds of the great leaders of history as well as those of the common man. Speaking on behalf of Moira, Steve's eldest daughter, Stephenie Ambrose-Tubbs, reminded us that while her father regarded those who fought in that war as heroes, he "wanted us to learn, as the citizen soldiers did, that war is hell, that war is a serious business, and we should never enter into it lightly." She added her father would say, "Study war and then go out and make peace."

Tom Brokaw said Steve had the "persona of a commander, a military man, but what he did was mobilize the citizenry of this country, commanding it to understand its past and to celebrate its heroes." Tom described Steve as a having "a football lineman's demeanor, an academic's discipline, a boy's enthusiasm, and a thespian's heart for the story well told." I could not describe him better. Tom said it best for all those gathered: "Stephen Ambrose's voice has been stilled, but his song will go on forever." Len Lomell, the Army Ranger veteran who stormed the cliffs of Pointe du Hoc on D-Day, confirmed Steve's eternal "song" with some emotion in saying that he "gave voice to the combat soldiers who were actually on battlefields, or at sea or in the air . . . he has filled the void left by those men who couldn't talk about war to their families." Nolan Marshall thanked Steve and the Museum for hosting the New Orleans Double V parade in 2001, saying that it was the first time he and many other African American veterans had been thanked for their service. Speakers honored Steve for rescuing the memory of Andrew Higgins, whose boats helped to win the war, thus restoring the rightful place of New Orleans in WWII history. Hugh Ambrose spoke of his father as a man who gave generously, loved dreamers, and gave away much of what he earned. "The riches that he treasured were the love in his heart and the wisdom and knowledge that he carried with him. And he had both of those in abundance."

I closed the program with the weight of Steve's loss heavy on my heart. I spoke first of Steve Ambrose, the historian and his special abilities to touch the hearts of Americans, who had the ability to "write about something familiar, and to let us discover it for the first time in a new way." Steve, I said, was "America's storyteller," and I shared a similar refrain from my poet brother, Jack Mueller, who had known Steve as long as I did, who wrote me to say Steve Ambrose was the "American Lighthouse." Indeed, he was and still is today. For me, everything revolved around the deep friendship and love we felt for each other. He wrote about our friendship in his book *Comrades,* just a few years earlier, and I read a few of Steve's words to the audience, as he described friendship in its purest form "Friendship is different from all other relationships . . . it is free of jealousy . . . it knows neither criticism nor resentment . . . [it] has no status in law . . . it is freely entered into and freely given."[24] Those words described my relationship with Steve, which gave us both a life of adventure in history, travel, and meaning; a friendship that resulted in the unlikely story of this Museum.

The most inspirational words I read at the service about the impact of Steve Ambrose were not from me, but from a phone call I received a few days earlier. A father had called me to say his 16-year-old son, an avid reader of Steve's books with a passion to be a history major, was distraught about hearing of the death of Steve. He asked his father, "Dad, who will write all these wonderful stories now?" His father told him, "You will, son." Steve's song would not be stilled. The Museum would become the words of his song. As Boysie and I carried on in the days following the memorial, we felt a renewed commitment to expanding the Museum to cover all of World War II. The torch was now in our hands to tell that story. Steve's legacy lived on as we became The National WWII Museum. His spirit helped us prevail over every adversity that faced us as his Museum materialized around those three blocks in New Orleans.

LORD CONCEPT PLAN

In February 2003, once things had settled and everyday life began to resume, Lord Cultural Resources submitted its full concept plan, including recommendations on the Museum's exhibits and attractions, the physical planning, and a feasibility analysis of the market demand for the expansion. Their interpretive strategy provided overarching themes that would appear throughout the new exhibit spaces. The concept plan traced content ideas for the exhibits and multiple attractions. Most importantly, Lord worked hard to create a unifying idea to portray the American experience of the war.

The first major challenge for the charette group, which reconvened in New Orleans for the Lord presentation, was finding the connective tissue to convey the epic story of World War II. After hours of debate at the charette, we were stuck. Then, Van Romans quietly raised his hand and said, "At Disney, we always talk about the 'journey,' so let's think about that." It was a eureka moment, a single word that carried a big idea. I seized on Van's idea to frame our story as the "journey" all Americans took through World War II. Every individual, from the home front to the front lines, experienced the journey in different and yet very personal ways. Everyone in the charette embraced the concept at once.

The idea of portraying World War II as a journey influenced every aspect of the concept plan Lord presented to us that spring. This journey led us through the entire American story, from the isolationism of the 1930s to the national fear after the attack on Pearl Harbor. It brought us through our national response in the face of total unpreparedness for a global conflict, to our sacrifice and fight for survival, and finally to victory. We envisioned visitors traveling metaphorically through all stages of the war, as they witnessed the courage and sacrifice of families, soldiers, and leaders at home and abroad.

In Lord's plan, visitors pass through a major re-creation of a train station in the main entry pavilion, as this was the place where the journey began for so many. These stations conveyed the great bustling energy of the war years. They were emotional places, filled with tearful goodbyes from mothers, fathers, brothers, sisters, wives, and lovers. These farewells were both sad and full of hope. There were joyful homecomings, but also many reunions that were filled with grief and tears when families arrived at train stations to retrieve their sons' caskets. Visitors would board the train and follow in the footsteps of departing troops through the major campaigns of the war, witnessing the stories of citizen soldiers fighting for their lives and their country. They would end their journey by seeing the celebrations of V-E and V-J days, the liberation of POW and concentration camps, and America's role in creating peace after the war.

Lord proposed a complete immersion into the social, economic, and political scenes of America of the late 1930s and 1940s within galleries described as a "Cinematic Museum." Exhibits and shows were linked in a coherent storyline with veterans telling their personal stories of major events and battles. Historical personalities and journalists would keep visitors "in the moment" as they progressed through the Museum. Multisensory re-creations of wartime environments and simulations would enhance the memories of historical events and battles.

Lord shaped our initial ideas by dividing the story into three parts: 1) Prelude to War and America in Crisis; 2) the War Years; and 3) Liberation and Winning the Peace after 1945. Prelude to War covered the run-up to the war that America tried to avoid. The exhibits would show how President Roosevelt held our country together amid the Depression and prepared the country for war by restoring the draft. Despite the violent expansionist wars in Europe and Asia, Congress wanted to stay out until the attack on Pearl Harbor, the iconic crisis that quickly led to America's entry into the war.

Next came the war years, with the charette identifying the additional campaigns the expanded Museum would cover, including North Africa and Sicily. We would also document the war on the ground, at sea, and in the air, as well as all service branches. A home front exhibit would tell the story of workers in the United States who built the weapons and supplies to sustain our troops across vast distances. For the European Theater, we would design exhibits on the Allied defeat at Kasserine Pass in North Africa and our narrow victory in the Battle of the Bulge, both displaying America's strengths and weaknesses. For the Pacific Theater, we identified the Battle of Guadalcanal and the development of the atomic bomb as two pivotal and controversial events to highlight in exhibits because of their importance to the eventual Allied victory.

The final chapter would comprise the stories of the victorious Allied armies of liberation and of Holocaust survivors and freed POWs, along with graphic depictions of the horrific price paid to achieve peace. The exhibits would describe the fruits of victory as well as the challenges for those changed by the war. We would highlight America's role as a new superpower in the nuclear age, with new responsibilities to keep the peace, and how the United States promoted democracy abroad through the Marshall Plan and by leading the United Nations. Lord asked us to think about how we would answer the "so what" question regarding the meaning of the war. What lessons would we present to future generations a century from now? What would our victory in World War II mean to them? Answering these questions in our final exhibits was perhaps our most challenging task and of greatest importance to our future exhibit designers and architects.

The final element in our concept plan was a proposal for a larger-than-life domed theater experience that would surround visitors with the sights, sounds, and the story of the war on an epic scale. The theater would feature eyewitness accounts to convey the veterans' memories and feelings of the conflict. We envisioned this as a unique cinematic experience that would immerse the visitor in stories of individual endurance, courage, sacrifice, and grief that would serve as exemplars of the American Spirit. No war is good, but the final exhibits needed to make visitors recognize that World War II was a necessary war and help them understand the American role in turning horrible conflict into the catalyst for a freer world. The final takeaways should be personal, provocative, and educational. We wanted the exhibits to enlarge the national memory of World War II with a trusted narrative of the American experience in the war and provide a template that would help guide visitors on decisions about war and peace in their own time.

MASTER PLAN COMPETITION

The members of the charette and our Board of Trustees were pleased with the direction of the concept plan from Lord. When calculating the entire scope of the future Museum, the concept plan provided a core narrative to stimulate education and discovery, including the original D-Day exhibits, and addressed circulation, special exhibits, restaurants, a USO experience, and special events. We would need to add more than 225,000 square feet on top of the 70,000 square feet of the existing D-Day Museum exhibits. This was much larger and far more costly than anything we imagined a year earlier. Boysie took on the task of convincing the board to approve the concept plan early in 2003. Many trustees were skeptical and needed assurance that this was not a pipe dream. Boysie's stature as CEO of a major shipyard and the general respect he garnered from the local business community made him a formidable champion. With nearly $30 million in funds already appropriated since 2000, he convinced the board that this was the only path to recognition as The National WWII Museum. Next came the real thing: a fully developed Master Plan.

With the Lord scope and concept plans defined, we launched a national competition to find the best architects and museum exhibit designers to vie for the contracts to be the Museum's master planner of record. Thirteen architect firms and seven exhibit design firms responded to our Request for Proposals (RFP). These included some of the top firms in the nation with reputations for extraordinary architecture and exhibit design. All were impressed by our 119-page concept plan, which included carefully detailed specifications of exhibits, size, and feasibility projections. The level of interest our RFP garnered from design teams was impressive for a three-year-old Museum that struggled for survival for so many years. We formed a design competition jury consisting of Arthur Davis, several board members, and me. Our task was to narrow the list to fewer than five architect and exhibit firms. With funds available from Congress to support the planning process for the Museum, Lord began to manage the competition. We made it clear that the finalists, regardless of the outcome, would be generously compensated for their submissions of architectural and exhibit design plans for the competition and review by the jury. The presentations were breathtaking and the competition fierce. Among the finalists were Voorsanger Architects from New York and Gallagher & Associates from Maryland. While other competitors were impressive, the Voorsanger and Gallagher firms stood out.

Bartholomew Voorsanger, a New York architect who was prominent in the museum field, offered a daring and imaginative architectural vision in a stunning presentation. His building concepts were bold, evoking a fractured look with interlocking concrete elements shielded by slivers of glass and ribbed metal. He said the design would "metaphorically offer protection for our troops but with a visual density bridging on intimidation."[25] Unlike other competitors who proposed a single monolithic building for the entire Museum, Voorsanger understood our fundraising challenges and presented a series of smaller, individual pavilions, which could be completed and opened one at a time. This design approach allowed us to build exhibit spaces, visitor amenities, and educational facilities in phases. We could build one pavilion at a time, depending on when funds became available. We knew the expansion would take years, so this tactical approach was appealing to us. Boysie told me later that approving the Voorsanger plan was probably the best decision we ever made in that early stage, "rather than trying to create a box that was big enough to house this whole story."[26] Each pavilion was designed around a central parade ground with landscaping and space for the public to gather.

By far the most distinctive element of Voorsanger's design was the unifying Canopy of Peace, which would soar above the pavilions and give the Museum a national scale. Voorsanger designed the canopy as "a lightweight structure of geometric panels woven from Teflon-coated fiberglass strands."[27] It would be massive, stretching over two city blocks and soared twelve stories above the parade ground. Practically, it would provide a connection between all the pavilions. Aesthetically, its unique, artistic structure allowed for individual interpretation of its meaning. We saw the towering structure projecting the strength of democracy, with its elegant dovelike wing as a symbol of peace. For some, it signified the unification of the allied nations who fought for our freedom in World War II. The striking use of imagination was a breath of fresh air for the jury and won the competition for Voorsanger. Bart agreed to our request to incorporate the distinguished New Orleans firm Mathes Brierre Architects to oversee the implementation and construction of the future buildings as our official architectural master planners.

Alongside Voorsanger, Patrick Gallagher of Gallagher & Associates made an impassioned and enthusiastic case to become the master planners for the exhibit design. Patrick and his team had a thoughtful, sensitive approach to storytelling in exhibits. Most importantly, it was clear they shared a similar philosophy in the use of technology, multimedia, and immersive concepts as outlined in the Lord exhibit plans. Gallagher wanted to take the Museum into the next generation by employing modern techniques to engage visitors in personal and experiential ways. "Technology becomes the backbone for interpretation," he told the *Times-Picayune.* "You can layer the content, allow a visitor to go deeper into a subject area."[28] Gallagher's creative signature would be story-driven, with artifacts adding individual and authentic dimensions to engage and motivate young people to discover the rich history of World War II.

At the same time, Gallagher made it clear that his team was not interested in developing technology just for the sake of having high-tech galleries. A major concern with this new expansion was that it might cross the line between education into entertainment. We needed an exhibit design team that would be able to walk that line with us and carefully employ cutting-edge elements without diminishing the seriousness and depth of the story.

Gallagher's winning idea was to create electronic "dog tags" that linked the visitor to a soldier, sailor, airman, or home front worker at each listening station, using personal accounts from the Eisenhower Center's Ambrose Oral History Collection in the galleries. The proposal was a home run for the jury, which loved the use of oral histories in our *D-Day Invasion* exhibits. Individual accounts would now be directly linked to the journey of visitors who carried the name and story of a veteran. We could see that Gallagher's vision perfectly aligned with ours. Gallagher & Associates was the jury's unanimous choice to be the master planner and designer of our exhibits. In January 2004, we publicly announced the results of the design competition. We required the involved firms to collaborate in partnership to executing the Master Plan; Voorsanger and Mathes Brierre formed Voorsanger Mathes LLC to ensure a close working relationship with one another. The Museum was the "lead" in the project in order to ensure collaboration between the architecture and design firms satisfied our mission requirements, which was no small point and meant a greater role for our staff. I felt it was necessary to control costs while also assuring the highest standards of historical authenticity, which was paramount in our vision of the Museum's future. Luckily, the firms welcomed our collaboration requirements.

We could now go to Senator Stevens and other federal and state leaders with the confidence of possessing a clear vision of design, cost, and timeline estimates. A national governance structure would allow us to deliver on the promise to build The National WWII Museum. The wind was back in our sails.

CONGRESSIONAL DESIGNATION OF THE NATIONAL WWII MUSEUM

Securing national designation from Congress was the last step before launching the campaign. We had the firm backing of our powerful WWII champions in the Senate, Stevens and Inouye, as well as critical support from the Louisiana delegation to help us achieve the coveted title as America's National WWII Museum.

We sorely needed boots on the ground on Capitol Hill, and Rep. Bob Livingston designated his trusted legislative assistant, Paul Cambon, to work as our pro bono point person to coordinate our efforts across various congressional offices to help us obtain national designation. Paul worked tirelessly in the effort to reach our coveted goal, often updating me daily on his work in the halls of Congress.

US Rep. David Vitter of Louisiana introduced the bill in the House in May 2002. Momentum grew throughout 2003 as Senators Stevens, Inouye, and Landrieu worked to link Congressional support for our annual appropriation to our official designation. Boysie and I went back and forth to Washington, DC, often to meet with the senators as well as with Billy Tauzin and other members of the Louisiana delegation. Stevens and Landrieu also urged us to meet with other WWII veterans of Congress to secure their support, and we did—again and again. We emphasized that we were slowly losing the "Greatest Generation" and nothing official had been built to honor their story except the World War II Memorial at the National Mall in DC. The latter was a place to remember; our Museum would be a place to learn. Thus far, there was no comprehensive museum to preserve and teach what this passing generation had achieved for America. Our message and mission had a sense of urgency and agency. By 2003, Congress had appropriated $13 million to the project in four consecutive Congressional budgets. The 12 WWII veterans in Congress, both Democrat and Republican, along with Rep. Tom Lantos, a Holocaust survivor, helped us win bipartisan support for the Museum.

On the afternoon of September 25, 2003, I learned our efforts had come to fruition when Paul called to tell me that Congress passed Public Law 108-87 to designate the Museum as "America's National World War II Museum." Paul read me excerpts over the phone. The resolution's intent was to express the United States Government's support for "the operation of a premiere facility for the public display of artifacts, photographs, documents, and personal histories from the World War II years . . . ensuring the understanding by all future generations of the magnitude of the American contribution to the Allied victory in World War II, the sacrifices made to preserve freedom and democracy, and the benefits of peace for all future generations in the 21st century and beyond." [29]

The words rang in my ears for days. We had never been sure the bill would pass both the House and Senate, and it would never have happened without the strong commitment of Stevens, Inouye, Landrieu, and Vitter. It was a great day for the Museum and me. My first wish upon hearing the news was that Steve Ambrose could have lived to see this day. As the Baton

Rouge *Advocate* quoted me after the news broke, "this was Steve's dream, and we are grateful to the entire Congress."[30]

Meanwhile, we worked feverishly to recruit trustees to our new national board. At the officer level, Boysie agreed to continue as Chair, but Herschel Abbott had new job responsibilities with BellSouth and deferred his Chair-Elect position to David Voelker, one of the top entrepreneurs in New Orleans. Harold Bouillion, a former Managing Partner of KPMG who succeeded Tom Snedeker as Treasurer, prepared our accounting systems to manage the significant infusions of expected federal, state, and private funds. Our new Secretary was Rich Pattarozzi, President of Shell Oil Offshore, which had just donated $1.5 million for our Steven Spielberg documentary, *Price for Peace.*

At the national level, we enjoyed a string of success, attracting trustees of great national stature. We recruited corporate executives, such as Jim Barksdale, who held leadership positions at FedEx, Netscape, and AOL and was President and CEO of Barksdale Management Corporation. We drew in future board Chairs such as Phil Satre, CEO of Harrah's Casino; Pete Wilson, former Governor of California; and Richard Adkerson, President of Freeport-McMoRan. We also enlisted museum professionals, such as Marc Pachter, Director of the National Portrait Gallery, to our board. We deepened our talent pool nationally with a diverse group of corporate leaders who were either World War II veterans or had family members who served. All were excited by our mission and agreed to join with gusto.

Though we had a string of new faces on our board, we had several steadfast local members who remained on our board. Old friends such as Arthur Davis, Teddy Solomon, John Kushner, Howard Gaines, Herschel Abbott, Greg O'Brien, Rep. Jackie Clarkson, and Frank Stewart believed in us and supported our transition from D-Day Museum to National WWII Museum.

The creation of the national board was critical to sustaining our momentum and providing credibility to key supporters in federal and state governments, as well as to major donors in the private sector. The transition was one of my proudest achievements. I was honored to have played a significant role in creating our national board and personally recruiting many of these trustees who assumed the responsibility to help carry the Museum into the future. We needed leaders who were not afraid of risk, had weathered corporate disasters, and brought courage and leadership to the table. We had come a long way from the 1990s, when major business and government leaders gave Steve and me the cold shoulder. To understand the success of the D-Day or National WWII Museum, one must recognize the quality and dedication of the board of trustees, past and present.

We took our story to Washington, DC, with a kickoff gala on February 4, 2004, honoring the WWII veterans in Congress and announcing our capital campaign. The dinner event was held in the imposing National Building Museum, an architectural landmark just blocks from the Capitol. Tom Hanks was the Honorary Chairman of our capital campaign, and co-hosts were senior statesmen Inouye and Stevens. Six hundred attendees came to the event to honor them and the other ten WWII veterans still serving in Congress. Among the guests were Secretary of Defense Donald Rumsfeld, titans of the defense industries, and CEOs from across the nation. A highlight of the evening came when all 12 Congressional veterans came on stage in a very poignant moment.

Boysie lauded them as citizen soldiers, noting that their stories would be told in our Museum because "these men have exhibited the values of the American spirit, the values of teamwork, optimism, courage, and sacrifice throughout their lives' work."[31] Just 10 years prior, there were 25 WWII veterans serving in Congress, so their diminishing numbers made it all the more important to recognize them. "We're dying left and right, so I guess it's important if we're going to remember all that happened that we do it now," said Rep. Cass Ballenger of North Carolina, a Naval Air Corpsman in World War II. "Today's generation hasn't experienced the kind of unity that brought Americans together for a single goal: defeating the Nazis and Imperial Japanese forces in World War II," said Rep. John Dingell Jr. of Michigan, the longest-tenured House member, who served in the Army in World War II. "I think people of this generation want to learn from those who know that feeling of being united."[32] The event was a smashing success. The *Washington Post* called it a "five-star patriotic dinner." Moira Ambrose attended and was quoted as saying, "I know my husband would be flying [high] to know so many people are here to support his dreams."[33] We were very pleased at the effort, which netted $617,000, a big number that helped our operations enormously that year. With the 60th anniversary of D-Day quickly approaching, I proposed to the board that we charter a luxury cruise ship to Normandy for the occasion. The financial conditions to pull that off were onerous. We needed to sign a $1.2 million, non-refundable contract with Silversea Cruises to charter a ship for nearly 300 passengers for the anniversary. But the payoff could be huge: if we filled the ship, we stood to raise $1 million for the Museum.[34] The cruise was not an easy sell, and Boysie put me through the wringer. Aside from the significance of being there on D-Day, I argued this venture would jump-start future travel programs in Europe and the Pacific, support our educational mission, attract new supporters, and create a new revenue stream for the Museum. To help persuade Boysie and the board, I secured an in-kind donation from Tim Forbes for four full-page ads in *Forbes* magazine to promote the cruise. In return for these free ads, which were worth $200,000, Silversea agreed to discount the charter by the same amount, so the contract was reduced to $1 million with a $200,000 deposit.[35] It was sounding better and Boysie was getting fired up.

Aside from the financial risks, I had to design a program that would be irresistible to prospective passengers who would pay a lofty admission for the cruise. We had some advantages. Steve and I had our long-established relationships from two decades of D-Day tours, including with potential speakers, D-Day veterans, and French museum and tourism officials. We also had travel companies in New Orleans, including Peter McLean Ltd. and Stephen Ambrose Tours, Inc., which agreed to underwrite the marketing and management of the tour and accept some of the risk.

Regardless, the risk was still huge for a new Museum just getting on its feet. The total cost of the entire marketing, speakers, and ground program approached $1.5 million. The price was steep, with a per-person price tag between $7,990 and $19,990. To the skeptics on the board, I argued that it would be wrong for a recently designated National WWII Museum to not be front and center in these ceremonies. We needed to raise our Museum's flag at a time of great national attention and publicity about aging D-Day veterans and to demonstrate leadership in preserving the public memory of World War II. The board approved the venture, the deposit was sent, and the contract chartering the *Silver Cloud* for $1 million was signed.

I was confident we would sell out the ship. I began to secure verbal commitments from more than 40 board members and donors, employing a form of guerilla marketing via phone and personal emails to get them excited about the speakers and itinerary well before signing the contract and the marketing push for passengers. The move was bullish, but it worked. The most expensive luxury suites sold out the fastest. Momentum for the cruise built long before the ads hit *Forbes* a few months later. We filled up the ship by the end of 2003.

The tour turned out to be everything we hoped it would be. We had 18 D-Day veterans on board, among them Hal Baumgarten and Walt Ehlers, who gave talks, spoke to tour-goers on the beaches, and shared memories. John Keegan, the famed British military historian, gave a riveting address as we sailed from London down the Thames. Andy Rooney, a *Stars and Stripes* reporter during the war and later a CBS *60 Minutes* contributor, offered the trenchant views of a journalist who was there. In Normandy, Tom Brokaw, Steven Spielberg, and Tom Hanks broke away from other duties and spent time chatting with our group. Gen. John Raaen, who went in on Omaha Beach with the 2nd Rangers as a Captain, gave an officer's view of the battle. We had reserved seats to hear inspirational remarks by President George W. Bush as he addressed the assembled veterans and leaders from many nations who came to honor the Allied troops who stormed those same beaches 60 years before.

I reflected back ten 10 years to 1994, when I had been in the same cemetery with Brokaw and Ambrose, facing the growing responsibility of building the National D-Day Museum. I had no idea I would be there again as President and CEO of that same Museum, which had just been given Congressional designation to be the nation's Museum for all of World War II. This time, without Steve by my side, I could not help thinking of the many agonies and ecstasies on my journey to this day, now with a thriving new Museum and a ship full of Museum supporters giving their voice and support to a much larger mission.

Our cruise was a great success. I learned once again how important it was to connect our members, donors, and board members directly to the heroic battles and individuals who led the Allies to victory. The secret to our success, past, present, and future, was to engage ever larger numbers of the public in the personal and authentic story of World War II. From the start, victory always meant risk, engagement, and building ownership in our mission. The 60th Anniversary of D-Day cruise met those tests, winning new friends, donors, and trustees to take on the challenges ahead. We always set expectations that seemed beyond our reach, and, by 2004, we knew our Master Plan needed to create a National WWII Museum experience to rank with the best in the world.

After returning from the cruise, we got back to work on carrying out the first steps of our Master Plan. Three years earlier, Boysie asked me to lead the planning process, and this had been my top priority. I knew it was imperative for the story of the American experience in World War II to be historically authentic in the use of every medium to document the journey with artifacts, media, oral histories, scripts and text, environments, and engagement technologies. Early on, I told Patrick Gallagher that we were designing these exhibits for younger audiences, while also honoring the "Greatest Generation" veterans who were visiting our Museum in droves in those days.

I insisted, and our designers agreed, that the story came first, and we would rely on the best historians to add value to the planning and design choices. With Steve no longer at my side, I turned to my friends, colleagues, the Presidential Counselors, and authors of great histories who were experts in different theaters of the war. As we began to flesh out the main ideas of the story, the process was not unlike writing a book or making a movie. The first step is to bring in a lot of content, and then unpack the density and streamline the narrative into visual dynamics. The goal was to immerse the visitor in a few elements that reveal the essence of an exhibit or gallery, with just enough photos, text, maps, artifacts, or oral histories to illuminate the central event of the narrative flow. For every exhibit, my challenge was to extract the central theme, fact, or event that made the story readily comprehensible for visitors from ages 15 to 60. Chronology of the major exhibits was the approach of choice. Turning points of a battle and individual actions were important, as was the geography or terrain of the campaign. We pushed to find four or five strategic challenges that had to be overcome in the conduct of the war in Europe, the Pacific, and at home. These challenges and solutions had to be crystal clear. The exhibits had to be designed to create shock, amazement, and discovery about the sacrifices, courage, fear, deaths, and horrors of war. I insisted to the Gallagher team and to the board that this was no "triumphalist" American story; that we would also include the mistakes made, the military defeats, and the victories. We would face up to the irony of our segregated military fighting racist dictatorships and our own sad story of incarceration of Japanese Americans. We would always focus on the personal stories that brought this history to life.

By early 2005, after 18 months of intensive work with our exhibit design and architecture teams, we were ready for prime time. On March 8, 2005, the new board Chairman, David Voelker, convened a special board meeting in the Willard Hotel in Washington, DC. The Master Plan was the only agenda item. This was the pivot point to our future. Final decisions had to be made on the entire Master Plan, phasing plans, and the expansion budget. Boysie opened the meeting with disappointing news from Senator Stevens: he could not promise more earmarks beyond the $13 million over the past four years. But Stevens was on board with my suggestion to ask the WWII veterans in Congress to introduce a $50 million authorization bill for the US Pavilion, designed to be the new entry pavilion across the street from the original D-Day Museum. Voelker indicated that Louisiana Gov. Kathleen Blanco was willing to commit a 50–50 state match of federal funding.[36]

In my presentation, I reviewed the planning process and content decisions and shared a digital "fly through" of the planned buildings and exhibits. Bart Voorsanger spoke about the phasing plan for multiple pavilions. Phil Hettema, Executive Producer and CEO of The Hettema Group Company, described a 4D film in the domed theater as a stand-alone exhibit of the entire war providing an astonishing visitor experience but noted that it could wait for the second building phase. Patrick Gallagher reviewed the extraordinary design proposals for exhibits from the home front to America's fight in the European and Asia-Pacific Theaters. He described the innovative use of interactive technologies, such as the "dog tag experience," to link visitors to the personal accounts in the exhibits as well as the opportunity to engage with these stories via the internet after their visit. He said the Liberation Pavilion would challenge visitors to reflect on the meaning of World War II in their lives and to focus on the fruits of victory at home in the years since Allied victory in 1945. In all, the presentation was breathtaking.

The board debated every detail, including decisions that were approved two years earlier after accepting the Lord Concept Plan. Now, there were suddenly questions about the multiple pavilion strategy instead of a single museum box, building in phases instead of all at once, the cost of the canopy, cost of escalators, traffic flow, the total square footage, the hotel and parking, circulation space, and, of course, the budget, which was now presented at $282 million. There were many questions about the enormous cost and projections of visitors and future revenues for operations and fundraising, but in the end their questions were thoroughly answered with the best information from museum consultants and attractions specialists.

The board approved the entire Master Plan at $282 million. They also approved the phasing plan, as the entire budget was based on the phasing concept with the goal to finish the entire project by 2012. Accordingly, Louis Freeman, Chair of the Capital Campaign, secured approval of a new campaign goal of $120 million in private funds, with the hope that the other $162 million would come from state and federal sources. Louis noted we had already received nearly $12.5 million in private funds since we announced the expansion in Washington, DC, a year earlier.[37]

In addition, Louis and I flew to visit Jim Barksdale at his home in Brandon, Mississippi, and received a major campaign gift of $5 million to fund what would become known as the Barksdale Parade Ground in the new expansion. The Barksdale pledge was the biggest private gift we had ever received to this point and, taken together with other strong private funding, was dramatic and encouraging news. We continued significant discussion of how the pavilions would be prioritized for construction. Some thought the US Pavilion should be built first, while others thought the Campaigns Pavilion should be given priority before the dome theater and USO Canteen. We finally agreed upon a building plan, and the board approved the operating budget to support the new project to be completed between 2005 and 2012. After years of planning, we finally had a clear Master Plan for The National WWII Museum.[38]

The board's actions that day took great courage. David Voelker managed the process carefully to allow everyone's voice to be heard. This was important, as David and I agreed that it was essential for the board to "own" the expansion decision and the fundraising responsibility it carried as we moved forward. It marked the beginning of a new era. We succeeded because of sound planning, the tremendous growth in our national profile, the success of our Normandy cruise, and our strong visitation and operational revenues. The growing momentum for the expansion and success of the Museum operation since 2000 were all factors in the board's bold decision to build a 300,000-square-foot Museum, adding five pavilions in a seven-year span with a phenomenal price tag.

The year ahead looked bright indeed. David was equally engaged as Boysie, Museum staff were gelled, planning was completed, the Museum was humming, and excitement and optimism for the Museum's future were beyond expectations. We were riding high.

9

HURRICANE KATRINA

Everyone has a plan until they get punched in the mouth.

—MIKE TYSON

MID-MORNING ON SUNDAY, August 28, 2005, I was putting up shutters as a monster Category 5 hurricane named Katrina barreled across the Gulf of Mexico directly for New Orleans. I planned to stay, but Mayor Ray Nagin came on the news late morning and announced that the National Weather Service in Miami insisted that he order a mandatory evacuation of the entire city. This was unprecedented. My plans shifted immediately to getting my wife, Beth, our son John, and our dog in the car to evacuate with tens of thousands of other cars that were streaming out of Louisiana at a snail's pace. Evacuation routes and traffic jams forced us north instead of east, and lines of bumper-to-bumper traffic filled both sides of the interstate in one direction. Strong hurricane bands of 60 to 70 miles an hour winds shook the car violently as we crossed the 26-mile causeway on Lake Pontchartrain, hoping to find a place to stay by nightfall. By late afternoon, it had taken six hours to travel 40 miles.

I had been worried about the Museum since August 23, when we began to hear rumblings of a tropical storm brewing near the Bahamas. By August 25, the storm developed into a Category 1 hurricane and was slowly making its way westward across southeast Florida into the warm waters of the Gulf of Mexico. There, it rapidly developed into a full-blown Category 5 hurricane and started tearing through the Gulf.[1] Everyone in the city held their breath, waiting to see where the behemoth would land. As I headed north for safety, I reflected on the decision that Steve and I made years earlier to champion New Orleans as the best place to commemorate WWII history. We always knew that the city of New Orleans presented a unique vulnerability but never gave it much thought as the city had survived hurricanes for nearly three centuries. We had weathered several smaller storms before, but I always hoped our Museum would never have to face a truly destructive hurricane. Now, only five months after our board approved our Master Plan, Hurricane Katrina was hitting New Orleans with devastating force, turning our plans and world upside down—as it did to so many others in the Gulf region.

We had made all the usual preparations to safeguard the Museum, and employees were urged to evacuate and leave emergency contact numbers for communication with their supervisors. We locked down the Museum with steel barricades to block entry to the valuable exhibits on the upper floors. Jake Staples, our Assistant Director for Facilities, insisted on spending the night in the Museum as he had done during previous hurricanes. He would stay in contact with me and senior staff after the storm with the only reliable landline in the Museum, a pay phone on the first floor. We arranged to call him at 2 p.m. every day for reports.

After twelve hours, my family finally made it 150 miles to a friend's house in Crystal Springs, Mississippi, south of Jackson. By the time Katrina hit New Orleans overnight, we learned it had weakened to a Category 3 as it made landfall in southeast Louisiana with sustained winds of 125 mph.[2] We heard early reports of heavy rain and powerful winds, but the storm surge is what we feared the most. Media went silent overnight as the storm battered the coast. The next day Katrina barreled through Crystal Springs with its spent force of 60 to 70 mph winds, taking down trees and knocking out power around us. That morning, I could not reach anyone in New Orleans until I remembered Bob Farnsworth, our Vice President for Capital Projects, lived just across the New Orleans city limits and had a land line at his house. He picked up when I called and said the storm was furious, but they were okay. I was relieved. By Tuesday morning we prepared to return to the city. I tried to call Jake on the pay phone but got repeated busy signals. I called Bob again and got a very different response. "Nick," he said, "it's awful today. We are getting out now. Water is rising on the street and is up to my doorstep and in my house on the ground floor level." Bob had no time to speak but made it clear there was no sense in coming back.

My heart sank. This was a major disaster. Bob was my last call to anyone in the city. There were no communications, just vague reports that said no one could go back to New Orleans anytime soon. We heard rumors that the levees had broken, and the city was filling with water. At first there were no TV or radio reports directly out of New Orleans, just silence and sketchy reports from national networks via Jackson's television stations. Those who stayed in the city could not communicate with the outside world, nor we with them. It was shocking. I feared for the lives of friends, my house, our employees, and the Museum.

News accounts from New Orleans got worse by the day. The television networks broadcast the scope of the broken levees and flooding that covered most of the city in ten to twelve feet of water. The devastation was horrendous. In addition to the physical destruction, the situation was deteriorating fast for the desperate residents who remained and were now trapped by the floodwaters. There was no electricity, no food, no communications, and no drinking water. The heat sweltered in the high 90s, and thousands of survivors found their way to high ground downtown near the river, only blocks from the Museum. The situation began to improve after Joint Task Force Katrina, under the leadership of Army Gen. Russell L. Honoré, came to town with troops from the National Guard and the 82nd Airborne Division. They delivered medical and food supplies to the city and began plans to rescue thousands of trapped citizens.[3]

Once reporters and cameras gained access to the area, the national media showed the ghastly results of flood and wind that destroyed buildings and homes and created life and death situations for those who remained. TV reports indicated that many had drowned in the storm, and we saw survivors on rooftops, waving sheets and hoping for rescue in scorching heat. It was depressing to feel so helpless, and I could only wonder about the future of the Museum, or if it even had a future. The only good news came from reports showing that the flood waters had not reached the Museum. It was on high ground, which fortunately protected most of the Central Business District and French Quarter, as well as Uptown sections of the city.

We finally reached Jake, who told us he experienced some terrifying moments during the storm, but he was okay. He reported that the Museum was secure and in decent shape. Looters had broken into the Museum store and smashed it up and stolen much of the merchandise. The main thing was that our exhibits were safe. Jake had hidden deep inside the Pacific exhibits protected by the steel gates that blocked the looters from accessing the galleries and artifacts.[4]

I had to make new plans for lodging accommodations for my family and dog for probably weeks to come. I could not contact any staff by phone, as the entire 504 area code phone exchange was wiped out. Nor could I reach them via email because the Museum servers had no power. We were off the grid and isolated from staff and friends. We drove to Orlando where our oldest son, Dave, was starting his MBA at Central Florida University. After we arrived, our son John got on a computer and found satellite images of our house near the lake and discovered that our roof was half blown off, but there was no visible water on the street or our patio.

Miraculously, Stephen Watson, Associate Vice President for Membership, was able to reach me on my cell phone. Stephen informed me David Voelker and some of the senior Museum staff had found their way to Baton Rouge. He gave me an email address so we could communicate that way and said the best option was for me to get to Baton Rouge as soon as possible and find a place to stay. Stephen had already found his way along the river to get into the city and said the Museum suffered some roof damage from the storm. Learning that Jake and the Museum were safe was a big relief, though we still knew nothing about other employees who might have stayed in the city.

We drove straight to Baton Rouge, arriving September 5, eight days after the storm. We stayed with an old friend, Gladys Solomon and her family. It was good to join David and Stephen in Baton Rouge to compare notes, begin assessing the consequences for the Museum, and locate our staff. We felt helpless as we joined the whole world to watch the unfolding tragedy on television 24 hours a day. We had some 61 employees scattered far and wide, and while most had been accounted for, the whereabouts of others remained unknown. They surely were running low on funds, wondering about their flooded homes, and trying to survive day to day. We needed to find some way forward, both personally and for the Museum. We were facing a disaster of historic proportions. Our Master Plan seemed a distant memory. Our first priorities were to find our employees, get access to Museum bank accounts to pay staff in the coming weeks, and get relief from our insurance companies. Most importantly, I had to find a way to get into the city as soon as possible to assess the damage myself.

There were a few senior staff members in Baton Rouge. We were able to find a few others, such as CFO Jim Green, by phone. We talked almost daily to figure out the next task that needed to be tackled. A few board members, including David Voelker, T. G. "Teddy" Solomon, and Louis Freeman, also found houses in Baton Rouge. I began meeting every few days with David to brief him on our initial plans to keep the Museum running. David quickly approved my decision to keep all employees paid through mid-October, when I knew I had to make significant layoffs before we ran out of funds. We were poised to face plenty of unexpected financial challenges, the most immediate being our next WWII cruise aboard the *Seabourn Legend,* scheduled to depart in the Mediterranean that October. Like our cruise the previous year, we had signed a nonrefundable contract with the cruise company for nearly $2 million. At that early stage, all I could hope for was that an "act of God" hurricane clause in our insurance policy would cover our losses, but that was a battle for later.

By the middle of the second week of September, I managed to get into the city to see the Museum with our technical consultant, Steve Gandolfi, who had a medical pass that got us through one of the only checkpoints into the city, on dry ground by the river. That gave us access to St. Charles Avenue, which was free of water all the way downtown. Seeing the Museum as a littered mess was a shock, but there was minimal building damage as Stephen Watson described. My immediate task with Gandolfi was to retrieve the Museum computer servers and get them relocated to a high-rise office building a few blocks away that had a large generator on the tenth floor of the parking garage. This lone building acted as the single technology hub in the city. It was an abandoned Enron technology center being used as a communications center for the Mayor's office, the National Guard, and the arriving FEMA workers. The powers that be understood our plight and allowed us to place our servers in a room full of computers and server racks. That enabled us to get back online, restore our email accounts, and get access to our databases, accounting, banking, and payroll information. This was a blessing.

After returning to Baton Rouge, we retrieved our financial information with the help of Jim Green, and we could finally produce a snapshot of the Museum's financial situation. After subtracting our expense commitments, we had $2.9 million in unrestricted funds on hand, enough to give us a little breathing room. However, our salary budget was $2.5 million, almost half of our total of $5.1 million cash balance. So the financial outlook for the coming months was grim. There would surely be no visitors for the foreseeable future. We would quickly run out of cash if we did not implement draconian measures that would certainly affect many employees but would determine the Museum's future. Our most significant revenues, not affected by the disaster, came from Stephen Watson's national membership campaign, which was luckily managed by a direct-marketing firm in the Northeast. We had 120,000 members and were just starting to generate positive earnings. These figures were astonishing and our only source of predictable revenues. Citizens across the nation became one of our main lifelines.

Aside from those revenues, we had a rainy-day reserve fund of only $750,000. That was it. With an estimated $10 million operating budget and only $2.9 million in unrestricted cash, the reserve fund would not help us on the operations side unless the board approved its use.[5] We also needed to address the ongoing construction and capital projects that fell outside of our operations budget but needed to be dealt with quickly.[6] The stark reality of the disaster was palpable for the city and the Museum. We had just approved an optimistic budget a few months earlier, along with our new Master Plan for the expansion. We had taken one hell of a punch.

The fighter's challenge is always to move on from that punch to recovery and counterpunch as fast as possible. That was our challenge as a Museum team. Setbacks in battle, business, or life do not resolve themselves. Fortunately, my core team was young and resourceful. Our Chairman, David Voelker, was an amazing entrepreneur with an astute business mind. He quickly seized on our bottom-line priorities. There was no panic in him. David also counted on me to figure out what to do regarding our capital expansion commitments, contracts, and operational needs. We needed answers fast so David could convene the Executive Committee by phone in October and then assemble the national board for an emergency fly-in meeting at the Dallas-Fort Worth Airport hotel by early November, if possible. He asked me to work out our key decisions, staff reductions, and expansion plans in the coming weeks to give the board options for the Museum's path moving forward. We worked on the basic assumption that it could be a year or longer before many residents or tourists could return to the city, so we would only count on meager revenues from our national membership and donations.

There were some bright moments amid the dark clouds over the city and Museum. Offers of help came in daily as we sent out our new phone numbers and contacts to trustees and friends. Others across the nation and even my colleagues in Innsbruck, Austria, saw our plight on television and made contributions. Tom Brokaw called me soon after I arrived in Baton Rouge, and it was reassuring to hear his strong voice of concern and hope: "Nick," he said, "I'm coming to help, NBC is flying me down tomorrow with a camera crew to get a firsthand look. Can you get me into the Museum? I'm going to cover the Museum first and then get my crew in boats to see the devastation in the Ninth Ward." I assured Tom I knew how to get into the city and would meet him at the Museum. He showed up the next day and we met in the Louisiana Memorial Pavilion to assess the damage to the Museum.[7] Tom immediately met Jake Staples, who was an eyewitness to the storm and mayhem of those harrowing days. Tom rolled the cameras as he interviewed Jake for the national news to tell his frightening story of sleeping in the exhibits during the storm and then experiencing the break-in of the Museum by some 50 looters a few days later. The famous news anchor was deeply touched by Jake's tears and his patriotic pride in protecting the Museum's treasured exhibits and artifacts in America's National WWII Museum. Later that afternoon, Tom toured the city by airboat and noted the presence of the 82nd Airborne Division, which fought in the D-Day invasion. They had come to the beleaguered city and the Museum that was built to honor their fight for freedom in Normandy in 1944, Tom said on the evening news. Before he left, Tom invited me to come to New York in a few months when he would host a fundraiser for the Museum with D-Day veteran and former Chairman of Goldman Sachs, John Whitehead.[8] Tom's promise was a bright ray of light amid a lot of grey.

Of course, the Museum was not the only concern for me or our employees and friends. The widespread devastation impacted our daily lives with big personal decisions about the depressing condition of flooded homes, insurance claims, massive cleanups, and finding contractors or demolition crews to tear down houses after waters slowly receded. My house was spared from flooding, but with half the roof torn away, rainwater from above ruined the walls and floors throughout. All our employees faced major decisions about damage to their homes and how to repair what was left. This compounded their anxieties about their jobs and the Museum's future. Luckily, my house was accessible and dry, so I quickly received insurance money to begin restoration work with the hope of moving back in by January 2006, months before most residents could even enter their watery homes.

In some ways, the situation felt very surreal. For months after Katrina, the weather was hot and sunny, and life seemed normal around Baton

Rouge and surrounding areas where most of us were living. By contrast, New Orleans was in disastrous shape, devoid of life without power and with only a trickle of the population able to return, with many commuting in and out as I did. Without power, nights were pitch black for months, except for those with generators and fuel to keep them running. There were no lights, no birds chirping, and no traffic in a major American city. In the Lakeview neighborhood, the streets and playgrounds looked like another planet, with mud, debris, and fallen trees everywhere. As water drained from the city, the National Guard went house to house to determine if any occupants or animals remained inside. Codes chalked on front doors indicated how many, living or dead, resided in each house. It was a grisly sight that I endured during my daily journeys to the Museum to determine what our rump staff and I could do to start managing repairs. A few hardy souls cleaned up the entire Museum, and we slowly found contractors who could do the major work.

My principal job was to work with David and our few senior staff to prepare for a mid-October Executive Committee meeting in Baton Rouge. Our goal was to lay the groundwork for the emergency fly-in meeting of our national board, which David scheduled for November 10 at the Hyatt Hotel in the Dallas airport. We located our scattered employees and got everyone paid through mid-October. However, David and I agreed we would have to make drastic cuts to reduce a $10 million operating budget nearly by half before we went to the board.

We convened the Executive Committee on October 12, 2005, in Baton Rouge with six local trustees present and four others via teleconference.[9] We briefed the committee on all aspects of the Museum's condition and explained our preliminary plans to cut the $10 million budget. David presented a full report of Economic Research Associates (ERA) from Chicago, which had reported the best estimates of the economic outlook for downtown and tourism. Harold Boullion reviewed our financial situation and the end report of the previous year to establish a baseline for the new budget amendments to be made for the balance of our fiscal year. He also secured approval to appoint a Trustee Recovery Task Force to assist management in monitoring the quickly changing conditions and providing major budget adjustments as needed.

In my President's report, I gave a recap of the 40 days since Katrina. I covered the state of Museum damages, personnel, and fundraising. I reminded the committee that an emergency budget would need to be approved at the board meeting in Dallas just a month later. On the operating side, the outlines were already clear. Harold agreed with my proposal to reduce our staff from 61 to 26 to reduce our $2.5 million salary budget by nearly half.[10] The committee approved this very difficult decision in the face of the stark budget realities before us. I stressed that David and I could cut no deeper if we wanted to sustain core personnel, get the Museum open in a few months, and meet our current contractual commitments to fight another day. To bring us closer to a balanced budget, I said our current negotiations indicated we would receive $750,000 in December from the Museum's business-interruption insurance, cutting the deficit to $574,457. To balance the budget, we would still have to seek approval of the national board to dip into our $750,000 rainy day reserve fund.[11] I said it was fortunate the board had the foresight to set aside these funds for emergency purposes, though I hated to rely on it.

The looming question was the current capital expansion budget of $282 million with construction suspended on Discovery Hall as well as the contracts with architects and exhibit firms designing the first pavilions. Maintaining exigency budgets for construction and minimal operations were the two immediate priorities, but many other initiatives hinged on the outcome of these three decisions by the board: getting the Museum open, finding a way to sustain operations, and approving the short- and long-term plan for capital expansion were the do-or-die decisions facing the board. I promised the Executive Committee that I would present at least four long-term scenarios for the board to consider in its decision on the future of the Master Plan and capital expansion. I noted that some were already calling for us to abandon the Master Plan entirely and return to our status as the National D-Day Museum. I was receiving questions from donors as well as government leaders at both state and federal levels about our capital funds, both monies received and those in the pipeline. How we decided on these matters would determine the fate of the Museum.

We were all hands on deck for the next four weeks preparing for the November 10 fly-in board meeting in Dallas. We had to get it right, and David knew it. Big bills were due soon, contracts were on hold, employees had to be paid, and without a viable plan, the Museum would go bust. We could not go forward without the full support for decisions and plans that had to be made amid enormous uncertainties. The operating budget and the capital expansion were the first decisions to take on, but there were many other decisions that hinged on those two. David and I were encouraged after the Executive Committee meeting. We felt we had gotten off the mat and were ready to unleash the Museum's first counteroffensive.

"IT'S NOT OMAHA BEACH. NO ONE IS SHOOTING AT US."

The day of the emergency board meeting quickly arrived, and the trustees flew into the Dallas Fort Worth International Airport from all over the country. As we filed into the meeting room at the Hyatt, there was a mixture of joy and anxiety from national trustees who greeted the battered New Orleans contingent. Tension filled the room as all were aware of the gravity of the situation for the city and the Museum. I prepared a full agenda to provide the foundation for all decisions related to the Museum's proposed strategies for survival. It felt like an existential moment for the Museum and the new board of trustees. We were all being tested for our courage, commitment, and judgment. Having the advice and support from such a seasoned group of trustees, many of whom had other crises in business and government was reassuring.

I presented the board with briefing documents with the latest professional assessments for the recovery of the city. These documents, provided by ERA, estimated the economic and tourism outlook downtown, expectations for the travel industry, and the unprecedented large-scale rebuilding efforts.[12] From these documents, the board could see beyond the devastation. On the tourism front, FEMA and other recovery workers occupied approximately 7,000 of the city's hotel rooms. The airport had only 37 scheduled flights the week of October 24, and our sources predicted that the airport would not even reach 50 to 60 percent of pre-Katrina capacity by March 2006.[13] Public safety concerns persisted, yet city officials tentatively entertained the idea for a very limited Mardi Gras as the first signal of a city comeback. Even a toned-down Mardi Gras was uncertain with so few residents in the city at that time.

In this atmosphere, David opened the meeting with the first order of business to ensure future leadership of the board with the election of former California Gov. Pete Wilson as Chair-Elect and Phil Satre and Bobby Savoie re-elected to the Executive Committee. David commented on the state of the Museum and his request for the approval to create the Trustee Recovery

Task Force to work with him and the President in addressing the best options in the dynamic environment we faced in the months ahead. The task force would reexamine the Museum's strategic planning commitments and budgetary assumptions. The board needed to determine the major financial issues on the revised operating budget and capital expansion options in this meeting so the President could proceed to execute based on new plans.

David outlined his broad goals: he wanted to assure cash for operations, personnel, and fundraising initiatives, as well as sufficient marketing funds, to place the Museum in the vanguard of the recovery with a December 1 reopening and to attract those visitors who might return by spring. On the advice of the Ehrhardt marketing team, several messages were already in the works, including "Operation Comeback," reinforce a positive image of the Museum's resilience to donors and those in government who may consider future support. David referred to the ERA report, giving evidence that bringing back creative and cultural resources to the city could help restore confidence and create a renaissance to help jump-start the recovery.

David then got into the heart of the meeting, explaining that I had prepared a bare-bones budget that he believed would support the Museum's recovery, providing several options to consider as modifications to the Master Plan. We needed board approval of the revised fiscal year 2006 operating budget, along with a strong commitment from trustees to help management prevail through the crisis and deep revenue cuts ahead, he said. David's urgent appeal was for the board to use this extraordinary moment in the Museum's history to demonstrate resilience and leadership of our trustees to assure our survival as an institution. For better or worse, the future of the Museum depended entirely on the board's acceptance of my recommendations. He then gave me the floor.

My motto was we are down, but not out. I drew from the Museum's historical roots, reminding the board that we needed the "can-do" spirit that Andrew Higgins and all the Rosie the Riveters showed during World War II. "It's not Omaha Beach," I noted. "No one is shooting at us." I declared it was my goal to be among the first cultural institutions to reopen in New Orleans, and we aimed for December 1. We would operate on a five-day weekly schedule with reduced admission. I also announced we planned a block party on November 11, Veteran's Day, for volunteers, veterans, and first responders. Our reopening would make clear to donors, government officials, and staff that we were determined to move ahead.

Nick Mueller (*left*) and Steve Ambrose retracing the Lewis and Clark Trail on their trip to Montana in 1999. Courtesy of the author.

The 1983 Opening Ceremonies of the UNO-Innsbruck International Summer School, in Innsbruck, Austria, which the author founded and is still in operation today. Here, he stands with fellow colleagues. *Left to right:* Dr. Edward Socola, UNO Dean of Liberal Arts; US Sen. Dick Clark; Dr. Josef Rothleitner, Rektor of the University of Innsbruck; Dr. Joe Logsdon, Summer School Director; and Dr. Nick Mueller, Dean of Metropolitan College. Courtesy of the author.

Steve conducting his "D-Day to the Rhine" tour in Normandy, France, in 1984. Courtesy of Grace Ambrose-Zaken.

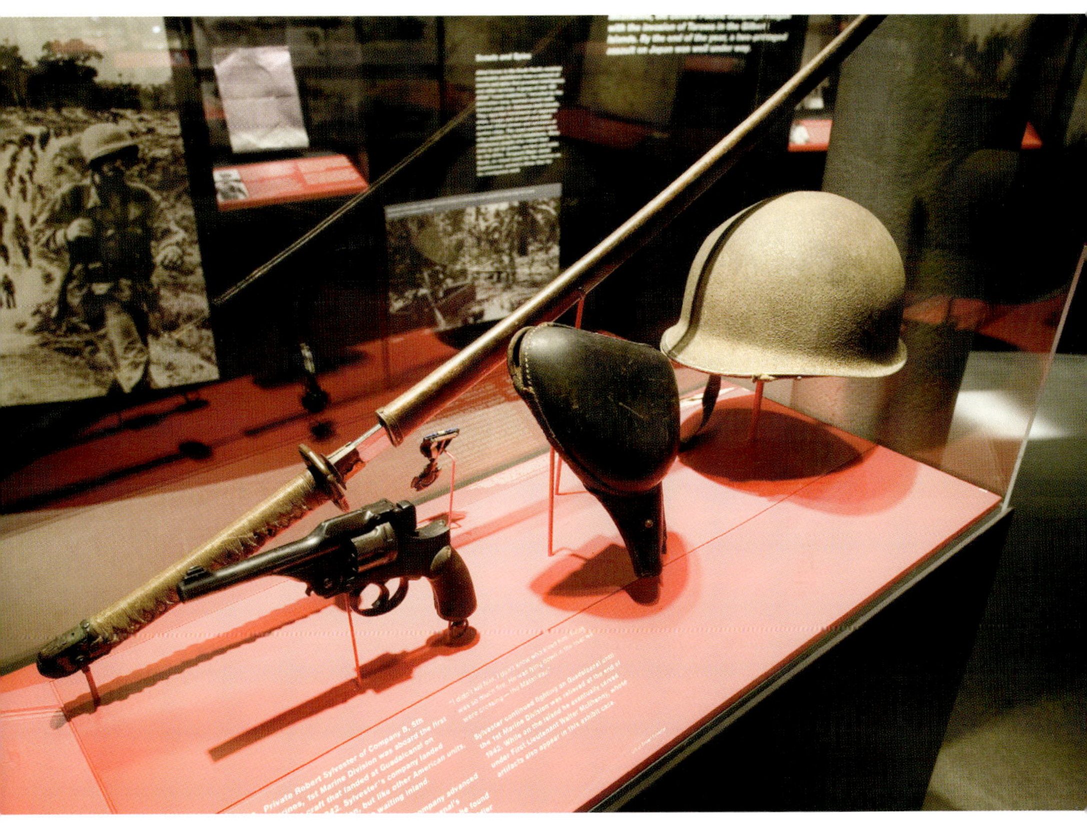

WWII veterans often gifted Steve with artifacts from the war after he had captured their oral histories. These artifacts given to Steve embody an encounter 1st Lt., 1st Marine Division Walter S. McIlhenny had with a Japanese officer on Guadalcanal. In a surprise attack, McIlhenny killed the officer with his pistol at the very instant the man struck his sword on McIlhenny's helmet, knocking him unconscious and denting the helmet. Displayed here are McIlhenny's dented helmet and the Japanese officer's katana. These one-of-a-kind artifacts are a constant at the Museum—first appearing in *D-Day Invasions in the Pacific*, then in *Road to Tokyo*. Courtesy of Jeffrey Johnston Photography.

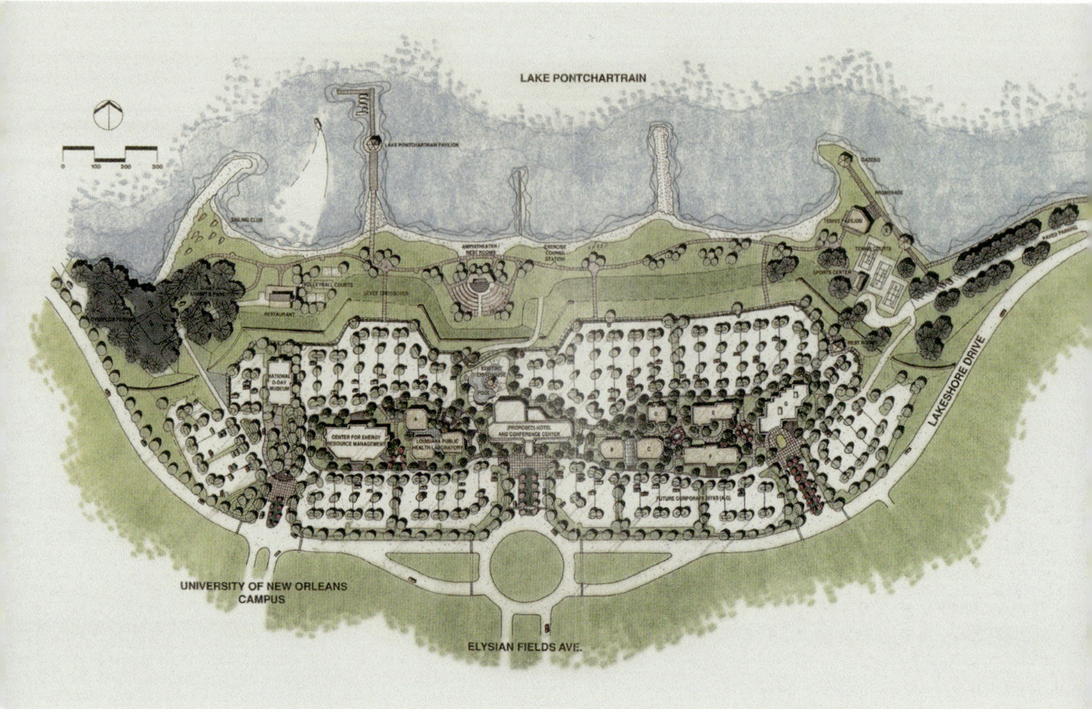

A rendering of UNO's Research and Technology Park Master Plan, created by architects Davis and Associates. The first location of the D-Day Museum is sited on the far left, where it was originally planned to be built on the park's western side. Courtesy of John C. Williams Architects.

A 1991 rendering of the National D-Day Museum building for the lakefront location in the Research and Technology Park, as created by local firm Eskew Filson Architects. Courtesy of EskewDumezRipple.

Steve Ambrose (*center right*) visited Normandy in 1992 with his wife, Moira (*right*), exhibit designer Jack Masey (*left*), and filmmaker Charles Guggenheim (*center left*). Here they tour the same beaches the troops stormed on D-Day. Courtesy of Lee Schlesinger.

Steve at the White House in May 1994. He was invited to give a historical briefing to President Clinton before the 50th anniversary of D-Day. Courtesy of Grace Ambrose-Zaken.

Above: Before the National D-Day Museum opened, a dedicated group of volunteers led by board member Jimmy Duckworth built a seaworthy Higgins Boat using original blueprints secured by Higgins biographer Jerry Strahan. These volunteers consisted of WWII veterans and former Higgins Industries workers. Courtesy of Jimmy Duckworth.

Steve Ambrose, Nick, and President George H. W. Bush with a sketch of the exterior of the Louisiana Memorial Pavilion. Designed by Lyons & Hudson Architects, the pavilion was funded and built by the state of Louisiana as the grand entrance to the Museum to accommodate macro artifacts, such as fighter planes, military vehicles, and the Higgins landing craft. Courtesy of Jackson Hill Photography.

At the *Saving Private Ryan* premiere in 1998, Nick and Steve introduce director Steven Spielberg to Dick Winters, Captain of the "Easy Company" of the 101st Airborne Division during World War II (*second from left*). Spielberg later produced *Band of Brothers*, a dramatization of Steve's history of the same name, which depicts Winters and the Easy Company in the European Theater of the war. Courtesy of Institutional Archives of The National WWII Museum.

One of the original exhibits in the National D-Day Museum. Miniature soldiers represent the number of Japanese and German service members on the eve of World War II compared to those of the active-duty US soldiers. The size of the Axis militaries dwarfs that of the United States, showing how America's isolationist policies and weak defenses left the country unprepared when it declared war in 1941. Courtesy of Institutional Archives of The National WWII Museum.

Facing page: Massive crowds lined the street of the Warehouse District on June 6, 2000, to celebrate the grand opening of the National D-Day Museum and to view the military parade with trucks carrying veterans from all D-Days of World War II. Courtesy of Grace Ambrose-Zaken.

Poydras
1ST INFANTRY DIVISION

"We did it!" Nick and Steve proudly celebrate ten years of hard work just after the ribbon cutting at the grand opening of the National D-Day Museum. Courtesy of Institutional Archives of The National WWII Museum.

The author and Steve Ambrose give a tour of the D-Day Museum during the grand opening celebrations in June 2000. They show longtime Museum supporters Sen. John Breaux (*left*), Secretary of Defense William Cohen (*center left*), and his wife, Janey Langhart Cohen (*center right*), the animated maps of the D-Day invasions in the galleries. Courtesy of George Long Photography.

WWII veterans greet crowds at the *D-Day Invasions in the Pacific* grand opening in 2001. Courtesy of George Long Photography.

Chairman Boysie Bollinger stands with Joe Foss, MOH Recipient and Executive Officer of Marine Fighting Squadron 121 (VMF-121) in World War II, who was honored at the grand opening of *D-Day Invasions in the Pacific*. Courtesy of George Long Photography.

A US Navy sailor interacts with the *D-Day Invasions in the Pacific* exhibit during its grand opening in December 2001. Courtesy of Institutional Archives of The National WWII Museum.

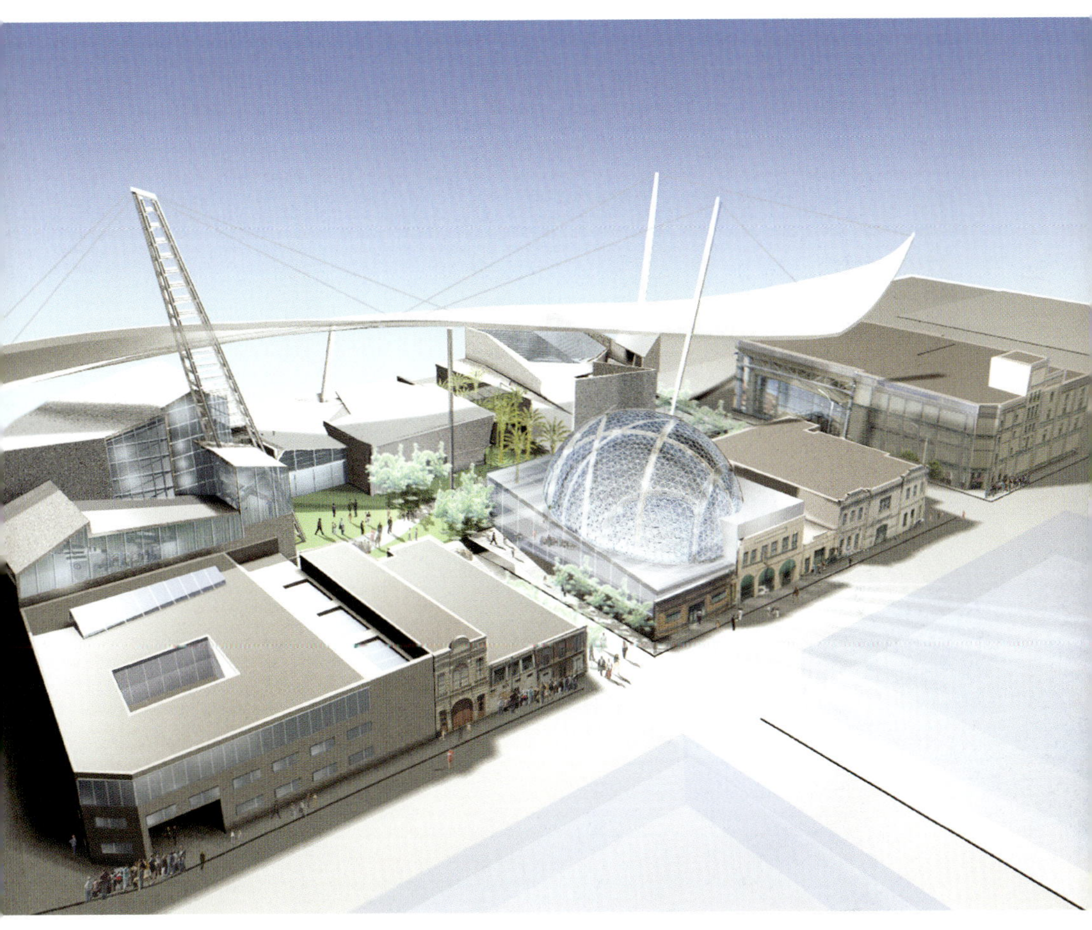

The Master Plan as designed by architects Voorsanger-Mathes and exhibit designer Gallagher & Associates in 2003. Though it would evolve over the years, major elements of the design remained intact. Courtesy of Voorsanger Architects PC.

Steve with Senators Ted Stevens (*center left*) and MOH Recipient Daniel Inouye (*center*), along with Senators John Warner (*right*) and Bob Graham (*left*). The Congressional support Stevens and Inouye offered was key to the Museum expansion and Congressional designation as America's National WWII Museum. Courtesy of Grace Ambrose-Zaken.

Hugh Ambrose speaks at Steve's memorial service in 2002. Among the mourners in the front row were President H. W. Bush, Boysie Bollinger, Tom Brokaw, Archbishop Philip Hannan, and the author. Courtesy of Rudy Bierhuizen.

The first International Conference on World War II in November 2006. Here, historian Don Miller interviews WWII veteran Andy Rooney. This conference was the first major sign of recovery of the Museum and New Orleans after the destruction of Hurricane Katrina the previous year. Courtesy of Institutional Archives of The National WWII Museum.

In August 2009, a group of board members, staff, and volunteers traveled to Baton Rouge to advocate for the Museum to receive funds from the Louisiana Recovery Authority Board. Pictured are D-Day veteran and MOH recipient Walt Ehlers (*center*), 82nd Airborne D-Day veteran and Museum volunteer Tom Blakey (*right*), and Pacific war veteran and board member Paul Hilliard (*left*) before the Museum's presentation. Courtesy of Institutional Archives of The National WWII Museum.

Tom Hanks films the narration for *Beyond All Boundaries*. The film was studded with major film stars like Hanks which attracted major audiences, essentially reviving the Museum after Hurricane Katrina. Courtesy of Institutional Archives of The National WWII Museum.

At the grand opening of the Solomon Victory Theater in November 2009, WWII veterans got an exclusive showing of the new film *Beyond All Boundaries* as part of the celebrations. Courtesy of Institutional Archives of The National WWII Museum.

My Gal Sal, the iconic Boeing B-17 bomber aircraft, is towed down Magazine Street toward its new home in the US Freedom Pavilion: The Boeing Center. Courtesy of Institutional Archives of The National WWII Museum.

Facing page: The open floor of US Freedom Pavilion: The Boeing Center provided space for the display of large vehicles, including a Sherman tank and a GMC CCKW truck. The lower screens run a special interactive experience, *What Would You Do*, challenging visitors to make difficult decisions related to strategic or moral situations of the war. Courtesy of Institutional Archives of The National WWII Museum.

ARMY

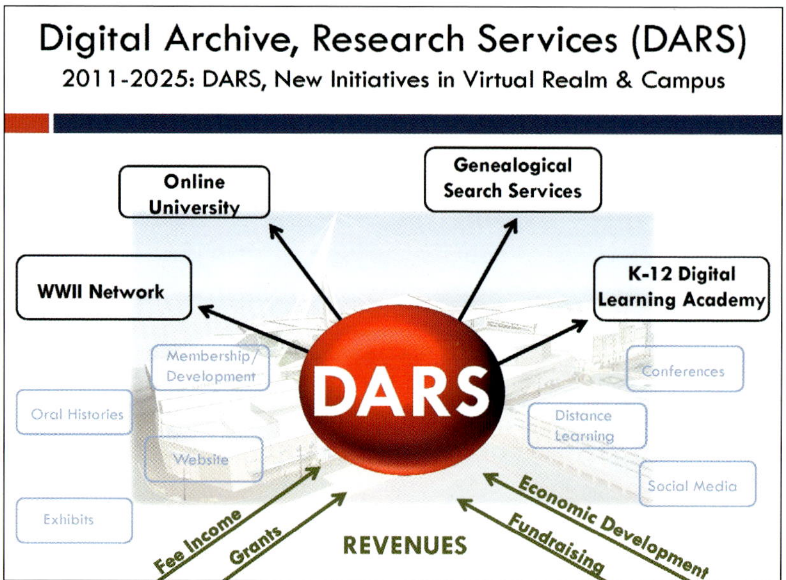

A graph developed by the author to help persuade the board to invest $10 million in the DARS initiative to digitize Museum collections and create programs to make WWII history accessible to global audiences via distance learning. Courtesy of Institutional Archives of The National WWII Museum.

The Air War gallery in *Road to Berlin*. This gallery is a recreation of the Thorpe Abbotts, a Royal Air Force Station in England that also hosted the US Army 100th Bomb Group in the final years of the war. Courtesy of Jeffrey Johnston Photography.

The Guadalcanal gallery in *Road to Tokyo*. Dense vegetation fills the exhibit spaces and veteran oral histories play on screens. This experience immerses visitors in one of the most intense and decisive jungle battles of the Pacific War. Courtesy of Jeffrey Johnston Photography.

Visitors in the *Arsenal of Democracy* exhibit. Guests learn about life on the home front as they move from a re-creation of a Main Street USA into a typical 1940s American home. Courtesy of Jeffrey Johnston Photography.

Chrissy Gregg, Associate Vice President of Education, films an electronic field trip in the *Road to Tokyo* exhibit. Every year, thousands of students from across the country learn about WWII history in engaging and interactive ways through these streaming programs. Courtesy of Institutional Archives of The National WWII Museum.

The late Marc Pachter, former Smithsonian Director, Presidential Counselor, trustee, and longtime friend of the Museum, interviews the author. Pachter always pushed his colleague to write the story of creating the Museum. From 2008 to 2012, Marc filmed the author and recorded his memories of the project as a foundation for his research and future book on the Museum's history. Courtesy of Institutional Archives of The National WWII Museum.

Meg Cahill, the author's longtime Executive Assistant (*center*), helps "pass the baton" to Nick's successor Stephen Watson (*right*) at the party celebrating the author's transition to part-time President and CEO Emeritus in 2017. Courtesy of Institutional Archives of The National WWII Museum.

Facing page: The lobby of The Higgins Hotel and Conference Center. Inspired by the art and architecture of the 1930s and 1940s, the building features major conference facilities that allow the Museum and other groups to host high-quality conferences and symposia throughout the year. Courtesy of Jeffrey Johnston Photography.

The exterior of the Liberation Pavilion. To some, the design of the structure evokes that of a Higgins landing craft—the boat that began the liberation of France on D-Day and all D-Days of WWII. Courtesy of Institutional Archives of The National WWII Museum.

The *Four Freedoms* exhibit in the Liberation Pavilion. The Four Freedoms were integral to America's postwar policies at home and abroad and are the central theme of the exhibits in the pavilion. Courtesy of Institutional Archives of The National WWII Museum.

Tom Brokaw films a celebratory toast to honor the author, Steve Ambrose, and the completion of the Museum Master Plan during the Road to Victory celebration dinner at the Liberation Pavilion grand opening events. Courtesy of Institutional Archives of The National WWII Museum.

Boysie brings the author up on stage during the Road to Victory celebration dinner. The author reflected on the multidecade journey to build the Museum with donors, board members, and other dignitaries. In 2016, Boysie told the author that when the Master Plan was finally completed, "they would both be there at the end." This photo shows Boysie's prediction came true. Courtesy of Institutional Archives of The National WWII Museum.

The completed campus of The National WWII Museum, 2023. Courtesy of Institutional Archives of The National WWII Museum.

Then I dove into the tough financial choices the board needed to make, outlining significant budget and personnel cuts with my recommendation to use much of our rainy-day fund of $750,000 to balance the budget. Everyone could see that 26 employees were barely enough to manage the Museum, even one without visitors. If we could not retain those few key employees, we might as well close. Fortunately, no one suggested that we cut personnel any further, but after animated discussion of the bare-bones budget, someone on the board (forever unnamed) objected to my reliance on the rainy-day fund as it would deprive us of any emergency cushion in the future. This remark caused spontaneous chuckles among trustees. "If the Katrina disaster does not qualify for use of this rainy-day fund, what else would ever qualify?" I retorted. The comment broke the ice, and the board quickly approved the revised budget with reliance on the reserve fund unless other unexpected revenues made it unnecessary.

There was other encouraging news that, despite our condition, boosted the morale of the board. I reported on Brokaw's national NBC coverage in mid-September and his promise to host a fundraiser for the Museum in New York City in December. Louis Freeman then brought up the $5 million capital campaign pledge that new trustee Jim Barksdale had made the previous spring. Louis told the board he had called Jim in the weeks after Katrina to ask whether his pledge was still firm in the face of the ravaged city. Jim said that he fully appreciated the candid communications and actions so far and that "he was more committed than ever." That lifted everyone's spirits. "The fact that he reassured us about his commitment was even more important to us than the $5 million," Boysie later told me. Louis also reported that we had raised $19.5 million since the start of the capital campaign with $1.2 million in new pledges since Katrina, mostly from individuals. He cautioned that fundraising was likely to slow down with all the social and economic needs in the city but announced that there was a new pledge of $1.5 million for Discovery Hall from E. J. Ourso, a wealthy WWII veteran.

All this news was positive, but I cautioned that $14.5 million of the $19.5 million in cash and pledges for the capital campaign were restricted to endowment, so we could only count on $5 million to sustain our current capital commitments. Congress could not provide relief, David said, as our hope for a $50 million federal appropriation would not happen "because of the massive federal monies now needed for the flooded city." [14] David felt optimistic that the $4 million in state funds were still solid, and he was working hard to double it. Still, we could only spend these capital funds on construction, not on day-to-day operational costs, which we desperately needed.

The best news of all was that our membership had grown from 70,000 the past year to over 120,000 nationwide and had generated a gross income of $820,000. This was the largest and most predictable source of revenue, given the minimal income expected from visitors for 2005 and 2006.[15] Without these new revenue streams, we could never have proposed the revised $7 million operating budget, which projected the small deficit covered by the reserve account.

We also had other plans already in the works on the education front. I reported that Kenneth Hoffman, Director of Education, was developing programs for local teachers and schools. I also confessed that it took Hurricane Katrina to wake me up to our pressing need to ramp up our distance-learning initiatives to reach beyond the physical walls of the Museum. How I missed this opportunity years earlier was embarrassing. As Vice Chancellor for Extension at UNO for almost 20 years, I had built the university distance-learning programs, but it was only after Katrina that I wondered why I was not doing more in that regard with the Museum. From that meeting onward, distance learning became a high priority for me, our senior team, and the board. It was the start of our commitment to develop digital content and technologies to extend our educational outreach on the WWII era throughout America and the world. Distance learning was a rich opportunity to fulfill the Museum's mission, and it had the potential to create new revenue streams to support education outreach via media and the internet. I promised the board new strategies and initiatives would be forthcoming in this area of our educational mission. But this was a very long-range plan.

The good news helped bolster trustee confidence to some degree, but Katrina anxieties remained top of mind on the financial front—especially our significant, over $6 million contractual commitments to ongoing construction of the Discovery Hall, as well as the design work for the Master Plan, CSAS, and the 4D theater. In the last few weeks, I had asked Bob Farnsworth, Patrick Gallagher, and Bart Voorsanger to explore the elimination of some of the buildings in the Master Plan and redesign of others to reduce our $282 million capital campaign costs. I promised the board I would come back with a detailed reduction of the Master Plan by the May 2006 board meeting.

Meanwhile, I proposed two steps to address our immediate contractual commitments for current construction and design. To sustain some forward movement, I recommended the first step was to use $8.6 million of capital funds already available in our budget to complete construction on Discovery Hall by next April as well as the approved Master Plan redesign. These funds would also fund the continuance of the architecture and design work for the 4D theater, which was included in the first phase of our Master Plan. For step two, assuming the State Bond Commission approved an additional $4 million, I proposed we increase the expansion budget to $12.6 million for the coming year and keep these projects moving forward. This was much better news than board members expected, and they approved these proposals for short-term action.[16]

For the immediate year ahead, I proposed several scenarios with the caveat that we would make no commitments beyond the $8.6 million capital expenditures until the following summer. Anything beyond that would depend on the pace of the city's recovery and our ability to fund construction, which was estimated at more than $55 million for the 4D theater, a USO-style experience, and the restaurant. Funds of that magnitude were not in view at all. I advised the board that this attraction could wait until we had a better understanding of our financial situation as well as a firmer agreement with creative designer Phil Hettema. We counted on future private and state funds to build the theater, create a movie, and construct related buildings. We were just starting the thematic planning for the 4D film, and I still had unresolved issues with Hettema regarding the arc of the story, the length of the show, as well as the contractual costs for development and production. The theater and show together were going to cost more than $30 million, as much as the entire D-Day Museum had cost when it opened in 2000. Digesting these big numbers was tough for the board just two months after the storm.

There were also longer-term challenges that had to be addressed to give me direction for developing the strategy that would define the Museum's future. The most contested issue at the board meeting was the viability of the entire Master Plan. The scope of the Katrina catastrophe deeply concerned trustees, who worried about the outlook for long-term recovery for the city, and these concerns clearly put a cloud over the future of the Museum. Everyone had different opinions about our ambitious $282 million Master Plan; some proposed we revert to the original D-Day Museum and sell the land we had purchased for a large endowment. Others, mostly local trustees, believed in the city's ultimate recovery, took a longer view, and hoped to keep the Master Plan largely intact, though many were agreeable to eliminating some pavilions and lowering the campaign goal substantially. The most optimistic were the visionaries who wanted to keep the entire plan.

I proposed four contingency options with graphic renderings derived from the approved Master Plan, and I named each scenario to reflect the theme of the proposed changes. The first scenario was the "National D-Day Jewel," which would suspend the entire Master Plan indefinitely after completion of Discovery Hall and revert to the original D-Day Museum. Second was the "Cinematic Journey," which envisioned completion of the 4D Theater, a USO-type experience, the restaurant, and a large hangar for macro artifacts and events. The issue with these two scenarios was that we would not fulfill our commitments to Congress for appropriations to expand our Museum to cover all of World War II. The third option was the "Halt at the Elbe" scenario, which meant stopping at Poeyfarre Street in the middle of the property, keeping everything in the second plan but adding the US Freedom Pavilion and Campaigns of Courage Pavilion. This scenario would encompass much of our original Master Plan but without a macro gallery, Liberation Pavilion, 4D Theater, and the additional space for Collections and Administration. The final scenario I named "The Grand Vision: Stay the Course." It pushed the completion date from 2011 to 2015, retaining everything in the Master Plan, minus the planned elimination of one building and reductions to others that Gallagher and Voorsanger were already undertaking. Even with the reductions in the last scenario, I reminded the board that construction inflation would likely keep the capital campaign budget the same for this scenario.

Neither David nor I asked for approval of any of these conceptual options but said the board needed to make a final decision by June 2006, when the architects and designers completed their revised plans and we had a better view of the recovery of the city and tourism. Privately, I hoped for the third or fourth scenario, but at the very least we were financially committed to the second scenario. I considered this a victory, since there were many trustees who preferred the first scenario, namely, scrubbing the entire expansion. That big battle was behind us.

The November board meeting was the failsafe point for the Museum's future survival and expansion hopes. We had approval for the revised budget for operations and the capital expansion for the next 12 months. We also won approval of a new plan and Museum reopening date with a blueprint for future decisions that gave me the freedom to operate in concert with the Chairman, the Trustee Recovery Task Force, and my senior staff. The board's commitment was inspiring to our staff members whose jobs now appeared secure for the coming year. Volunteers drifted back to help as well. It had only been 10 weeks from the day that Hurricane Katrina destroyed the city to the November 10 emergency board meeting in Dallas. We were coming back and counterpunching above our weight class in a city looking for signs of life.

REOPENING DECEMBER 1, 2005: "WE'RE ALL IN THIS TOGETHER"

Just over three months after our forced closure on August 27, 2005, we officially reopened to the public on December 1. We waited until Saturday, December 3, to celebrate our reopening under the WWII rallying cry, "We're All in This Together." We invited everyone in the city and were delighted that over 300 residents showed up to cut the ribbon for the reopening and nearly 1,300 came during the day to see the Museum and join our festivities.[17] We even organized a symposium on what we could learn in the aftermath of Katrina from the rebuilding of German cities after World War II. The crowds were a great boost to our spirits and morale, despite the contrast with our grand opening in 2000, when 200,000 enjoyed our parade and festivities. We were in the vanguard of the city's tourism rebound at a time when recovery still seemed years away, and we got attention in the media as one of the first cultural institutions to reopen after Katrina.

Our reopening was a bright light in the blighted city, albeit like a Roman candle that fizzled out quickly the following week. Visitation slowed to a trickle. By December, less than half the population had returned and estimates were that only about 15 to 20 percent of those returnees were living in the city limits.[18] National Guardsmen roamed the empty streets. We gave them free admission, and we loved having them in the Museum. Emergency workers and individuals and families were our target market. With our marketing budget cut in half, a skeleton staff, and a few volunteers, we planned a variety of USO-styled evenings, WWII films, special exhibits, and conferences in the coming year.[19] Normally we could expect about 20,000 guests per month, but now we hoped these events would attract 20,000 visitors over the first six months of 2006.[20]

Without a full staff, everyone had to take on duties normally performed by others. We agreed that every three weeks, all 26 staff members, including myself, would come to work in jeans to clean the entire facility, from top to bottom. My assignment was cleaning the bathrooms. We had to display the same can-do spirit exemplified by others who were cleaning up 40-foot-high mounds of debris throughout the devastated city. Relief and comradery resulted from the basic duties of keeping the large Museum running, albeit an empty one. As we entered 2006, we projected forward-looking optimism about the Museum's future, planning as if a brighter tomorrow was just around the corner.

REFINING PLANS:
EARLY 2006 AND DISCOVERY HALL

Our national board convened again on January 13–14, 2006, the first time since the Dallas meeting. For our national trustees, this was their first look at the city other than what they were seeing every day on television. They were shocked just driving in from the airport. Chairman David Voelker and I recapped our progress and reviewed our major commitments for the year ahead. I assessed our progress and the challenges I saw from my vantage point. We still had strong cash reserves, I said, and our rump staff was managing the Museum well with only the barest trickle of visitors. Yet, I happily reported that our national membership had now grown to 122,000. We had strong assets, I said, recapping the last five years. Going forward, we planned a strong calendar of events for the year ahead, which would make us attractive to tourists and residents as they returned. I also outlined the marketing strategies proposed by the Ehrhardt group. But all was not rosy despite my positive report.

We knew it was going to be a difficult year, but with the board's November approvals regarding operations and the capital expansion, I could now focus on execution of the most important goals to sustain the Museum. Harold Bouillion, our Treasurer, was confident we would meet our 20,000-visitor goal by June 30. And our membership campaign and other fundraising had already reduced our projected operating deficit by half to $250,000, though we were still dependent on our "rainy day" reserve fund. Regardless, Harold cautioned that our budget for 2007–8 needed to assume a dramatic jump to 150,000 visitors to sustain operations. Daunting as it seemed, this was about 60 percent of our pre-Katrina visitor level. We were unsure where those visitors would come from, or if the city would be ready for them. We were still operating on a shoestring. I reminded the board that members of our staff were dealing with wrecked homes, families and schools in disarray, and insurance worries, which all added to the daily stress and anxieties of keeping the Museum open.

To give trustees another dose of the gravity of our situation, David and I had busses take them on a tour of the devastated sections of the city, notably the destroyed Ninth Ward, but also the lakefront and other neighborhoods, where homes had been under ten feet of water and suffered terrific wind damage as well. Trustees were shocked. Mud, blackened lawns, and piles of housing debris stretched for miles and miles along empty streets, devoid of traffic or people. The sight was disheartening and even more meaningful to trustees as they grasped the magnitude of the challenges the city and the Museum faced. When we returned to our meeting, I did my best to buck everyone up with allusions to the resilience of the soldiers who fought so courageously in World War II. "We're like our soldiers facing the great Nazi offensive in the Battle of the Bulge—when you are in the trenches you have to fight the battle in front of you every minute, every hour, every day; setbacks don't mean you have lost sight of the mission to cross the Rhine and achieve victory!" I said, "That's the way our Museum staff is facing the days and months ahead. We need you in this battle with us." I believe seeing the reality of the devastation on our tour through the city helped convince those trustees who were still skeptical. It became clear they were ready to grapple with the Museum's short- and longer-term priorities beyond day-to-day survival.

The capital expansion redesign and construction were the most pressing objectives. Previously we had asked Voorsanger and Hettema to continue their work on phase 4, including the 4D Theater, a USO experience, and the restaurant. We had also resumed the construction of Discovery Hall and instructed Mathes Brierre and Gallagher to continue their work. Even as we considered contingency scenarios, I convinced trustees that funding construction of phase 4 was essential to our forward momentum and our overall expansion goals. Expansion was the sine qua non of our endeavor. At this January board meeting, trustees were completely focused on achieving this objective in the coming year, but everything boiled down to the same thing: money! We had to raise a lot of it in the next 12 months—far more than our

$12 million campaign goal for the year. Louis Freeman reported again that we had raised $5 million in private funds.[21] Phil Satre stepped up with $500,000, and Boysie announced a $1 million planned gift, and I secured a $1 million donation from Raymond E. Mason for our endowment, the latter to support an annual lecture series.[22] These gifts gave us a big lift and indicated confidence in our future, but private donations were not coming in fast enough to fund construction of phase 4, which we broadly estimated to be about $35 million for the theater, plus at least another $20 million for the adjacent USO live entertainment hall and the American Sector Restaurant. Funds of this magnitude could only come from the state or federal public sector in amounts larger than any single appropriation in the Museum's history.

During this time, we were very fortunate to have Boysie working the federal side of the funds, and David Voelker was working with Gov. Kathleen Blanco to secure more state funding for the Museum. "[David] was the right guy to be the chairman at the time." Boysie later said. He was extremely close to Governor Blanco and was looking out for the city's recovery and the Museum.[23]

David focused on getting the State Bond Commission to move up the other $4 million for the theater complex and worked on getting more. Blanco appointed both David and Boysie to the Louisiana Recovery Authority Board, giving us two very influential leaders on the board that distributed billions of dollars for the Road Home program. The program financially assisted owners of damaged homes. David believed that some of these federal economic development funds might also be available to the Museum in 2007 or 2008. We mobilized everyone behind David in a full-court press on a statewide strategy for a major appropriation.

In January 2006, the board settled on The National WWII Museum Foundation, Inc., as our official new name. This step was our response to our Congressional mandate to cover the entire war, which was made into law in 2004, but Katrina delayed the adoption of our new name. We also adopted new bylaws that finally completed our transformation to an entirely new structure, composition, and responsibilities, both financial and mission-related.[24] It felt surreal to pause for this work in the middle of our recovery from Katrina, but the new name and governance were important to planting the flag for our vision to become America's WWII Museum. Every step like this one drew the board another step closer to officially approving the "Grand Vision: Stay the Course" scenario.

Along with our name change, we shifted operational strategies, since we could not attract visitors who were unable to come to the city. We focused instead on a robust schedule of programs and events that generated stories and kept the Museum visible to our national members, donor prospects, and the state of Louisiana. The legislature and people of Louisiana were proud of the Museum and were naturally drawn to our ambitious vision despite the Katrina disaster. Continuing support from the state was vital, as private donors were more likely to contribute if they saw continued investment from the state.

On April 21, 2006, we held the most unusual ribbon cutting in our history for the E. J. Ourso Discovery Hall, named for the WWII veteran who provided the capstone gift for the building that would host these educational programs.[25] We had a few dignitaries on hand, including Governor Blanco, former Rep. Bob Livingston, and Jesse Arboneaux, President of the E. J. and Marjory B. Ourso Family Foundation. It was a strange celebration. The Museum was devoid of visitors, other than those of us who cut the ribbon. That red ribbon's slender fabric seemed representative of our slim resources but strong heart that held the Museum together that day. The E. J. Ourso Discovery Hall focused primarily on K–12 education, with a classroom, mini-library, special exhibit hall, and orientation room that gave a boost to our educational outreach program plans. We had already moved the Eisenhower Center from UNO's campus to the building next door, and it included space for research historians and our oral history collection. These steps were small by any measure, but in our deserted city the openings were victories.

In an effort to build confidence in our national audience, we held the American Spirit Award Event in San Francisco for former Secretary of State George Shultz. This was a way to carry our flag across the country and generate funds from untapped donors. Former Gov. Pete Wilson, a good friend of Shultz, led the way in organizing this tribute on May 3, 2006, with a Marine band and more than 400 contributors in attendance. Pete and I took the opportunity to tell the comeback story of The National WWII Museum and sought support for our continued recovery and vision for the future. When all the sponsor contributions were counted, we netted $300,000 for an endowment that would support an annual symposium at the Museum named the George Shultz Forum on World Affairs.[26]

On the Museum leadership front, the board elected Pete Wilson as the new Board Chairman at the annual meeting on June 3, 2006. Pete and his wife, Gayle, had become fast friends of ours from the moment Pete was elected to the board in the fall of 2002 as one of our first national trustees. Steve Ambrose had already begun to recruit him, but I did not meet him until Gayle surprised him with a birthday visit to the National D-Day Museum shortly after Steve's passing. Wilson was the first nonlocal Chairman of the board and, as a former Governor, had friends in high places of business and government across the country. His national profile meant the world to us as we fought our way through recovery to maintain our expansion goals. Pete's election sent a strong signal to our national stakeholders that we were serious about our commitment. He brought vast experience dealing with natural disasters during his term as Governor of California and provided reassurance for decisions that David and I made in the months following Katrina. Pete had experience in every level of government as Mayor of San Diego, a US Senator, Governor of California, and a Presidential candidate, which meant there was nothing he had not seen in public or private affairs. He opened doors for us in our fundraising and lobbying efforts. CEOs across the country and members of Congress would always take his call. He was a Marine Corps veteran and had an avid interest in American military history. He had become a fervent champion of the Museum's larger mission and ambitious expansion plans. Just prior to his election as Chairman, he spoke to a joint session of the Louisiana State Legislature on behalf of the Museum and received a standing ovation. From state, national, and business perspectives, Pete Wilson was the perfect Chairman to help lead our recovery in tandem with David's state strategy and the federal initiatives pursued by Boysie and me. It felt like we had retaken the beachhead in the last nine months since Katrina, and now General Patton had arrived to help lead our drive to Paris. With Boysie and David still active on the battlefield and Phil Satre as Chair-elect, we had an all-star team to carry the Museum from crisis to victory.

A few months later, our June 2006 meeting was another milestone in the Museum's recovery. We earned sufficient revenues to finish the fiscal year with a surplus and therefore with no need to dip into our rainy day reserve fund. I also proposed a new budget for the next fiscal year that restored all voluntary salary reductions that current staff accepted in 2005. Around that time, we elected a new group of distinguished trustees, including Norman Francis, President of Xavier University, who was also chair of the Louisiana Recovery Authority Board. The boost in support from our newly elected trustees meant that we were going to survive.

David Voelker reported that he had more confidence in a substantial increase in funds from the state in the coming year, entirely dedicated to construction of the 4D venue, or Victory Theater, as we called it. There had been some questions from the board about prioritizing the Victory Theater ahead of the Campaigns Pavilion, which would cover military operations, but the possibility of additional funding quashed any doubts about the Victory Theater as our top priority. As recommended by the ERA report, local board members believed that the 4D cinematic experience would be a spectacular first addition of the Master Plan and held our greatest hope of drawing visitors back to the Museum. I persuaded the board that the state was more likely to fund a theater, as there was a precedent for the state supporting similar projects in the past. State politicians could easily see how the state could benefit from a stand-alone theater instead of additional galleries, which were much more expensive. For these reasons, David and I championed the approval of the theater as the Museum's primary focus for state and private funding in the coming year. This decision was perhaps the most important choice that determined the next phase and future direction of the Museum.

The board voted to proceed with phase 4 of the expansion that included the final construction plans for the theater and 4D film experience and the USO-style venue and restaurant. I assured the board that we could delay construction until we raised most of the $30 million needed. Then came the big decision on the Master Plan. Inflation drove up costs for the "Grand Vision" scenario, which were now estimated to exceed the original goal of $282 million, even with significant reductions to the Master Plan. Despite that reality, a confident board voted to support my recommendation to increase our capital campaign goal to $300 million with the agreement to postpone completion of the campus until 2015. I was surprised and relieved by the solidarity of the board to support these decisions. Ten months after Hurricane Katrina destroyed New Orleans, our tenacious decision sustained momentum and charted our path forward.[27] With the decision to stay the course, we could sink our teeth into rebuilding and growing the Museum.

THE C-47 SKYTRAIN

Many events cropped up unexpectedly in 2006 that demonstrated the vitality of the Museum. The city began showing signs of life, and tourists started to return. Programming picked up with plans for a Medal of Honor Exhibit in late fall. On October 15, 2006, the Museum made national headlines with a screening of the new film, *Flags of Our Fathers,* with actors Ryan Phillippe and Reese Witherspoon in attendance.

A combination of individuals, luck, vision, and initiative sustained the Museum at critical moments after before and after Katrina. Such was the rare chance to purchase a Douglas C-47 Skytrain transport plane. This was one of those sudden and opportune events that literally dropped in out of the sky. The C-47, like the jeep, Sherman tank, and Higgins boat, was among the iconic American artifacts of World War II. The plane was often called the workhorse of the Army Air Corps, and after the war was flown worldwide, carrying freight and passengers under the DC-3 moniker. Our curators and historians searched for a C-47 for years, but they were all too expensive—in the $500,000–$700,000 range—for one with an authentic wartime provenance. In the months after Katrina, we certainly had no budget for artifact acquisitions of any amount.

Getting this plane was a great story. In late January 2006, as I got off a sailboat to return home from a long-delayed vacation in the British Virgin Islands, I received a call from an excited Tom Czekanski, our Director of Collections. Tom told me that a Douglas C-47 was up for sale on eBay with the auction closing at noon. He said he had already checked out the plane from the owner in Hondo, Texas, who was auctioning it off. Tom said the tail number of the plane told an amazing history. This plane had flown in the four major engagements of the war in the European Theater. "This exact airplane," Tom said, "was assigned to the Pathfinders of the 82nd Airborne Division that flew the paratroopers into Normandy the night before D-Day." I knew the Pathfinders went in first to set up the radio direction finders to guide an armada of 1,000 planes and 13,000 paratroopers to their designated landing zones that night.[28] It was one of the boldest and riskiest actions of the war. The story got better. This same C-47, Tom said, also carried Pathfinders in Operation Market Garden, dropped supplies to troops in the Battle of the Bulge, and then flew its last mission in Operation Varsity in March 1945 to support the Allied forces pushing across the Rhine River into the heart of the Third Reich. "It's a prize artifact," Tom said breathlessly. "The starting bid on eBay is $150,000, so can you authorize me to bid on it?"

"I don't have any funds at all, but this is too great to pass up," I told Tom. "Put in a bid for $155,000 and go for it. I'll find someone to donate the money if we get it." Tom called a few hours later before I boarded my plane home: "We got it!" It was thrilling news; now I had to find a donor fast, and I knew just the person to call.

Paul Hilliard was a rear-seat gunner on a Dauntless Dive Bomber in the Pacific turned successful oilman in Lafayette. He was my "plane guy." I had grown fond of Paul when I got to know him on our 2004 D-Day cruise to Normandy. He was so interested in all WWII history topics that I began cultivating him to come on the board of trustees that spring. He often pestered me about purchasing some of the iconic WWII warbirds before they were too expensive or got picked up by other museums. Paul knew I agreed with him, and he also knew we had no money, but he promised to help. I called and told him I had just authorized the purchase of a C-47 from eBay but had no money. "Could you help?" I asked. Paul responded immediately, "I'll put up the cash, and I need no recognition. Once we have it, offer the C-47 naming rights to another donor for half a million." I laughed. That was Paul. Never looking for recognition. He would advance the dough for any plane we could buy, and then let me go find a donor for that plane so we could use Paul's money for the next plane we wanted to purchase.

The C-47 was a bargain. We replaced an engine, added original seats, gave her a paint job, and new windows, and flew her to New Orleans. I had the big thrill to fly over the city and tip our wings to onlookers below before Tom disassembled the plane for her last journey to the Museum—on the ground instead of the air. Tom and our staff took off half of each wing and towed her downtown through the French Quarter in front of Jackson Square en route to the Museum. Seeing the old warbird against the backdrop of the famous Jackson Square and St. Louis Cathedral was quite a sight.

Patrick Gallagher persuaded me to hang her in the Louisiana Memorial Pavilion after beefing up the steel members of the ceiling. We squeezed her through the large pavilion doors with only an inch to spare and hoisted her to her spectacular resting place, suspended 40 feet in the air. Paul was thrilled, as were we all. We already had the Spitfire and the Higgins landing craft; now, with our C-47 Skytrain, we had three key artifacts that played an enormous role on D-Day. Ambrose would have been so proud.

During this time, I asked Paul if he would like to join the board. He had a can-do attitude, was used to meeting big challenges, and he still carried the same undaunted spirit exemplified by his service in the Pacific. He also owned Badger Oil Company in Lafayette, Louisiana, as well as a chain of regional banks. Paul told me that, with the recent passing of his wife, he was looking for a cause he could embrace wholeheartedly. By this time, we were already becoming good friends. Like all others who knew Paul, I enjoyed his sharp wit and insights into history and other people. He joined the board in June 2006, destined, I thought, to become one of the great leaders of the board. We could not have added a better trustee in those recovery years after Katrina.

All this good publicity preceded our October 18, 2006, Executive Committee meeting, when we announced that the Louisiana Bond Commission approved $23 million in state funds for the Theater/USO phase.[29] Even in the wake of tremendous spending needs after Katrina, David Voelker, Governor Blanco, and legislative leaders came through with the largest single appropriation the Museum had ever received. It was a magical moment for our board, staff, donors, members, volunteers, and me—but mostly for the WWII veterans who were counting on us. This grant was undoubtedly the most significant contribution toward making The National WWII Museum a reality. Katrina was a huge setback, but now, just fourteen months later, there was no doubt we could complete the first phase in the next two to three years.

PRESIDENTIAL COUNSELORS AND INTERNATIONAL CONFERENCE ON WORLD WAR II

After our rapid expansion plans began after Katrina, I decided to form a new advisory group, the Presidential Counselors, for the Museum. The decision to create this group was perhaps the best idea I ever had in advancing the Museum's exhibit content, research, programs, and educational outreach beyond the walls of the Museum. The group comprised the most distinguished experts on World War II, consisting of 15 top historians, authors, journalists, filmmakers, and museum directors. I recruited a Smithsonian director, along with international experts from Canada and the director of the Churchill War Rooms at the Imperial War Museum. I only promised expenses and some great New Orleans cuisine in exchange for their advice on future opportunities for the Museum. We would convene once each year for two days to review our emerging plans for exhibit content, design, media, outreach to new audiences, and even our overseas tours. I also invited their assistance as presenters at our International Conference on World War II.[30]

We sought their expertise on artifact collection, the latest media technologies, as well as research and education initiatives to assure the historical integrity of all that we present at the Museum. I charged them to help us deliver the most authentic public history of the American experience in World War II to our various audiences.

The Presidential Counselors became a veritable think tank that helped us shape the strategies for a Museum that aspired to be the world's best museum on World War II and its enduring legacy. Their support and willingness to give us their time and intellectual embrace was a godsend and gave us a vote of confidence. They all understood that our Museum mission was to portray the American experience in World War II, both in our contribution to its lasting consequences and memory of the war for the United States and the world. We will always need the best historians and museum leaders to help the Museum shape America's authentic place in our historical memory and meaning of that conflict.

All the Presidential Counselors, especially Don Miller, helped me plan and promote our first blockbuster conference on World War II in 2006. I initially broached the idea with Don in spring 2005 at his home Easton, Pennsylvania, asking that he help me create a major annual WWII conference that focused on public audiences with the top historians of that conflict, at home or abroad. As we envisioned it, the inaugural International Conference on World War II would be the biggest event at the Museum since Katrina. He was easily convinced. We both thought we could do something unlike the typical academic conference for professional historians. I believed enthusiasts would pay to come to New Orleans for a program that featured the most exciting WWII historians and public speakers in the world. We would not shy away from controversial topics. We brainstormed about popular historians we knew would be a hit, keeping in the tradition of spellbinding speakers like Steve Ambrose. Don was a great historian and speaker himself, so he understood just the kind of speakers I wanted to recruit.

That very day, Don and I moved from idea to action, making phone calls to our famous historian friends to sign on. We sold them with the idea of being part of the first great conference on World War II; one that would reach new audiences, attract national media, and sell their books. Almost everyone we approached enthusiastically agreed. We told them we wanted to reach avid WWII readers who we thought would want short presentations, rather than 45-minute lectures or peer-reviewed papers. We promised prospective speakers a large audience of non-historians who were genuine fans of history and sought to learn, question, debate, and socialize with bestselling authors, as well as with veterans of World War II. The target audience were some of the same ordinary citizens who streamed into the Museum before Katrina, so this was another way to get them to return despite the devastation still manifest in the city. The conference demonstrated our commitment to our mission and to our expansion simultaneously.

The conference was a big gamble to sell to the board at a time when we were understaffed, without tourists, and had only a meager marketing budget. Regardless, I knew our visitors kept asking for more content about the war—they wanted more exhibits, tours, information about their families, and especially more programs. They could not get enough of the history of World War II as we told it: fresh, authentic, personal, engaging, and accessible to non-historians. The first pitch for any new venture is always the hardest. I convinced the board that our marketing risks were minimal, and I promised we would get enough attendees and sponsorships to cover the expenses and generate revenue.

Indeed, more than 800 attendees filled the Museum over a four-day span in the Louisiana Memorial Pavilion and the adjoining auditorium in the Contemporary Arts Museum. We divided the program into two parts: The World of History and Memory Hall. The former featured top historians who debated history and controversies of the battles, leaders, and strategies of the war. The presentations were terrific and electrifying. In the sessions, we had panels of American, German, and Japanese veterans who had served in World War II, despite deep-seated animosity between the wartime enemies. Though some objected, we stuck to our guns and invited both Japanese and German vets to bring their contrasting memories of famous battles like D-Day and Iwo Jima. Everyone loved the exceptional debates that followed between panel members, historians, and attendees. American and Japanese veterans gave poignant and contrasting accounts of the use of atomic bombs, and we also had testimony from those on the ground who survived Hiroshima and Nagasaki. The controversial A-bomb discussion was punctuated by the Norwegian Counsel General Svein Andreassen, who presented the Museum with a German Heavy Water barrel, artifactual evidence amid the controversial discussion by giving his view on the race to build the first atomic bomb.[31] During the war, Germans moved barrels of heavy water from a Norwegian factory to Germany, where the water's unique atomic structure could have helped Nazi scientists create a nuclear bomb. Norwegian resistance fighters placed a bomb on the transport ferry and sank it, sending its payload of barrels to the bottom of a very deep Norwegian lake. The barrel had only recently been recovered from the lake with its heavy water still in the barrel, a remarkable artifact. The gift and the conference received heavy media coverage, raising the Museum's credibility and national profile. The entire conference exceeded all expectations, demonstrating again how the Museum was pressing through the Katrina disaster by taking bold risks and delivering revenues to cover our bets.

EDUCATIONAL INITIATIVES, 2006–9

These various Museum activities so soon after the city's devastation helped us regain momentum, visibility, and the funds needed to rebuild our personnel. We sorely needed to replenish our bare-bones staff after our massive layoffs after Katrina, which drastically limited our operational capacity. As we moved from 2006 to 2007, our number-one priority was retaining the employees we still had and gradually restoring those employees we lost after the storm. The mantra was get a plan for new revenues and then hire the staff to get the revenues. Our education positions were at the top of our list to fill as we recovered. By 2007, we restored most of the positions in our education department, putting us at nearly 55 full-time employees, who enabled us to reinstate the educational initiatives we suspended after Katrina.[32]

After we opened the first Discovery Hall in 2006, we put serious energy into ramping up our outreach and distance-learning capabilities. Our handful of education staff, still led by talented Director Kenneth Hoffman, reinstated our virtual field trip program. They spent countless hours crafting thoughtful programs for students across the country. To our delight, the virtual field trips were immediately popular after the storm. By the summer of 2007, our education team organized twenty virtual field trips for classes in seven states and one in Ontario, Canada. We used technology to make America's role in World War II a part of school curriculum, a perfect fit for our mission. Our education department also threw itself into creating other programs and initiatives for K–12 students. We did not turn our attention away from local New Orleans schools either. By the summer of 2007, we reinstated our Red Ball Express program, which allowed staff to travel to local schools and introduce WWII artifacts to students. These activities helped breathe life back into the Museum and keep us forging ahead on our big-picture agenda.[33]

The benefits of our hard work were threefold. First, we reaped revenue from educational initiatives, making them a vital part of our Katrina recovery process. Second, our educational programs helped bring some national attention and economic activity to the city of New Orleans in a time when we needed those things most. Third, and most important to our big picture as an institution, resumption of our educational outreach helped legitimize the National WWII Museum as an effective source for learning about America's role in World War II for students and scholars alike.

In those years, we worked every day, counterpunching to recover from the damage done by Katrina. We made progress towards recovery, but there was still much to be done. Our staff, board members, and volunteers came together after Katrina determined not only to save our Museum, but also to build it bigger and better. What made the biggest difference in our success in those years was not necessarily how much money or influence our team brought to the table, but the incredible commitment of time they gave to us: board, staff, members, and volunteers alike. We thought about Steve a lot in those days. We knew we were working to preserve his legacy with this Museum, as well as our commitment to illuminate the values, integrity, and spirit of unity exemplified by the WWII generation. It was how I phrased it in one of our board meetings after Katrina. This Museum and all the work we put into it were our "love song to democracy," a fond callback to Steve's famous remark about the Museum on the day of the grand opening.

But as we moved through 2007 into 2008, it became more and more obvious that a full recovery from the storm required more than determination. We needed to make a statement by opening the new National WWII Museum with a major attraction—a "wow" experience to motivate tourists and locals alike to flock to us. We had to create a must-see exhibit to live up to our Congressional billing as the nation's Museum of World War II.

BEYOND ALL BOUNDARIES

My attention turned fully to resume work on the nascent concept of creating a unique cinematic experience for the Museum. I had titled it *Beyond All Boundaries* as a placeholder to help frame my vision for World War II in this dramatic media show. It was going to be expensive and so wedded to new media technology that it could only be shown in a custom-designed 4D theater—which was also expensive. The theater and 4D film together would cost $30–$35 million to present a single show that would play for years to come. Unlike many ballyhooed Hollywood films, we could not afford a box office flop or endure serious criticisms from veterans or WWII historians. Any replacement show would take years of design and would incur new costs. It was also important that we did not miss on the historical memory of America in World War II or the impact that cinematic experience would have on our visitors and public stakeholders. I was counting on this single attraction to be a rocket booster for our visitation.

No one yet knew what this might look like, including me. I only had a general outline in mind for some highlights and chronology, so we had yet to define a compelling historical narrative at the core of the show. And I knew less about the movie business than about starting a museum, by a wide margin. I thought I had a big idea, but I knew I needed help.

I think Steve would have been delighted to know that his wake in 2002 provided the spark that led to our collaboration with Tom Hanks. During my conversation with Tom that evening at Moira's home in Bay St. Louis, I described my vision for the theatrical presentation and the arc of a story that would immerse visitors into the dramatic story of World War II. I explained my concept was to portray the war that took America and the world beyond all existing boundaries in every way imaginable—a war fought to save democracy and civilization. He was intrigued. I described the essentials of my idea to enlarge the WWII show and story to a visual scale never seen before in any theater, much less in a museum theater. We would portray America engaged in a global war that exceeded the limits of wartime experience on every level known to humankind. I outlined my ideas quickly. America was the "hero" of the story set against a broad tapestry of the war spread across every continent, fought in every kind of climate and terrain, from the freezing temperatures of the Arctic to the desert heat of Africa; from the stormy beaches of Normandy and Mediterranean to the wintry battles of the Bulge; from the islands and jungles of the Asia-Pacific to the peaks of the Himalayan mountains. Both Allies and Axis powers fought on land, at sea, in the air, and even in the outer atmosphere, with Hitler's V-2 rockets. The war's campaigns, weapons of war, and genocide exceeded every boundary of human killing and mass destruction, culminating in the industrial-scale bombing of cities and the use of the most powerful weapon of all, the atomic bomb. Victory meant the preservation of democracy, a new era of prosperity, and great advances in human rights and freedom. This was our story, I told Hanks, "A war beyond all boundaries known to mankind," presented in a format that also pushed cinematic boundaries.

Above all, I said, the film would reflect the Museum's mission, presenting a positive narrative, a celebration of the strength of the American spirit, and a story of hope and liberation from tyranny. I wanted future generations to know that contrary to misguided public opinion about the efficiency of totalitarian regimes, our messy democratic institutions and systems emerged superior in battle, weapons, troops, technology, leadership, and home front support. Our audiences should understand what General Eisenhower meant when he said that "Hitler should beware of the fury of an aroused democracy."[34] The film would reveal the unifying strength of our democracy when we are resolved to a common purpose, I said. So, for me and the Museum, *Beyond All Boundaries* was not just a dramatic multimedia experience, but a preview of the historical themes in the rest of the Museum exhibits yet to be designed and built.

I admitted to Tom that this was a lot of history to encompass in a 40- or 50-minute show, but I felt it could be achieved without trivializing the story. To my knowledge, there was no film that conveyed the scale, power, authenticity, and significance the war and American memory deserved. My knowledge of Disney and Universal amusement parks provided clues as to how these technologies could be used to convey serious history instead of entertainment, but I surely did not want this show to cross the line into mere entertainment. "So that's the idea," I said to Tom, "but I have no idea if it's crazy or where to begin. What do you think?"

Tom put on his serious film hat and, to my relief, expressed interest in the idea. We agreed that some combination of theater, film, and technology might be used to create a large-scale experience, an impressionistic show that was authentic, astonishing, and beyond the imagination of the audience. Top WWII historians would help shape the story with me. Tom seemed to agree that a theater designed for such a show might work. He saw the value in an immersive, human approach to the film. Our discussion focused more on the content of a show that drew people into the story with images, sound, scale, senses and was grounded in personal accounts, touching people on an emotional level during a climactic war. In the end, we agreed that such a dramatic multimedia attraction would be unique and could be an essential foundation for our future expansion plans.

I was thrilled to have Tom's attention and enthusiasm for the story idea and the use of new, large-scale cinematic technologies for the presentation. I hastened to add that I knew these types of productions were his world and not mine. I had no clue about what was feasible for the Museum in this realm, only that it was going to be costly. His agreement to help that evening at Steve and Moira's home gave me enormous confidence that there was a path forward. With the memory of my late friend heavy in my heart, I knew Steve would have asked Tom for help if he were still alive.

My next task was to find someone in the world of cinematic attractions that could turn the creative concept into a reality. Our master planner, Patrick Gallagher, introduced me to Phil Hettema, founder and President of the newly formed The Hettema Group. Patrick was confident that Phil could execute the "wow" attraction I was gunning for. Phil had already learned about my ideas from Patrick, and when we met, Phil immediately knew how to create what I could only imagine in story and format. He struck me as very confident in his creative imagination, his focus on the story above all else, and his use of multimedia technologies. Phil had a 14-year career as Vice President and creative designer for many of the world-class attractions at Universal Studios. Universal theme park rides were not exactly the normal models for a serious history museum show. However, I had been on those rides with my kids and seen how technology could transport the visitor through sensory and emotional experiences. Harking back to my meeting with Hanks, I told Phil that I believed there was a fine line for a history show to use new technologies while preserving the authenticity of historical content. Phil was brilliant on that score. His father was a B-17 pilot in World War II, and he would never approve of anything that diminished the seriousness and meaning of his father's experience in the war. That was the perfect response. Phil understood our desire to capture the drama of the war and our commitment to historical accuracy. He also understood how to convey emotional meaning and my desire to elevate the strength of the American Spirit in the story with personal accounts. The next step was for him to develop a conceptual proposal with estimated costs.

By the time we finished the Master Plan for The National WWII Museum expansion in late 2003, Phil gave a full presentation in the Museum's Purple Heart Conference room with all senior staff in attendance. Phil was at his best. It was a breathtaking proposal with a sweeping storyline of the war. Phil began the story with the origins of World War II, the Depression in America, and isolationists in American business and government, with our military totally unprepared for a global conflict. Then, with creative use of a digital spinning globe, historical film footage, a B-17 bursting through the screen, animations of firebombing of Japan, all linked to personal accounts, Phil gave us a taste of how a 4D experience would dramatize the story and the visitor experience in ways never done before on such a scale in a theater. I finally understood how Phil achieved 3D effects without special glasses. He used multiplane screens (the 120-foot-long primary screen placed a foot in front of secondary screen) with 21 advanced projectors and lighting that allowed visitors to occasionally see through the primary screen and be drawn into the middle of wartime environments illuminated on the rear screen. The 4D effect, as Phil explained, was the Fourth Dimension, the sensory realm that engaged visitors through the introduction of the smell of cordite from gunpowder, touch of snow falling on visitors in the wintry Battle of the Bulge, motion of seats that shook as tanks rumbled over the full screen and the sensation of wind blowing in the theater at certain points of the show. There would be a wartime radio on stage to broadcast news, machine gun turrets and a guard tower of a concentration camp, rising from sunken pits before the audience.

Phil's team proposed to tell the story that we historians would provide for their script writers, an impressionistic story of America's journey through the war. He gave a glimpse of how technology would blend seamlessly with archival images, sound, music, and sensory experiences to simulate battles, events, and personal experiences of troops fighting in the trenches, the ships, jungles, and planes. Visitors, Phil said, would both understand and feel the scale and power of the military campaigns as well as moments of personal trauma of the war taken from our oral accounts that are woven into the story. While this conceptual idea came from me and Phil's excellent writer, Chris Ellis, Phil said he would look to the Museum curators and our WWII historians to authenticate every frame of the show.

Phil's presentation was astonishing. We all stood and cheered at the end. Of course, we had many questions, especially about length, cost, and the mysteries of how these exotic technologies could work. Our initial budget for the show was only $6 million, plus another $25–$30 million for the custom-designed theater, and he thought he could work with that until we determined the length of the show. We finally agreed to a contract for $9 million and began to exchange the draft outlines of scripts to flesh out different approaches to the story. I flew to Pasadena with Bob Farnsworth on several occasions in 2004–5, before Katrina, to understand how the show and technology could work together in very Rube Goldberg–type presentations in an empty theater. It was still much of a mystery to me, but I had ultimate faith in Phil's cinematic experience and his deep appreciation of the story. In almost any field of professional competence, I could usually probe the confidence and depth of expertise of talented people who could do what they promise. Phil was one of those rare talents who was instrumental in our success in those early years.

Progress on the concept development with Phil slowed down in 2003–5, as we were building the new national board of trustees, starting a new capital campaign, pushing Congress for The National WWII Museum designation, and leading the 60th anniversary D-Day cruise to Normandy in 2004. And there were issues to be worked out with Hettema on the length of the script and the historical story line. It was an interactive process that took time. We needed board involvement, given the cost of the theater and the film, so I asked Boysie to appoint Trustee T. G. "Teddy" Solomon, our "Mr. Hollywood," to chair the task force with me and a few select trustees to oversee the project. My job was to put flesh on the bones of any historical concept as outlined a few years earlier to Hanks. Phil relied on his historians and writers on staff to initiate some conceptual outlines to link any historical themes to the larger story, but the early content was too historically dense for an impressionistic treatment in an hour, much less 20 minutes. In addition to my own ideas, I consulted with historian friends to help define the broad themes and historical beats of the WWII story. Phil developed several mockups for review in his Pasadena offices, and I flew to Santa Monica to meet with Tom Hanks to gauge his continuing involvement in the project. I also wanted to meet with Phil and discuss the emerging history outline. The first meeting, joined by Teddy Solomon, was encouraging: Tom offered good ideas on the WWII story line and agreed to help. I asked Hanks if he would narrate the final show. He agreed but said it was far too early to think about narrators. Instead, he suggested that we use the words of combat journalists or broadcasters, like Edward R. Morrow and Ernie Pyle, who could keep the story in the present tense. It was a brilliant suggestion, exactly the sort of insight I had hoped to gain from Tom. Phil and our team began to look for journalists and personal accounts from our oral histories to see if we could stitch the larger narrative together with their recordings or accounts of the key moments in the war.

Later, in early 2005, Phil met us at Hanks's Playtone offices in Santa Monica to review some of his ideas with T. G. Of course, anything visual was on a flat screen, not multiscreen panels with depth, so it took some imagination, but the presentation was nevertheless disappointing. All of us agreed it was too historically dense and needed a much more impressionistic approach to the history, so we went back to the drawing boards. Then Katrina hit, and, while Phil gave us a sketch of the concept as it stood after the storm in October 2005, he was still stuck on a 20-minute format with no progress until late 2006.

Hugh Ambrose, Bob Farnsworth, and I were reviewing multiple draft scripts of varying length without much satisfaction. Phil always thought we were at final script, and I kept making revisions and pushing for a longer show of 45 to 50 minutes. The bones of the story were emerging, but they were not hanging together. At this point in 2007, I once again called Don Miller for reinforcements. Don had also written American history scripts and helped produce dozens of documentaries on World War II for WGBH-TV in Boston, as well as for the History Channel. Don was just who I needed for sound historical judgment combined with script-writing ability, a gift not found in many historians. By 2008 we had already reviewed some 12 to 15 scripts when Don suggested the hinge of the story should come when the tide turned in favor of the Allies for the first time since the war began—during three weeks of 1944. These were the deciding battles: the D-Day Normandy landings on June 6, the Allied seizure of Rome on June 4, and the landings on the island of Saipan in the Pacific on June 15. Don and I won Phil's agreement to incorporate the war's turning point into another draft script. Phil soon felt confident enough for us to invite Tom Hanks to join us at Phil's offices in Pasadena to finalize the script in the summer of 2008. On paper, I still felt the show was too short and compressed, at 24 minutes, to reflect an authentic account, but Phil assured me that his visuals and media would help bring it together and that Tom could help put on the finishing touches.

We arrived in Pasadena in the early evening in time for Don, Hugh, Bob, and me to preview the latest draft script before the full working session with Tom the next morning. To our dismay, our viewing of the narrated show with the visuals was a disaster. The images made it clear that we did not have a compelling story; it was too dense and compressed. We needed a longer script that was allowed to breathe. It was going to take a lot of work, not just "finishing touches." We spent the evening debating whether to waste Tom's time by coming in to look at something still so rough. Phil called us at the hotel at midnight strongly urging us to cancel Tom's visit. I decided to go ahead despite the deeply flawed script and visual presentation. I reasoned this was exactly the situation that called for Hanks's expert, independent advice. We were also under the gun. We needed to get into production in the coming months, and we were still unsure of how major elements of the story could be told. This was mission critical. We could not complete Voorsanger's construction documents for the building, or the technology embedded in theater design, until we had resolution on a solid script linked to the supporting visuals and physical objects. We were floundering and needed fresh advice, and Tom was the best and most trusted source I knew.

Tom arrived promptly at 9:00 a.m. the next morning. Phil and the Hettema managers plus our Museum team were all there. Before we began, I decided I had to brief Tom on the situation. Instead of my promise of a nearly finished script, I confessed that we almost canceled the meeting because the script and visual supports were in such bad shape. I told him the historical content was far too heavy and dense, that it was our opinion that the short 24-minute script could not resolve those issues. "It's a mess, and we need your help right now if we are going to get a show ready for opening in fall of 2009," I told Tom. To my great relief, Tom started to roll up his sleeves, and said, "Let's get to work and fix this." The next four hours were the turning point in our entire script and show development. We cut, slashed, trimmed, and added fresh content to the script. By the end of the session, we had a longer show outline that had breathing room—preserving the epic narrative I had outlined to Tom six years earlier. We shied away from American bravado and instead simply told the dramatic history with heart and meaning, a story that would make Americans feel justly proud of how our country rallied, fought, and helped win an existential war that saved our freedom. Tom Hanks made all the difference in the outcome that day. He provided the creative and artistic insights, deep experience, and production knowledge that allowed us to shape a credible, crisp, and compelling draft outline.

With Tom's thumb on the scale, Phil finally agreed to the longer version of the script, but said he needed several million more than his contract provided to produce a longer show. I did not have the money in the budget, but the clock was ticking and said I would find the money. I was ready to do whatever was necessary to produce a show that met my expectations for quality, authenticity, and impact.

In that meeting we also settled the question of the show's narration. It became clear that our selections of war correspondents' reports could not carry the story without a common narrator to link them to our other veteran accounts and the larger themes. Luckily, Tom agreed to provide the narration to tie them all together from the pre-show to the larger format show. This was a huge contribution. There were 25 eyewitness accounts from veterans and correspondents that were already integrated into the new story. Tom also stressed the importance of finding top film actors on the younger side, closer to the age of the 18-year-old veterans and combat journalists, to read their first-person accounts of the battles and campaigns as these eyewitnesses experienced them. "It would lend authenticity and drama," he said. He immediately proposed Gary Sinise to portray Ernie Pyle. Tom then offered to recruit another 10 or 12 actors to voice the different veteran accounts. We would find the rest, he suggested. Tom never asked for any compensation for himself for the entire project over four years of intermittent work. He also promised to attend the premiere of the show and the grand opening.

We believed we were at the turning point in the making of *Beyond All Boundaries.* There were another 18 months of work led by the Hettema team on the creative production and direction, while I worked with Don, Hugh, Bob, and Tom on distilling the key historical moments.

In the final production stages, Phil designed and built extraordinary sets with multiple screens, along with environments between screens. He designed moving elements within and in front of the screens—all controlled by computers. He oversaw the recording of an original orchestral soundtrack to surround the visitors within the entire multisensory 4D experience. For the role of director, Phil hired David Briggs, an amazing script writer who took the lead on fine-tuning the final script for the last year of production. Don, Tom, and I labored over each new draft in the closing months, right up to the final recordings. Tom brought so much to the final script revision that we insisted he be listed as the executive producer of the show, not that he needed the credit. He understood his name would add credibility and market appeal to the show, so he agreed. But we all felt he would never have agreed to narrate and advertise his name as executive producer if he were not proud of what was emerging in the final production.

ROAD HOME TO OPENING: GETTING OFF THE FISCAL CLIFF

Finally, by the summer of 2008, Becky Mackie, who at that time was our Chief Financial Officer, figured out the complex financing mechanisms to use tax credits to secure $10 million of the funds needed to supplement some private funds and the $26 million in state funds from Governor Blanco and her successor, Bobby Jindal, to assure construction of the theater and production of *Beyond All Boundaries.*[35] By then, the total project cost had grown to $58 million and we were still some $15 million short of funds to complete the Stage Door Canteen, and the American Sector Restaurant.[36] Nevertheless, we were close enough and I authorized Bob Farnsworth to keep those latter projects moving with the expectation that we would find the funds in time to meet our new opening date of November 9, 2009. By then, Phil Satre would be our new Chairman, bringing great leadership skills to the race to complete the fundraising. It was going to be a cliffhanger, not unlike the last 18 months before we opened the D-Day Museum on June 6, 2000.

It was not until the summer of 2009, as we were closing in on the opening date of November 9, 2009, that we had two major breakthroughs on the funding for our new complex. On the private side, T. G. Solomon and his family had been considering a $5 million donation for naming rights to the theater.[37] He was a natural choice, given his deep involvement on behalf of our film and in the theater industry. Our Vice President for Institutional Advancement, Alma Jane Shephard, had been working with his sons, Gary and Glenn Solomon, to persuade all the others in the family. And as a close friend of 30 years, I had been urging T. G. and his family to make this gift. I pointed out to his children that the donation would honor their father for all he had done for the community, serve as a tribute to his WWII service, and establish a legacy for his distinguished career in the theater business and this Museum. Alma and I pressed them as it was getting late in the construction to put the Solomon name on the building façade, but at the last minute the entire family agreed. The generosity of Teddy and his family was crucial to the completion of the Solomon Victory Theater and assured that the opening would be a major celebrity event.

The second breakthrough was the work of former board Chairman David Voelker, who was now Chairman of the Louisiana Recovery Authority Board (LRA). As he promised me several years earlier, he identified some LRA funds dedicated to economic development and invited me to make a presentation requesting funds at an LRA board meeting in Baton Rouge in August. He said to ask for what we needed: $10 million. "Pull out all the stops; bring the troops," David told me. "You will have 20 minutes." I did what he asked. We bussed in 60 Museum volunteers, who were mostly WWII veterans and Higgins Industries workers. We also flew in Medal of Honor Recipient Walt Ehlers from California. Phil Satre arrived from Nevada just in time for the presentation. The volunteers crowded into the small board room, cheering and wearing construction hard hats. Phil stepped up to the podium and delivered a paramount justification for receiving LRA funds. He reiterated that the Museum had an impeccable record of keeping its commitments to "invest the financial support of private donors and public financial support prudently, responsibly, and as promised."[38] His argument carried weight, as he was the CEO of a major entertainment company. After Phil, I made the case for the economic impact of the Solomon Victory Theater, *Beyond All Boundaries,* and the related canteen and restaurant. I promised a spectacular opening and presented marketing data on the predicted influx of tourists who would respond to the new attraction. Walt Ehlers was the closer. Once he started talking about his harrowing D-Day landing and the tragic loss of his brother on that day, you could hear a pin drop. We were there for an hour longer than the 20 minutes David gave us. It was one of those memorable moments. The board voted to grant us the $10 million we needed for the final funding of the entire complex in time for our opening in November. This was another poignant example of the way the unlikely story of The National WWII Museum came about—it was personal, it took persistence and contributions from volunteers, and veterans, along with Museum and state leaders who recognized the importance of saving that history.

RUN-UP TO THE GRAND OPENING

We could not wait to see the full production of *Beyond All Boundaries* in the Solomon Victory Theater, the only place where the technology, physical elements, and integration of multiple screens could be brought together with the dramatic imagery and narrative voices. Computers and custom software drove the entire show with the turn of a switch. It could not be shown anywhere else. At the same time, all the other actors from around the country were in recording studios reading the personal accounts of veterans and correspondents. With Tom's help, we had landed a glittering group of celebrity movie stars to read the gripping stories embedded in the show. Among them were Voila Davis, Brad Pitt, Elijah Wood, John Goodman, Patricia Clarkson, Tobey Maguire, Gary Sinise, Neil Patrick Harris, Kevin Bacon, and Wendell Pierce.

Everything was coming together in the final months before the grand opening and excitement was building, especially mine. The opening was gaining traction in the media as well, and feverish work was going on in every part of the building as we raced to November 9, 2009. Phil Hettema was on site for six weeks installing the film. After a few weeks of fine-tuning all the moving parts, our senior staff got to watch the first preview of the show in early October. It is impossible to describe the impact of the full presentation in the 250-seat theater with all the special sensory effects before the 120-foot-wide screen. It was stunning, historically authentic, and visually arresting. Parts were difficult to watch, with the roar of battles and the fear generated by the concentration camp scenes, as well as tanks and planes bursting through the screen in full 4D. Soaring symphony music with the surround sound and lighting rose to a majestic climax, as the young soldiers transformed into aging men of the greatest generation giving their last salute to the audience. It brought tears to my eyes. From my conception of the idea to execution had taken seven years, survived the devastation of Katrina, and multiple production, funding, and writing challenges. I was both relieved and confident that *Beyond All Boundaries* would rank among the greatest media presentations on World War II of any museum in the world.

SOLOMON VICTORY THEATER GRAND OPENING

We kicked off the ceremonies with a private premiere of the film on the evening of November 5, 2009. The night was a wonderful, star-studded event that featured several cast members from the film, including Patricia Clarkson and James Cromwell, local and national politicians, several WWII veterans, and special guests Tom Hanks and Tom Brokaw. I waited outside the theater doors as the audience spilled out of the show, and I was relieved to hear the emotional responses from veterans who said, "You got it right, Doc." Then out came Tom Brokaw, who sat down on the bench in the lobby. "I'm overwhelmed," he said. "It was stunning and true to the memory and sacrifice of the Greatest Generation. Everyone in America should see it." We both agreed that Steve Ambrose would be so proud and amazed. The rave reviews kept coming. It was truly a wonderful moment for me personally and for all who had worked so long to tell the World War II story in this amazing format. Tom Hanks felt the same. He later told the press that after seeing "every mock version . . . to finally see it fill up the space was great."[39]

The next day we held the ribbon cutting ceremony for the theater complex and hosted the official premiere of *Beyond All Boundaries* for donors and invited guests. The day was jam-packed with events to commemorate the ribbon cutting. The dedication event that morning was filled with moving words from Museum leadership, highlighting the challenges and successes in the great leap from D-Day to The National WWII Museum. Perhaps no words were more poignant than those of Stephenie Ambrose-Tubbs, Steve's daughter and a historian herself, who recalled how her father would ask that the servicemen and women of World War II stand to be recognized in nearly every audience he encountered. "For us, his children, that is the legacy of this Museum," she said. "History lives on, respect will be paid; and the stories, however painful, will be shared."[40]

The highlight of the ribbon cutting was the tribute to our guests of honor: 350 WWII veterans from all service branches and all theaters, plus 150 active-duty members of the military.[41] We opened the Stage Door Canteen and the American Sector Restaurant, both offering more options for food, beverages, and live entertainment. After visitors experienced the intense and emotional *Beyond All Boundaries* for the first time, they were treated to more light-hearted entertainment in the Stage Door Canteen. We designed it as a USO-style venue to present live 1940s musical performances with educational programming and other public functions. Our own Victory Belles got a new venue, where they covered WWII–era song and dance acts, such as the Andrews Sisters, Bob Hope, and other entertainers who boosted troop morale in World War II. Our new restaurant, the American Sector, adjacent to the Stage Door Canteen, gave a nostalgic nod to the past by offering more modern takes on classic Americana dishes. We hoped that with these nostalgic additions, members of the WWII generation could be transported back to their youth, while younger generations might experience these cultural touchstones for the first time. When crowds experienced all these new amenities that opening weekend, it was a proud moment for all of us who helped design and build them.

The opening gave credence to our reasons to build the Museum in New Orleans, and it was testimony to how New Orleanians remained resilient in the face of the near total destruction of their beloved city. It was an exceedingly difficult road that New Orleans had to tread after Katrina, one full of suffering and hardship for so many. If our Museum played a part in reviving this tough old city, then this project meant so much more than what Steve and I ever imagined 19 years prior.

We exceeded all expectations for the impact of the opening of The National WWII Museum and new attractions. *Beyond All Boundaries* became an immediate sensation. The show played every hour of the day to a full house. Visitation to the Museum skyrocketed. We heard from visitors and hospitality leaders that people were coming to New Orleans specifically to see *Beyond All Boundaries;* it was a "destination" attraction. The tremendous increase in visitation exceeded every previous benchmark. With the healing tourism industry in New Orleans and improving visitation numbers, the future looked bright once again.

We knew, however, that we could not be complacent. I had learned several lessons during our Katrina ordeal. First, I especially learned the importance of perseverance and sticking to our mission and a solid Master Plan, albeit with some modifications. Second, I learned how the Katrina disaster brought out the best of the leadership of our board and staff in our survival decisions and our commitment to pursue the Museum mission and vision for the future. Third, I learned that we had friends and supporters in Louisiana and around America who wanted to help us succeed and believed in the Museum and the importance of the WWII story we were telling. Fourth, I learned that the diversification of our revenues beyond visitation saved us: the spectrum of funding from national membership, retail sales, D-Day tours, grants, reserves, and donor pledges kept our heads above water just long enough in those critical early months and years. Finally, I relearned an old lesson: the Museum had to invest more in historians, educators, curators, and technologies that would support distance learning and public access to the Museum's growing educational resources.

As the Museum regained a healthy attendance and financial footing, I charged our board to envision a national campus that was available to a wider public. I wanted visitors to have access to WWII content and research from our historians and curators, aided by advanced digital technologies, both on and off site. It was my firm belief that we could not fulfill the Museum's educational mission by relying solely on visitors who came to see our exhibits. Interest in WWII history far exceeded the number of visitors who could come to New Orleans to the Museum. We now had to think of the Museum as a global leader in education on World War II, for a vast audience of enthusiasts as well as for higher education and K–12 teachers and students. I began to speak to Chairman Satre and other trustees about creating a task force to explore opportunities in higher learning, on site and off site, which might even include online graduate degrees in WWII Studies, as well as research, popular history publications, and digital resources for teachers and students across the nation. On a smaller scale, this was foreseen in the original CSAS, even before Steve died. Now, with Katrina behind us, those early ideas gained clarity and force. As we moved forward, the Museum staff and board were ready to explore these new opportunities to expand our Master Plan, once again—this time, beyond the boundaries of our physical campus.

As we entered 2010, there was a mountain of work ahead. We enjoyed a moment to revel in our accomplishments; we had taken a hard punch from Katrina, beaten the odds, and were stronger for it. But the road ahead was steep. The Master Plan called for four more major pavilions, including the US Freedom Pavilion with macro artifacts, a Campaigns Pavilion with the *Road to Berlin* and *Road to Tokyo* exhibits, and in the Louisiana Memorial Pavilion, the addition of the new Home Front exhibits called *The Arsenal of Democracy*. Our Master Plan also called for a hotel and conference center, a Hall of Democracy for a research center staffed by WWII historians, a Special Exhibit Hall, the Canopy of Peace over the campus, and the Liberation Pavilion to portray the legacy of the war through the victory and peace that followed.

The official goal of the board was to raise enough funds to have this all completed by 2015. A new plan was put forth to pursue our immediate goal of constructing the US Freedom Pavilion. This magnificent pavilion would house iconic large artifacts from various air, land, and sea campaigns alongside personal stories that revealed the meaning of these relics. Our plan envisioned an architectural structure of significance, and its size and volume meant we needed at least $25 million to build it.

At the same time, as we basked in the exhilaration of the grand opening of the Solomon Victory Theater, we understood the country had been in the grips of a deep economic recession since 2008. Hank Greenberg and John Whitehead, our major donor friends in New York, told Pete Wilson and me that this was not a time to ask corporations and foundations for money. The stock market had dropped like a stone and fortunes were lost. Their advice: "Keep coming to visit, tell corporate leaders and foundations of your progress, but don't ask for money now; just remind them of your mission and vision and hopes for future support." That was sobering news that underscored the dim prospects of raising significant funds from the private sector. We had new momentum, and the state had done its part. Now the Museum's best chance for funds to build the US Freedom Pavilion rested with our friends in Congress.

10

SURGING FORWARD

How the Museum Remembers

LOOKING BACK, ONE would never guess that the funeral services for Sen. Edward Kennedy in Boston in late August 2009 would impact the future course of the Museum, but it did. Almost every US Senator was in attendance, including Daniel Inouye, one of the Museum's patron saints, and one of the last WWII veterans serving in Congress. With the Democrats in the majority in Congress, Inouye had become Chair of the Senate Appropriations Committee and served as chair of its Defense Appropriations Subcommittee. He was our last best hope for a major earmark in the defense bill that fall.

With everything on track to open the Museum's first major expansion in November, Pete Wilson and I had agreed over the summer that we needed to make an urgent appeal for a $25 million defense appropriation to fund the US Freedom Pavilion, the next major building in our Master Plan. The request was huge, but I worked with the staffs of Inouye and Mary Landrieu all summer to arrange a meeting with Inouye before the Defense Appropriations Subcommittee met on September 10, 2009. The Senator agreed to meet with us on September 9 to hear our proposal. Just before Kennedy's memorial service, I was notified that the subcommittee meeting had been moved up to the day before our scheduled meeting with Inouye, which would be too late to get a Museum earmark of that amount into the bill. By rule, if you were not in the bill when it went to the committee, you were dead in the water for that year.

This was a crisis. All our work would be for naught. There was no one around in Senator Inouye's office to change our meeting time. Everyone with the authority to adjust his calendar was either in Boston or out for Labor Day weekend. I was desperate. I had pulled in every chit I had to get that meeting before the Defense Appropriations Subcommittee meeting. My heart sank as I watched Kennedy's services on television and saw Senator Inouye and his wife, Irene Hirano, sitting in the front row. Over the summer, I had enlisted David Voelker and Pete Wilson to fly in to attend this all-important meeting in Washington, DC, with Inouye and Landrieu. Our pro bono legislative consultants, Paul Cambon and Dick Egle, were also coming. Everything was teed up, except now the scheduled meeting would be too late.

I knew only one person who could reach the Senator in Boston, and that was his wife, Irene. She and I became friends in the years before she married the Senator, when she was Director of the Japanese American National Museum in Los Angeles. We shared a mutual interest in portraying the shameful story of America's incarceration of Japanese Americans during World War II, and I regarded Irene as one of the most influential leaders in American history museums. We stayed in touch after she married Senator Inouye, and now she was my only hope. With the memorial services underway, the timing was terrible, but I sent Irene an email explaining my plight. I asked if she could speak to the Senator about moving our meeting up on his calendar to the evening before the Defense Appropriations Committee meeting. She did it. I was quickly notified we would have our meeting with Senators Inouye and Landrieu on Monday, September 7. This was yet another instance when the fate of the Museum hinged on a personal relationship.

We were ready for the decisive meeting with the Senators. The Museum had not received an appropriation from Congress since 2003, and this meeting felt like our last big chance for a federal grant to motivate state and private donations in order to move forward with our expansion. I asked our architects at Voorsanger Mathes and our exhibit design firm, Gallagher & Associates, to greatly enlarge the land, sea, and air pavilion to create an imposing architectural structure to justify the federal funding. The plans included a 75-foot floor-to-ceiling glass wall, which allowed for awe-inspiring views of interior spaces from outside from the Col. Battle Barksdale Parade Ground. With a large, open floor plan, the pavilion was designed to showcase each military service's iconic weapons of war from American industry, including aircraft and large vehicles, with stories that highlighted how these weapons helped win the war. I also instructed architects and exhibitors to design the building so that it could host large public programs with technology capable of video streaming events across the country. We planned exhibits and macro artifacts to recognize Medal of Honor recipients, to represent every theater of the war, and to honor all WWII veterans who went on to be leaders in public service. We designed it to be a stunning national tribute to our veterans in Congress who returned home to serve their country in government. We estimated the construction cost alone to be around $33 million, and the pavilion could not be built in phases. A large federal appropriation was crucial to getting it built.

We gathered in Inouye's large conference room around 6 p.m. on September 7. The tension was palpable. Our plan was for me to make the initial presentation and the request for a $25 million appropriation, acknowledging that this was a huge ask, but reminding the Senator we were about to open the Solomon Victory Theater. Although the state and private sector had raised just over $60 million for that current phase, we could go no further on the US Freedom Pavilion without this Congressional appropriation.[1] Landrieu warned us that there was sure to be pushback from Inouye for a request this big, so I asked Pete Wilson, Inouye's former Senate colleague, to make the final close for our request, Senator to Senator and veteran to veteran.

The room was packed with at least 30 Senate staffers, along with Voelker, Wilson, our consultants, and me. The greetings were amiable, though the large number of their people in the room heightened the atmosphere of anticipation. Landrieu made sure that all the key staff appropriators were there to field every question on the spot. I opened my pitch as planned, and Inouye listened intently. "We recognize we are coming with an enormous request of $25 million that exceeds the bounds of a normal earmark," I said, "but if anyone in Congress can make it happen, you as a decorated WWII veteran and senior Senator from Hawaii are our best hope." I made the case that the pavilion would recognize the tremendous contributions of American industry, technology, and engineering to the war effort. I stressed the urgency of our request with the dwindling of the WWII generation. I also noted that the pavilion would accommodate all the Medal of Honor recipients of World War II. I further emphasized that only this federal funding could enable us to build the entire structure, while private donations could support the exhibits and the acquisition of aircraft and macro artifacts.

The future of the US Freedom Pavilion hung in the balance as we awaited Inouye's response. "I don't know if we can do it," he said. "I know you need it, but I don't know if we can do that much money." This was the critical moment. Pete stood up and walked over to his side and spoke directly to Inouye. "Danny, you're a Medal of Honor recipient," Pete said. "You served, you were wounded, you're one of the last World War II veterans [in Congress]. You are the Chair of the Defense Appropriations Committee. If not you, who? If not now, when?" With those words, Inouye paused, rolled his eyes, and then looked directly at Landrieu. "Okay, Mary, I'll put forward $5 million," he said. "What can you do?" Landrieu looked to her staff members to find out how much she had left in her defense allocation, and they said $13 million. "Well, I will put it all in,"[2] she told him. "That's $18 million," Inouye said. He then added a stipulation that we had to secure support from the Republican Senator from Louisiana, David Vitter, for the remaining $7 million to display bipartisan support. "It is all or nothing," said Inouye. He did not want any pushback from the other side of the aisle for such a large and visible earmark. He said we had until midnight to persuade Vitter to provide the remaining sum and to send word to Inouye's staff upon agreement. We left Inouye's office elated but began a frenzied evening burning up our cellphones trying to reach Vitter, to no avail. We called Boysie, who luckily found him at a banquet. After speaking with Boysie, Vitter put Zak Baig, his Legislative Director, in touch with us, and Pete Wilson and I debated with him late into the evening. Vitter's staffers were afraid we were "setting them up" with an embarrassing earmark, but just minutes before midnight Zak agreed, and we sent the news to Inouye's office with seconds to spare.

It was a huge victory. I'd never been through such an intense six hours when the fate of the Museum's future expansion hung in the balance. The $25 million appropriation passed the committee the next morning, but it was reduced by $5 million a few months later when the House reconciled the bill.[3] This was enough to ensure the pavilion construction could move forward. In my memory, this was the pivotal point to sustaining momentum for the Museum's expansion. The state of Louisiana helped pull us through the Katrina years with huge support for the Solomon Victory Theater and related attractions. However, the private sector was reeling from the 2008 recession, and we could have easily run out of gas in 2010, settling in for a long, slow grind to fund the new pavilions that were already on the drawing board. This appropriation assured us we could open our US Freedom Pavilion by 2013, and design plans could proceed for future pavilions along with the funds to acquire artifacts to fill them.

Soon after the appropriation, we launched a full-court press for a multimillion-dollar gift from the Boeing Company to help us add a B-17 Flying Fortress and to secure the remaining funding for the US Freedom Pavilion. We had to move fast in 2010, as we had nearly finished the construction documents to accommodate five iconic aircraft in the pavilion, and we would need to raise the roof by 15 feet to create space to hang a B-17, the most famous Boeing bomber. The building foundation would need to be strengthened, as would the roof and ceiling structures. A B-17 weighed over 30,000 pounds, and a plane that heavy had never been suspended in the air before; moreover, the roof structure would also have to carry the weight of all the other aircraft. Pete and I had been cultivating Boeing for a major gift for some time, and we invited two top Boeing executives, Rick Stephens, Vice President of Human Resources, and Dennis Muilenburg, President and CEO of Boeing Defense Space & Security, to visit the Museum. Muilenburg was a promising candidate to become Boeing's next CEO after the eventual retirement of current Chairman and CEO James McNerney Jr. With these powerful executives coming to New Orleans, this was our best shot.

Before the visit with the Boeing executives, I asked Scott Evans with Voorsanger Mathes to calculate the costs of making significant architectural changes to the building in order to accommodate the aircraft. I also asked him to create a presentation for the Boeing executives, showing our existing five aircraft hanging inside the pavilion, and a new version showing the pavilion with the roof raised by 15 feet and the B-17 Flying Fortress hanging from the ceiling. We calculated it would take another $6 million for the taller building, plus the cost of the plane. We were well prepared for the visit, but I was nervous about the size of our gift request, which I pegged at $10 million. I consulted Patrick Gallagher the day before, as I always trusted him for sound advice on big fundraising and design decisions. He asked me: "Nick, what do you need?" I said $10 million would cover the minimum added costs, but Patrick said, "Ask for $15 million. Boeing is doing well, and that number should be acceptable to them if they want to do it." So that was my new number. The pressure increased, but I was ready to swing for the fences.

After Stephens and Muilenburg viewed *Beyond All Boundaries* and toured our D-Day exhibits, we rendezvoused with Patrick and Scott, as well as Bob

Farnsworth, Stephen Watson, and a few of our senior staff. We gave the presentation, which dramatized the taller structure with the suspended B-17. We showed angles from the high catwalks and from the parade ground through a 90-foot-high glass wall. It was stunningly beautiful. I also spoke about the $20 million Department of Defense grant appropriated by our champions in Congress, including Senator Inouye and recently retired Ted Stevens. Muilenburg and Stephens remarked that the significance of such support "is not lost on us."

In the end I summoned up all my courage and boldly asked for a gift of $15 million. I promised that a gift of that magnitude would cover the costs of raising the building height and restoring a B-17, which we had reserved in California pending their gift. I was relieved that they both expressed enthusiasm for the proposal and accepted my calculations for the funds requested. They did not say no immediately. I was impressed by their appreciation and their pride in Boeing's contribution to the war effort. They understood that The National WWII Museum and Boeing both would benefit by having the most iconic bomber of World War II hanging in the Museum. I stressed this was our last chance to quickly redesign the pavilion from the ground up and get the B-17 under contract for restoration to stay on schedule for opening by 2013. Without the gift from Boeing, we would not have the funds to move forward with the changes, so I said I could only give them 30 days to reply, or we would have to stick to our original plan, which did not include the B-17. That was the hardest part of the request. I had never asked for that much money and never dreamed of putting such a hard deadline for a major corporation to decide. But these were power hitters with Boeing, and, if anyone could do it, they could. In any event, I had little choice.

Everyone at the Museum was on pins and needles as the 30-day deadline approached. I spoke to Brokaw after our presentation with Boeing, and he offered to help with CEO McNerney. I called Tom again in the last days before the deadline to remind him of his offer. Lady Luck must have been smiling on us. "Great that you called to remind me, Nick," Tom said. "Coincidentally, I'm having breakfast with McNerney in the morning and will push him to support your request." As I heard later, the meeting to decide on our request was the next day at Boeing headquarters in Chicago. According to Rick Stephens, McNerney burst into the room and exclaimed, "What's this I hear from Brokaw that we may be giving $15 million to the WWII Museum in New Orleans?" Stephens recalled that "We all smiled and said, 'That's right, it's a great opportunity, the Museum is getting a B-17 and naming the building, the US Freedom Pavilion: The Boeing Center. We are all supportive.'" McNerney agreed, and a few minutes later I got the call from Stephens to say it was a yes! You could have scraped me off the ceiling.

There was one big problem: We did not have a B-17 yet. Stephen Watson, who had assumed responsibility to oversee the purchase and restoration of the bomber, had connected with a vintage aircraft collector in California who had assembled what looked like an old plane graveyard in Los Angeles. He had already delivered a restored B-25 for the pavilion, so we trusted him. The collector said he had a B-17 he could restore within our budget parameters of $3–$4 million within two years. He also offered us a TBM Avenger, a P-40 Warhawk, and a P-51 Mustang. All those aircraft would be valuable additions to our collections, so we agreed to have the collector restore them and sell them to us.

The offer was exciting, but when Stephen Watson and Tom Czekanski, our Director of Collections, went to California to check on the planes, they found a disaster. The B-17 consisted of little more than a fuselage and some assorted parts, including half of one wing, which was held in the backyard of a rental property in Los Angeles. The P-40 was essentially a few bits and pieces of metal from the fuselage with no engine, and the "P-51 Mustang" was only a box of parts the size of a footlocker stored in a garden shed. Stephen and Tom were absolutely shocked. Stephen called me with the bad news, and my heart sank. It got even worse. The next day, they headed down to San Diego, where the Avenger torpedo bomber was supposed to be under restoration by a volunteer crew with the USS Midway Museum, but Stephen and Tom found the work had stopped because of a lack of funding. When they checked on the B-17 fuselage, which was being restored by airplane salvage expert Gary Larkins, they learned that the job would require very extensive work. Stephen and Tom left California knowing they had no planes and little more than a derelict B-17 fuselage.

Back in New Orleans, Stephen provided funding to get the restorations back on track, and he and Tom took regular trips out west to keep a pulse on the projects. The Avenger was coming along well, with slow but steady progress by the USS *Midway* Museum team. However, Stephen received a grim report from Gary, who concluded that the B-17 fuselage was so cut up and damaged that there was no way it could be suspended in the air, which was the whole reason we were redesigning the US Freedom Pavilion. The news was devastating. Then, out of the blue came one of those miracles that happened so often in building this Museum. Stephen got another call from Gary, who heard from a Cincinnati businessman who had a restored B-17 that was about to lose its home.

Stephen, Tom, and Associate Vice President Owen Glendening immediately flew to Ohio to meet with Bob Ready, the owner of an international lighting company in Cincinnati. Stephen reported that the first meeting went well, so a few weeks later I flew with them to meet Bob and see the B-17 for myself. Bob recounted the amazing story of *My Gal Sal,* a B-17 that had been downed in a storm en route to England in 1942 and landed on an icecap in Greenland.[4] The plane was rediscovered in the 1960s and salvaged in 1995. Bob purchased it in 2000 and, along with his family and company volunteers, worked every weekend over 10 years to restore the plane to its original state. When we met him, he had *My Gal Sal* 95 percent restored and on display in a hangar at a private airport near Cincinnati. Bob was passionate about the plane and wanted to tell the heroic story of how the plane's crew was found and rescued, the plane's recovery, and his subsequent restoration of the aircraft. He had recently learned that the city of Cincinnati, which owned the airport property with the hangar and plane, decided to repurpose the property—meaning he needed to find a new home for *My Gal Sal.* After a one-hour meeting and a handshake, we had our B-17. The entire affair was a stroke of pure luck. Bob donated *My Gal Sal*—a restored plane worth at least $5 million—and only asked us to cover his $1.5 million of costs for parts and shipping. This was a huge relief. We all celebrated our angel from Cincinnati and the acquisition of the marvelous *My Gal Sal.* The plane was an extraordinary artifact with an amazing human-interest story.

We had our B-17, the Boeing executives were thrilled, and I breathed a huge sigh of relief. As work on the Avenger continued to progress, Stephen managed to get restoration underway on the Warhawk as well as on a P-51 Mustang that we acquired from a collector in Nashville. Stephen teamed up with Rolando Gutierrez, one of the USS *Midway* Museum volunteers, who proposed leasing a hangar in San Diego to set up a small restoration company working with a group of recently returned Iraq and Afghanistan veterans, who were getting their aircraft mechanic certifications from Miramar Community College. With our financial support, Rolando set up Flyboys

Aeroworks, which successfully restored the Warhawk and Mustang over the course of the next year. With his typical flair for finding solutions, Stephen helped them form a company that met their needs and solved our problem.

Now, all there was left to do was to get the restored planes to New Orleans, into the Pavilion, and hoisted into place. We hired professionals to lift the planes in place, one by one, to their positions 30 to 70 feet in the air. We had to hang them all in the span of 5 days between Christmas and New Year's Day, 2012, two weeks before the grand opening on January 12, 2013. One mistake would be a disaster. Years of work and millions of dollars could be lost in an instant. My heart was beating hard, especially while hoisting the B-17, which had to be raised initially with only half of one wing attached to get past the visitor catwalk halfway up. When they raised the 30,000-pound bomber the first five feet off the pavilion floor, the crane hydraulics stopped abruptly for a moment, as did my heart. The wing of the heavy plane bounced almost to the floor before the plane settled in her stirrups. Then she was hoisted until she cleared our 40-foot-high aerial catwalk. Hanging from the steel rafters, the crew rappelled down with the other half of the wing, which they attached to the B-17 in midair. We held our breath, but it all worked flawlessly. Once the B-17 was in place at the highest point in the pavilion, all the other planes were hung in sequence over a 24-hour period. Stephen, Tom Czekanski, Bob Ready, Rolando's team, and the professionals who lifted the planes were the heroes of the effort to secure and install these magnificent warbirds in time for our opening.

The US Freedom Pavilion: The Boeing Center was a brilliant new addition to the Museum's campus. Beyond the iconic aircraft and vehicles, visual displays on three enormous screens told the story and scale of America's industrial war production. The Medal of Honor exhibit included enlarged photos of every WWII recipient, with an interactive database to explore their valorous actions in combat. On the mezzanine level, oral histories and media tables enabled visitors to search through all the major campaigns and battles of the war.

The grand opening on January 12, 2013, was another spectacular event filled with WWII veterans, each escorted by schoolchildren to their reserved seats of honor. Sen. Mary Landrieu and Lt. Gov. Jay Dardenne were present, along with the Vice Presidents from Boeing. The two Senators primarily responsible for the pavilion, Daniel Inouye and Ted Stevens, had not lived to see its completion. Their widows, Irene Hirano Inouye and Catherine Stevens, were there to represent their husbands, our two magnificent champions. Inouye and Stevens, like Stephen Ambrose, were among those who had passed their torches to me and to future generations to sustain the vision of the Museum.

INTENSITY MOUNTS

We could scarcely rest on our laurels. Two major pavilions and the Canopy of Peace were still on the drawing board, plus a hotel and conference center we planned to build with a developer. The Campaigns of Courage Pavilion and *The Arsenal of Democracy* exhibits were up next, along with early design work on the Liberation Pavilion.

Visitation increased dramatically after the November 2009 opening of the Solomon Victory Theater. Group rentals also gained traction, along with tours, conferences, and educational programs. Everything was happening at once, so I had to restructure the Museum leadership team and bring on new positions in almost every department to keep up with the expansion rate. My crack leadership team now included Becky Mackie as VP and CFO; Stephen Watson, now promoted to VP and COO; Bob Farnsworth, Senior VP for Capital Projects; and Mike Carroll, our new VP for Institutional Advancement. By now I had come to know many Museum leaders across the country, and I believed that there was not a more entrepreneurial team of museum professionals in the nation.

I was fortunate to hire and retain such a loyal and extremely capable team of professionals who had a can-do spirit in service of the Museum. Our national membership grew exponentially under the leadership of Watson to around 150,000 from every state in the United States. *TripAdvisor* began ranking us annually as the number-one attraction in New Orleans. By 2013, it ranked us the number-seven most popular museum in the nation, and number 14 in the world.[5] These stunning numbers helped recruit a new class of distinguished trustees and bolster our private fundraising. Our 55-member board began to shoulder more responsibility in raising money for the Master Plan, including sponsorship funds for major Museum events held around the country. Equally important was support from the board for getting it right, the best that could be done, regardless of the cost. When asked to approve exhibit content and themes, the board members always asked important questions and openly debated the financial choices and historical authenticity but left the final decisions on design and how to tell the stories to me, our Museum team, and professional design consultants.

THE CRESCENDO

In the 1990s many skeptics doubted our ability to complete the D-Day Museum. Now, with three pavilions attracting audiences in droves and another pavilion under construction, the voices of skeptics were seldom heard. Our trustees, donors, and our government leaders in Louisiana began to share my confidence.

Between 2011 and 2013, the board approved an extraordinary expansion of the Master Plan, committing serious budgets to move forward with plans for the Campaigns of Courage exhibits, renovations to the Louisiana Memorial Pavilion, the Union Pacific Train Car experience, *The Arsenal of Democracy* exhibits, a Merchant Marine gallery, the Canopy of Peace, and the capstone Liberation Pavilion. Together, these projects would fulfill our commitment to tell the story of the American experience in World War II. By 2012, all were in some stages of early planning and exhibit design by Gallagher, our architects, staff, and consultants.

Planning, constructing, and designing multiple pavilions at the same time we hosted half a million visitors a year was complicated. It put constant pressure on the staff, the board, and me to plan, execute, and fundraise every day. Any single construction project or operations alone would have been more than enough for most nonprofit boards to oversee. On the operations front, our staff grew to over 200 employees to manage visitation and plan future programs.

To meet these challenges, the Museum undertook a crescendo of activities, planning, and studies in these years to sustain our momentum. Multiple planning groups of trustees, staff, and consultants engaged in converting our exhibit ideas from the 2004 Master Plan into solid exhibit treatments that could be defined with clear purpose, content, and costs. Fundraising for the capital campaign had to ramp up significantly. Private funds flowed a bit faster than earlier years, with nearly $10 million raised in 2012; further, the state of Louisiana committed $15 million over three years for new pavilions on the drawing board. Our board also maintained its national stature with the election of Dennis Muilenburg, future CEO of Boeing, as a member. The local trustees were so encouraged by our successes that even these expansive new plans seemed achievable, and, at the board meeting on June 9, 2012, we raised our capital campaign goal from $300 million to $325 million.[6]

By 2013, construction on the Campaigns of Courage exhibits was underway and scheduled to open in December 2014. We were out over our skis again. I told the board we needed another $10 million and needed it fast. The clock was ticking for a development and financing plan for the hotel and conference center to be built in the next 4 to 5 years. Even with the funding challenges for Campaigns of Courage, the board agreed to establish an ad-hoc committee led by John Koerner to explore size, feasibility, costs, and a developer for the hotel.[7] We had volunteers working on the restoration of a patrol torpedo boat, PT-305, originally built by Higgins Industries, to be commissioned for charter in Lake Pontchartrain. In a few years, we also planned to create a special permanent exhibit to house the most iconic WWII artifacts in our collection. For me, the most important task was the daunting intellectual effort to create the story narrative for all the WWII exhibits still to be designed in the core historical exhibits.

Looking back, choosing Bart Voorsanger's plan in 2003 to build the Museum one pavilion at a time was a godsend. Building in stages now allowed us to prioritize our planning according to the pavilions we had funds to build and to take our time with those that had a longer planning horizon. In 2012, we estimated that we would need $150 million to complete the rest of the Master Plan.[8] As challenging as this effort appeared to be at the time, I was confident that we would succeed, and I made a personal commitment to see these projects all completed or approved with most of the funding in place by 2018.

REACHING A GLOBAL AUDIENCE

By 2011 I believed it was time to engage our board in redefining the scope of our education futures, a process I began after recovering from Katrina. I was convinced we had to develop strategies for expanding education and outreach initiatives beyond the completion of the campus. We also needed to identify the costs and sources of revenue to support such a venture. The campus completion date was still years away, but any plans for investments in new educational technologies were going to take planning, time, and money. To launch the planning effort, I looked to longtime Trustee Herschel Abbott Jr., who had succeeded Phil Satre as Chairman in 2011.[9] When I proposed to Herschel that he chair a strategic planning task force of the board to explore our distance-learning opportunities, he readily agreed.

In the early 1990s, when Herschel was President of BellSouth Louisiana and I was UNO Vice Chancellor, we worked together to get a BellSouth grant to support a New Orleans universities and public-school endeavor to telecast live classroom instruction to students in their homes via dedicated television channels. Given Herschel's background and vision, he was the natural choice to lead this board task force.

We were behind the technology curve. All public and private television stations began converting to digital technologies in the 1990s; it was time for the Museum to make a similar push. With the board's approval, Herschel and I asked the task force to define the scope of a new plan to digitize all the Museum content and collections and integrate them with new digital platforms that would provide access to these learning resources for a global audience interested in WWII history. These goals were ambitious and went far beyond our 2003 Master Plan. Accordingly, the task force was charged with determining how we should fulfill one of the Museum's key vision statements: "To engage worldwide audiences by providing access to our collections, exhibits, and oral histories through creative museum experiences supported by innovative outreach, distance learning and new media relationships."[10]

The task force, which included trustees, consultants from the Smithsonian educational technologies division, and Ford Bell, the President of the American Alliance of Museums, was staffed by Stephen Watson and me.[11] Stephen was the driving force in preparing the meetings, leading national research on museum digitization projects, and supporting Herschel and me with the documentation and cost analysis needed for the final plan. Stephen's fine work clearly signaled to me and the board that he was destined for greater leadership responsibilities at the Museum.

The challenge was to define a scope that was suited to the Museum's vision and to identify the investment costs of implementation over a phase-in period of 10 years. It soon became clear that the costs of the scope were daunting; they were estimated at around $10 million. The Museum's collection was vast and growing, filled with images, oral histories, artifacts, and our storehouse of historical films. We had to assess how to make these educational resources available to anyone interested in World War II, either at the Museum or online. We also needed to invest in new infrastructure technologies to digitize our collection and then produce content and deliver or provide access to the digital media through every portal available to the Museum.

The plan presented to the board in December 2011 recommended approval of $10,000,000 to digitize most of the Museum's collection.[12] The organizing concept was to create a new program called Digital Archive Research Services (DARS), which was amusingly nicknamed "DARS-VADER" for the threatening challenge it presented to staff and board. The plan bore the characteristic entrepreneurial spirit of the Museum. The DARS plan not only defined the detailed investments needed, but also showed how ongoing programs could benefit new distance-learning, research, publications, and media programs.

The $10 million estimate for the digitization and phase-in plan was just the tip of the iceberg. We also needed to plan and redesign campus buildings with new technology infrastructure, virtual classrooms, and studios. The Hall of Democracy would have to be increased in size with the addition of a third floor and additional construction costs to accommodate the distance-learning technologies, along with professional support staff. A few current and former board members, including Jim Barksdale, Pete Wilson, and Dick Duchossois, were already excited by the distance-learning opportunities. They touted my idea that the Museum should think of itself as a "World War II U," which could one day offer our own accredited online university graduate degrees on such topics as World War II, Museum Studies, and Leadership. I strongly believed in this goal and promoted it often. Dick, the CEO and founder of Duchossois Industries in Chicago, fought as a Captain with the 610th Tank Destroyer Battalion during the Lorraine Campaign in France during World War II and was a staunch advocate of military history. I befriended him in Chicago, and we invited him to join our board in May 2014. With Herschel, Dick, and Jim leading the way, our new chairman Richard Adkerson and the board stepped up to the larger opportunities inspired by our updated vision. It was astonishing that these board leaders were willing to accept changes to a plan that had already grown to cost a projected $325 million and without funds in sight. They accepted ambitious new ideas that would substantially expand the campaign goal; it was a gutsy move by the board.

As we entered the Museum's second decade, we found new ways to advance our educational outreach and impact, particularly for teachers and high school and university students. One of these initiatives, done in partnership with Nicholls State University, was the Normandy Academy, a reflection of the Museum's D-Day roots. This program took high school and university students from around the country to the Normandy invasion beaches, where they confronted the difficult decisions made by military leaders in the heat of that climactic battle. For younger students, summer camps and customized onsite field trips provided opportunities to learn more about the war's history and to dive into the scientific and technological advances that led to Allied victory.

To improve the teaching of World War II in classrooms across the country, we established several summer professional development seminars on each of the major theaters of the war, bringing high school history and social studies teachers to our campus to learn from Museum educators, curators, and WWII veterans. For science teachers of younger students, Real World Science, a curriculum development company, provided tools to help educators integrate World War II stories into math, science, and social studies lessons and train other educators in their hometowns. This, in turn, created a grassroots effort to improve the integration of WWII history into school curricula. At the same time, our International Conference on World War II and overseas tours for adults and university alumni were gaining in popularity and numbers. Our planned second charter cruise, commemorating the 70th anniversary of the Normandy D-Day landings in June 2014, sold out nearly six months in advance. Momentum grew from every side of the education front.

PERSONAL PLANS

By now, I considered how many more years I could, or should, continue in my role as President and CEO. I was in good health and still had the energy for a few more years, but by 2017 I would be 78, which I thought would be a good time to retire and help the board find my successor, a leader who shared the Museum's vision and who was young enough to do the heavy lifting in the massive operational and fundraising challenges through the Master Plan completion and beyond. By then, I believed I would have most of the funding in place to finish the remainder of the Master Plan. The pavilions and exhibits would be largely completed or under construction, and new leadership would be needed to finish the job and lead the Museum into the future. By 2017, I would have been engaged in the Museum's development for more than a quarter century since its conception in 1990.

The board would need time to determine whether there was an internal candidate or to reach outside for a historian or museum leader with the required leadership skills and experience to extend the Museum's vision and relevance for future generations. With these thoughts in mind, I sent a confidential memo in 2012 to then Chairman Abbott to advise him of my intentions to step down in five years, along with a promise to help guide the board leadership in a confidential planning process for my transition and to find my successor.

Even with my retirement on the horizon, we still had work to do, and funding continued to be a juggling act. In 2012 I had secured an appropriation of $17 million from the state of Louisiana for the Campaigns of Courage exhibits, and we wanted to start construction immediately. But that sum was only enough to complete *Road to Berlin,* not *Road to Tokyo.* Once state officials realized this, they balked at releasing those funds, so I struck a deal with them. I promised to construct the entire building but delay completing the *Road to Tokyo* gallery by one year to December 2015, when I believed I could raise the funds for that exhibit. The state agreed, and we got construction and exhibit design for *Road to Berlin* underway.

Somehow, I had to raise another $15 million to complete the *Road to Tokyo* exhibit. I asked the past board chairs to help me recruit Richard Adkerson, President and CEO of Freeport-McMoRan, a prominent oil and mining company that supported us in the past. Richard was a Board Director in 2002, but he resigned from the board when his firm moved its headquarters to Arizona in 2007. My thought was to lure Richard back to take on the Chairman role and help attract private funding from major corporations. With Abbott and former Chairs Wilson, Satre, and Bollinger on the phone with me in my office, we had the "A-Team" making the ask, and Richard accepted. We were all elated and believed it was a huge step to recruit another top CEO from outside New Orleans.

Richard's father served in World War II as a Seabee in the South Pacific and was often stationed on islands with no infrastructure and overrun with jungles. His family connection to the Museum was personal and fueled his enthusiasm for Campaigns of Courage, which stimulated private funding for the project. Additionally, he and the Freeport-McMoRan company gave the Museum $5 million to support *Road to Tokyo,* which helped us add to the match we needed for the $17 million from the state of Louisiana. Richard was the perfect choice at yet another critical moment for the Museum, not only financially, but because of his passion, leadership, and dedication to our mission. To further close the funding gap, Dick Duchossois donated an additional $5 million towards *Road to Berlin.* His capstone donation and other contributions allowed us to complete our goal of opening both galleries exactly a year apart, in December 2014 and December 2015 respectively.

THERE WAS A WAR, LONG AGO: ONCE UPON A TIME

For years I pondered how the Museum should tell the story of America's experience in World War II. The question was, how would I capture the scale and complexities of America's experience? How does one portray the epic story of such a gargantuan struggle waged globally and do justice to the deaths, campaigns, and battles, momentous decisions of great leaders, strategies, and the blunders? We also had the challenge of bringing the visitor into the trenches and battle sites to understand and feel the trauma of the citizen soldiers who encountered the brutality of a war without mercy—a war animated by racist beliefs of an enemy that changed the rules of warfare, especially in the Pacific. Museums often tell stories with words, artifacts, and visual treatments that must condense the story for the visitor. As Patrick Gallagher always reminded me, the exhibits needed to be engaging for adults and teenagers alike.[13]

We had to do so without losing authentic documentation and the feelings of the participants. Museums rely most heavily on visuals to tell their story, much like war correspondents who delved into the emotional stories in words to help their readers see the personal side of the conflict. The best correspondents passed along the pain and constant fear of death through their writing. The great John Steinbeck, who covered the war as a correspondent for the *New York Herald Tribune,* described seeing "a small Italian girl in the street with her stomach blown out, and . . . an American soldier standing over a twitching body, crying." and smelling "the sharp cordite in the air and the hot reek of blood." His description causes you to realize that the war was not just strategy and tactics and generals, but a reality of how very fragile life is. We had to find the balance of describing the big picture strategy and still helping visitors "see" the war that Steinbeck saw and veterans remembered. Museums must capture memories large and small to keep the story both visual and authentic.

The master narrative we developed called for a balanced historical account that highlighted the voices of eyewitnesses, in particular veterans. Their personal viewpoints were buttressed by the best contemporary journalism, with contextual information about the policies and strategy pursued by our civilian and military leadership. We often relied on illuminating words of those with agency, including some of the most momentous speeches by President Roosevelt and the recorded thoughts of General Eisenhower and other military and civilian leaders. These seminal passages help reflect the collective mood of the nation, together forming the public memory of the war. I felt it was important for the Museum to provide a strong narrative of what happened and how it happened from the American perspective, and how the events of the war, both successes and setbacks, helped shape the character and values of the nation that emerged from the war.

For the individual American combatant, the war was intensely personal, for those who survived and for those whose stories we know from their oral histories, letters, and diaries, from their buddies in combat, or from journalists, such as Ernie Pyle and Martha Gellhorn, and war photographers like Robert Capa. We had to tell those stories of courage and sacrifice. At the highest levels, the war was an epic conflict that most Americans remember as the "Good War," a view sometimes tinged with triumphalism and an overreach of patriotic memory. Historians and authors such as Steve Ambrose, Tom Brokaw, and Victor Davis Hanson leaned into that narrative, but moderated it with the recognition that the war was an existential conflict against racist regimes, a necessary war, and that the forces of freedom and democracy prevailed. Our government and military leaders, along with the men and women who served, believed there was a moral commitment undergirding our struggle against the extreme racist ideologies of Nazi Germany and Japan.

While some historians argued against the notion of the "Good War," we hold that most Americans viewed the war as a life-or-death fight between the forces of mostly good and certainly evil, that our military victory was also a moral victory.[14] This view endures today in American memory. However, we document an American journey through World War II that is not always heroic. The war was brutalizing, and ideals were sacrificed for survival. America made many blunders and subjected its own citizens and soldiers to racial discrimination.

Historian Stephan Jaeger is critical of The National WWII Museum for drawing the visitor into a "collective journey" that provides a "gaze" of a "master narrative of the heroic war to free the world. . . . The New Orleans WWII Museum allows the viewer to experience what is at stake, while didactically controlling its messages that the war was good, both for freedom and humanity."[15] I agree with Jaeger on the master narrative of the story we tell of the American experience in World War II. The Museum does indeed reflect a "collective gaze" and memory of the war as it was lived and experienced. We do not glorify the war nor ignore our own issues with racial and social issues at home, or the more cynical views expressed by soldiers about the war, which can be heard in our listening stations. Some of the best WWII historians in the United States and abroad gave advice and helped reach a consensus on the broad story we chose to present in our galleries, including balanced accounts from individual troops and home front workers as well as from leaders. The latter views have agency in establishing national policies and messages that reflected military and political actions. The policies and speeches of government leaders and reports from combat journalists rallied Americans to fight a war that they believed was just, a war they knew was more destructive than any other war in human history. Our exhibits also show our defeats and the disturbing issues of the day, but we do not apologize for our efforts to preserve the memory of the American experience in the war as it was widely experienced by our leaders, our citizen soldiers, and our various publics. This public memory of the war and what it meant to those inside the war is worth preserving for future generations of visitors.

FINDING THE STORY

Our Master Plan envisioned portraying America's journey through World War II in two massive galleries, each to follow in the footsteps of our soldiers, sailors, and airmen. This gave us a roadmap to guide our exhibit design. The plan called for us to begin America's war in their respective campaigns: the *Road to Berlin* for our crusade against Nazi Germany and the *Road to Tokyo* to trace our campaign against Imperial Japan. While we used major battles and campaigns as signposts on these roads, our Presidential Counselors and I believed the course of the war was determined in many ways by the Allied goal to demand unconditional surrender from the Axis powers. There was to be no negotiated peace. It was going to be a fight to the finish. Digging beneath these broad goals was my task. From the home front to the front lines, the Museum's intention was to convey a fact-based historical narrative of the crisis our leaders faced at the end of 1941.

Ever since the 2004 Master Plan, we envisioned the Campaigns of Courage exhibits to be the pounding heart of the WWII story, carrying visitors into the battle against the Axis powers on land, sea, and air. The plan called for telling the story of World War II as a journey of Americans travelling through the war. The metaphor meant beginning a visitor's Museum tour in a typical Union Train Station, where our troops began their journey to war and where visitors had a short, simulated train ride through the United States, with views of 1940s cities and landscapes outside the windows. In those moments on the train, visitors met their soldier, sailor, or airman on a video screen at their seats and signed up for their digital dog tags, which enabled them to follow a single veteran, who in his or her own voice would narrate a story, taking visitors on a personal journey through World War II. Working with this framework and the advice from historians and our Presidential Counselors, Patrick Gallagher and our Museum team began in 2010 to design exhibits in earnest for Campaigns of Courage.

Visitors needed to start their journey through Campaigns of Courage by understanding how defenseless America was at the outset; moreover, the Axis powers thought the United States could never build, equip, and supply a modern military before they conquered Great Britain, the Soviet Union, and China.[16] At a minimum, Campaigns of Courage had to help visitors understand that America's military challenges were so great that Axis powers believed our defeat was assured. Every strategic challenge demanded extraordinary leadership, innovation, every resource of American ingenuity, and a commitment to defeat powerful enemies on opposite sides of the globe.

The first of these challenges was to win control of the seas, both in the Atlantic and Pacific Oceans. Rebuilding our naval fleets, defeating German U-boats, and building transports were the essential conditions for any chance for success. Second, the United States had to develop landing craft that could place soldiers in massive numbers on enemy shores and take the battle to these forces. Third, the citizen soldiers had to overcome the logistical challenges of sending our military and supplies tens of thousands of miles away from home to fight on various terrains, such as the oceans, islands, mountains, deserts, and foreign territories. Fourth, we had to gain command of the air in Western Europe and the Asia-Pacific by conquering enemy territory to build bases that could put our army air corps in position to reach deeper into enemy territory. Finally, we had to win the battle of science and technology to achieve superiority of weapons, aircraft, vehicles, ships, and bombs with systems to build them faster and better than the enemy.

Campaigns of Courage had to tell the story of how America met these challenges so that visitors would understand how we defeated the Axis powers. We also had to show how we mobilized our armed forces through recruiting, drafting, and training green troops to fight a war in the Pacific and in Europe at the same time. We had to take the fight to the enemy and on every terrain and any climate of the world. We designed our exhibits to show America's resilience, how we rebounded from our lack of preparedness, where the battles were fought, and how the war was won. Just as we had done prior, we put emphasis on the stories of the men in foxholes, inside ships and planes, and storming beaches from their Higgins landing craft.

Ultimately, the exhibits had to capture the character, doubts, and courage of those facing combat. "No one, least of all themselves, knows what they will do when the terrible thing happens," Steinbeck wrote. "No man there knows whether he can take it, knows whether he will run away or stick, or lose his nerve and go to pieces, or will be a good soldier."[17]

THE DUCHOSSOIS FAMILY *ROAD TO BERLIN*: EUROPEAN THEATER GALLERIES

The *Road to Berlin* gallery begins in North Africa, where the Allied amphibious assaults hit the beaches in Higgins landing boats in November 1942, an invasion that succeeded despite mistakes, bad communications, and poor execution.[18] Our exhibits place visitors in desert environments with dust-covered jeeps and simulated arid terrain where American troops fought their first pitched battle against the Wehrmacht at Kasserine Pass, with original maps and listening stations to help tell the story. Our green troops and commanders suffered a disastrous defeat and an embarrassing setback. Disasters and mistakes were aplenty in World War II, and we present America's share of them as part of the story, but we also show that one of the keys to ultimate victory was how the US military learned from its mistakes in combat and corrected them more quickly than the enemy.

After Kasserine, the US Army recovered slowly and slugged its way into Sicily and mainland Italy. We suffered horrible losses in these landings, shooting down some of our own planes carrying paratroopers during the invasion of Sicily, but nonetheless succeeded. The exhibits on Sicily and Italy use animated maps, media, and interactives to describe our aggressive counterattacks. Visitors walk through reproductions of Roman archways and faded stucco homes, reminiscent of scenes that Allied soldiers walked through. Listening stations use the personal accounts of veterans to narrate the story of Allied advances up the bloody boot of Italy. Correspondents' photos and films of the battles convey the intensity of the fighting and endless battles in the rugged mountains around the Abbey of Monte Cassino. Personal artifacts in the gallery tell individual stories, including a metal cigarette case with a dent that stopped a bullet from piercing the heart of PFC Andrew Sexton, a random instance of saving grace. Similarly, we display Capt. Oscar Henry Reinboth's portable altar, which he used to deliver mass on a loudspeaker on Easter Sunday 1944, during the fighting in Anzio. Soldiers on both sides paused their fighting to observe the mass but resumed immediately after it ended.

Then broader displays with maps and media shift attention to the capture of Rome on June 4, 1944, along with the defeat of the Wehrmacht in southern Italy and the capture of Italian airfields at Foggia. These exhibits provide context to a strategic turn in the war that put the 15th Air Force's B-17s and B-24s within bombing range of targets in Germany, Austria, and Nazi-held oilfields in southeastern Europe. Historian Don Miller consulted on all aspects of the air war exhibits in *Road to Berlin,* providing advice on how to communicate its strategic importance to Allied victory in Europe through design elements.

Around the corner from the Italian campaign, visitors are introduced to the air war. A media screen introduces the 8th Air Force in England and its bombing missions into Germany, pulverizing German cities and rail yards beginning in 1943. To further immerse visitors in the Allied push to gain air superiority over Germany, our designers fabricated a Quonset hut from the Thorpe Abbott airfield in England. Looking up reveals a hole in the roof with a view of 8th Air Force bombers flying overhead on media screens. Maps track Allied raids deep into Germany as the tide of the air war began to turn in the Allies' favor. By utilizing this tactic, superior fighter planes and Allied bombers cleared the Luftwaffe from the skies above Normandy before D-

Day, an action that was vital to the success of the invasion. General Eisenhower promised his commanders and troops that "if you see fighting aircraft over you, they will be ours."[19]

Since our original D-Day galleries had about 8,200 square feet devoted to Operation Overlord and the Normandy invasion, the new *Road to Berlin* gallery treats D-Day as the hinge of the larger Allied campaign against Hitler's Third Reich. The dog tag listening stations support the story with personal memories from soldiers, such as J. J. Witmeyer Jr., a native New Orleanian who fought with the 4th Infantry Division on D-Day. Witmeyer describes the brutal fighting in the hedgerows in the French countryside. After seeing a close friend killed, he describes his deep grief. "And at that time, I changed . . . first I had to change from a civilian to a soldier . . . and then I had to change from a soldier to a killer," he said.[20] After the Normandy landings, exhibits turn to the hard fighting in the hedgerows beyond the beaches that cost more lives and slowed the progress of Allied troops. Visitors next follow the rapid drive of Allied troops across France to the liberation of Paris in August 1944 and then through Belgium near the German border in the fall.

Then the exhibits come to the surprise German counteroffensive in the snow and ice of the Ardennes during the Battle of the Bulge. We selected the fighting around Bastogne, Belgium, to illustrate the drama of the near defeat of the Allies in the crushing counterattack of Hitler's best Panzer divisions. Visitors first glimpse the snowy scene through an abandoned German bunker. Then, visitors enter the thick Ardennes Forest, where we project snowfall and a colder feeling in the battle scene. Minimal radio chatter of miserable soldiers sitting in foxholes in the sub-zero temperature fills the room moments before the German attack. All is calm and quiet, until suddenly the lights dim, and the space is filled by the unsettling sounds of machine gun fire and the flashing lights of artillery bursts. As the battle erupts, sounds of advancing German Panzer tanks and frightened GIs barking orders back and forth on radio phones in the chaos of the surprise offensive are projected through the scene.

The exhibit shows the deep advance of the attacking German forces and their encirclement of the US Army's 101st Airborne Division at Bastogne. General Patton's 3rd Army raced north to the rescue the surrounded American troops as Eisenhower poured a quarter million troops into the battle to stop the German advance. The multisensory environment of the snowy forest exhibit combines with large film screens of maps tracking the Germany offensive to replicate the chaos and freezing cold of the American fight for survival. The Battle of the Bulge is the most intense sensory experience in the exhibits on the *Road to Berlin,* with stirring personal accounts adding to visitors' understanding of the largest battle fought by American forces in the war; the US Army suffered over 80,000 casualties after a month of fighting.

For Museum goers, the prominence of our exhibit signifies the importance of this near-catastrophic defeat of US forces, which showed clearly that the defeat of Nazi Germany was not inevitable. From the Bulge, visitors follow American troops into the heart of Germany, where the story of war gets even darker. Museum visitors find themselves in the footsteps of the soldiers as they fought their way through the rubble of bombed-out buildings. The exhibits are evocative, with floor-to-ceiling photos of destroyed cites, such as Cologne and the Ruhr Valley industrial sites. After seizing the last remaining crossing of the Rhine River at Remagen, American forces fought across Germany through cities like Frankfurt and Munich, cities that were subjected to the massive blows of the Allied bombing campaign. Visitors understand the necessity, but sometimes wonder about the total destruction of the beautiful Baroque city of Dresden in February 1945, so close to the end of the war. "How this thing's going to work out, nobody really knew," noted Don Miller.[21] Roosevelt knew that Hitler had his own scientists working on an atomic bomb, and there was talk about other super weapons. We hold the visitor in the same suspense about the war's end, with exhibits using dim lighting, ominous music, and rubble underfoot to illustrate the agony of the last days in Berlin as the Soviet Army closed in from the east.

The death throes of the Third Reich included the shocking discovery of Hitler's concentration camps, containing the bodies of murdered Jews and emaciated survivors. The virulently racist Nazi ideology is revealed in our exhibit by photographs enlarged to enormous scale to show what our soldiers saw as they opened the gates and what the Signal Corps photographed for the world to see and remember. What our troops found at concentration camps such as Buchenwald and Dachau give a partial answer to the Museum's mission to explain why the war was fought. Certainly, seeing the camps changed perceptions for many Allied troops. Eisenhower asked correspondents to keep cameras rolling to document what they saw.

Maj. Gen. John C. Raaen Jr. put it best during the Museum tour to Normandy on the D-Day anniversary in 2004: "In Normandy I think we all thought we were fighting German soldiers, but as we came into increased contact with their views and atrocities in Germany, we began to understand we were fighting Nazis."[22] Our exhibits reflect these darker views expressed by our troops in the closing days of the war on German soil as the consequences of racist atrocities became clear.

The *Road to Berlin* ends with the suicide of Adolf Hitler on April 30, 1945, in his Berlin bunker and then the unconditional surrender of Nazi Germany. While Allied victory was necessary to preserve freedom and democracy, it came at the cost of immeasurable loss to fighting forces, unimaginable destruction of cities, the deaths of countless innocent civilians, and a lifetime of trauma for many survivors. American soldiers and civilians alike celebrated the victory over Germany, but the Museum ensures that visitors know that victory came with heavy costs to those who had seen the face of war. Richard Proulx, an 18-year-old American infantryman at the Battle of the Bulge, recounted years later that his traumatic experiences left him with dreams that he would be back in "that nightmare world and be lost there forever. . . . One cannot go to war and come back normal."[23]

RICHARD C. ADKERSON & FREEPORT-McMORAN FOUNDATION *ROAD TO TOKYO:* PACIFIC THEATER GALLERIES

The surprise Japanese attack on the US Pacific Fleet at Pearl Harbor on Sunday morning, December 7, 1941, sank seven US ships sitting at harbor and left 2,403 dead, shocking Americans to their core and thrusting the nation immediately into World War II.[24] President Roosevelt's "Day of Infamy" speech on the next day, December 8, called for a declaration of war against an enemy he characterized as "depraved" for its unprovoked attack. From the outset, Roosevelt relentlessly impugned the character of the enemy, exuded determination, promised revenge, and described the war to come in moral terms, depicting the Japanese attack as an act of treachery and declaring that the "American people in their righteous might will win through to absolute victory."[25]

This enduring public memory of the start of war with Japan informs how the Museum presents *Road to Tokyo,* the story of the war in the Asia-Pacific.[26] The racial and fascist undertones of the war colored the personal experiences of those in combat, while propaganda inflamed America's emotional and political impressions and its public memory of the enemy. Similarly racist propaganda in Japan inflamed their perceptions of Americans as "beasts." From the outset, it was clear that this was going to be an ugly, savage war.

As visitors begin their journey in the *Road to Tokyo,* they find themselves on a replica of the bridge of the USS *Enterprise,* where they learn of the strategic challenges that the United States faced in 1942 and beyond. The first major American victory in the Pacific, at the Battle of Midway in June 1942, is presented in a theater, which tells the dramatic tale of American Douglas Dauntless dive bomber planes sinking 4 major Japanese aircraft carriers, a devastating blow to the enemy.

The war in the Asia-Pacific, dominated by naval battles, was quite different from the lengthy land campaigns fought in Europe. The Pacific Theater was beastly hot and featured mosquito-infested jungles, which brought malaria, dysentery, and psychological trauma that harmed morale among our ground forces. The fighting often bordered on barbaric, with combatants on both sides in a brutal fight to the finish. The arbitrary torture and murder of American POWs, kamikaze air attacks against ships, and ritual hara-kiri introduced American troops to new ways of warfare. In the last years of the war, American military leaders accepted high casualties of Japanese civilians and used napalm bombings that burned whole cities to the ground. *Road to Tokyo* documents this violence with images, artifacts, personal testimonies, letters, and media assembled to create an experience as immersive as *Road to Berlin.* The experience sometimes shocks and at other times evokes empathy and questions, with increased knowledge and understanding as the goal.

In the *Road to Tokyo,* I wanted the orientation of the war to present the same bleak outlook for the Pacific as the United States experienced in the first year of the war in the European theater. After the destruction of American battleships at Pearl Harbor, we lost the Philippines in following months, culminating in the largest surrender of an American army in history. Japan initially reigned supreme in the Pacific Ocean.

The landings of the 1st Marine Division on the island of Guadalcanal on August 7, 1942, were the first major land offensive against the Japanese and succeeded in capturing an airfield the Japanese had been building for its next strike against Australia. For six months, intense naval, air, and jungle fighting raged for control of the island and the airfield, with heavy casualties on both sides. The Museum's Guadalcanal exhibit simulates the thick green jungle vegetation, complete with 25-foot-tall palm trees, while translucent screens carry the battle action on film. Between the dense foliage are sandbags and machine guns embedded as defensive positions to simulate the Marines defending the airfield on the famous perimeter called Bloody Ridge, where they held off thousands of attacking Japanese soldiers. Years later, I visited that site on Guadalcanal with Richard Greer, an acting First Sergeant and ammunition carrier with a 1st Marine Division machine gun squad in those night fights. While standing at the defensive position where his squad fought, I asked him: "How did you feel in the moments before the attacks?" In Richard's slow Virginia drawl, he described the midnight battle scene, and now his words are the first our visitors hear as they enter the ferocious jungle battles to hold Bloody Ridge: "You know the Japanese are coming . . . and fear sets in . . . your mouth is dry, and your heart is racing, and you wonder how you're going to perform. . . . But when they come, fixed bayonets, dynamite throwing, grenades throwing, your training sets in, and you do your thing."[27]

Sounds of machine gun fire and flashing lights accompany the visitor through the jungle exhibit, with artifacts and personal accounts to amplify the multisensory experience, giving a sense of the six months of hard jungle fighting that was required in order to preserve US control of this strategic island. The final Japanese defeat and withdrawal from Guadalcanal stopped Imperial Japan's southward conquests. This American victory allowed the start of US island-hopping counteroffensive campaigns, which pushed northward toward the ultimate goal of defeating Japan on its home islands.

The *Road to Tokyo* exhibit presents a variety of evocative ocean, jungle, and mountain environments, providing context for visitors to understand the naval operations, amphibious assaults, and intense land and air battles of the Pacific Theater. The 40-foot ceiling height on the building's second floor were critical in portraying these diverse campaigns, allowing our recreated jungle landscape and enormous photo images and maps to convey the sense of distance and scale in the Pacific War, something that the American public often did not fully grasp. As historian Rich Frank, our consultant on *Road to Tokyo* noted, the overwhelming impression for visitors going through these exhibits was one of revelation.

A 40-foot-high media wall illustrates that scale, displaying the Himalayas in the China-Burma-India Theater, thousands of miles to the west of the fighting in the southwest Pacific. Allied supply routes stretched thousands of miles from New York to India and over the Himalayans and into mainland China. Hanging in this exhibit is the P-40 Warhawk and the story of Lt. Gen. Claire Chennault, a Louisianian whose "Flying Tigers" of the First American Volunteer Group supported the Nationalist Chinese armies prior to Pearl Harbor.

Moving north, maps and ruins bring the visitor into Saipan and Manila, follow American forces in retaking the Philippines, regaining Japanese occupied territories, and winning supremacy of the seas in the Battle of Leyte Gulf, shown in a dramatic film in a mini theater. Then come the intense battles for Iwo Jima and Okinawa in the spring and summer of 1945, bringing Allied forces ever closer to mainland Japan.

Victories came at a heavy price in lives, ships, and aircraft. B-29 firebombing raids burned 69 Japanese cities to the ground, which is shown graphically in the final exhibits. The planned Allied invasion and conquering of Japan's home islands was expected to cost one million American lives by some estimates. Body bags already came home in great numbers, and Americans on the home front were exhausted, with some in favor of negotiating a peace with Japan to end the war without unconditional surrender. In June 1945, President Truman's choices were few. Either invade Japan at a horrific cost in American lives or blockade the islands and bomb the nation into submission. Operation Downfall, the invasion of Japan planned for fall of 1945, would be larger in scale than the Normandy invasion and was projected to last through spring of 1946.[28] As President Truman arrived at the Potsdam Conference with Stalin and Churchill in July, he learned that an atomic bomb was successfully tested in New Mexico and was ready to end this brutal war. The destruction and subsequent defeat of Japan is laid out in the final exhibit of *Road to Tokyo.*

The exhibit on the birth of the nuclear age has walls on either side reaching to the 40-foot ceiling, holding historic photos enlarged to 15 by 20 feet, showing the utter devastation of Japanese cities. The photos on the left wall show Hiroshima and Nagasaki; the photos on the right wall depict cities including Toyama, Omura, Tokyo, and Osaka, incinerated by the B-29 firebombing raids months earlier. A map on the wall shows the location of 69 firebombed Japanese cities. Visitors are struck to see firebombed cities that looked no different than those destroyed by atomic bombs. No commentary is provided or needed.

This first use of nuclear weapons in an armed conflict ushered in a new era in world history and remains a dominant legacy of World War II. Visitors view the images of the aftermath of the nuclear bomb's devastation on a vertical screen 20 feet high, projecting historic film footage of the moments after the second atomic bomb fell on Nagasaki, sending huge plumes surging upwards to 30,000 feet. A flash-burned porcelain vase from Nagasaki shows the bleached effect on the half exposed to the blast, while the other side retains full color. Photos in the exhibit also show the ghastly human effects of the blast and radiation burns over the bodies of several Japanese survivors. The moral question about whether the use of the atomic bomb was righteous is left to the viewer. Just beyond the exhibit, alongside the Japanese unconditional surrender signing aboard the USS *Missouri,* are the words of Gen. Douglas MacArthur: "It is my earnest hope, and indeed the hope of mankind, that from this solemn occasion a better world shall emerge out of the blood and carnage of the past . . . a world dedicated to the dignity of man and the fulfillment of his most cherished wish for freedom, tolerance, and justice."[29]

With those words, World War II came to an end. Hitler was dead and his thousand-year Third Reich was in ashes, and the Imperial Japanese regime had met its demise as well. Years later, Sgt. Debs Myers reflected a viewpoint of the average citizen soldier of World War II: "Maybe he didn't know what fascism was—maybe he did. [He] did not destroy fascism. But he helped defeat the fascists and took away their guns. . . With his allies, he saved the world and hoped to God he'd never have to do it again."[30]

Campaigns of Courage makes clear that the war was barbaric, brutish, racist, and "so savage it turned many soldiers into savages, human beings who had to kill in order to keep on living."[31] The Museum story reflects the prevailing American memory that it was an existential war, a war to preserve our nation's freedom, democracy, and respect for human rights. One learns that after World War II, we quickly came to the aid of nations we fought and defeated. Under the Marshall Plan, we helped many of those countries rebuild as more free and democratic nations. In the words of Stephen Ambrose, "America's young men had gone to Europe not to conquer, not to enslave, not to destroy, but to liberate."[32] The Museum holds that there was a redemptive and moral tone to World War II as promised in President Roosevelt's prewar vision of Four Freedoms that should prevail in all nations of the world. America also demonstrated that its democratic system of governance and military command was superior to all the vaunted claims of the nationalist military, economic, and domestic systems of the dictatorships that took the world into war to expand their fascist empires.

THE ARSENAL OF DEMOCRACY: THE HERMAN AND GEORGE R. BROWN SALUTE TO THE HOME FRONT

On the day the United States entered World War II following Japan's attack on Pearl Harbor, Brig. Gen. Dwight D. Eisenhower wrote a letter to his brother Milton, "Hitler should beware of the fury of an aroused democracy."[33] Ike's prescient words sum up the essence of *The Arsenal of Democracy,* the Museum's exhibit on the American home front.

The Arsenal of Democracy captures the outburst of patriotic sentiment and moral outrage that came with the shock of the Japanese attack.[34] This was reflected in a slogan that was commonly heard across the country during the years when Americans were called upon to accept the sacrifices demanded by the war: "We're all in this together." Most Americans who lived through the war remember that feeling of national unity as one of their most satisfying memories of those years. This feeling of unity prevailed despite the irony of fighting racist empires with our own segregated military and despite discrimination toward minorities, America mobilized for war. Yet, many minorities who felt the brunt of injustices wanted to join the fight against a common enemy and demonstrate their worth as Americans.

Wars are crucibles of change in societies, both during and after the conflict. War also helps define the values and identity of a nation, for better or worse. Americans' experiences on the home front and the front lines shaped our memories of World War II. These Museum galleries immerse visitors in memories of the war, including memories of shameful behavior and policies contrary to our values, as well as those that reflect our higher ideals of freedom, democracy, and human rights. War brings difficult questions to the surface of a society but does not answer them. The Museum's broader narrative documents an authentic public memory of unity, hope, and patriotic support for the war effort. *The Arsenal of Democracy* is filled with stories that America can proudly preserve in its public memory, but our exhibits also reveal the cracks in society and expose issues that were dealt with poorly or papered over for the sake of the war effort.

America's mobilization to support the war effort was extraordinary and is indispensable to understanding how the war was won. Even before the United States entered the war, President Roosevelt began gearing up American industry through the Lend-Lease Act, which sent supplies, trucks, and other war materials to our allies fighting the Axis. FDR first declared that America would be the "arsenal of democracy" in a speech to the nation on December 29, 1940, almost a year before Pearl Harbor. The President spoke of "a world crisis" and warned that the fate of nations already defeated by Axis powers "tells us what it means to live at the point of a Nazi gun."[35] Roosevelt did not mince words when calling out the racist and anti-democratic ideologies of the Axis powers that threatened our freedom. "The plain facts are that the Nazis have proclaimed, time and again, that all other races are their inferiors and therefore subject to their orders," he said. [36]

Roosevelt made clear that to keep war away from our shores, the US needed to support European nations and stated that these Europeans "who are defending themselves do not ask us to do their fighting. They ask us for the implements of war, the planes, the tanks, the guns, the freighters which will enable them to fight for their liberty and for our security."[37] Roosevelt set a tone for a moral struggle against "evil forces," while delivering an urgent message to the American people to prepare for the war he believed was coming.

Roosevelt's speech exuded confidence, honesty, and clear-eyed warnings of what was needed to support our friends—and our own nation if the war came to America. "We have the men, the skill, the wealth, and above all, the will . . ." he declared. "We must be the great arsenal of democracy."[38]

The Arsenal of Democracy exhibits follow the President's blueprint for the mobilization and leadership challenges he described. They portray how the nation mobilized and transformed its military, weaponry, and industries. By capturing this sense of urgency, patriotism, and sacrifice, the Museum sets the stage for the trials and tribulations the home front faced. It was indeed a fight for freedom.

The 2004 Master Plan provided conceptual ideas for what would become *The Arsenal of Democracy* galleries. However, serious planning and designing did not begin until I sought board approval for a more detailed plan in June 2013, even as fundraising and construction efforts for Campaigns of Courage were in full swing. I worked with Patrick Gallagher, our Presidential Counselors, noted historian Lynne Olson, and our staff historians to bring the home front exhibits into their final design. We reserved just over 8,000 square feet on the second floor of the Louisiana Memorial Pavilion for *The Arsenal of Democracy,* near the Museum entrance and the Pete Kent Train Car Experience. For once, we did not require a new building, but the exhibits were still expensive. True to form, we began the design work without the funds to pay for the fabrication and installation of the exhibits. Fortunately, longtime supporter and charter Museum member Walter Negley, with his mother, Nancy Brown Negley, helped us secure a $6.8 million capstone gift from the Brown Foundation of Houston, Texas, to fund these galleries. The grant honored the wartime contributions of Herman and George Brown, Texas brothers who transformed their construction company, Brown & Root, into a shipbuilding juggernaut during World War II, building warships of all kinds despite having no previous experience in ship construction. The Brown brothers were awarded the Army-Navy "E" Award for Excellence in Production during the war, reflecting their entrepreneurship and commitment. The Brown Foundation grant ensured that the entire permanent exhibit would be funded in time for opening on June 10, 2017.

World War II affected every aspect of American life, from industry and the workforce to Americans' relationships with one another, down to their home lives. *The Arsenal of Democracy* portrays these complex social and economic transformations of the nation. In the galleries, we show how our disparate society coalesced into a nation united under the banner of war. We built a replica of Main Street, USA, the kind of place an average American might have walked through. Here, newsstands show historical newspapers reporting the attack on Pearl Harbor and other milestones of the war, and there are comic books and radio broadcasts reminding Americans to "Remember Pearl Harbor." Shop windows display household items like pins and plates with patriotic slogans. A movie theater exterior, complete with a marquee and a box office, displays posters of war-era films, as well as featuring period records and musical scores.

Americans felt the impact of the war in their daily lives and their homes. The government encouraged them to conserve resources like soap, metal, and gasoline and asked them to buy war bonds to support the military. Many families created "victory gardens" to grow their own food so mass-produced crops could feed GIs overseas. Radios delivered news of the war and carried Roosevelt's famous Fireside Chats. *The Arsenal of Democracy* includes a replica of a simple 1940s-style home. Kitchen drawers are filled with ration books, wartime recipe books, sewing supplies, and other household items.

The closet holds uniforms and children's toys, many of them war-themed, such as toy soldiers, play guns, or other items to match the news. In the living room, photos of loved ones in and out of uniform are displayed prominently. These exhibits show how simply Americans had to live, and they capture their volunteer spirit, homespun virtues, religiosity, and ideals in a perilous time.

The drums of war reverberated everywhere, including in the entertainment industry. Hollywood helped the military make propaganda films that sought to get everyone "in the fight." The gallery on training troops includes examples of the sophisticated films produced by the War Department that educated new recruits on the "evil" nature of the enemy and characterized the enemy as brutal dictatorships, fueled by racist ideologies and determined to destroy our freedom and democracy. Roosevelt authorized the films be shown in movie theaters around the country to inform citizens and soldiers alike of the nature of the struggle for civilization that we were waging and to help unify the nation in the fight.

World War II also brought significant changes to the daily lives of Americans, sinking into the social fabric of the nation. Strikes and racial unrest enflamed war time pressures on the economy and social system. *The Arsenal of Democracy* galleries do not shy away from these conflicts in American society. War often exposes weaknesses and strengths of every nation, victors and vanquished alike. World War II became a crucible for social tensions and changes in American society. In the galleries, we highlight the irony of over 1.2 million African American asked to serve in a segregated military for a country that did not treat them as equals. Even more minorities contributed via industrial jobs on the home front. Double V became a popular rallying cry among Black Americans, calling for victory on the front lines against the Axis powers and victory at home against racist laws and attitudes. Hispanics, Native Americans, and Asian Americans also faced similar discrimination at home; yet, they still answered the call to fight for their country. We dedicated space in the galleries to the struggle for civil rights, not just for its importance for the war effort, but for the social changes that followed the war. People of color returned home to face discriminatory laws and continued their struggle for civil rights, making these stories critical to American history, not only to the history of World War II.

Other sad commentaries of American missteps are presented in our galleries. One notable case is the incarceration of Japanese Americans, who were declared aliens by Roosevelt in his Executive Order 9066, which was issued in February 1942 amid the paranoia of Americans after the Pearl Harbor attack. By this disgraceful order, the President "authorized the forced removal of all persons deemed a threat to national security from the West Coast to 'relocation centers' further inland. . . ."[39] These incarcerations were done without due process, and Japanese Americans were forced to leave behind businesses, homes, schools, and their whole lives. They languished for weeks in crowded, makeshift assembly centers before the War Relocations Authority moved them to confinement centers. The shoddily constructed camps consisted of flimsy, overpopulated barracks surrounded by barbed wire. Armed guards looked down from imposing towers, constantly reminding detainees they were presumptive enemies of the state.

In *The Arsenal of Democracy,* Japanese Americans who endured incarceration tell their stories of property loss, humiliation, and incarceration as aliens, although most were American citizens. Oral history clips of detainees are featured, including that of future US Representative and White House cabinet member Norman Mineta, recalling life in overcrowded buildings lacking bathrooms.[40] Detainees were determined to create a sense of normalcy and community within these camps, especially for their children. They built baseball fields, grew gardens between the barracks, and did what they needed to create a livable community. Despite the severe discrimination, 33,000 Japanese Americans served in the military to fight the Axis, even while many of their families lived behind barbed wire in America. This dark and complex moment in American history is critical to understanding an unhappy chapter in the social and racial context of the war.

The Arsenal of Democracy also highlights how the sudden need for wartime weapons and goods caused a spike in innovation, creating new production processes, more efficient machines, and more. The exhibit provides a scaled-down version of an assembly line, showing an example of factory production during the war. In the center of a large room, visitors find jeeps in various stages of production. In front of the jeeps, they can peer into welding masks to see war-era footage of welding and other production processes. Tools, equipment, machinery, engines, and models of ocean liners convey the scope and scale of the supply and transportation feats Americans accomplished.

Perhaps the greatest logistical miracle and scientific innovation during the war was the Manhattan Project, the secretive program to develop, test, and deliver an atomic bomb before the Axis powers could. Led by Dr. J. Robert Oppenheimer, and Army Lt. Gen. Leslie Groves, the program coordinated the work of thousands of scientists, engineers, and factory workers at sites across America, including secret cities in Oak Ridge, Tennessee, Hanford, Washington, and Los Alamos, New Mexico. We use the setting of a scientific laboratory with chalkboards showing mathematical equations, equipment, designs, and plans to allow the visitor to experience a wartime laboratory. The Manhattan Project led to the creation and use of the atomic bomb, the weapon that ended the war. As our exhibit shows, it is a legacy of World War II that first brought hope, then fear of a new nuclear age that could destroy all of humanity. It was a weapon that changed the world forever.

Roosevelt's arsenal of democracy metaphor became a reality for Americans during World War II. "They believed that, as a popular saying of the times had it, 'we're all in this together,'" Steve Ambrose once wrote about the legacy of the war and the Americans who fought, stating, "Their sense of duty, of right and wrong, their teamwork and their courage embody the American Spirit. The National D-Day Museum celebrates the American Spirit. Young and old will come to learn of their proud heritage. Since 1945, democracy and freedom have been on the march. But visitors will learn not just of what we have done. They will learn what we can do. They will learn that we are still in this together."[41]

Though Steve wrote those words about our original D-Day galleries and the brave citizen soldiers who won those days at Normandy, the same spirit flowed through those on the home front and those fighting across the globe. Above all, Campaigns of Courage and *The Arsenal of Democracy* recognize and honor their spirit and strive to keep that spirit alive for the next generations.

11

PUSHING THE BOUNDARIES OF THE MUSEUM

AFTER THE OPENING of the US Freedom Pavilion in 2013, Museum visitation was soaring, programs were booming, and the core content exhibits were entering intensive design development phases. Our desire to be the best WWII Museum in the world meant much more work lay ahead. We needed revisions to buildings to accommodate changes to exhibits and new ideas to improve the overall experience. We especially needed to accommodate our expanding vision for education programs, research, publications, and global outreach.

The Master Plan sorely needed an update. The general plan was largely intact, but elements had changed dramatically. More spaces were needed, and I felt we were approaching the point of no return for big and expensive decisions for the final design and build-out for the remaining campus. We had many smart designers and builders, but neither they nor I had a clear idea back in 2003 when the Master Plan was conceived of all that was needed to fulfill such an ambitious vision, much less create an institution that pushed beyond all boundaries.

The most significant changes resulted from our growing commitments to digitization, distance learning, education, and access to our collections and programs. Just as the Allied planners had not anticipated the problems that hedgerows posed for troops trying to advance through Normandy, I found we were often confronted by unexpected barriers, some sent by nature and some devised by people. From the start, we made significant errors that came from a mixture of naivete, lack of museum experience, and funding restraints that precluded doing anything more than what was necessary for our core exhibits. Now those mistakes had to be corrected.

Early decisions to add buildings for storage and collections were ad hoc and not part of our strategic plan. Similarly, other buildings on the drawing board had to be redesigned, enlarged, or repurposed to accommodate emerging needs for historical research, publishing, and oral history collection. Conferencing activities that were originally envisioned for the now-scrapped Center for the Study of the American Spirit had to be completely reimagined. The entire education center had been eliminated after Katrina with the intent to revive the conferencing functions in a future hotel and conference center. But the virtual classrooms, production studios, and distance-learning technologies were not as robust in the 2003 Master Plan as they became by 2011 when we began to look beyond the completion of the Museum's core exhibits. We also needed to fill out the Hall of Democracy with space for a research institute with historians who could assure the integrity of future programs, publications, and the historical record of the war and its legacy.

We faced two hugely challenging other big projects, the Canopy of Peace and Liberation Pavilion. Both needed attention and planning even though their funding and construction were years away. It became clear to me the original plans and cost estimates for the Liberation Pavilion, the key to the last part of our mission, were sorely lacking at the conceptual level. On top of that, we had to add an additional floor to the Liberation Pavilion for exhibit space that was lost when the US Freedom Pavilion expanded in size to accommodate the B-17 and submarine experience.

The Canopy of Peace, meant to be the Museum's iconic architectural statement, faced major challenges. We needed financially feasible engineering designs, and we had no donor in place. Decisions on the foundation pilings for the Canopy had to be made soon, or it would not be built at all. With these ideas in mind, I also believed we had not yet scratched the surface of inventing what the Museum could become on the education outreach, research, and programming front. A career spent extending the boundaries of the University of New Orleans combined with the jolt of nature's fury in Hurricane Katrina inspired an expanded vision with new education horizons for the Museum.

JOHN E. KUSHNER RESTORATION PAVILION

As early as 2010, we were desperate for space for our mushrooming collections. As we filled out the first pavilions in the Master Plan, we realized that we miscalculated the amount of space needed to store artifacts and collections. In the late 1990s, with no funds for storage, we accepted a policy to limit our collection to our core exhibits. At the time, the board believed that we could never afford to be a significant collecting Museum. Initially, we only built a few thousand square feet for personal artifacts and some basic weapons and uniforms that were mostly linked to our D-Day exhibits. We also believed that we would house a few selected vehicles and aircraft permanently in the main pavilions or in the exhibits, not in some offsite warehouse. We could not have been more wrong. From the start we were on the receiving end of an avalanche of artifacts. I was slowly learning a dimension of museum development I had not anticipated.

It was very difficult to say "no" to personal artifacts that came linked to an important story of husbands and wives, fathers and mothers, or grandparents. Every day brought not-to-be-missed opportunities to receive donations or chance purchases of iconic planes, tanks, jeeps, boats, and even an ambulance. Accepting them was a huge challenge with no space in our plans to store them, let alone restore large artifacts to working condition. We were not the Smithsonian Institution with an annual infusion of operating funds or enormous warehouses to accommodate its vast collections of the nation's history. As a self-sustaining, nonprofit Museum, we had to live within rigid financial limitations.

That said, we quickly succumbed to the needs for additional storage space, which became our most pressing need by 2008. With the aid of some state and private funds, we purchased an old 17,000-square-foot warehouse three blocks away for the storage of the macros, with a portion reserved for overflowing retail inventory for our store, another need not fully identified in the Master Plan. This warehouse space was a boon for our big rolling stock of macros, but since it lacked air conditioning, it was not usable for restoration projects that required a controlled environment.

Fortunately, the Museum owned a building that could serve as a Restoration Pavilion, located at the intersection of Magazine and Andrew Higgins Drive, directly across from our original galleries. The building had 14,000 square feet and 30-foot-high ceilings. The space was perfect for tasks such as welding, painting, and woodworking, plus moving large objects in and out of the building. The façade featured giant storm-resistant glass panels on the Andrew Higgins side to give pedestrians a sneak peek of ongoing restoration projects.

The building lacked a major donor until the summer of 2010, when Boysie and I led a campaign to raise funds in memory of the late John Kushner, a longtime board member and close friend, who used his shrewd real estate skills to acquire the Museum's first warehouse for the D-Day Museum in 1996 and then overseen the purchase of three city blocks for the Museum's expansion. The Museum would not be what it is today without John's passion for the expansion mission. John passed away in 2005, and we felt it right to honor him with one of the properties he helped purchase. The John E. Kushner Restoration Pavilion opened in the summer of 2011.

TIP OF THE ICEBERG: LIBERATION, *MONUMENTS MEN*, CANOPY OF PEACE, HALL OF DEMOCRACY AND HOTEL

The addition of the John E. Kushner Restoration Pavilion was just the tip of the iceberg of all the adjustments to the Master Plan. Even as we continued to develop the US Freedom Pavilion and Campaigns of Courage in 2010, the board agreed to new additions to the Liberation Pavilion, including a faith in wartime exhibit, an interfaith chapel, and a *Monuments Men* exhibit. None of these were envisioned in the 2003 Master Plan.

I realized by 2009 that I had completely overlooked the spiritual dimension of the war that families and troops felt so deeply. After listening to hundreds of oral histories over the years, I came to appreciate the important role faith played for Americans throughout the war. Religion was so central to the lives of the generation that went to war in 1941 that I could not believe I had not realized it earlier, particularly as the son of a church historian and former Baptist minister. After recognizing this was a big miss on my part, I won board approval to add the faith in wartime exhibit and chapel. Herschel Abbott suggested I ask the New Orleans–based Baptist Community Ministries Foundation (BCM) to support the gallery, and that group donated even though we were in the earliest planning stages for the Liberation Pavilion. BCM's willingness to support this idea so early in its conception confirmed my belief that the topic was significant to the Museum's story.

The way we came to the idea of the *Monuments Men* gallery was unusual. In 2009, Guenter Bischof, now a history professor and my successor as UNO's Director of Center Austria and a Presidential Counselor, gave me a lead on Robert Edsel. He was working on a book entitled *The Monuments Men,* a story that few people knew. I called Robert's office and left a message. A few days later, while on vacation, I received a call from him. He told me the amazing story of how the US Army helped recover thousands of masterpieces of art and sculptures that Hitler's henchmen stole from Jewish homes and museums across Europe. Hitler secretly hid these masterworks in castles and salt mines across Germany and Austria. Edsel called it the "biggest art heist in history."

Late in the war, as Allied troops advanced into Germany, a gallant band of curators, art historians, professors, and museum experts were recruited into the US and British armies with officer rank, creating the Monuments, Fine Arts, and Archives Unit. Their mission was to find these precious works of art in all their hiding places, rescue them before they could be destroyed, and return them to their rightful owners. The so-called Monuments Men had their orders and authority from the Supreme Commander himself, as General Eisenhower charged them to safeguard these cultural monuments and to make every reasonable effort amid the war "to preserve and protect these products of man's creative instinct."[1]

This daring story of courage and intrigue was a perfect way to illustrate an extraordinary aspect of the American and British war effort, as they were the only wartime nations seeking to rescue these stolen cultural treasures and restore them to their rightful owners. I quickly invited Robert to make a presentation to our board in June 2010. His story had the trustees spellbound, and they enthusiastically supported my recommendation to make space for a new exhibit in the Liberation Pavilion. Immediately after Robert's presentation, Bob Hayes, one of our most enthusiastic trustees and major donors, rushed up and pledged $1 million toward the exhibit.[2] The board roared its approval and by the next year, the adjustments to fit the story into the Liberation Pavilion were being designed. Soon after, Robert was elected to the board.

This is not how museums typically plan or design their exhibits. The addition of the *Monuments Men* and *Faith in Wartime* exhibits, as well as the interfaith chapel, added at least $10 million to the cost of the Liberation Pavilion, making it one of our most expensive and difficult elements to design. I was always pleased by the willingness of our board to accept cost increases when justified. Everyone understood that there would never be another WWII museum in America that would exceed what we aimed to build in New Orleans.

The decision on whether to build the Canopy of Peace was also fraught with high drama. Plans for this striking structure, rising 148 feet above the campus, was one of the reasons Bart Voorsanger won the competition to be the architect of record in the 2003 Master Plan. Boysie and I, among other board members, saw that it would change the skyline of the city, especially at night, when lighting would bathe the Canopy in changing colors. The Canopy would be a landmark in the city and a symbol of the Museum, seen worldwide on television during the many international events held in New Orleans, like the Superbowl. In 2002, everyone loved the idea of the Canopy, and in his bid Bart promised it could be built for $6 million. It turned out this estimate was far off the mark.

Over the years, Bart redesigned the Canopy three times to keep the costs down close to his original projection. Nothing worked until 2010, when Bart proposed a final design with estimated costs of around $10 million. Without a donor for the Canopy in sight, the issue became urgent in 2011, when we were about to drive pilings for the US Freedom Pavilion. Bob Farnsworth reported that if we drove the pilings for the Canopy at the same time, it would only cost $750,000, as opposed to $2 million if we waited for a donor and a second construction event.

An immediate decision to spend up to $750,000 for the Canopy pilings struck some board members as a risky investment and a waste of money. They were skeptical we would ever find a donor to fund the completion of such a project, rendering the pilings useless. We were already scraping together all available funds in hopes of starting construction of the Campaigns of Courage later that year.

These reservations sparked a fiery debate at the board meeting of June 3, 2011. With strong support from others, Bob Hayes believed that the Canopy was outside of our mission and its excessive costs could be used for higher priorities, while Frank Stewart expressed concern about insurance and maintenance. If we could build it safely with a donor to meet the budget, I and others remained ardent supporters. A motion to kill the project failed.[3]

Six months later, with no funds yet expended or raised, the issue came to a head again at the board meeting on December 10, 2011. Bob Hayes continued his adamant opposition. As one of our $2 million donors, Bob had earned respect for his passion for our mission, his active board participation, and his generosity. John Koerner endorsed the recommendation to approve the expenditure for the pilings. I voiced my continued conviction regarding the importance of the Canopy to our national museum. "It fired the imagination," I said, arguing it "was worth the risk." As the debate heated up, I was glad to hear Boysie strongly endorse the Canopy as an iconic, visually powerful signature addition to the New Orleans cityscape that would attract visitors. He also argued that there were donors who would only give for such monumental architectural works and were not interested in funding exhibits. At this point, both Bob and Boysie rose from their seats and argued across the boardroom table. Boysie, as board chairman from 2000–2004, and part of the architect selection committee, was as passionate as I was in favoring it. Our most prominent board members joined the fray, but almost all the local members supported building the Canopy. In the end, the vote was strongly in favor of funding the pilings.

It was a healthy debate that spoke to the passion and dedication of trustees on both sides of the issue. Many shared my belief that the board emerged stronger from having such candid and emotional discussions on strategic decisions. Sometime later, Bob confided to me that he was okay with the vote because he understood "it was a local issue." He saw that the Canopy was more important to those from New Orleans than for the trustees from around the country.

This open review process was critical to the success or failure of achieving our larger mission. There was no extra federal or state government funding around to bail the Museum out of costly mistakes. The National WWII Museum had to live or die by its research, debates, and decisions. There were financial risks going into each project and pavilion. The leadership I provided since 1998 was always premised on the reality that the Museum functioned more like a growing private enterprise, albeit governed by nonprofit regulations and policies. Instead of shareholders, board members were invested as stakeholders with personal contributions in the many millions. Their credibility was as much at stake as mine. And we were all determined that donations from both private and public sectors would not be squandered. I always felt more confident in my leadership and the future of the Museum when this group of smart businessmen and women debated tough decisions and emerged unified. Hurricanes and economic conditions might force big adjustments, but this board was not afraid to make bold decisions, laden with multi-million-dollar obligations, and once made trustees seldom went back to question the path chosen. They did what great boards do. They rallied behind every decision, contested or not, and resolved to support me and our staff in the execution and success of those decisions. This commitment to a common cause sounds like an obvious path to success, but it is a central challenge for nonprofit boards. In our case, the board members trusted a process that was fair and open and took bold actions to build one of the great museums in the world. It was quite remarkable.

We faced numerous other daunting challenges, all converging in the same period of 2011–15. The pace of designing and constructing new pavilions intensified, even as we continued to expand our programming. Outside of pavilion construction, I kept the board focused on feasibility studies for the hotel conference center. When we eliminated the Center for the Study of the American Spirt (CSAS) from the Master Plan after Katrina, Boysie and I agreed to use the land opposite the Museum on Magazine Street to develop a hotel and parking garage that could support a state-of-the-art conference center to replace a major element that was initially envisioned for CSAS. We believed that a hotel could enhance our educational mission through the conferences and groups we wanted to attract to the Museum. We understood the mission components well but had to learn how to fill the hotel with Museum visitors and conference programs.

We needed professional help to assess the property purchased in 2002 for future Museum parking and a hotel site. Bob Farnsworth and I attended the nonprofit Urban Land Institute (ULI) convention in Las Vegas in 2011 to present our hotel development concept to hotel developers who selected several projects each year. To our disappointment, they ranked our site as a C- as a prospect for hotel conference center development, given the poor image of surrounding warehouses and street conditions. They did, however, recommend retail and parking amenities that would make the site more attractive to our proposed uses.

We returned to New Orleans determined to make the improvements recommended by ULI. Bob worked with the New Orleans Regional Planning Commission to get commitments for sidewalk and street improvements around the Museum. Boysie and I convinced Gov. Bobby Jindal to procure most of the funding for a parking garage that could serve the Museum and a future hotel and conference center—adding to our visitor and tourist appeal. We made good progress and then out of the blue, Bob got a call from a local developer who wanted to buy the property for a hotel. We were not interested in selling, but the fact that the property was attracting other potential developers was the best kind of feasibility study.

We had important guidance in our exploration from a young hotel developer on the board, Brandon Berger, and from Robert Merrick, who was President and CEO of Latter and Blum Real Estate New Orleans. Explorations with other local hotel developers and feasibility studies became more encouraging. With the garage in the pipeline and the streetscape improving, we occupied a rapidly improving location in a city and district that was heavily invested in tourism. Our project was complicated by our need to meet mission-related education requirements for conferences at a standard of quality that matched our Museum experience. This made it challenging to find a developer to partner with. Many did not want to build a large conference center in a small hotel.

The growing popularity of our conferences and group programs boosted the case for a hotel and expanded meeting rooms to support onsite programs. Accordingly, in June 2012, the board approved searching for a developer for the hotel and conference center, and we formed a task force to begin formal feasibility studies on the project.[4] As was common with all our capital projects, the hotel idea made some board members nervous. However, few questioned its importance as a pathway to achieve our educational mission.

EMERGING IDEAS FOR LIBERATION

While the immediate challenges revolved around the Canopy and the hotel, long-term issues about the design and the creation of a coherent theme for the Liberation Pavilion, the last of the content pavilions, were already at the forefront of board planning in 2012–15. This pavilion would focus on the final part of our mission statement by attempting to answer the postwar question of what World War II means today. The legacy and lasting consequences of the most destructive war in human history had to be clearly defined, at least in the broadest terms. Did we fulfill our war aims? How did Allied victory benefit America and the world? Answering these questions was the biggest challenge we faced.

In 2003 we had framed our conceptual designs for the Liberation Pavilion around a very American-centric scheme. We focused almost entirely on

America's domestic legacies from the war: an expanding economy, the GI Bill, the struggle for civil rights and women's rights, extension of our defense systems, growth of suburbs, innovative technologies, the race to the moon, and quantum leaps in medicine, science, research, and higher education. These historical legacies were evident and needed significant treatment as all these advances could be traced directly or indirectly to our victory in World War II. But by 2009 I was worried that our inward-looking theme was too narrow. I advised the board that the Liberation Pavilion should also recognize America's larger legacy as a world leader for the rest of the twentieth century. We should emphasize how America led advances in democracy and human rights abroad as well as at home. I argued that the Museum's mission, enshrined in our Congressional designation, committed us to help visitors understand not only how our victory in World War II changed America, but how it changed the world. The United States emerged as a superpower after World War II and helped shape the world order in the twentieth century and beyond. It was a supreme achievement that should be recognized, along with mistakes that inevitably came with the responsibility of leadership. We took on a new role as leader of the free world and promoter of democracy, a role that was critical in our competition with the Soviet Union, which lasted for much of the rest of the century. I firmly believed we needed to add these stories to the Liberation exhibits.

As a prelude to the shift in emphasis, in early 2008, incoming chairman Phil Satre and I visited Sara J. Bloomfield, Director of the United States Holocaust Memorial Museum. We wanted to understand how that museum kept the story of the Holocaust relevant in exhibits that extended the legacies and lessons of that horrific genocide to the present day. She advised us that they were most successful when they grounded their exhibits in historical roots of events or ideas that preceded the central event itself, with examples such as Hitler's racial laws, censorship, book burnings, and other attacks on human rights that led to the Holocaust. This was the kernel of advice that led me to consider the ideas in President Roosevelt's "Four Freedoms" speech in January 1941. The President's State of the Union address came 11 months before the attack on Pearl Harbor and US entry into the war. This speech was a historic source for his vision of victory and became a significant American legacy in the postwar world. But there were other historical themes to consider, and I would need much more investigation and engagement from the board and historians to re-envision the legacy themes for the Liberation Pavilion.

BATTLING ON ALL FRONTS

By 2012, as I looked towards the next five years, I felt much more confident than in those worrisome days after Hurricane Katrina, when it felt like we might never complete the Master Plan. We had a top-notch team and could see a world-class Museum taking shape. Funds were sufficient to begin construction of the Campaigns of Courage Pavilion with the two core content exhibits already in design and fabrication. It felt like a turning point in our campaign.

My push for expanding our education frontiers for the future became a new driver of the capital and programming opportunities that were under review. Even as exhibit design, construction and fundraising remained the highest and most immediate priorities, the market demand for online visitors and education markets was still untested. We hired the Edge research firm to help us quantify the size of the national audiences, and their findings were both disappointing and encouraging. Its major finding was that the Museum had very low brand awareness around the country.[5] The research also showed we had a tremendous opportunity with those who mostly had not heard about us. The survey methodology showed that 55 percent of polled individuals were interested in engaging with us online, skewing to enthusiasts and younger audiences interested in the war. If we could find more ways to drive awareness and traffic to our website, Edge reported, these populations were open to engaging with Museum online programs that could generate interest and revenues from younger audiences as well as from older adults. The results reassured the board and me that we had not exaggerated the potential for our digitization and distance-learning plans. We also learned that there were 34 million Americans in the cohort age who were interested in World War II—an exponentially larger population than knew of the Museum.[6] That was big news and complemented our research into our online education opportunities.

Our staff and I had already gathered information about launching an online higher education plan, with the hope of creating an academic program in military history or WWII Studies. With a dramatic decline in graduate degrees in military history over the last three decades, we saw a gap between continuing student demand for such programs, both from the undergraduate level, as well as from military history enthusiasts, such as those who attended our International Conference on World War II every year. I believed the Museum could become an accredited degree-granting institution and could help fill the widening gap in World War II and military studies in higher education. Research from a Boston marketing firm we hired, Eduventures, indicated a strong opportunity for an online MA graduate degree program in military or World War II studies as no history museum had entered the field yet.

This seemed to me a promising way to advance the Museum's educational mission at the university level and generate new sources of income to support education, research, and publications. It would be innovative, making us the first WWII history museum in the world to enter the field of K–12 and higher education in such significant ways. We felt these new opportunities justified a significant increase in the size of the Hall of Democracy to accommodate a media center with production studios, virtual classrooms, a library, and professional offices for historians and media professionals. By the end of 2013, the board agreed to add the spaces and new technologies that these initiatives required.

The Canopy, Liberation Pavilion revisioning, hotel and conference center planning, and expansion of the Hall of Democracy were now all consuming for me. These were ambitious and costly ventures that added new risks and big increases to our capital campaign. Richard Adkerson, who became Chairman in June 2013, was no stranger to risk, and if there were ways to demonstrate the need for adjustments to the Master Plan, his leadership record inspired confidence.[7] The decisions about changing the Master Plan were so consequential that I thought it important that the board's core leadership team needed to understand the choices before the Museum and share in the responsibility for leading trustees to consensus on major issues. Soon after Richard became chairman, I recommended a first-ever executive meeting of all the past chairs to consider the scope of the impending changes to our Master Plan, as well as my personal plans.

Richard supported the ideas but understood the risks and the process we needed. In the fall of 2013, he invited all of us, including Boysie, Pete, Phil, and Herschel, to his home in Phoenix. First, I confided my plans to retire in 2017 and commit to a reduced emeritus position should they approve. The board would need to decide whether to search nationally or select one of our Vice Presidents to succeed me. My recommendation was to look internally at those who were already helping to run the Museum, as we finished financially in the black every year, and we wanted that to continue. I asked that these plans be kept strictly confidential until Richard could vet the succession plan with the Executive Committee and then with the board. There was too much going on for our staff to be distracted by my retirement and future replacement.

Before we adjourned in Phoenix, I briefed the former Chairmen on the looming decisions on multiple projects that were sure to impact our capital campaign and made the case for revisiting the entire Master Plan in order to include proposed changes to future buildings that best reflected our mission. The Canopy was still unfunded, and the design, development, and decisions for the hotel and conference center and Hall of Democracy had to be made soon to bring clarity to potential state funding sources and private donors. My marching orders were to support the Chairman and board committees while they vetted the major transition decisions in a comprehensive manner. For me, this felt like a turning point for the Museum from a personal and planning perspective.

PIVOT TO THE FUTURE

Richard and I devoted much of the ensuing year to wrestling plans to the ground for the Hall of Democracy and the Liberation Pavilion. "These two pavilions," I told the board in May 2014, "will define our Museum's identity and interpret the legacy of World War II."[8] The modifications to the Hall of Democracy would be costly, as they involved adding a third floor to an existing building. The space was needed for the historians, professionals, and digital communications experts to support our online education objectives. The plans included a major store on the ground floor, an expanded library and Rare and Iconic Artifacts Gallery on the second floor, and offices for a research and media center on the third floor. The board agreed with my push to enlarge the library and increase its height to accommodate a mezzanine level for books, but all these needs began to crowd the available space in the Hall. We agreed to move the Iconic Exhibit room to the Louisiana Memorial Pavilion in the Forbes Theater, where the public could easily access the treasured artifacts. That move also created more space for the library, the media center, and the virtual classrooms. In my mind, it was important to give the highest prominence and visibility to the core historical foundations of the Museum as well as to the media center, which afforded global outreach of our programs. These changes were ready to submit to Gallagher and Voorsanger Mathes for preliminary concept design and cost estimates in 2015.

The Liberation Pavilion was another story, however. The board struggled to grasp the themes and legacies of the pavilion, so I encouraged Richard to form a Master Plan update task force to review both Liberation and the best uses of every campus space. It was critical to make these decisions for the entire campus now while we were halfway through expansion. We could not secure funding for the remaining buildings without a clear plan of how everything fit together to advance our long-range educational mission and vision for the completed Museum. Richard and I knew that we needed a process to bring the board along with the ideas and costs for that final vision.

This Master Plan Update Task Force had to be a formidable group of leaders to meet these challenges. On my recommendation, Richard chose Boysie to chair the task force, with John Georges leading a subcommittee to review the final concept themes for the Liberation Pavilion and John Koerner heading a subcommittee to recommend final uses for existing and proposed spaces. These three trustees were all influential board members and CEOs with experience in making judgments on big, creative ideas.

Going forward, what I needed most was a board consensus on a single unifying theme for the Liberation Pavilion and its third-floor cinematic experience. While our historians would lead the thematic development, we needed an imaginative director to create the show. After some discussions, we commissioned our Beyond All Boundaries partner Phil Hettema to do the job. Unlike other exhibits that traced the course of the war on the home front and the front lines, the Liberation Pavilion was to focus on the meaning and legacies of World War II in the postwar era. The reality is that public memory evolves over time from various sources in media, personal accounts, and public policies and is colored by current mindsets. For the Museum, the lasting meaning of the American experience in World War II had to be manifest in well-documented outcomes of the war. As a historian, I strongly believed that the chosen legacies needed to be historically sound and consistent with our mission. It was critical that the board, staff, and designers were all on the same page.

We were juggling many big projects at once. The hotel and Liberation projects were most vexing, and we had little idea of the engineering complexities we might face with the Canopy of Peace, which still had no donor in sight. The changes to the Master Plan kept moving the goalposts of the capital campaign. Going into 2015, we knew we might need to raise another $50 to $80 million to reach our capital campaign goal, which now stood at $325 million. Pushing the educational boundaries of The National WWII Museum was going to be expensive.

CHANGES IN TRAJECTORY

Boysie gave me an unexpected phone call in my office one afternoon in early 2015. I planned to call him that day anyway, so I began the conversation with my immediate concern that we were approaching a decision point on whether we could build the Canopy of Peace. Boysie interrupted me. "Stop right there, Nick," he said. "I'm about to be your largest donor." I took a deep breath and was silent for a moment. At that point, as I knew and Boysie knew, Boeing was our biggest donor at $15 million. After I caught my breath, I said, "Boysie, do you know what you are saying?"

Boysie was never one to beat around the bush. "Yes," he replied. "I'm donating $20 million to the Museum to fund the construction of the Canopy of Peace." Just like that. I was stunned and almost fell off my chair. I could barely say, "Thank you." I knew Boysie was grinning on the other end of the phone. I think he was happier to surprise me with the news than about his enormous gift. He later said, "I always told the board that one day, someone would donate funds for the Canopy, I just did not know it would be me." The size of the gift from Boysie and his wife, Joy, enabled the Museum to name the canopy as well as BB's Stage Door Canteen in honor of them. Boysie's gift also provided funds to recognize his friend, John Alario, a longtime state legislator and Museum supporter who was then President of the Louisiana Senate, with the Senator John Alario Jr. Special Exhibition Hall. Boysie's surprise phone call and huge gift were among the greatest moments in the history of The National WWII Museum and for me personally.

The news came at exactly the right time. The Canopy had to be funded with firm commitments in the coming months, or else it could not be built at all. It had to be nearly complete before the last pavilion began construction. The gift energized the board and inspired everyone with renewed confidence that the Museum could overcome every fundraising obstacle in the years ahead. A few weeks later, Boysie came to my office and typed out the $20 million check, using Stephen Ambrose's personal IBM Selectric III typewriter, the same one Steve used to write most of his 30-plus books. I think Steve must have been watching from heaven in amazement. This single check was nearly the amount that took us 10 years of struggle to raise for the National D-Day Museum from 1990 to 2000.

LEANING FORWARD: LEADERSHIP AND BIG DECISIONS

By early 2015, Richard and I felt it was the right time to prepare the board and staff for the transition to a new and younger leadership. Since the opening of the Museum, the trustees and I always assumed my successor would have similar qualifications to mine: a PhD in history with senior-level executive experience in a history museum. I turned 60 the year we cut the ribbon on the D-Day Museum, so I was not the typical age for one to start a second career, building a national Museum. From time to time, various chairmen asked me for thoughts about my eventual replacement. I always kept my eyes open for a potential successor. Indeed, one reason for forming the Presidential Counselors group was to ascertain if any of them might be future candidates. I also queried the Presidential Counselors about others they might suggest among museum leaders and historians around the country. The needs of our Museum were unique in conception, funding, and operations. Very few museums were independent nonprofits, and even fewer had military history as part of their missions. Out of necessity, the Museum was an entrepreneurial institution that had to survive on its own resources.

During my tenure, senior staff and I were always searching for new revenue-generating opportunities outside of visitor-based income, which helped keep the Museum afloat during troublesome periods and advanced our mission to create state-of-the-art exhibits and programs. From the day I became Chairman and CEO in 1998, I was always motivated to reinvent what the Museum could become, and what it must become to generate excitement and community learning in unique environments. When it came to my successor, we needed someone who embraced the entrepreneurial culture I had instilled in our employees, especially in my core leadership team, though none of them were historians. When my scouting for an ideal candidate with historian credentials proved unsuccessful, I gradually began to look internally at my own senior staff. There were three top candidates: Stephen Watson, Bob Farnsworth, and Becky Mackie. All of them were impressive, making their marks in different ways, and contributing mightily to the Museum's success.

Stephen Watson stood out, even among our accomplished senior staff. As is often said of certain basketball players, he always "wanted the ball" when emergencies struck. In the crisis months during Hurricane Katrina, he stepped up and demonstrated leadership, undaunted by the challenges we faced. At other times, he excelled in every area of operations, marketing, management, budgeting, travel, education, digitization, distance learning, and a host of other initiatives I sought to advance. He personally led the direct marketing campaign since 2002 that grew our membership to over 147,000 by 2016.[9] He was always in the middle of major decisions and implementation of our plans for our exhibits, fundraising, and construction. He rose through the ranks performing at a high level, exceeding expectations at each position and task along the way, culminating in his promotion in January 2015 to Executive Vice President, my number-two position. Through performance, position, and leadership, Stephen gradually emerged as our most deserving senior executive, and I advised the board that his appointment would result in the smoothest transition possible. I did not believe there was anyone in the nation who was better prepared to complete the remaining campus buildings, raise the remaining funds, and extend the Museum's mission into the future. Stephen Watson exemplified all the entrepreneurial and leadership traits I wanted from a successor. Indeed, I told the board leadership, he was already succeeding at many things that I was getting credit for doing. However, I did take some credit for hiring and promoting someone so capable.

Agreement on hiring internally, instead of conducting a national search, did not come without a lot of soul searching. It took more than a year of confidential deliberations before Richard and a small group of board members agreed with my argument that Stephen was the best and most natural choice. They finally concurred, pending Executive Committee approval.

My suggested transition plan was unusual, but it made sense. I proposed working a reduced load as President and CEO Emeritus for a few more years after stepping down to write the Museum history, participate as a speaker on tours, help with our conferences, and advise on the three remaining major projects that were central elements of my vision for the Museum's future, including the hotel and conference center, the Hall of Democracy, and the Liberation Pavilion.

In spring 2015, Richard convened the Executive Committee in a special fly-in meeting in Phoenix to finalize the succession plans and make decisions on other key projects. The March 17, 2015, meeting was one of the most consequential of the decade for the Museum and for me. Fortuitously, it came just days after the Bollingers announced their $20 million donation for the Canopy of Peace. The mood of trustees was upbeat and forward looking. It was a good thing, because taken together the threshold decisions before the Executive Committee would define the Museum's future path for years to come.

The Executive Committee officially approved Stephen's candidacy for President and CEO at the March 2015 meeting, though formal action by the board would wait until fall 2015. Additionally, the Executive Committee approved my request to continue as President and CEO Emeritus until 2017. Richard and a few other trustees were worried this would not work, but I assured them that I had been working closely with Stephen in recent years, and we had always found common ground and mutual respect on major decisions. Since Stephen was not a historian, he welcomed my continuing role in standing up our research center and helping to recruit WWII historians. He was fully on board with our strategic push for conferences, distance learning, and research, all needed to support our ambitious plans for higher learning and education outreach. I assured the board that the choice of Stephen would assure a seamless transition through a period of the Museum's greatest expansion.

We passed more milestones in Pheonix. Boysie reported on the results of a three-hour meeting of the Master Plan Task Force in February at one of our favorite restaurants, Ralph's on the Park. John Georges, John Koerner, Boysie, and the rest of the Task Force reached a final consensus on a single theme that united all the exhibits in the Liberation Pavilion. The group debated many historical consequences of the war before coming to agreement on a single word to recommend to the board. That word, Boysie told the Executive Committee, was "Freedom." It summed up what World War II means today. The freedom theme gave the entire pavilion a hopeful and positive imprint on the meaning of victory for America. We came out of that Executive Committee meeting with approval of our new concept.

Later, in June 2015, John Georges presented these findings in greater detail to the full board. He and his subcommittee worked for years to shape the themes of the Liberation Pavilion, working with our historians, Gallagher, and Hettema, and now their key ideas were on full display to the board. He also provided a better look into Hettema's vision for the third-floor cinematic experience, which we now called the Freedom Theater. John said the theater would be "a revolving immersive presentation to provide visitors with a deeper understanding of postwar American objectives such as FDR's Four Freedoms and to incorporate famous quotes from leaders on what freedom means today." [10]

Patrick Gallagher described the overview for the first two floor exhibits that we had hammered out with our staff and Presidential Counselors. These exhibits would be media-heavy experiences. After many discussions together, Patrick and I proposed we plan these exhibits to be powerful experiences, both emotionally and educationally. We wanted the exhibits to stimulate visitor introspection, causing them to ask, "Could we do it today? Why did we fight? How could we prevent it from ever happening again?" I promised that the exhibits would be historically grounded in public memory, with the Four Freedoms as a connecting thread throughout the pavilion. The exhibits would present America in the postwar era as a global superpower with the responsibility of leading the free world in advancing and protecting our hard-won freedoms at home and abroad. At that meeting, we finally achieved a board-approved direction for the coming years of design work on the Liberation Pavilion. John Koerner also broke several logjams in his report on the space and use subcommittee for the Master Plan and won board approval for expansion of the Collections Department's space and storage, adjustments to the Hall of Democracy, and repurposing the ground floor of the parking garage.

The last major project report from the Hotel and Conference Center Committee came at the June 2015 board meeting as well. While we were still considering a contract with a hotel developer, the hotel task force began to examine moving forward with the Museum as the sole owner and developer. Financing prospects looked promising. Once we contracted with architects, hotel designers, and marketing consultants, our task force raised our sights to a higher-grade hotel with a major franchise, which meant the cost would skyrocket to just over $68 million, largely because of the cost of the conference center. The task force later recommended I be authorized to issue a Request for Proposals for a joint venture developer.

The Executive Committee approved the basic terms to develop the hotel and conference center as a nonprofit subsidiary of the Museum. We thought that by having an experienced hotel developer and operator as a co-owner, with the Museum as the dominant partner, we could prescribe our terms for the hotel class and number of rooms to reflect the results of our feasibility studies. The size of the conference center was a critical consideration for the Museum to determine our anticipated needs for future education programs, conferences, and Museum groups needing residency on the Museum campus.

These approvals at the Phoenix Executive Committee meeting in March and the June 2015 board meeting gave me the green light to guide the design and funding changes needed for the home stretch in completing the Master Plan. There was a lot of work ahead on every project, but I believed that we had turned the corner, and we were empowered to plan, design, and build the remaining multiple projects. Richard forcefully put the full weight of his Chairman's goals for 2016 behind the board recommendations. I could not have asked for more support from a Chairman at a more critical time in the Museum's development. Every Chairman had helped get us to this moment, but Richard's leadership helped us fight our way through some tangled hedgerows.

PUSHING FORWARD

Canopy construction began in 2016 with a budget increase to nearly $12 million, with many more to follow. The project was plagued by engineering, shipping, and assembly issues over the following years, and we would need every cent of Boysie's $20 million gift to complete it. Meanwhile, modifications to the Hall of Democracy raised its cost from $18.3 million to $25 million.[11] The state government committed $18 million to the project, but we needed find the remaining funds before June 2017 to receive the state's money for construction in that year. Representatives from the Wayne and Gladys Valley Foundation heard about our expansion needs and offered a capital construction grant to complete our funding and satisfy the match for the state.[12] The commitments from the state and the Valley Foundation in 2016 secured the essential funding we needed to begin construction in

2017, with the cost of the pavilion totaling $30 million. This was a huge relief to me, as this meant that the completion of Hall of Democracy was assured, including all the new media technology, the library, and research spaces for historians.

The research center was slowly emerging under a new name that I felt was more appropriate to the Museum's mission—the Institute for the Study of War and Democracy. It would not only revive the CSAS project scrapped after Katrina, but it would also transcend it with some significant additions. We envisioned a research center full of top historians to advance both our educational mission and our commitment to historically sound exhibits and content. These public historians, together with educators, media producers, and other specializations, would draw on the Museum's vast resources and oral history assets to become an international center for research, programs, and publications on World War II—delivered on site and online. Our team would establish partnerships with universities for joint degrees and create a community of scholars to keep the study of World War II fresh, accurate, and relevant. With some internal reorganization, we started staffing the new department with a few historians from our oral history and collections staff. The Institute's scholarly pursuits include a range of topics in American WWII history, but we also charged it with paying special attention to the principles of freedom, democracy, and human rights, as well as our military history.

To lead the Institute, I wanted a World War II historian with superior credentials to match those of our founder, Stephen Ambrose. I envisioned a senior historian who could assure accuracy of our future projects and programs and to assist in the development of the Institute. Some years earlier, I secured an endowment from the Zemurray Foundation in New Orleans to support a Chair for Research and Education at the Museum, something I could offer to entice a major WWII historian.[13] For several years, I had been recruiting Dr. Rob Citino, one of the most notable WWII historians in the United States. His scholarship on the German Wehrmacht placed him among the top military historians in the country. A few years earlier, *USA Today* had ranked Rob as the best university history teacher in America.

I invited Rob to be a featured speaker on our 70th anniversary of D-Day cruise to Normandy in 2014, alongside Tom Brokaw, distinguished historians Rick Atkinson and Don Miller, along with 19 D-Day veterans. Rob held our passengers spellbound with superb presentations. After the end of the tours, Rob and I sat on a bench outside Churchill's home at Chartwell when I told him he was my choice for the endowed chair. Two years later, I was finally able to offer him the Samuel Zemurray Stone Senior Historian endowed chair position, the first major hire for the Institute. I was as excited to offer him the job as he was to accept. We hit it off as colleagues and friends from the beginning. I felt confident we had the start of a top team of historians to complement the national stature of the Museum.

In October 2015, I was stunned and humbled to receive a letter from the President of the French Republic notifying me that Tom Brokaw, Tom Hanks, and I would be recognized with the French Legion of Honor, the highest award for a civilian. The Legion of Honor symbolizes "France's profound recognition of your eminent career as President and CEO of The National WWII Museum . . . and your personal role in honoring the memory and the heroism of the American veterans who fought on French soil during World War II and contributed to the liberation of France."[14] Brokaw and Hanks would receive the decoration in recognition for their contributions to the success of the Museum and for bringing international attention to the story of the Allied victory in Normandy. We were invited to Paris for the ceremony in May 2016 to receive the decorations from Gen. Jean-Louis Georgelin, the Grand Chancellor of the Legion of Honor. I later learned that Dorothea de La Houssaye, head of the Normandy Institute in Chateau Bernaville near Ste Mere Eglise, forwarded our nominations to the President of France.[15]

Our group, which included Stephen Watson, Trustee Mike Bylen, my wife, Beth, fellow historians, and other friends closest to me and the Museum, traveled to Paris for the ceremony.[16] The two days of events were memorable, starting with a magnificent dinner organized by Dorothea and Mike and held in the Circle du Union Allied Club, in a building Thomas Jefferson called the most beautiful in Paris. The Circle was established by General John Pershing in 1918 to provide a club for officers after World War I. The official award ceremonies were held the next day in the historic museum of the Legion of Honor. The elegant building exuded history and ideals in the birthplace of the *Legion d'Honneur* under Napoleon Bonaparte in 1802. The museum listed displays and names of all previous recipients since Napoleon, as an honor for freedom-loving people around the world, whether military personnel or civilians. It was thrilling for all of us to receive the prestigious decoration in this historic Grand Chancellery.

In a quiet moment, I reflected on all those who had helped bring me to this place of honor with two of our Museum champions after nearly 20 years of pursuing the Museum's mission. Who could have imagined? In my remarks, I drew attention to the person who should have stood at our side, noting that it was Stephen Ambrose's idea to tell the story of the Allied landings on D-Day and build a national Museum to honor the American sacrifice in liberating France. I said it was his vision for our Museum to give "close attention to America's critical role in helping to end tyranny and restore freedom in Europe, in alliance with our embattled friends in France . . . in 1944."[17] As result of our victory, I added, "We share a bond with France in our love of freedom and democracy." Following the award ceremony, Brokaw said to Hanks, "You and I are offered more awards than we can accept, but this one counts." Indeed, it did and still does. The US Ambassador to France, Jane Hartley, made the occasion even more memorable when she invited us all to a reception and dinner at her magnificent residence in the French Embassy. This was a high point of recognition for the Museum, for me, and my two friends, who had given so much to help the Museum over many years when success seemed like a distant dream.

HOME STRETCH, 2016–2017

Back at the Museum, there was much still to celebrate, but more work laid ahead in my last year. Stephen Watson was at my side for all the major challenges before us. Jim Courter succeeded Richard Adkerson as Chairman in June 2016, and his tenure would continue through my last year and Stephen's first year as President and CEO.[18] Jim served as a New Jersey Representative in Congress from 1979 to 1991 and later as CEO of the IDT Corporation before joining the board. "I'm going to be your best board member," he told me on my first visit to his office in Newark. He was excited to join the board, and he donated to the Museum on the spot. While in Congress, Jim had been colleagues with then Sen. Pete Wilson, and, some years after joining the board, served as Secretary before rising to Chairman. We still had big public and private fundraising goals to meet, as well as threshold decisions on the remaining Master Plan, but Jim was up to the task. At the June board meeting, I gave my last report as President and CEO on my final year ahead. The funding for the last two pavilions was partially complete, and plans were on track for the hotel and conference center.

After ten years of restoration, we launched our prized PT-305 in Lake Pontchartrain in March 2017. Named the USS *Sudden Jerk,* this Higgins PT boat served in the Mediterranean off the coast of France and is credited with sinking three Axis ships. She is the only remaining Higgins Industries–built patrol torpedo boat that saw combat in World War II. After the war, PT-305 was sold as surplus and used for sightseeing tours in New York City. Later, she was used for hauling oyster shells in the Chesapeake Bay. Finally, after a collector bought the boat and sold her to the Museum, she came home to New Orleans. Then, a group of our volunteers began restoring *Sudden Jerk* to her original specifications.

She was a big boat, and the opening of the Kushner Restoration Pavilion in 2011 provided a large, climate-controlled space that was required to continue the restoration of this prize artifact. Our volunteer group was talented and savvy and included some former Higgins workers who helped build PT boats during the war. After more than 120,000 volunteer hours and support from many sponsors, our boat team completed the restoration and secured US Coast Guard Commissioning for open-water operation. Soon after, the Museum began offering rides and tours aboard the fully restored and operational vessel, giving Museum guests the thrill of riding full speed in one of these famous PT boats. These tours were a prime example of the creative programs that depended on volunteerism, expertise, and passionate companies who made donations in cash and in kind.

Additionally, Trustee Ted Weggeland reported that in 2017 we planned to complete the Founders Plaza, an unexpected and pleasant surprise. My senior staff had secretly commissioned a monument that recognized Steve Ambrose and me by telling the story of the moment in 1990 when we conceived the idea of building the D-Day Museum. Our creation story is now forever preserved in Founders Plaza. Founders Plaza also paid tribute to Pete Wilson with a flagstaff monument that added to the impressive entryway of the campus. Also featured there was a prominent tribute bench with a bronze sculpture of President Franklin Delano Roosevelt, honoring his steadfast leadership of America during the uncertain years of the war. The plaza includes a Wall of Honor, listing all those who have contributed at least $1 million to the Museum, with room to add more names.

We all felt like we were riding a wave that was cresting as we entered my final year, but two big projects needed resolution: the Liberation Pavilion exhibits and the hotel and conference center. First came the Liberation

Pavilion. Despite more than seven years of work on Liberation with historians, the Gallagher team, Presidential Counselors, and board committees, lingering issues remained. By now, previous authorizations had led to final construction cost estimates of $38 million for the Liberation Pavilion with another $14 million for exhibits.[19] This was more than double the projected cost from the original master plan.

To achieve final resolution of the remaining exhibit ideas and themes, I convened a distinguished group of twelve historians, museum leaders, and international professionals in the visual arts to spend two days at the Museum in June 2016. We hoped they could help our team establish the historical framework for both the pavilion exhibits and the Freedom Theater show.[20] The specific charge for the charette was to verify the core postwar themes that trace their roots to the war and to American values, so that visitors could consider the war's repercussions for the nation and world—and in their lives. With those recommendations and board approval, design work began in earnest.

The final authorizations for both the Liberation Pavilion and the hotel & conference center came to a head at the January 25–26, 2017, Board of Trustees meeting. Boysie, the Task Force Chair, reported "unanimous consensus" for a story arc focused on the legacy of freedom and democracy and the struggle to extend and defend them both at home and abroad. The theme would be grounded in FDR's Four Freedoms speech, with a narrative "built around a solid research methodology that tracks the advance of (or lack of) freedom and democracy in the world since 1945."[21] John Georges followed with a detailed review of all the work his task force performed to define the advances of freedom in the postwar era. Next came presentations on the Freedom Theater from Phil Hettema and the exhibit design from Patrick Gallagher. The entire board enthusiastically approved the plans with the understanding that they would see the final designs before construction started on the exhibits a few years hence. Now at least, the road was clear for our staff and exhibit firms to finalize design and construction plans.

THE HOTEL AND CONFERENCE CENTER DEBATE

Next on the board's agenda was the hotel and conference center project. BB's Stage Door Canteen was filled with nearly 50 trustees along with consultants and hotel experts. The air was filled with anticipation. After years of study, it was time to make the final decision. By this time, the board was comfortable with the project for all the mission-related reasons, but they awaited the final details on the financing package, size of hotel, and its benefits to the Museum's long-term future. After all, no museum had built its own hotel and conference center.

The Hotel Task Force, the Museum staff, and I had worked for six months prior to the board vote to resolve the final conditions on the scope, mission, operations, and financing. Our recommendations did not leave any loose ends. We organized the meeting into two parts: the presentation and a Q&A session so trustees could ask questions and discuss any contentious points.

In his introductory remarks, John Koerner, Chairman of the Hotel Task Force, summarized the years of due diligence on this project.[22] Brandon Berger noted that our financial plan and partnership with a hotel operator made great sense. He outlined a commitment from Hilton to be part of the company's Curio Collection soft brand, a relationship that would allow the Museum to design the hotel and conference center with historic themes reflecting the WWII era. Brandon's compelling presentation emphasized that the upcoming recommendations were guided by the Museum's mission and laid out the financial viability of the project.

Bob Farnsworth reported that the hotel would have 230 rooms, with 20,000 square feet dedicated to a full-fledged conference center. Our standards for the hotel had risen significantly, as had the total cost, now pegged at $66.5 million. The Hotel Task Force, designers, and our marketing team were in full agreement that we should name it the Higgins Hotel, honoring the New Orleans boat builder who inspired Stephen Ambrose to envision the D-Day Museum.

Lead architect John Nichols, of Nichols Brosch and creative designer Alexander Julian proposed a modernized art-deco style for the building's exterior. Our lead interior designer, Kay Lang, delivered a stunning presentation that highlighted the deco theme throughout the interior spaces. Her presentation included plans to display historical photographs and artifacts in common areas, along with the ability for guests to view oral histories in their rooms to utilize the Museum's collection and reflect its mission.

After 90 minutes, the Hotel Task Force recommendations were turned over to the board for discussion. Chairman Courter's opening remarks were met with surprise, given all the years of groundwork and prior approvals. Jim raised concerns about financing at less than 100 percent, and now understood that this was not possible without relying on our education endowment for our equity. He also noted that approving the motion would mean increasing the capital campaign goal again, this time from $370 million to $382 million. Jim's concern over raising more capital funds sparked several hours of discussion. Despite the need for some capital, most trustees, senior staff, and consultants expressed confidence that the hotel would enhance the "world-class destination" status the Museum had reached in recent years. The addition would allow Museum guests to visit for multiple days and be completely immersed in our content for the duration of their stay.

The board discussion went into high gear. Herschel Abbott reiterated his belief that the "conference center was crucial to fulfilling the Museum's mission as determined years ago, and [that] nothing speaks more clearly to the mission of the Museum than a conference center." Mike Bylen then noted the much-improved quality of the hotel since the first presentations, praising a design that reflected the WWII era as well as our mission. Mark Rubin, a Holocaust survivor and real estate developer, strongly approved of the hotel, noting that it would be the key to success of our education and conference initiatives. While there was some concern about weathering an unforeseen economic downturn, that would be no different from challenges Museum operations had already survived after multiple hurricanes and economic downturns. Trustees discussed such risks openly in this meeting and brought up every one of the previous pavilions we had constructed. The prevailing refrain from trustees was that the priority should be on expanding our educational mission through new conference center space.

I reported the plan embraced by the Hotel Task Force provided multiple safeguards through creation of a Higgins Campaign Fund. It would have the potential to raise $19 million in private funds for naming of hotel rooms and conference center spaces around World War II themes and individuals. Additionally, we had created a Higgins Reserve Fund to hedge against any unexpected financial issues, such as those suffered after Hurricane Katrina. I also reminded the board that the Museum had raised $270 million in the last 14 years, and $10 million in 2017 alone; with another $10 million expected by the end of the year.

The addition of the hotel to support our conferencing mission was only a minor modification to our original vision. Each year's conference grew larger than the last and having meeting spaces in proximity to the Museum was paramount to continuing that success. I pointed out that the feasibility studies we conducted on the hotel were more rigorous than any we did for a single pavilion on our campus.

From the start, diversification of revenue sources was the lifeblood of the Museum, I argued. "The board always had the courage to take calculated risks, from the very beginning. This was a prime reason for our success to date. It was part of our entrepreneurial spirit culture."

Richard Adkerson inquired about the use of $12 million of naming opportunities as a sound financial backstop, which garnered trustee responses that our business plan was "well structured, a very good investment and worth the risk." I weighed in once more to say if anyone had an idea for a sustaining source of revenues to the Museum endowment that was better than this hotel and conference center, "I was all ears."[23] Ted Weggeland argued the hotel would provide educational value and boost visitation, in the same way that *Beyond All Boundaries* and BB's Stage Door Canteen raised our reputation for destination-worthy educational experiences.

Boysie made the final proposal that brought the discussion to an end. As he often did when board members worried about risks, he first said that "if we approve this project, we on this board won't let it fail." Boysie was right. The board never failed to fully support any approved project. He concluded by asserting that "the hotel promises tremendous returns even at moderate projections," and, in the best spirit of philanthropy from our largest donor, Boysie offered his personal guarantee for losses up to $5 million in the first five years of hotel operations.

It was time to vote. John Georges called the motion, seconded by Pete Wilson, to approve the project. The vote was overwhelmingly in favor. The victory was a shining final moment for me as I prepared to step down. Boysie and the board did what they always did when faced with big decisions: they had rigorous and open debates, had all the data before them, were prepared to deliver sound answers to tough questions, and stood firm in making a final decision. The diligence of the Hotel Task Force could not have made me prouder. They worked tirelessly with me and the consultants, bankers, lawyers, hotel developers, exhibitors, architects, and designers for three solid years. During all those years, the board focus on the Museum's education mission was always paramount. The vote was a culmination of the dedication, commitment, and savviness they put forth in service of The National WWII Museum. The board approval never would have happened without Stephen Watson, Bob Farnsworth, the Hotel Task Force and the board all working together for years. It took a team, the comradery was special, and we again felt a part of creating something larger than ourselves.

"WORLD WAR II-U"

Before stepping down, I was determined to make more progress on the "World War II-U" distance-learning concept that I had conceived years earlier in the aftermath of Hurricane Katrina. I believed a strong higher education partner to deliver a joint online master's degree in World War II history would add credibility to our educational outreach capabilities. For several years, I scanned the higher education landscape through my old university contacts to find institutions that offered nontraditional course offerings—online and off campus. I was searching for a public university partner with a big national online reach, one that would have lower tuition rates than private university degree offerings, one that was also offering MA degrees totally online. It was important that a partner history department did not have an MA in military history and was entrepreneurial enough to consider partnering with a history museum. By early 2017 I found a single university that met all my requirements: Arizona State University (ASU).

As the second strategic planning task force got underway in the spring of 2017, I asked Richard Adkerson to arrange a meeting with ASU President Michael Crow to consider a partnership with the Museum to offer jointly an online master's degree in WWII Studies, relying on our faculty, digital assets, and marketing reach. Richard's firm was headquartered in Phoenix, and I was aware that he knew President Crow well enough to secure a meeting with me. I also knew that ASU offered massive online degree programs for over 40,000 students, one of the largest commitments to online learning of any public university in the nation. Richard quickly got the meeting scheduled, and in early May 2017 Richard, Stephen, and I met with a group that included Crow, ASU history faculty, and the directors of their online programs. I made the case for the joint venture, pointing out that our distinguished historians matched up well with the standards of the ASU history department.

Crow immediately saw the potential and directed his team to work out the details. I believe he and the ASU professionals welcomed the partnership partly because of the Museum's rising national reputation for programs and conferences on World War II. I think he liked our entrepreneurial spirit, too. But most important to ASU was the Museum's significant investment in top

WWII historians to provide the knowledge and credentials needed to deliver distance-learning programs at the graduate level. Stephen finalized the partnership a year later, resulting in one of the fastest-growing MA degrees among ASU's online graduate programs.

LAST HURRAH: MEANINGFUL MEMORIES

My final months as President and CEO were special for other reasons as well. In January, we celebrated the completion of Founders Plaza and dedicated the Horatio Alger American Spirit Bridge, making the symbolic link between the original pavilions at the Museum's birth to our new pavilions and expanded mission. The bridge carried our visitors to the rest of the campus, including pedestrian transit into the Ralph E. Crump US Merchant Marine Gallery, named after the board trustee and generous exhibit sponsor who served in US Merchant Marines in both the Pacific and Atlantic theaters during the war.[24] The gallery portrays the extreme dangers and losses incurred by mariners who carried lifesaving supplies to our troops overseas.

I also had special opportunities to enjoy the company of many WWII veterans coming through the Museum that spring. The most notable event was the annual birthday party we held in January for 107-year-old Lawrence Brooks, a New Orleanian who was the oldest living veteran of World War II. His birthday celebration had become an ongoing tradition at the Museum for a man who modestly shared the secret to his long life, simply saying, "Be nice to people."

Some years earlier, the Museum formed a relationship with the Gary Sinise Foundation's Soaring Valor program, bringing WWII veterans to New Orleans to tour the Museum. Gary, the acclaimed actor and director, was inspired by his uncle, Jack Sinise, a navigator on a B-17 Flying Fortress, who flew 30 missions over Europe.[25] By 2017, Gary's efforts helped us capture the accounts of many veterans who would never have been recorded. Notably, at one of his Soaring Valor events, he joined me in welcoming Dick Cole, the renowned co-pilot on Jimmy Doolittle's daring raid on Japan in the spring of 1942. Dick joined several of our programs, conferences, and airshows, and at age 90 he participated in the Soaring Valor event with more than 40 WWII veterans. Gary and Soaring Valor kept the Museum in the forefront of our national efforts to save these stories and honor those who fought for our freedom. After Jack Sinise passed away at the age of 90, Gary said, "It was comforting to know that his story was part of the Museum's oral history collection, and that he had the opportunity to visit such a remarkable institution."[26]

As we moved toward my last board meeting, we had groundbreakings for the Hall of Democracy and the Bollinger Canopy of Peace. They were capped off by the June dedication and opening of *The Arsenal of Democracy* exhibit. The full campus was coming into view. As I looked in the rear-view mirror at the last 19 years as Chairman and Founding President and CEO, I felt proud of all those who had come into my life to become part of this unlikely story. The transition was underway, future leadership was in place, and the revised Master Plan would be completed in coming years. The Museum was already a national treasure, and its growth was phenomenal, despite past disasters and unforeseen challenges.

The Museum was reaching new heights with 685,721 visitors in 2017 and over 156,000 members from every state of the country. The revised Master Plan would encompass over 650,000 square feet in nine buildings, double the number estimated in the 2003 Master Plan.[27] We employed over 300 people in a national Museum that was in development long before some of them were even born.[28] There were also some 400 dedicated volunteers who joyously supported our mission and programs every day. Our overseas programs were growing and generating new revenues. On the capital side, since our initial campaign set our first goal at $180 million in 2003, we raised nearly $324 million in cash, pledges, and appropriated funds from state and federal government.[29] I trusted no one more than Stephen Watson to meet the challenges and finish the capital campaign, which had now increased to $400 million. Stephen still needed to raise $70 to $100 million to reach that goal; a tall order, but I knew he would succeed. In addition to a great board that could see the goal line, Stephen would enjoy the continued support from one of the most talented museum teams in the nation—all high performers with deep experience and commitment to the mission. The new Institute, Media Center, and Education Department were all gearing up. Mission accomplished—almost.

STRATEGIC VISION FOR THE FUTURE

Before passing the reins to Stephen, we worked to create a new plan to advance all the changes to our institution since our last planning effort. We launched the Chairman's strategic revisioning process to push the boundaries of the Museum's distance-learning and education programs far beyond anything imagined in the original Master Plan of 2003. Stephen and I framed the goal of the strategic plan I proposed to the board in the meeting of June 2016: I remarked that "we were pivoting from being the best Museum on World War II to being the best source of knowledge and information on World War II."

Stephen and I agreed that the planning process should start in my last year and continue to completion during his first year as President and CEO in 2018. Chairman Courter understood that the results would be as much his legacy as it would be mine and Stephen's. To execute this planning effort, I proposed that Stephen and I invite a distinguished task force of WWII historians, media, and museum professionals to advise us.

Working with this group and our old friends at Lord Cultural Resources, Stephen and I charged the participants to recommend specific strategies the Museum might pursue to help shape new education and learning futures. With these goals we asked "What made sense for the Museum?" "What did not?" "How could we achieve the impact we needed to achieve our ambitious vision?" Herschel Abbott's task force report in 2013 had set out the board's vision "to engage and inspire all generations by broadening awareness and appreciation of America's role in the war that changed the world." Our task was to convert that vision into a concrete plan that utilized our personnel as well as digitized WWII content and our new technological resources.

In its first year, the task force agreed on two big ideas that would shape the future direction of the Museum. First, the Museum would become the most accessible resource for trusted knowledge about the American experience in World War II. Second, the Museum would embrace a "Society of the American Spirit, serving communities, learners, and institutions." With these broad goals established, Stephen and the board had the signposts to guide the Museum toward more expansive goals for future WWII education, both on campus, online, and overseas.

In my last days as president, I felt satisfied that I had met my commitments to the Museum. From the origin of the idea in 1990 with Steve Ambrose, to Chairman and CEO from 1998 to 2000, to Founding President and CEO from 2000 to 2017, my major goals for the Museum were being realized. At my last board meeting as President and CEO, the board presented me with framed copies of President Roosevelt's Four Freedoms Speech from

January 1941, the foundational theme and beacon for the Liberation Pavilion. The Board of Trustees expressed their warm and emotional gratitude for my 27 years of leadership.

PASSING THE BATON

Once Stephen took control of the helm, he hit the ground running, spearheading the completion of the strategic revisioning project. At the November 2018 board meeting, led by new Chairman Paul Hilliard, Stephen and Task Force Chair Chip Goodyear presented the final planning document. As approved, "Learning in the 21st Century: A Strategic Vision for Outreach & Accessibility" provided the blueprint for the Museum's educational future beyond its physical borders.

In its report, the task force envisioned the Museum becoming a national leader in K–12 WWII history education, research, and leadership. To activate the two big ideas of the plan, the task force identified specific strategies around five opportunity areas: K–12 Education Programs, Leadership Development, Higher Education and Lifelong Learning, Affiliate Networks and Force Multipliers, and Content Production and Delivery. We believed these initiatives would lead to partnerships and affiliates that would increase the Museum's national profile. The strategies also aimed to increase our capacity to produce high-quality WWII content by drawing upon our collections, programs, and personal stories to magnify the Museum's impact on public memory of the war.

With a new strategic vision for the Museum in place, Stephen led an aggressive fundraising effort to finish the capital campaign and complete the construction of the remaining campus. Building on the success of private donations in the previous years, trustees and new donors stepped up rapidly with larger gifts to help fund the remaining programs and pavilions. Paul and Madlyn Hilliard generously donated to support the Museum's educational mission by sponsoring the research library in the Hall of Democracy, as well as the entire conference center in the Higgins Hotel. The families of other WWII veterans, home front workers, and Holocaust survivors stepped up to assist with hotel fundraising by sponsoring hotel rooms to honor loved ones or other members of the WWII generation.

Jenny Craig, the famous nutrition guru and a fierce advocate for veterans, together with her daughter Denise and son-in-law Peter Merlone, a Museum trustee, gave a signature gift of $5 million to advance the higher learning goals of the Institute. Jenny wanted her contribution to help educate young people about the consequences of war. With two brothers who served in the armed forces during the war, Jenny believed her family's support of the new research and education center would be a tribute to all who served in World War II. "I have my name on several things; however, there is none that I am prouder of than The National WWII Museum," she said. Her donation added credibility to the Institute and to the Museum's reputation as a global gateway for research and programs on the study of World War II.

The Hall of Democracy opened in October 2019, and the Media Center began to bear fruit immediately as its production capability attracted new donations, including an important grant from the American Battle Monuments Commission to produce classroom curriculum on World War II. The Higgins Hotel and Conference Center opened a few months later in December 2019. In the following years, Stephen relocated our International Conference on World War II from offsite hotels to our own conference center in the Higgins Hotel, and the Institute was able to make good use of the conference rooms and technology.

When viewed together, the Madlyn and Paul Hilliard Conference Center, the Jenny Craig Institute for the Study of War and Democracy, the technological infrastructure of the Media and Education Center, the Madlyn and Paul Hilliard Research Library, and the Education and Access Departments enabled the Museum to conduct research, instruction, and distance-learning programs to reach millions of teachers and learners nationwide.

Paul Hilliard's veteran status and commitment to the Museum made him the overwhelming choice to become Chairman in 2018. His experience gave him a unique edge, as he brought business acumen, a veteran's perspective, and an enormous passion for learning about "his" war to the table. He became one of the Museum's most generous trustees and, over the years, contributed over $13 million toward exhibits, artifacts, the hotel and conference center, our educational mission, and more. In addition to supporting our acquisition of macro artifacts, and joining Museum tours, Paul's good-humored leadership saw us through the opening of the Hall of Democracy and the Higgins Hotel and Conference Center.

Stephen's campaign to complete the funding for the remaining campus also bore fruit for the Liberation Pavilion. Over the next few years, the Museum received multiple generous gifts to support the galleries in the pavilion. The first came from longtime Museum supporters Pam and Mark Rubin, who supported the Liberation Theater, which explores the testimonies of both the liberators and survivors of the Holocaust. Both Pam and Mark were passionate about preserving the memory of those who were liberated from the camps, as Mark, a Museum trustee, was a Holocaust survivor liberated from the Terezin camp in 1944.[30]

Byron Trott and his entire family donated to the first floor of the Liberation Pavilion to honor his father, David W. Trott, who served in the European Theater under Gen. George Patton. David W. Trott, who was a private first class, embodied the "citizen soldier" that Steve Ambrose admired so deeply. Instead of a great general or politician, we are proud to have named the first floor, *Finding Hope in a World Destroyed,* after Byron's father. Byron also was a lead donor as President of the Horatio Alger Association campaign to build the American Spirit Bridge linking the original D-Day exhibits to the expanded National WWII Museum.

In 2022, the Priddy Family Foundation also supported a critical element of the Liberation Pavilion: the Freedom Theater. Robert, a Museum trustee, and his wife, Kikie, understood our bold vision for the theater, and they also had a deep understanding of the crucial role the Freedom Theater would play in the Museum. After they made their generous gift, Robert Priddy said: "We hope that the central theme of human freedom and the exploration of 'what World War II means today' will inspire all who see it to reflect on the meaning of freedom and their role in preserving it."[31]

Together, all these major donations totaled nearly $15 million and contributed substantially to the completion of the exhibits in the Liberation Pavilion, the final piece of the Master Plan—a testament to the attractiveness of the Museum mission to private benefactors as we neared the completion of the campus. Their gifts came during another national crisis that once again placed the Museum in jeopardy.

A NEW CRISIS

Museum operations came to a grinding halt in mid-March 2020, when the Covid-19 pandemic became a national crisis. In New Orleans, the tourism industry, which sustained most of the city's economy, came to a standstill and Stephen ordered our doors closed on March 14, 2020. With the pavilions and campus empty for the foreseeable future, the outlook for the Museum was grim. Just as Hurricane Katrina paralyzed New Orleans and the Museum 15 years earlier, now Covid-19 cast doubt on the campus completion as well as on the survival of the Museum and the recently opened Higgins Hotel and Conference Center. It was a full-blown disaster.

Stephen moved decisively to assure staff of their continued employment and salaries for at least three months. He immediately reduced all professional staff salaries by 25 percent for the next 18 months and began to leverage the Museum's previous investments to expand our online educational programs. Stephen assembled a team of subject matter experts in various departments to deliver an unprecedented level of online WWII programming on our website. Then, after just 10 weeks with hardly any visitors, Stephen found a way to reopen to the public on Memorial Day 2020, regrettably with a draconian survival budget that resulted in the layoffs of one-third of 300 Museum employees. He called on the hotel management to reduce its staff to 10 to keep the doors open. He also secured federal Covid relief funding, as well as state and federal pandemic funding earmarked to revive museums and tourism industries. Amid great turbulence and uncertainty, Stephen led a gradual recovery, allowing the return of some visitors, while keeping the Liberation Pavilion and exhibit designs moving forward, albeit with opening delayed to 2023. He followed a bold and deliberate strategy amid an extraordinary national crisis. With precautions and restrictions in place, visitors slowly trickled into the Museum.

The pandemic changed many other planned events, including the Museum's 20th anniversary birthday, set for June 6, 2020. We expected to celebrate the milestone with multiday events, fanfare, and crowds. Instead, the Museum hosted a variety of online events. Everyone pitched in to provide historical talks, a session on the Museum's 20-year history, and a culminating program featured the Dr. Hal Baumgarten D-Day Commemoration Ceremony on the morning of June 6. Although the Museum had scarcely any onsite visitors that day, 4,000 people viewed the events online.

Echoes of Katrina hung in the air. Stephen discovered that the pandemic caused many to feel doubtful about the Museum's future. Then, on August 29, 2021, Stephen got a hurricane as well, Ida. It was a scary time, and Stephen, Becky Mackie, and others in our "remain behind team" stayed in the Museum through the night during the height of the storm. Though not on the scale of Katrina, Ida caused significant damage to the city and to the Canopy. In coming weeks, Stephen gradually got the Museum back on its feet with staff mostly working remotely; as visitors slowly returned, he found ways to begin restoring Museum jobs. Throughout the pandemic, the staff strove to emulate the same can-do spirit displayed by the men and women of World War II whose memories are preserved in the Museum.

During this challenging time, the Board of Trustees provided unwavering support. Chair Paul Hilliard established a Covid-19 Response Fund, which was instrumental in keeping the Museum operating. By obtaining federal grants and private support, Stephen moved forward with new projects that had been planned before the pandemic. If the pandemic boosted anything at the Museum, it was our online master's program with ASU. Between 2019 and 2021, we helped educate a new generation of scholars by producing more than 100 graduates. The Museum staff began to get a strong hold on online content. After three years of planning, we held an online Museum conference, entitled *Memory Wars: World War II at 75 and Beyond*, in 2022. Conducted virtually because of Covid-19 and damage from Hurricane Ida, the program drew nearly 14,000 registrants worldwide for the two-day online conference, which examined how national memories of World War II around the globe differ in how they are remembered, preserved, and portrayed.

On July 1, 2020, the chairmanship passed from Paul to John Koerner, who led the board through the pandemic's continuing challenges and into recovery. A lifelong New Orleanian, John had been president and CEO of Barq's Root Beer before selling the company to Coca-Cola. Afterwards, he applied his business leadership skills by forming his own investment firm and devoting his energies to the Museum. John sustained our capital expansion and oversaw multiple major projects during his Chairmanship, including the building of the Canopy of Peace as well as the construction and final exhibit design of the Liberation Pavilion. All the while, he helped Stephen navigate the Museum's recovery from Covid-19. John's Chairmanship was defined by his ability to inspire cooperation and harmony among board and staff.

Stephen and John supported Vice President of Education and Access Pete Crean and his team, who delivered an astonishing number of programs in those years. We recorded 17.5 million hits on the Museum website in 2021.[32] The Higgins Hotel received favorable reviews; it was ranked by *USA Today* readers as number eight among the best new hotels that opened in 2020 and rated the sixth best hotel by *US News and World Report.* Twenty years of work came to fruition despite the pandemic, a testament to the strength of the Museum's mission and its leadership.

The Jenny Craig Institute for War and Democracy also hit its stride after the hiring of its new Executive Director, retired Col. Michael S. Bell, PhD. Under his leadership, the Institute became a national educational force in the study of World War II and the relationship between war and America's democratic system, known for its top-notch programs and exhibits on the war's enduring legacy. The Education and Media Center combined to train hundreds of teachers on World War II via a one-week, fully sponsored online Summer Teacher Institute, while college and high school students received college credit in the Normandy Academy in France and thousands of students watched the 75th Anniversary D-Day Electronic Field Trip. Through our exhibits, programs, and outreach, as Tom Hanks remarked to me, "We are making a dent in the Zeitgeist."

CANOPY DEDICATION AND *EXPRESSIONS OF AMERICA*

The dedication of the Bollinger Canopy of Peace, the Museum's signature architectural structure, on the evening of December 9, 2021, was an emotional night for me. Standing boldly 148 feet above the center of the campus, 481 feet long and 133 feet wide, the Canopy unites the campus's pavilions and signifies a symbol of hope and America's commitment to peace through strength. Spectators enjoyed the ceremonial lighting of the Canopy, which transformed the New Orleans night sky into multicolored illuminations. The sight was stunning, and I was so proud to witness the triumphal display after 10 years of struggle. Joy Bollinger spoke about hers and Boysie's reasons for their donation: "For Boysie and myself, we wanted to do something that would commemorate the 16 million men and women who served in World War II and who gave us those precious gifts of freedom, democracy, and peace."[33] I wished Steve Ambrose had lived to see it. Through many disasters and setbacks in its short history, the Museum not only survived but always emerged stronger with renewed energy for the future.

Less than a year after the dedication, the illuminated Canopy served as a fitting backdrop for unveiling a creative application of the campus developed under Stephen Watson's leadership. On Veterans Day 2022, on the soon-to-be-dedicated Col. Battle Barksdale Parade Ground, the Museum debuted *Expressions of America,* the Bob and Dolores Hope Foundation–

funded night-time experience. Using the exteriors of the pavilion buildings, the Museum offered an innovative sound and light experience that combined cutting-edge outdoor projection technology, an original score featuring 1940s-era songs performed by local musicians, and 90-foot-tall images that immersed viewers in the stories told by members of the World War II generation in their own words. Narrated by Gary Sinise, *Expressions of America* is a musical and visual tribute to Bob Hope and his USO performances that brought hope to troops all over the world.

CONCLUSION

On October 17, 2019, the same day the Hall of Democracy opened, we broke ground on the Liberation Pavilion. The dual milestones finally put the finish line in sight for completing The National WWII Museum, but plenty of work remained. Everyone involved understood that the Liberation Pavilion exhibits and media had to be our best work to withstand the test of time. Our duty was to document the deeper meaning of America's triumph over tyranny, a final pavilion where future generations learn from the tragedies and consequences of war. Liberation was the hardest pavilion to plan and execute. It had to reach new frontiers of learning and experience. The story it told needed to be a beacon from the past, shining light on the victory of the American Spirit as well as illuminating the deeper and darker stains that led to the war and its aftermath. It was a profound challenge.

12

LIBERATION

Preserving Memory and Meaning

"WHAT DIFFERENCE DID it make that we won World War II? Who will care or know in 50 years?" That was the final question that Barry Lord, President of Lord Cultural Resources, posed to me and the exhausted members of the Master Planning charette in 2003. We had just spent 19 months planning all the exhibit ideas and concepts for the proposed expansion to an epic National WWII Museum. We thought we were done. We selected and developed rudimentary content and outlines for the major battles, campaigns, and events from the front lines to the home front. However, Barry insisted that, before we finished our work, we needed to answer that question for our visitors. Thus, was born the idea for the Liberation Pavilion and the challenge to describe the American legacy of the war. I began the long process of answering that question nearly four years later. Finding a consensus among our designers and historians, many of whom could not even agree on when the war really ended, was not easy. Gradually, the challenge was to go beyond the domestic legacies of America to document an expansive and relevant portrayal of the war's lasting meaning.

The war was fought globally, and we had to view its legacy globally, albeit from an American perspective. Some elements were obvious from the start. We had to tell the story of America's leadership role as a global superpower after 1945. America made the difference in victory and led the transformation of the world order after the war. Our role as a global leader meant we needed partners to defend against new authoritarian attacks. We emerged with superior economic strength: we led the world in military strength, technology, science, education, and government, and the country emerged as defender of the free world and eventually won the Cold War against communism. We championed the rule of law that led to the expansion of equality, women's rights, civil rights, and human rights globally albeit not always consistently. We became champions of free trade, spearheaded the creation of the Universal Declaration of Human Rights, the United Nations, and the World Court to adjudicate crimes against humanity. Despite the odds against us, we proved in victory that our democracy was superior to fascist dictatorships. During our Museum planning, we believed that these lessons were part of the dominant legacies of World War II that drove our foreign and domestic policies and movements of change for half a century. Those lessons provided fertile ground for the Liberation themes that grew rapidly in the postwar era. America entered an age of affluence, passed the GI Bill that led to a renaissance in education, and became the envy of the world.

Not all nations were liberated or tasted the freedom that we did in 1945; many just exchanged one dictator for another. Soon again, a home front and a "front line" developed, this time in the form of a cold war. Decolonization, inspired in part by Roosevelt's Four Freedoms and war aims, created new and independent nations. A revolution in weaponry and warfare introduced the atomic bomb, missiles, jet aircraft, naval power, and computers, areas where American innovation stood first.

These observations are not new. Many historians have described these achievements that shaped the enduring meaning and memory of World War II from our national perspective. Yet, it was a difficult challenge for our historians, Museum leadership, and me to agree on how to authenticate the public memory of such recent history. In the realm of public memory, even if one takes issue with the motivating ideals and policies that shaped our recent past, finding firm consensus was difficult. As William Faulkner once wrote: "The past is never dead. It's not even past."[1]

Documenting dominant themes of the recent past required us to conduct considerable research to create a historically sound and holistic view. The complex dimension of any single theme is layered with individual and collective memories as well as the course of events over time. Collective memories are certainly formed and discernable from policies, media, symbols, history, events, memorials, and even museums. Our work was to uncover that history since 1945 and to portray how Americans largely remembered what happened, actions based on those memories, and how we gave meaning to Allied victory in our individual lives and the history of our nation. Within these complexities were the answers to that final question Barry posed to us at the master planning charrette in 2003: What difference did the war make?

Our public memory of World War II does not yet have a rigorous historiography to support it. Memories change as new facts come to light, and Hollywood, historians, journalists, and government leaders spin their own versions. When a veteran dies, his memories go with him. People look back at history through the prism of their own memory, through lived experience, through the emotions of pride, loss, and trauma. In the best cases, they widen the prism of their personal memory by what they learn from historical sources. Through experience, actions, events, documents, and historical research we begin to see the common thread. The mission of the Liberation Pavilion is to find the seam to compose an authentic story of World War II's principal legacies.

CONTESTED MEMORIES

Nations remember World War II in different ways, depending on whether they were victor, vanquished, or victim. The Liberation Pavilion portrays the enduring legacies and meaning of the war through the American experience. We settled on Freedom as the primary legacy, the silver lining that gives meaning to the stories we tell in these exhibits—stories of pain, sacrifice, purpose, courage, optimism, celebration, and renewed faith in our national values. At its core, we have added meaning to justify why we infused a moral tone to our victory. We came home from the war with hope and a new commitment to protect and extend the Four Freedoms. However, we did not pursue those ideals with perfection. America's policies and vision for the postwar era were not evenly applied, and we made mistakes at home and abroad. In words and actions, we agreed with Eisenhower that World War II was a crusade and that our victory was vital to the destruction of fascism and the preservation of our democracy and freedom. As a result of our victory, America became the richest and freest nation in the world. How that story emerges through the crucible of conflict is at the heart of the Liberation Pavilion. We describe the broad changes in our social, economic, and foreign policies; changes that were shaped by ideas before the war and influenced Roosevelt's vision of victory. America's policies and ideas in shaping the peace reflect a country standing on a commitment to freedom. That is our story.

From the earliest years of planning the Liberation Pavilion, our goal was to create exhibits that allowed visitors to comprehend the war's vast destruction and the price that was paid for our freedom. We wanted them to understand that our way of life was at stake and that our nation fought to survive, prosper, and ultimately lead the world with democratic values and to oppose autocracies that threaten democracy. I believe, just as Steve Ambrose did, that the strength of American Spirit made a difference to victory in World War II. As hard as this spirit is to define, most know it when they see and feel it. That American Spirit and our values gave meaning to our fight in World War II. Veterans infused the war with a moral quality in our defense of freedom. We believed then and now that these values and qualities of civic virtue must always be nourished as we confront other threats to our democracy and our commitment to human rights.

The journey to find consensus and distil these themes over fifteen years was exhaustive but in the end rewarding. The board validated our decision recommended by historians and by Boysie Bollinger's committee to establish "Freedom" as the enduring legacy of World War II. Most American leaders and citizens alike believed we fought for it in World War II. They agreed that America had to guard against all future threats to our freedom and democracy. These concepts would form the most visible themes rooted in American history and memory from the war, and we would display those themes in the Liberation Pavilion. President Roosevelt's 1941 vision of the Four Freedoms became the fountainhead for policies, domestic and foreign, by presidents of both parties and cited most recently in the opening of President Joe Biden's State of the Union address in March 2024.

After many animated debates, the Presidential Counselors gave broad support to the freedom theme. With final board approval in December 2020, we would need every bit of the next three years to open the Liberation Pavilion in 2023. Stephen Watson headed our internal team. Because of my long involvement in the project, he wanted me to participate in all design meetings to assure consistency with our concept plans. Mike Bell, who succeeded Rob Citino as Executive Director of the Jenny Craig Institute for the

Study of War and Democracy, led the work to transform the freedom theme into compelling exhibits. Mike was quarterback of our various teams working together with me, Rob, Assistant Vice President of Collections and Exhibits Erin Clancey, Oral Historian Hannah Dailey, and Vice President of Education and Access Pete Crean. Nina Luckman, our Project Manager, did a masterful job of keeping many firms, historians, curators working in concert week after week in intense collaboration. Bob Farnsworth served as the master coordinator of the project, supervising progress through budgets, timelines, and contracts with Voorsanger Mathes to assure that all the pieces fit together. Gallagher & Associates, the Hettema Group, and our media production firm led by Donna Lawrence Productions (DLP) were major contributors to our team. We held multiple meetings each week, bringing fresh research, feedback, and writing, with Stephen Watson's final approval required for each design and exhibit prior to construction and fabrication.

We answered our guiding questions by describing how the war changed the world around these inspiring ideals, mostly for the better. I promised the board that our honest portrayal of the mistakes and missteps the United States made in the postwar years should not diminish the story of the strength, the American Spirit, and the value of our national commitments to support national and individual freedoms across the world. Ultimately, our board and historians agreed. We believed that the values and American Spirit that carried us through the war also carried us through the Cold War and into the 21st century. Roosevelt's vision had an enduring positive influence at home and abroad, elevating America's image as that "city on the hill," a nation inspiring people at home and far beyond our shores by our publicly held commitments to human rights.

The United States carried these values under the banner that freedom and democracy had to be defended against the new authoritarian threats, whether communist, fascist, or radical theocracies. We understood that freedom was fragile, always under pressure, and that we could never return to isolationism. We emerged from World War II with the firm understanding that security in the nuclear age depended on a strong defense with allies ready to stand against enemies of democracy. Roosevelt and the leaders who led us through the war fully grasped the lessons of the failures after World War I. After World War II, those and future American leaders succeeded in preventing another world war for the next 80 years.

THE LIBERATION PAVILION OPENS, OCTOBER 30–NOVEMBER 3, 2023

By late fall of 2023, the Liberation Pavilion's 33,160 square feet of galleries and theaters were finished. Everything was ready for the grand opening of the last major piece of the campus, scheduled for the first week of November. After so many years of work by so many historians, I was nervous. Getting consensus on the historical themes embodied in the Liberation Pavilion was like getting a bunch of cats with PhDs to walk in unison. After I went through the completed exhibits, I felt we succeeded in our mission. The results were terrific.

Stephen and the Museum staff spent months planning multiple days of public and private events. Stephen wanted the events to introduce the new pavilion to the public in a big way, much as the opening of the D-Day Museum had in 2000. The grand opening's first official event was to be held at the heart of the campus on the 24,000-square-foot Col. Battle Barksdale Parade Ground, which would also be dedicated that day. This was a critical kickoff, as we were introducing Liberation's themes and relevance to the entire world. Things needed to go off without a hitch.

In the months approaching the grand opening, it was still unclear whether Tom Hanks would be able to attend. Tom had been a staunch supporter of the Museum since day one, so it was important to us that he be there. I wanted to add a personal touch to my invitation to an old friend, so I borrowed a World War II–era Royal typewriter from our collection and rolled in a piece of stationery while channeling Steve Ambrose, who always worked on an IBM Selectric typewriter. I hoped that Tom, being a collector of old typewriters, would appreciate the gesture of typing out a personal invitation on a precious artifact. I typed the letter, put it in an envelope, and sent it off to Los Angeles. We spent a few weeks awaiting a response, but it finally came, also written on an old typewriter. Tom said he was happy to come "home" to the Museum to see the completion of the Master Plan.

That same week in November 2023, we hosted the Congressional Medal of Honor Society's annual convention. Hosting 40 Medal of Honor Recipients at the Museum during our grand opening was a great honor and a major coup for us. Our board Chairman, Ted Weggeland, a longtime major supporter of the Medal of Honor Society, helped engineer the joint celebrations. Ted was critical to crafting the bid to host the Convention at the Museum, and he helped secure significant funding from his Museum trustees to support the events. All throughout the week, the society held its own events and joined us for our grand opening celebrations.

The Jenny Craig Institute for the Study of War and Democracy held a symposium with panels dedicated to telling the story of how we opened and built The National WWII Museum. I participated as a panelist alongside longtime Museum supporters Guenter Bischof, Don Miller, Boysie Bollinger, Jackie Clarkson, Marc Pachter, Eliot Cohen, and Diana Bajoie. We grappled with what it meant to build our institution and the implications of building an exhibit hall dedicated to the legacy of World War II.

During the second panel discussion, Marc made a compelling case for the themes and creative contribution of the Liberation Pavilion. The self-proclaimed "Nick Mueller specialist," Marc responded to criticisms that the Museum was too much of a Steve Ambrose memorial. "This is a good place to confess that history museums are not innately popular. . . . History museums had the habit of being reverential . . . but mostly people thought that history museums were boring; they would go out of obligation, that's the one thing you don't want. People coming in out of obligation. I mean that's nice if you get them in there, but then what do you do with them?"[2]

Marc's question was one he often posited during his tenure as a Trustee and Counselor. How can the Museum provide something more than an educational experience? Marc continued to address how our Museum did this like no other. "I felt from the first [moment] that you need, people need space and they need to learn together while they're moving through space, and they need to talk to each other. . . . Nick understood what Ambrose understood as a writer—people want to be entertained in the process of learning and that's not a bad thing. The storytelling component and the individual human component."[3] Marc praised Patrick Gallagher and his rare propensity for understanding space and how to utilize history through space. Marc was arguably one of the world's premier leaders in the museum field, and for him to acknowledge the complexity and uniqueness of our institution was heartwarming. [4]

The main event, of course, was the Grand Opening Ceremony of the Liberation Pavilion on November 3, 2023. All was quiet on the Museum's campus as we readied ourselves for the big day. Camera crews, news reporters, event crews, and Museum staff trickled into the Hall of Democracy in preparation. There were some anxious moments when smoke from a drought-induced marsh fire just outside the city reached the Museum and encapsulated the entire campus in a thick haze. The wretched smell and smoke threatened all our planning, and I had flashbacks to the early morning rains we faced at our D-Day Museum grand opening in 2000. Luckily, by 7:30 a.m., a light breeze swept through and cleared the air. By then, our halls and parade ground were filled with guests, dignitaries, military personnel, Medal of Honor recipients, donors, board members, members of the WWII generation, community members, and staff who found their seats, all eager to experience the opening ceremonies. The 82nd Airborne Division All-American Band and Chorus was on hand to perform. I had rarely seen the Museum overflowing with as many guests and supporters as it was on that day, and I swelled with pride.

Shortly before the start of the ceremony, we lined up on stage for our last major ribbon cutting. After a few photographs, I leaned over to Stephen and asked, "Hey, where are the scissors?" He hesitated and said, "What do you mean?" It quickly dawned on us that we forgot to bring scissors. We proceeded to have the ribbon cutting and had a good laugh because in a week's worth of events, the only overlooked item was a small pair of scissors.

At 9:00 a.m., Ted Weggeland stepped onto the stage on the Col. Battle Barksdale Parade Ground and welcomed all to the event. Louisiana Gov. John Bel Edwards and many other state and local leaders were on hand. Also in attendance were ABC News broadcaster Robin Roberts, daughter of Tuskegee Airman Lawrence Roberts, actor Wendell Pierce, and, of course, Tom Hanks. Ted also welcomed the 40 Medal of Honor Recipients, their families, and active-duty military personnel to the events. However, the most important people in the crowd, Ted said, were the 40 WWII veterans, home front workers, and Holocaust survivors in attendance.

Governor Edwards led us in ringing the Normandy Liberty Bell, which was first rung on the shores of Normandy for the 60th anniversary of D-Day in 2004. "Today, [the bell] rings in memory of the more than 400,000 Americans who gave their lives fighting for the cause of freedom in [World War II]," Edwards said, "And in honor of all the American citizen soldiers, sailors, airmen, and marines, whose brave efforts and sacrifice secured the victory and the peace that followed."[5]

The ceremony had a solemn tone, with speakers reflecting on the utter destruction caused by World War II. The legacy of the war includes its cataclysmic scale but perhaps a bigger part of its legacy is the peace that followed; one of the most remarkable aspects of the World War II generation was its ability to find hope in a world destroyed. Rob Citino, as the lead historian on the Liberation Pavilion, addressed this dichotomy eloquently in his remarks: "[W]hen it was over, the victors didn't just squeeze the losers dry as they had done in virtually every previous war in human history. They tried to build a better world through the Marshall Plan, through the new United Nations, enduring alliances like NATO. And perhaps the greatest success of all, the victors even turned their former enemies into allies—law abiding democracies, free societies. And that's what we're doing here in the Liberation Pavilion. We're celebrating, not just the military triumph, but the real victory, always the harder victory, winning the peace."[6]

In my remarks, I noted that The National WWII Museum did more than chronicle the battles, weapons, violence, and individual heroism, important as they all were. The Museum, I said, was also built "to measure the character and values of those who fought for freedom and democracy versus the totalitarian autocracies of the world that were bent on our destruction. This Museum, like all great museums, doesn't provide the answers or clear lessons for the future, but at our best, we honestly and with historical integrity document the course of the war and our moral fiber, looking at how we fought and why—and to find meaning in its legacy for us today."

The legacy of World War II is manifold and constantly evolving. We tried to capture this same complexity in the halls and galleries of the Liberation Pavilion, and it was captured perfectly by Tom Hanks in his keynote address:

> I invite you all to take in the Liberation Pavilion. It's an extraordinary, perhaps final, chapter here in the job, in the story of The National World War II Museum, but it is also an open-ended place because it does not have the finite ending of the end of the war and the surrender of the Japanese Empire and the Nazi regime. It actually leaves it open to understand that the real work of building a more perfect union in an imperfect world began the day after the war ended, and it continues now, and it requires vigilance, it requires attendance, it requires the desire to seek knowledge, and it requires, too, the accumulation of wisdom that will be found by anybody who attends this Museum, on any given day, for the rest of time.[7]

Then, just like that, the Liberation Pavilion was opened to the public.

LIBERATION PAVILION

We tell America's Liberation story on three levels. These exhibits move visitors through a first floor that shows a world in ruins in 1945 to the second floor, which presents celebrations of victory, accountability for the perpetrators of war crimes, through social and technological changes, and final expressions of US Presidents who supported freedom as the best defense against new enemies of democracy. The pavilion culminates in the third-floor Freedom Theater, an immersive cinematic experience that expresses our central themes. The exhibit impacts are at times shocking and at other times deeply emotional, evoking both grief, joy, and pride in the nation's achievements. The National WWII Museum stands at the intersection of politics, war, history, and public memory, and the Liberation Pavilion is right at the center of that intersection.[8]

In Honor of David W. Trott
Finding Hope in a World Destroyed

The first-floor galleries provide a view of the world in the immediate aftermath of a war that left cities destroyed, 65 million dead, nations exhausted, people traumatized and confronting the horror of loss and liberation as the victors and vanquished alike search for hope, reflection, and for millions the fruits of victory and peace are celebrated. *Finding Hope in a World Destroyed* revolves around themes of sacrifice and freedom, confronting Americans in the search for meaning and hope at the war's end. The nation was on a journey from darkness to light, from defeating tyranny to the restoration of freedom to people, including the treasured art of the western world. This introduction to postwar America offers promising hope in the broader story of coming home, winning the peace, and assuming responsibility and leadership for keeping it.[9]

We begin by connecting visitors on an individual level to the unfathomable scale of loss of human lives and myriad of other forms of destruction. The world is broken. Many families are broken, too. The entry walls are filled with thousands of dog tags representing 16.4 million Americans who served our country during World War II. The opposite wall contains photos representing a few from each service branch among those 414,920 Americans who lost their lives during the conflict.

The initial exhibits explore the enormous cost of victory with dramatic presentations of whole cities lying in ruins in Europe and Asia; these images provide visual reminders of grim statistics of the social, economic, and human losses in the combat zones throughout the world, with emphasis on the deaths of innocent civilians, which accounted for least two-thirds of the total 65 million lives lost in the worldwide conflict.

The dominant focus of the exhibit is a simple wooden coffin that contained the remains of Army Pfc. Gerald Williams, killed in action in Germany on January 15, 1945. This crate, shipped to his wife, Bernice, in Lorain, Ohio, is a poignant reminder of how personal tragedy arrived in the homes of families throughout America. The crate has a Christian cross and Star of David at either end and a marble tombstone from the American Battle Monuments Commission, like those found on graves in American military cemeteries near battlefields across Europe, Africa, and the Asia-Pacific.

Nearby are personal artifacts of POWs, such as a prosthetic arm fashioned in a Stalag, right next to the tearful film account of Vincent Losada, a B-17 crewmember from the 487th Bombardment Group, 8th Air Force, who lost his arm on a bombing raid over Germany. Graphics and interactives tell the grisly tale of torture and the death rate of 40 percent among captives held in Japanese POW camps. The cost of victory was high, and the exhibit creates a somber mood with feelings of shock from the scale of human misery.

The exhibits pose an all-important question: what were we fighting for? This was the same question our troops asked as they entered the gates of the death camps in the spring of 1945. Visitors fully grasp the consequences of Nazi Germany's racist ideology. Hitler's rabid antisemitism blamed the Jewish minority of Germany for all the country's social and economic ills. While the Holocaust is not an American story, it is impossible to understand the war and much of its meaning for Americans without opening a window to the Nazi evil that led to the systematic murder of six million men, women, and children across Europe, solely because they were Jewish. At least five million Soviet prisoners of war, Romani, Jehovah's Witnesses, homosexuals, disabled people, and other victims were also murdered.[10] Some 500,000 Jews fled Germany by 1939, but it was almost impossible to hide from Nazi terror after Hitler conquered most of Europe.

"And Then They Came for Me"

First they came for the socialists, and I did not speak out—
    because I was not a socialist.
Then they came for the trade unionists, and I did not speak out—
    because I was not a trade unionist.
Then they came for the Jews, and I did not speak out—
    because I was not a Jew.
Then they came for me—and there was no one left to speak for me.[11]

—Martin Niemöller's poem "First they came . . . "

Many on our creative team questioned the flashback to the Anne Frank story in this Museum of the American experience in World War II. I insisted on including this story in a small section of the Liberation Pavilion because the atrocities of the Holocaust shocked American morality and sensibilities when our soldiers and military leaders discovered the concentration camps in the last months of the war against the Third Reich.

The Jewish family of Otto and Edith Frank and daughters Margot and Anne went into hiding in 1942 in a secret annex behind Otto's offices in Amsterdam at a time when the Nazi SS rounded up all Jews and shipped them to death camps in Poland. Anne and her family were discovered and sent to Auschwitz in August 1944. Only Otto survived.

The exhibit immerses visitors into the living room of the annex and simulates the excruciating experience of the Frank family, living in fear and the terror of discovery and capture by the Nazis at any moment. With the sound of quiet music, the "voice" of Anne Frank reads from the diary she kept, sharing her innermost thoughts and feelings of the conditions of the outside world that forced the Franks into hiding. Visitors of all ages can feel and learn how quickly the lives of innocent families changed overnight. The overall experience provides a window into the internal lives of those trapped in the annex and the outside world that forced them into hiding.

The Anne Frank story became part of the American experience and is still an important reminder of the freedom that was taken from her. Anne Frank has a powerful impact on adolescents and adults who have read her diary. The Holocaust enters the American memory through Anne's heartfelt words. There are also clear lessons of the vigilance needed to defend individual freedoms in democracies and warnings against being a bystander when the rights of others are threatened.

Ronald Leopold, Director of the Anne Frank House and Museum in Amsterdam, told me in 2019 that the number of people who deny Anne Frank's story grows every year. The Anne Frank story in The National WWII Museum testifies to the truth of her story and reminds visitors with graphics, photos, and unequivocal evidence that six million Jews were killed by the Nazis in the name of Aryan purity. Anne's story also gives the world, and the Museum, the first ray of "hope in a world destroyed." This is a young girl who believed in the goodness of human beings despite the Nazi terror.

The Holocaust

Visitors walk out of the Anne Frank house directly into a re-creation of an extermination camp. The camp exhibit replicates prisoner living quarters with wooden bunks and cramped spaces. Large photos of the barracks at Auschwitz and other camps filled with emaciated Jews awaiting their trip to the gas chambers, reveal the horrifying face of extermination. Around the corner of the exhibit are more images and original film footage of General Eisenhower, together with his top Allied commanders, viewing one of the first camps discovered and liberated by American troops. The Supreme Commander was so incensed by the grisly scene of the bodies of murdered Jews that he invited war correspondents into the camp with instructions to document the atrocity with photos, film and reports so that the atrocity could never be denied. Eisenhower's words are projected on the exhibit wall to convey his anger and to help explain the reasons that the Allies sought to destroy Hitler and the Third Reich: "We are told that the American soldier does not know what he is fighting for. Now at least, he will know what he's fighting against."

Pam and Mark Rubin Liberation Theater

With those words, visitors enter the Liberation Theater, with its stories of Holocaust survivors and American liberators who opened the camp gates and restored their freedom. The war's end brought scenes of liberation: Allied armies breaking down the gates of political prisons and concentration camps. To the US soldiers, the horrific scenes they witnessed upon the discovery of the camps are evidence that they have indeed been fighting a "good war." Those rescued, many dazed and weak from hunger, gaze at their rescuers in a state of disbelief. Many weep, many drop to their knees in prayer. In many different tongues, they celebrate a forgotten word: "freedom."

The Liberation Theater presents compilations of powerful personal testimonies from the Holocaust survivors who were liberated from Hitler's death camps as well as the emotions from the soldiers who opened the gates. The film scrolls on a 30-foot-wide screen and exposes visitors to the complicated tangle of emotions felt by all in layered multi-image or sweeping panoramic scenes. The amphitheater is devoted to these singular testimonies, which, for survivors and Museum visitors, offer great promise of freedom and hope following the deadliest catastrophe of World War II. I initially envisioned this exhibit in 2001 during a brief visit to the Shoah Foundation archive located on the Universal Studios complex in Los Angeles. Steve Ambrose was at Amblin studios that day recording oral histories for Spielberg's *The Pacific* series. I knew Spielberg funded the Shoah Foundation after he produced the movie *Schindler's List* a few years earlier, and they had already recorded over 50,000 testimonies of Holocaust survivors. I knew that the foundation was located at the back of the Universal lot, a short walk from Amblin studios. Out of curiosity, I left Ambrose after a few recordings and walked to the back of the lot to the trailers to speak to the collection curators. I had previously seen the scrolling testimonies of Holocaust survivors at the National Holocaust Memorial Museum and was deeply moved by their testimonies. We were just starting to formulate ideas for the Master Plan of the expanded Museum, and I had to find where the wartime American story intersected with the Holocaust. What I hoped I could find were testimonies from the very moment that the gates were opened by GIs who were confronted by the scenes of the camps, as well testimonies from prisoners who were surprised to see the Americans approach.

I asked one of the Shoah curators if she could retrieve a few excerpts of personal accounts by survivors that fit that description. To my great surprise, the curator replied, "Yes, we have over 300, but do you want to see the testimonies of the liberated or the liberators?" I was incredulous: "You have both?" I asked. She said, "Of course, sit down in that booth with the computer screen, and we will pull some from our database." Fifteen minutes later I was watching several testimonies of survivors and liberators, two to four minutes each, just at their exact moment of liberation. They were emotionally powerful, and I was elated. From that moment until 22 years later, the theater presentation I envisioned remained in the core exhibit experience of the first floor of the Liberation Pavilion.

In the final years before opening, we received more oral testimonies from the Shoah Foundation in addition to those we recorded ourselves. Our media production firm, DLP, worked with our Museum professionals for over three years to carefully select, edit, and review testimonies. We viewed dozens of filmed accounts of moments that brought shock, tears, and grief for American troops, as well as feelings of hope and joy during survivors' first taste of freedom. Every review left us all in silence. It was hard, emotional work. With the help of our researchers, the DLP team produced visual testimonies with photos that matched the camps of each testimony of the liberated to help our visitors grasp the stark reality of those survivors' experiences. This careful curation allows visitors to feel present in that very moment of liberation. Donna Lawrence put her heart and soul into creating one of the finest films in the Museum, one that will forever honor the survivors and liberators in that meaningful moment of freedom. For me, the liberation film accomplished everything I hoped for when I first saw these testimonies at the Shoah Foundation in 2001. The following excerpts tell the story in their own words and feelings, never to be forgotten:[12]

> I saw human beings . . . beaten . . . starved, tortured . . . skeletal faces . . . some on ground dying. I said, "My God, Who are these people? What have they done that was so terrible that could cause anyone to treat them like this?" They're Jews, gypsies, Jehovah Witnesses, some are Catholics . . . The Nazis said they weren't good enough. They weren't fit to live. They could be terminated, murdered. I said, "My God."

Leon Bass, born Philadelphia, 1925, a member of the 183rd Engineer Combat Battalion, he helped liberate Buchenwald Concentration Camp near Weimar, Germany, April 11, 1945.

> Suddenly, there was a tremor . . . like an earthquake. It [the earth] began to shake. It got louder and louder . . . and all of a sudden, maybe a mile or two distant, tanks appeared . . . coming up the hill. And there was a white star on the tanks. And everybody yelled, 'American, American!' Such excitement filled the camps, and suddenly their tanks came in. . . . And a tanker stood up in the tank, and they began to kiss his hand . . . Americans were throwing crates of rations. I was dumbfounded. All of the sudden, the rain stopped, the sun came out. And it was such a beautiful morning. And the Americans, they looked like angels to me.

Survivor George Topas, born in Warsaw, Poland, 1924; he was liberated following a death march in Neunburg vorm Wald, Germany, April 1945.

> It must've been around 3 o'clock, all of a sudden we see the door opens (CRYING) and we see the American soldier. Must have been a young man, maybe 20, maybe 22, heavyset with a big helmet. . . . He looks at us and he starts crying. He cries. One of us—one of our boys, . . . comes out and starts singing "Yankee Doodle Dandy." (CRYING) And we all join in. And soon there's a whole battalion of American soldiers. . . . And they stand and cry. They look at us, and they cry. I men, battle-hardened soldiers. . . . They look at us and cry. . . . And we stand there, cry with them and sing "Yankee Doodle Dandy." The scene is something I'll never forget. It was like saying, "What took you so long? Where were you?'"

Survivor Max Durst, born in Ciescyn, Poland, 1927; he was liberated from Ebensee subcamp of the Mauthausen Concentration Camp in Upper Austria, May 6, 1945.

Faith in Wartime

Following the harrowing and emotionally taxing exhibits, visitors need a place for reflection. Just beyond the Liberation Theater, they find the Frank and Paulette Stewart Interfaith Chapel, a peaceful space with lighting that illuminates a ceiling of Florentine plaster painted with the gold of a setting sun. In this spiritual place, visitors can step out of the exhibits for a quiet moment to reflect on what they have seen, with a guest book to leave their thoughts and prayers.

Nearby, visitors find our *Faith in Wartime* exhibit. Freedom of religion was high on the list of American values. Whether Catholic, Protestant, Jewish, or of other faith, during World War II most Americans were from religious families and most of our troops went to war with their bibles and prayers as part of their daily lives. To be sure, the nation's dominant faith comprised the many branches of Christianity, but respect for all faiths was embedded in our Constitution. Eisenhower and others spoke of the war as a crusade against tyrants who would, among other things, destroy all our freedoms, including the freedom to practice a religion of one's own choice. A constant theme in the Liberation Pavilion is that those who survived must represent those who did not. In these spaces, we hope that visitors feel and accept that responsibility, too.

A sense of the spiritual—that one's existence was part of a higher plan—could help sustain the individual soldier in even the most trying times. The rigors of war, the terrors of front-line fighting, and the quiet worry of family members stressed the human personality to the limit, both at home and in combat. With life hanging by a thread, and with death occurring seemingly randomly at the front, faith could be a way to find some kind of answer to a question so many faced: why did I live, while my comrades died? This gallery offers spiritual respite to visitors. Veterans' reflections at listening stations offer poignant stories of how their faith sustained them through difficult times, helped them recover from their wartime ordeal, or described how wartime experiences helped strengthen and altered their faith.

The exhibits contain artifacts of chaplains of all denominations. They also contain items from Catholic chaplains, who carried their communion vestments, goblets, and other ceremonial relics to perform mass for the troops even in the fields of combat. Rev. Philip M. Hannan, the "Jumping Padre" of the 82nd Airborne Division, famously celebrated mass from the hood of a jeep for soldiers fighting in the Battle of Bulge. Later, when troops reached the bombed-out city of Cologne, Germany, he was given responsibility for protecting the famous Cologne Cathedral's precious relics during occupation. Reverend Hannan, who later served as Archbishop of New Orleans, offered prayers at all our grand openings before his death in 2011 and was deeply grateful to the Museum for including this exhibit and preserving the stories and artifacts of other chaplains.

The exhibit features stories and artifacts representing the deep beliefs of American troops, with service books, hymnals, and photographs of chaplains in combat tending and ministering to the dying and wounded. We focus on the story most well-known to all chaplains during the war and still today: the story of the sinking of the troop transport *Dorchester* and the selfless act of courage and faith by the Four Chaplains.

The USAT *Dorchester* was torpedoed by a German U-Boat in the Labrador Sea on February 3, 1943. Among the 674 who died in the attack were four Army chaplains of different denominations who gave up their life jackets so others might survive. Their names and selfless sacrifice are enshrined in the medals they received posthumously, and their story is part of the training for all US military chaplains today.[13] Together with descriptions of the incident and large photographs of the chaplains, our exhibit includes an artist study from muralist Nils Hogner, depicting the chaplains guiding men to the lifeboats. Hogner created the study in preparation for a mural for the Chapel of Four Chaplains on the grounds of Temple University in Philadelphia.

As we were developing the Four Chaplains story for the gallery, Stephen and I learned of the Immortal Chaplains Memorial Sanctuary, run by the Immortal Chaplains Foundation and located on the *Queen Mary,* an ocean liner used as a troopship in World War II. There we found artifacts, the Hogner artist study, a video, and, to our surprise, David Fox, head of the Immortal Chaplains Foundation and a nephew of Reverend Fox, one of the Four Chaplains who perished.

We spent hours talking with him about donating his entire exhibit and artifacts to our Museum for the Faith in Wartime gallery. Stephen befriended David, continued communications with him as well as those responsible for the Four Chaplains Chapel in Philadelphia and gradually won agreement from both groups that the story should be forever presented in our exhibit. David passed away before we opened the Liberation Pavilion, but the Four Chaplains story forms the heart of the gallery and remains a touching reminder of the deep spirituality of our troops and nation.

In the *Faith in Wartime* exhibit, the Museum strives to show how the WWII generation experienced the war and how both society and individuals dealt with the violence. The massive scale of the fighting affected everyone—combatants and noncombatants alike. With nearly 45 million civilian deaths, the war challenged American ideals of innocence and morality. However, in *Faith in Wartime,* a positive narrative emerges, which combines a spirit of civic renewal and, for many, religious redemption. Bonds of affection and compassion grew stronger in the postwar years among survivors and among ethnic and religious groups whose common sacred memories overshadowed the events.

The Monuments Men and Women

The remarkable story of how the Monuments, Fine Arts, and Archives Unit (MFAA) helped rescue priceless art stolen by the Nazis from museums, collections, and homes across Europe is a unique aspect of the American experience in World War II. The Monuments Men, as they were called, included 350 men and women from 14 countries who helped save the precious cultural heritage of Western civilization.

We open the exhibit with a photograph of Hitler gazing at the plans for his Führermuseum, an enormous art complex he wanted built in Linz, Austria, to hold looted art and serve as a tribute to him and the victorious Third Reich. Visitors then enter an immersion experience in a cave-like setting. The cave is stacked with digital art in large frames, with each piece transforming every few minutes into another famous artwork stolen by Hitler. A brief film relates the dramatic story in those last days of the war as US troops and Monuments Men raced to find the Altaussee art cache before it could be destroyed on standing orders from Hitler. Aided by the Austrian resistance, they located and saved some of the world's most precious art treasures just hours before the salt mine was triggered for demolition.

The results of their rescue efforts were astonishing. Major pieces recovered from the Altaussee salt mine included the Ghent Altarpiece, Michelangelo's *Madonna of Bruges,* and works by Vermeer, Breughel, and Rembrandt. Visitors learn that 700,000 art objects were recovered by members of the MFAA from over 1,000 repositories around Europe.

The final gallery is the account of the monumental task of finding the rightful owners and returning their art to them. Visitors learn that tens of thousands of works are still missing, and they can use interactives and search tools to follow ongoing efforts to locate those pieces and return them to their owners, a process that continues to this day.

The Goldring Family Foundation and Woldenberg Foundation *Forces of Freedom at Home and Abroad*

On the second floor, the *Forces of Freedom at Home and Abroad* galleries present broad themes reflecting the resilience of the American Spirit and assertive leadership in the postwar era.[14] Themes represented include patriotism, relief, reunions with loved ones, renewed pride in country, values, religious beliefs, and self-confidence that prevailed as our troops came home and celebrated across the country.

As visitors reach the top of the stairs, they enter a panoramic scene, hearing the immersive sounds of celebration with a surge of voices and music, moving images of the great moments of exhilaration as US servicemen and servicewomen step onto American soil again. Snapshots of homecomings and jubilant sounds of joy, laughter, tears, and indescribable happiness line the grand staircase. Images of sadness and uncertainty of what may lie ahead for individuals, for America, and the world are also shown. The world needed to heal, rebuild, and form a more just society. Just months after Roosevelt's death, Harry Truman inspired confidence, pride, and a moral righteousness in the words he gives to the nation: "This is a victory of more than arms alone. This is a victory of liberty over tyranny."

The United States stepped into a new role as global superpower, actively promoting freedom and democracy abroad in the face of a growing threat from communism and beginning to reckon with its own challenges at home. African Americans, women, and other groups who played a key role in forging victory and experienced expanded freedoms abroad now faced the bitter irony of returning home to inequality and the same racism of the prewar era. The question lingers: will America have the determination to respond to social change, as well as accepting the responsibilities of global leadership in peacetime?

I took a strong stand on behalf of affirming a moral tone throughout the Liberation Pavilion. This moral content to the themes is especially notable on the second and third floors, where America makes ever stronger commitments to individual and national freedoms. This moral sensibility reflects the national experience of the war and was the dominant legacy of World War II in American memory. We do not avoid the imperfections in our domestic and foreign policies, but we do not allow them to paralyze us from seeing positive elements in America's postwar achievements.

The remaining galleries of the Liberation Pavilion document a half century of American leaders and people committed to advancing democratic ideas, civic virtue, human rights, and the freedoms needed to support these principles in a world that was forever changed by World War II. Opinions today may not always warm to the policies and changes that marked the rest of the 20th century, but the Museum portrays what happened and largely reinforces the idea that these postwar policies and actions prevented another world war. The Museum narrates how the war and its motivating principles prevailed in American memory and are manifest in the actions of leaders for more than half a century: principles of justice, strong military defense, breaking out of isolation, antifascist and antiauthoritarian impulses, and efforts to combat racism and promote equality to make the country ever stronger against future enemies of democracy and human rights. As one journalist pointedly asked: "Is America 'exemplary' and 'honorable' or the reverse?"[15] Visitors are posed with this very same question after touring the

Liberation exhibits. We also hope the legacies that endured will have lasting meaning to those who visit.

Restoring Justice

The first galleries present an international perspective on foreign policy ideals that the Allies believed would establish laws of punishment and accountability to affirm undeniable human rights during periods of war and peace. Most Americans believed that the Nuremberg and Tokyo War Crimes Trials were essential to bringing nations back from the abyss of evil. A short media piece introduces the efforts of establishing international human rights laws and defining crimes against humanity. It opens with these lines: "Over the course of World War II the Nazis and Imperial Japan committed atrocities against millions of civilians and POWs. They imprisoned them, tortured them, worked them to death in factories, and murdered them in concentration camps and killing fields." With this overview, visitors learn about the International Military Tribunal, established by American, British, French, and Soviet governments, to try Nazi leaders at Nuremberg. Each Allied nation appointed its own judge and prosecution team and together drew up a list of new laws and legal categories, including war crimes, crimes against peace, and crimes against humanity.

On a large media screen, a short video presents the riveting words of Chief Justice Jackson at the opening of the Nuremberg Trials: "The wrongs which we seek to condemn and punish have been so calculated, so malignant, and so devastating, that civilization cannot tolerate their being ignored, because it cannot survive their being repeated."[16] The International Military Tribunal tried 24 high-ranking Nazi officials. After exhaustive testimony and deliberation, in which many of the accused claimed they were "only following orders," 12 were sentenced to death, 9 to long-term prison sentences, and 3 were acquitted.

The Tokyo War Crimes Trials were more complex and controversial, involving 11 nations. The Judge from India, Radhabinod Pal, voted to acquit all defendants as he opined the western powers were oppressors too, and all ruled vast colonial empires in Asia. Still, the Tokyo tribunal sentenced 7 leaders and military officers to death, including Japan's wartime Prime Minister Hideki Tojo, while 16 others were sentenced to life in prison. To provide other documentation aside from photos, and dramatic video wall, the exhibit displays personal artifacts and letters. For both sets of trials, visitors can see and hear historic film with voices of the accusers and the accused and hear accounts by American military guards from the Museum's oral history collection. We present the war crimes trials as a milestone of world history. For the first time, the entire world put aggressors and war criminals on notice and issued a warning to future would-be evildoers: your crimes will not go unpunished, you will be held accountable, and "I was only following orders" will no longer be a valid excuse for criminal behavior.

The next exhibit presents former First Lady Eleanor Roosevelt leading the United Nations committee in creating one of the most revolutionary documents in world history: the Universal Declaration of Human Rights (UDHR). We present this moment on an enormous video wall to signify the importance of the document with film and photo images of Roosevelt and the UN General Assembly meeting in Paris on December 10, 1948. Eleanor unified members representing both democratic and communist governments, including first-world countries, developing nations, and all different faiths.

The exhibit presents the words and language of the declaration as they were being framed. Motion graphics show the preliminary language being marked out and rewritten with amended text to illustrate key points that were debated and changed during the drafting process: "All men [scratch out "men"] human beings are born free and equal in dignity and rights. They are endowed by their creator [scratch out "by their creator"] by nature [scratch out "by nature"] with reason and conscience and should act towards one another as brothers [scratch out "as brothers"] in a spirit of brotherhood."

This document is clearly influenced by President Roosevelt's Four Freedoms speech and provides a powerful link to this legacy. "We will accept only a world consecrated to freedom of speech and expression . . . everywhere in the world," FDR said in his 1941 speech. Today, 193 member states of the United Nations have ratified at least one of the nine binding treaties influenced by the Declaration. Its influence is evidenced by its appearing in over 500 translations, the most of any document in history.[17]

Great Responsibilities Theater

As they continue through the exhibit, visitors can view an eight-minute film describing the new mantle of leadership the United States assumed between 1945 and 1950. The themes of the period reflect the growing tensions in a new cold war with Soviet Russia. It is a fast-paced and condensed presentation of the immediate postwar years, which saw America's consolidation of the lessons and legacies of World War II. "In 1945, the US is a superpower, the most powerful nation in the history of the world, and takes on a new mission: to champion global freedom." the narrator tells visitors.

With the Soviet Union installing communist regimes in Eastern Europe dominated by the Red Army, former British Prime Minister Winston Churchill warned during a 1946 speech in Missouri that "an iron curtain has descended across the continent," separating Soviet satellites from the "free world."

The United States responded to rising cold war tensions and the fear of communist takeovers in Greece and Turkey with a policy that became known as the Truman Doctrine, providing military aid to democratic allies threatened by totalitarian regimes. The war had left many people around the world struggling with poverty, and US leaders also knew that the global economy had to be rebuilt to prevent communism from becoming an attractive alternative to democracy. The solution was to offer unprecedented economic aid to both victor and vanquished nations alike. The policy proposed by Secretary of State George C. Marshall aimed to build prosperous, democratic, and free societies as the best path to peace and security. The resulting Marshall Plan poured massive economic resources into the devastated lands of Europe, even to those former Axis powers the United States had defeated a few years earlier. What nation does this?

To supplement the soft power of the Universal Declaration of Human Rights, the United States added hard power by leading the creation in 1949 of a new permanent military alliance, the North Atlantic Treaty Organization. NATO provided a unified front of the United States and West Europeans nations, designed to deter future Soviet expansion and respond to an attack on any one member as an attack on all.

The United States needed changes to end racial discrimination and promote equal opportunity within its own borders. Truman pushed to expand social security, create more public housing, raise the minimum wage, and end racial segregation in the US armed forces in 1948. His administration oversaw the implementation of GI Bill benefits, which provided free higher education and low-interest mortgages to returning veterans. These benefits accrued to people of color, one step in addressing the discrimination minorities continued to face in the country they fought to defend. Together, these reforms placed America on a trajectory to become a freer and richer country with greater opportunities for all its citizens—becoming a model for other nations of America's capacity to adapt and reform itself in response to new realities.

This film exhibit leaves our visitors with the same questions that faced our country in 1950: can the rights the United States seeks to spread globally receive the same protection and support on American soil? Can freedom and democracy survive the stresses of the Nuclear Age? Can American democracy ever again survive authoritarian threats without strong alliances of free nations that share our commitment to a common defense against the extremist ideologies of dictatorships, whether fascist or communist? It had taken the most cataclysmic war in human history to destroy right-wing fascist regimes in Germany and Japan.

So what? We ask. Why should we care about the meaning of World War II? Or the fruits of victory? In these exhibits, the links to the meaning and responsibilities of our past victory become clear. These events connect to our lives today, with the same hard questions and how our leaders responded to threats to freedom, not just in war but in peace as well.

Prosperity and Change

In depicting the enormous social, economic, and technological changes in postwar America, the *Prosperity and Change* gallery describes how the United States emerges from the war not only as a military superpower, but also an economic powerhouse, dominating the global economy. Media and graphics portray the transformation of the nation as it converts wartime production into an enormous economic engine of growth. The GI Bill created a renaissance in higher education that benefited eight million veterans. The GI Bill also created new job opportunities that greatly expanded the middle class and benefited all parts of the economy. Graphics and images trace the huge geographic and demographic shifts from south to north and rural to urban that largely followed the surging employment opportunities in expanding industries.

While most Americans felt these positive advances, some groups still faced a starkly different reality and were largely excluded from the prosperity of postwar America. Racial prejudice and gender discrimination were long-standing realities of American life, and, for many citizens, the Constitution's promises of equal rights remained unfulfilled. Minorities who served in the war now wanted equal rights at home—the Double V campaign linked their fight against fascism to their demands for democratic freedoms and civil rights at home.

We highlight several African American leaders, including US Army Staff Sergeant Hosea Williams, who was wounded in combat only to return home to be beaten by an angry white mob while still in uniform. He later joined Martin Luther King Jr. in the movement that led to the passage of the Civil Rights Act and Voting Rights Acts of the 1960s. We also feature Rosa Parks, who had a wartime defense job at Maxwell Field in Montgomery, Alabama, where she did not experience discrimination. However, when postwar segregation laws tried to force her to the back of the bus, she refused to give up her seat and changed American history by a simple act of resistance. Rosa Parks tells us in her own words: "Maxwell opened my eyes up. It was an alternative to the ugly policies of Jim Crow." Medgar Evers, who served with the Army's Red Ball Express in Europe, came home to become active in the civil rights movement, including voter registration drives for African Americans in his home state of Mississippi. His assassination on June 12, 1963, sparked unrest that ultimately led to the Civil Rights Act. These stories all have roots in World War II, where the experience of minorities and women led to their demanding equal rights and the end to discrimination based on race or gender.

Technological advances that originated during World War II to meet military needs found enormous applications in peacetime; the war accelerated advancements in the fields of medicine, aviation, computing, manufacturing, and nuclear technology. The first computer, Colossus, invented to decipher the Nazi Enigma code, later led to the mainframes of IBM and Commodore. Radar revolutionized aviation, marine navigation, and weather forecasting, while the transistor radio and other microwave technologies led to devices and appliances that transformed American life, including portable radios and microwave ovens.

Powerful rockets soon launched satellites into orbit around the earth, providing enhanced global communications for civilian and military use. Wartime advances in rocket science came largely from German engineers and scientists, who were recruited to lead the US space program. Among them was Werner von Braun, who developed the Nazis' V-2 rockets and later helped build the NASA rockets that took our astronauts to the moon. The same technology created new perils during the Cold War, as both American and Soviet scientists developed missiles that could reach any nation on earth with nuclear warheads. For the first time in world history, these new technologies made the annihilation of entire nations possible and soon a new term emerged: "weapons of mass destruction."

The exhibit's artifacts, oral history clips, and interactives track the evolution of ideas, policies, and innovative technologies that originated in World War II and became integral to the enduring freedoms extended to most Americans for the rest of the century, including changes that empowered individuals with new freedoms of expression and ways to solve complex social and economic problems. The legacies of the war are portrayed on the largest scale, but visitors also learn of varying personal experiences during the war that had a profound and lasting impact on individual lives, mostly for the better.

The Fight for Freedom

As visitors advance through the galleries, the focus shifts toward postwar Presidents of both parties who fought to extend Roosevelt's Four Freedoms in their foreign and domestic policies.[18] The exhibit displays large images that convey FDR's essential conditions for human freedom: freedom of speech, freedom of worship, freedom from want, and freedom from fear. The messages of these historic photos are clear without words. In the same gallery is a short media piece about successive Presidents whose famous public speeches and policies reflected national policies in meeting the challenges to defend these freedoms of their own time in their own way.

The media piece features moments of excellence from every President from Harry Truman to George H. W. Bush, highlighting moments of American power, such as when John F. Kennedy met the Soviet threat during the Cuban Missile Crisis, which took the world to the brink of nuclear war in 1962. Kennedy challenged Soviet Premier Nikita Khrushchev by dispatching US Navy warships to intercept Russian ships on the high seas to block their missile shipments to Cuba.

We show examples of soft power as well, including Kennedy's creation of the Peace Corps in 1961, sending America's youth around the world to bring modern farming techniques, medical care, and humanitarian aid to poverty-stricken lands. In Jimmy Carter's inaugural address in January 1977, he made the pursuit of human rights the cornerstone of his foreign policy. Human freedom was a "historical birthright" of the United States, he declared, a stance fully in accord with Eleanor Roosevelt's Universal Declaration of Human Rights.

Events portrayed reach their climax during the Presidency of Ronald Reagan, an ardent admirer of the ideals of Franklin Roosevelt and the Four Freedoms, who believed in peace through strength. The film features Reagan's defiant stance in 1987 before the Berlin Wall, where he challenged then Soviet leader Mikhail Gorbachev, with words that will live on forever among freedom-loving peoples: ". . . Mr. Gorbachev, tear down this wall. . . ." The Iron Curtain soon began to crack, and the Berlin Wall fell on November 9, 1989, and with it, Soviet control in Eastern Europe. In 1991, the entire Soviet Union collapsed. Our film presents a montage of events from the fall of the Berlin Wall to the liberation of Poland and other Eastern European nations. "This is freedom's greatest moment of expansion since World War II," our narrator proclaims. "The cold war ends in triumph for democracy." Here, some 45 years after the end of World War II the visionary ideals of FDR reached full bloom.

With the Presidential remarks from Harry Truman to George H. W. Bush ringing in their ears, visitors enter the concluding gallery of the second floor to see an enlarged and illuminated replica of the Victory Medal awarded to 16 million WWII American veterans upon completion of their service. Inscribed on one side of that medal are FDR's Four Freedoms to make clear what our American government and military leaders wanted every veteran to remember—that these were the ideals they fought for and that their service to their country was deeply honored.

Opposite the Victory Medal wall are the words of well-known veterans who offer their brief testimonies of the meaning of their service for themselves, America, and for freedom and democracy. On the other wall is a large interactive screen of some 15 feet wide and 8 feet high; before the screen are interactive hubs for visitors to give their own answers to the headline question emblazoned across the screen: how, in your view, did World War II change the world? Visitors' answers float immediately up to the screen mixed with responses from others in the exhibit. One question polls visitors on which of the Four Freedoms are most important to them—Freedom of Speech, Freedom of Worship, Freedom from Fear, or Freedom from Want? The polling results are immediate so visitors can consider the views of others compared to their own, and, through their participation, they become a living part of the story. Answers are varied yet provocative. One visitor typed, "World War II showed the value in rebuilding the economies and political systems of vanquished foes, something Western nations have forgotten." Another said: "It shows us that even though we won a war, doesn't mean evil is gone." One other said: "It [World War II] set the stage for people to consider their social responsibility to persons of the earth." This sampling of answers suggests that our exhibits in the Museum reach our visitors with content and meaning about America's role in World War II.

Priddy Family Foundation *Freedom Theater*

The final gallery on the third floor, the Priddy Family Foundation *Freedom Theater,* is a cinematic reprise of the Museum's mission in dramatic visual treatments that cover a century of American history.[19] We always envisioned the third floor as the capstone experience for not only the Liberation Pavilion, but also for the entire Museum. The Museum mission drove the concept for the exhibit, which was to move from the why and how the war was fought to a final question: what does World War II mean today? In my mind, this exhibit needed to be more than a celebration of victory. The exhibit transitions from narrative history to an exploration of dominant themes that give us an accepted meaning of the war. It places visitors as "players" in America's story and provokes them to answer questions themselves and add their own personal meaning to the outcome of the war. Perhaps they would answer the question in different ways than members of the WWII generation had. My fervent wish is that visitors take heart from the story of America's victory in World War II and see beyond the frontiers of learning and freedom in their current time in history. I also hope with the benefit of hindsight, the exhibit motivates visitors to take responsibility to be vigilant and prepared to fend off lurking threats to freedom and democracy. Mostly, I hope the third-floor exhibit helps visitors look beyond their immediate horizons to recognize both crises and opportunities in a future since freedom's hope now rests with them.

To carry our ideas forward after years of creative development, Rob Citino, our historians, and I developed several historical treatments for the film. Finally, in December 2020, the board gave its final approval of the conceptual treatment of the show before going into final design and production. That took another three years of intensive work with our historians, including our consultant for the Liberation Pavilion, Eliot Cohen, a renowned professor of strategic studies with the Johns Hopkins University School of Advanced International Studies. Rob, Mike, Eliot, and I interacted with Phil Hettema and his creative team to verify every word in the script for historical accuracy.

Phil and his lead script writer, Chris Ellis, initially focused on the rise of Third Reich and the failure of democracies in the 1920s and 1930s. The problem for us with this approach was that our story of Freedom, however defined, was not about how Germans lost their basic freedoms and human rights, but how Americans did not. We insisted that Phil shift the focus of the Freedom story to America, where the country faced similar extremist threats; yet, despite economic depression, domestic attacks from the right and left, our center held. Roosevelt's Four Freedoms were deeply embedded in Americans values, and the President believed these were a preferred path to peace and security for all peoples. This became the framework for the Freedom Theater.

After multiple drafts and research covering nearly a century, Phil, and Chris, working with an animation firm, Medici Media, produced the script and cinematic experience. Lighting, audio, and theater rotation are all synchronized for powerful effect. Stunning imagery moves visitors through a century of war and peace, with upheavals in between. The story builds to a crescendo with the voices of veterans and Presidents speaking of the sacrifice and the struggle, and with words that, in the end, inspire hope and commitment. American servicemen, nurses, and home front workers fill the screen, accompanied by music reflecting the pride, emotion, and sadness of people changed by war but resolved to look to the future. Words of Ernie Pyle echo from beyond the grave: "Thousands of men will soon be returning to you. They have been gone a long time and they have seen and done and felt things you cannot know. They will be changed."

Returning African American soldiers were still treated as second-class American citizens. "I had all kinds of ribbons, but it didn't seem to matter," veteran Chester White tells us. "To them you were just a black boy." In the following decades, the civil rights and women's rights movements gained momentum, powered by some of these same veterans. On the global economic front, America's commitment via the Marshall Plan is extraordinary: it was instrumental in rebuilding Allied nations as well as defeated nations as free, liberal, democracies. We were replanting ideas of freedom of thought, freedom of worship, press, and civil justice, along with strong economies. The Cold War, after verging close to a hot war with the Soviet Union, ends with the fall of the Berlin Wall.

We are reminded in the final act that the pressure on freedom never ends. A visual montage of celebrations is set to an uplifting musical score with images of American leaders filling the screen, their voices weaving in and out of the music: "We must not be confused about what Freedom is," Eleanor Roosevelt tells us. "Basic human rights are simple and easily understood: Freedom of speech . . . freedom of religion . . . freedom of assembly and the right . . . to be . . . free from arbitrary arrest and punishment." We hear John Kennedy saying, "Fellow Americans: Ask not what your country can do for you—ask what you can do for your country. My fellow citizens of the world: Ask not what America will do for you, but what together we can do for the freedom of man." And in the same spirt, President George W. Bush asks, "Did our generation advance the cause of freedom? And did our character bring credit to that cause?" Barack Obama adds, "Freedom without a commitment to others . . . without love or charity or duty or patriotism, is unworthy of our founding ideals, and those who died in their defense."

We learn as the show comes to an end that, thanks to the WWII generation and following generations who kept the flame alive, more people live in freedom today than any time in world history. As a flame ignites in the center of the stage, President Ronald Reagan reminds us that "Freedom is never more than one generation away from extinction. It is not ours by inheritance. It must be fought for and defended constantly by each generation." As the flame on the torch grows larger and brighter, President William J. Clinton lifts our eyes to the American Spirit: "The sun will always rise on America as long as each new generation lights the fire of freedom. Our children are ready. So again, the torch is passed to a new century of young Americans."

World War II was the most destructive and violent conflict in human history, but the story has a redemptive quality, and the Liberation Pavilion speaks to the moral tone of our nation, why we fought, and what we believe. We were fighting for freedom.

WE DELIVERED WHAT WE PROMISED

The grand opening events went by in a flurry of excitement and energy. Our guests spent the afternoon of November 3, 2023, walking through the galleries for the first time, and soon thousands more people visited the Liberation Pavilion. It felt strange yet satisfying, knowing that, for the first time, the exhibits were out of our hands and in the public eye.

The response to the Liberation Pavilion was overwhelmingly positive. People who saw each of our galleries told me this one was the best of all. The *Wall Street Journal* published a review, praising the exhibit for its "unflinching" honesty. "It's somewhat remarkable that in 2023, amid all our social upheavals and gnashing of teeth, there's a place that still celebrates all that we did," Mark Yost wrote. "And lest you think this is some patriotic whitewash of history, the museum does not shy away from pointing out our own shortcomings."[20]

With the Museum Master Plan finished, we had a chance to celebrate what we had accomplished. On November 2, 2023, the night before the grand opening, donors, dignitaries, friends, and families gathered in the Freedom Pavilion to enjoy our Road to Victory celebration dinner. We wanted to have a special event to mark the completion of the Master Plan and reflect on the 20 years we spent completing the capital campaign. Our speakers honored Steve Ambrose and his vision for this Museum. Steve's family was there, as was mine. In a special moment, Tom Brokaw surprised me with a video toast of sherry, commemorating the moment Steve proposed the D-Day Museum idea to me all those years before. Every speaker had a unique perspective on our journey to become The National WWII Museum, because each played a unique part in it. Boysie, who was there from nearly the beginning, noted our rare ability to keeping our eyes on the prize for so many years. "[It's] unusual thinking that in 20 years we didn't change directions," he said. "We surely didn't change mission. And we never have changed message."[21]

Throughout the dinner, we remembered all the challenges and triumphs of building the Museum. We remembered losing Steve, gaining our Congressional designation, enduring Hurricane Katrina, struggling to raise the millions of dollars we needed, the blood, sweat, and tears that went into designing and redesigning our exhibits, all of it. We recalled the countless people who championed the Museum throughout the years and how they shaped the final result. Over the course of three decades, our circumstances shifted, and our plans adapted to meet our immediate needs. We never lost sight of our goals and stayed true to our original vision of America's WWII Museum. Boysie once told me something that made me most proud: "We earned a reputation for delivering what we promised." It was easy to say, but hard to do.

The Road to Victory dinner was also about looking toward the road ahead for the Museum. Now that our permanent exhibits and the capital campaign were complete, the future holds so many possibilities for the Museum. In his remarks, Stephen Watson laid out an exciting vision:

"We know that this ending is really a new beginning," he said. "The beginning of the next phase of our work, to embrace the role of storyteller as fewer members of the World War II generation are able to share their experiences directly. To make sure that this campus continues to be vibrant and innovative and to inspire new and younger audiences with the significance of our mission and its continuing relevance. Our educational mission has never been more important, and with the opening of Liberation Pavilion tomorrow, we will be better equipped than ever to keep the lessons and the legacies of the war relevant for future generations."[22]

When Boysie called me up on stage to speak, I was flooded with memories, gratitude, and pride. "It's been an extraordinary adventure for me. A work of a lifetime," I said. So many of the friends who had been on the journey with me were there in the room. Many others had passed along the way, but they were not forgotten. First and foremost, I thought of my late and best friend Stephen Ambrose, who should have been there for this proud moment. "And I know he's whispering in my ear here saying, 'Nick, I told you it was going to be great,'" I said.[23]

The journey was 33 years in the making and now with the dedication of this seventh and final pavilion, that journey was ending. There were 6 million WWII veterans remaining when we started and now there were far, far fewer. "We had the chance, thanks to Steve's idea, to pay tribute to their generation before we lost them all," I said. "A tribute these veterans never asked for but deeply appreciated."[24]

I tried to sum up my love for Steve Ambrose and the Museum, my faith in democracy, and my hopes and optimism for the Museum's future: "The National World War II Museum is a place of history," I said. "It is also a place of memory where we come to know ourselves as Americans—and what we can accomplish together. . . . Stephen Watson has carried the torch forward in the last six years, and this museum is going to achieve things that you can't even imagine now."[25]

After viewing the Liberation Pavilion, I believe many visitors will leave our Museum pondering important questions. What would they do if called upon? What will they do today to protect our freedoms and sustain the expansion of human rights? Was World War II worth the sacrifice? How did we prevail? How will we preserve our freedom in the future? Their answers could help guide the future course of our democracy. There is also the question that we established as our mission to answer: what does World War II mean today? If visitors are better equipped to answer this question when they leave the Museum than when they arrived, we will have fulfilled our mission. While the next chapter for The National WWII Museum is still not fully defined, I know that we will hold to our mission and message and deliver on our promises, as we always have.

REFLECTIONS

> The mind, once stretched by a new idea, never returns to its original dimensions.
>
> —OLIVER WENDELL HOLMES

HOLMES, WITH FEW WORDS, tells us everything about how this Museum began, evolved, and never returned to the original dimensions of what Stephen Ambrose and I planned to do in 1989. The best our minds could imagine then was ambitious, even for us—to build a modest Museum dedicated to a single day in World War II, D-Day. In the following years, this idea propelled us on a journey that exceeded all expectations. It is indeed an unlikely story. I have traveled a long way since that day with Steve, a day that changed both our lives and has affected the many millions of people who have been touched by the personal stories and great history that now reside in The National WWII Museum. On a personal level, the Museum thrust me into a second career and brought me to this place that has now become an international site of historical memory of World War II and its legacy for America and the world. It is consistently ranked among the top ten museums in the world. But most importantly the Museum is an institution of higher learning that is becoming the most trusted source of accessible knowledge of the war that changed the world.

This story did not have to happen, and it almost ended several times because of doubters, funding shortfalls, poor decisions, natural disasters, economic recessions, and a global pandemic. There were many near-death experiences but also great triumphs that inspired us to forge ahead.

As I reflect on what has been achieved, I am most pleased by the excitement and education the world-class exhibits and programs present to people of all ages, especially the young. All of this is contained within our magnificent architecture and embraced by the Canopy of Peace. I am, of course, most proud that we have paid tribute to a great generation of Americans, veterans, and home front workers who helped win the war and gave us the peace that has not seen another world war for 80 years. I am also thrilled to see daily throngs of visitors, young and old alike, who swarm to this Museum to learn of America's achievements in a day and age when unity and common purpose seem like distant memories. The most frequent refrain I hear from visitors—"I had no idea"—is rewarding to this historian at the end of a long journey. I am very proud that we tell this American story with an allegiance to historical authenticity. I am honored that the Museum revives the ideals and values that inspired our children and leaders through the end of the last century—to this day. And I am very pleased we have documented legacies of the peace that made America the leader of the world, champion of freedom, democracy, and human rights at home and abroad. At this history Museum, we remain open to rigorous debate to understand the contributions of all Americans to allied victory, all races and religions, in what Supreme Commander General Eisenhower called the "Great Crusade."

World War II served as a crucible for America. We mobilized all the human, spiritual, material, and economic resources of our nation to defeat tyranny and the racist regimes intent on the destruction of our freedom and democracy. It was a fight to the finish for civilization itself. The American Spirit prevailed.[1] That battle of the twentieth century will always be with us. We learned the hard lessons of isolation and unpreparedness, the need for allies and partners to win out over fascism first, and then the necessity to overcome communism, too. Courage and commitment of our staff, historians, board of trustees, and donors all helped bring this great American story to life in brick and mortar, as well as in exhibits, programs, and ideas.

History museums do not predict the future; our exhibits and programs explore why the war happened, how it was won, and its enduring meaning. Whatever course our nation follows in war and peace in years ahead, it will have this great Museum to tell the story of what we can do when "we're all in this together"—united with a common purpose.

President Reagan told us that "freedom is a fragile thing and it's never more than one generation away from extinction . . . it must be fought for and defended constantly by each generation."[2] We are living in dangerous times, and there is no shortage of threats to freedom and democracy. We cannot cover up the persistent threats to democracy, but this national Museum can remind us of our great achievements, our generosity, and the best of the legacies of World War II. History is not static, and our memory of World War II will continue to evolve as we seek to understand the liberating power of the story and the dangers that lurk.

My successors, especially the leadership team and the national board of trustees, have inherited the role I have had most of the years since the Museum was created. They are now the curators of America's public memory of World War II, the most consequential war in human history. It's a heavy responsibility. We saved our freedom, gave new force to human rights, helped extend the gift of democracy to other nations, even to our former enemies. We extended civil rights and women's rights at home and gave birth to the greatest renaissance in research and higher learning through the GI Bill.

Steve Ambrose once wrote that the Museum we built would be "the place where stories of sacrifice, courage, and democracy will live forever." I feel we succeeded. We are a history Museum first and foremost, not a tribute museum or a memorial museum. Nonetheless, what we built in New Orleans serves as a tribute and a memorial to the men and women who served in World War II and beyond. Their stories are told in this Museum. They will never be forgotten and will and never fade from memory. You will find them here.

Five decades from now, even into the next century and beyond, visitors, historians, and government leaders will want to study and understand World War II. What will this Museum contribute to their knowledge? What story will we tell? What meaning did victory bring to the lives of our citizens and nation? What I believe will still matter to future generations is that America's leaders and citizens rallied to save our democracy and our freedoms in the most violent conflict in middle of the 20th century. My final vision was that our Museum's exhibits and programs will always be reminders of the liberating power of what America achieved and of the vigilance we need to remain free and strong. I hope this journey can be a guide to how that can happen. I've done my best and am indebted to many. The baton is passed.

ACKNOWLEDGMENTS

THIS BOOK, MUCH LIKE this Museum, was the product of many hands, and would not exist without the generosity and cooperation of numerous individuals. Those responsible for the success of the Museum are often the same people responsible for this book. First among many is the University of New Orleans, which provided Steve Ambrose and me with enormous support through the first ten years of the Museum's life. In those years when our project was in the incubator stage, UNO's Research and Technology Park, Eisenhower Center, and Foundation gave life support for our idea which otherwise would never have seen the light of day.

Enormous thanks go to the state of Louisiana, the city of New Orleans and our friends in the US Congress who have supported us since the beginning. These public institutions and officials backed the aspirations of two historians and a fledgling board at a time many thought we would never succeed. During those tough early years and beyond, leaders from the New Orleans business community gave their time, counsel, and personal contributions. I am humbled by the increasing support we received from the private sector. This book puts the final punctuation mark on the long journey that many have walked with me.

I have always been grateful for the spirit and commitment of The National WWII Museum Board of Trustees, the National D-Day Museum Board of Directors, and our Board Chairs: Arthur Q. Davis, Lee Schlesinger, Bob Howson, James Livingston, Boysie Bollinger, David Voelker, Pete Wilson, Phil Satre, Herschel Abbott Jr., Richard C. Adkerson, Jim Courter, Paul

Hilliard, John Koerner, Ted Weggeland, and Suzanne Mestayer. Their unwavering devotion to preserving the story and legacy of World War II helped transform a modest D-Day Museum into a world-class institution. No one was more important to me than Boysie Bollinger, whose vision and confidence often made the difference through times of adversity. He provided extraordinary leadership and added enormous credibility to the Museum by making the largest single private contribution to date. Boysie and many other key players in this story generously gave time to me for interviews that were foundational to the research for this book and added a dimension of personality and authenticity not otherwise obtainable. I also thank the many trustees, donors, staff members, volunteers, and especially the WWII veterans who occupy a special place in our mission and are at the heart of the legacy we preserve in this book.

There are too many building and exhibit designers to mention here, but our master planners should be recognized for their endurance and patience through 20 years of service. Bart Voorsanger, Master Plan architect, gave us the vision and beauty of the final campus. Bart's designs were inspiring and showed us how exterior architecture adds unity to the experience within. Our exhibits master planner, Patrick Gallagher, created immersive environments of a global war that always featured the personal word, image, or artifact. He was deeply committed to bringing the performance of art, history, and design together in ways that helped me preserve the integrity of the story of America's journey through the war and its consequences. The Museum's recently retired Senior Vice President for Capital Projects, Bob Farnsworth, coordinated the numerous designers, architects, builders, and construction firms to bring the $407 million WWII Museum to its physical reality. His unflinching optimism and his exceptional talents kept all the teams in unison through completion of the Master Plan.

Since 2006, the Museum has received sage wisdom and advice from our Presidential Counselors, the historians, museum professionals, and film producers who enriched our exhibits and programs beyond all expectations. I want to pay special tribute to the late Marc Pachter—Counselor, Trustee, and Director of the Smithsonian National Portrait Gallery, who had a profound influence on me, our Counselors, board, and designers on how to create a modern museum. Marc was a close advisor to me from the first months after opening the National D-Day Museum until his passing in February 2024. He was the first to press me to write the Museum's history—to tell the story from its origins to the present through my eyes and memory. Without his encouragement, this book would have never been written. Historian Don Miller played an outsized role as trusted advisor and close friend through every step of my journey. His contributions to our vision for the expanded Master Plan, to the history we portray in our exhibits, and the development of our conferences and WWII tours have improved the Museum experience and this book.

Several friends did not live to see this Museum finished; they guided me as the idea progressed from infancy to maturity, providing me with candid advice and support when most needed. Chief among them was my oldest friend of 60 years and fellow historian, the late Julian Pleasants. He was enthusiastically engaged with Steve Ambrose and me in the earliest brainstorming on D-Day, the war, and its aftermath, long before there was even an idea for a museum. Likewise, I thank the late Malcolm Ehrhardt, a friend and confidant, whose marketing firm generated national publicity for the Museum in the years before opening when prospects looked bleak. Malcolm's advice and marketing prowess piqued the public's interest and attracted droves of visitors to the Museum in the first five years of operations.

On the national spectrum, Tom Brokaw was our most ardent national champion from the very beginning. He gave Ambrose and the Museum national visibility at every given opportunity. The importance of his friendship, national influence, and commitment to our Museum cannot be exaggerated, culminating in his writing the foreword to this book. Likewise, Tom Hanks, Steven Spielberg, and Gary Sinise generously gave their time, funding, and creative expertise for over 25 years. Tom Hanks added to our national publicity in ways that only he could. His friendship gave us much needed expertise as we strove for visual authenticity in our cinematic productions. Steven Spielberg's support and films helped me find ways to give the personal voices to the horrors of the Holocaust and the meaning of liberation.

Stephen Watson, President and CEO of the Museum, has been a friend and co-conspirator in this great enterprise. He played a critical role in the Museum's growth, and he generously provided resources of people, records, and contributions from his senior staff to support this book. Stephen's keen memory of the last 22 years enriched many portions of the manuscript. I am indebted to him for helping me shape the history we tell in this Museum.

My wife, Beth, my sons, Dave and John, experienced the daily rigors of research and writing as well as the journey that led to the Museum. They remain a constant source of encouragement for me and always lift my spirits. The Ambrose and Mueller clans had a ringside seat to the adventures we traversed, and they all shared support when called upon.

Alisa Plant and her team at LSU Press have also provided support for this project and our previous work, *Building The National WWII Museum*. They have always been excellent partners and patiently guided us throughout the production of both books.

My staff deserves exceptional praise for their daily devotion to *Preserving the Legacy.* Former staff members Meg Cahill, Coleman Warner, Claire DeLucca, Robert Janous, Richard Brunies, Laura Journey, Connie Gentry, and Kali Martin Schick all helped get this project off the ground by providing initial ideas and collecting archival materials. Together, they organized and digitized over 25,000 pages of board documents and other resources. In recent years, Marisa Primeaux, Jason R. Van, and Taylor Lindner Dougherty worked through every step of getting me to the finish line. Marisa's duty of verifying all the various facts, figures, and dates, while constructing endnotes, was a monumental task; Jason kept me in check (likely the most difficult part of his job), managed our schedules, deadlines, and organized scores of oral histories, all while lending his editorial expertise to ensure this manuscript was in pristine shape; Taylor spent countless hours conducting research, writing chapter scopes, editing drafts, providing historical context and flow, and conquered every task necessary. Her writing and editing skills were of enormous help, as were Jason's. Their attention to detail, consistency, and commitment to excellence were key in completing this book, and I would not have been able to do so without them.

My principal editor, Steve Vogel, deserves special mention. As a well-known journalist and author, Steve was integral to the final product. He had the unenviable task of reducing at least 40 percent of what I wrote. Steve found the best and cut the rest, and he provided valuable historical judgment. His patience and thoughtful collaboration led to skillful reconfiguring and editing that helped bring the manuscript into its final form.

Most of all, I want to thank my best friend, colleague, and Museum founder, the late Stephen E. Ambrose, a great American historian. He and I had big dreams for the future of the Museum, and I think he would agree that it has exceeded his expectations—and mine. We traversed through the fog of our naivete and conquered adversities we never could have overcome without our shared commitment to an idea born in our hearts and minds and sealed in the deep bonds of our friendship. I hope Steve's vision shines through this story that he left me to finish. I suppose I should thank him for reeling me into his idea after serving me too many glasses of sherry. That afternoon led to one of the great adventures of my life. Without him, there would be no museum and no history of the unlikely story that is told within these pages. To Steve, his family, and mine, I am eternally grateful.

NOTES

1. THE IDEA

1. The quotation from Roosevelt appears in Stephen E. Ambrose, *D-Day June 6, 1944: The Climactic Battle of World War II* (New York: Simon & Schuster, 1994), 279.

2. Ambrose, *D-Day June 6, 1944,* 45–46.

2. PUTTING STRUCTURE ON THE IDEA

1. Materials of the Eisenhower Center Board of Directors Meeting, Oct. 2, 1991, Eisenhower Center Records, University of New Orleans. The Eisenhower Center Advisory Board of Directors in April 1991 comprised the following members: Ollie D. Brown Jr., John B. Dunlap Jr., James M. Cain, Arthur Q. Davis, Robert L. Dupont, John J. Graham, William A. Hines, Richard E. Holtz, Samuel G. Krauss, John N. Mangieri, Mary M. Mohs, Gordon H. "Nick" Mueller, Gregory M. St. L. O'Brien, Lee H. Schlesinger, and Richard B. Stephens.

2. "Agenda," Materials of the Eisenhower Center Board of Directors Meeting, Mar. 20, 1990, Eisenhower Center Records, University of New Orleans.

3. D-DAY

1. Stephen E. Ambrose, "Draft, D-Day Museum, "Eisenhower Center Records, University of New Orleans. The document was part of the materials from the Eisenhower Center Board of Directors Meeting on Mar. 20, 1990.

2. Ambrose, "Draft, D-Day Museum."

3. Ambrose, "Draft, D-Day Museum."

4. Ambrose, "Draft, D-Day Museum."

5. Ambrose, "Draft, D-Day Museum."

6. Minutes of the Eisenhower Center Board of Directors Meeting, Sept. 11, 1990, Eisenhower Center Records, University of New Orleans.

7. Minutes, Sept. 11, 1990.

8. Minutes of the Eisenhower Center Board of Directors Meeting, Apr. 11, 1991, Eisenhower Center Records, University of New Orleans.

9. Bruce Alpert, "D-Day Museum Is Backed." (New Orleans, LA) *Times-Picayune,* June 8, 1991.

10. Bob Livingston, interview by author, Jan. 18, 2023, The National WWII Museum Institutional Records and Archives.

11. The paraphrasing of the conversations between Ambrose and Livingston has been verified by Stephen Ambrose, Bob Livingston, and Paul Cambon, Livingston's Administrative Assistant, all of whom were present in the meeting.

12. Alpert, "D-Day Museum Is Backed."

13. Frank Donze, "Vote Due on Plan for Beach Project," (New Orleans, LA) *Times-Picayune,* Dec. 3, 1991.

14. Ed Anderson, "Outlay Bill Gives N.O. $166 million," (New Orleans, LA) *Times-Picayune,* July 24, 1991.

15. In the total funding, $9 million of $13 million were UNO assets, not the D-Day Museum's.

16. Ambrose had previously met Manford Rommel, Mayor of Stuttgart, on one of his D-Day to the Rhine tours.

17. Department of Defense Appropriations Act, 1992, Publ. L. No. 102–172, Stat. 105 (1991).

18. "Articles of Incorporation of National D-Day Museum Foundation, Inc." Materials of the Eisenhower Center Board of Directors Meeting, Dec. 12, 1991, Eisenhower Center Records, University of New Orleans. Paraphrased from the Articles of Incorporation, National D-Day Museum Foundation, Inc.

19. Minutes, Dec. 12, 1991, Eisenhower Center Records, University of New Orleans.

20. Joe Darby, "Normandy Relived at Pontchartrain," (New Orleans, LA) *Times-Picayune,* June 7, 1992.

21. Minutes, Dec. 12, 1991, Eisenhower Center Records, University of New Orleans.

22. Winston Churchill, comp. Charles Eade *The End of the Beginning: War Speeches,* 3rd ed. (London: Cassell, 1946), 215.

4. GROWING PAINS

1. Metaform is a subsidiary of the architectural firm Chermayeff-Geismar.

2. "Pacific Wing Owes Epic Touch to Veterans Museum Designer," (New Orleans, LA) *Times-Picayune,* Dec. 2, 2001.

3. Schlesinger, interview with the author, Sept. 27, 2021. Paraphrase of interview.

4. Schlesinger, interview.

5. Schlesinger, interview.

6. "Letter from Charles Guggenheim to Jack Masey," Materials of The National D-Day Museum Foundation, Inc., Board of Directors Meeting, Mar. 2, 1993, The National WWII Museum Institutional Records and Archives. Guggenheim's fee was later raised to over $1 million and 55 minutes to qualify for an hour-long national TV airing and to be eligible for a nomination for an Academy Award.

7. Schlesinger, interview.

8. Materials of The National D-Day Museum Foundation, Inc., Board of Directors Meeting, Apr. 14, 1993, The National WWII Museum Institutional Records and Archives.

9. Minutes of The National D-Day Museum Foundation, Inc., Board of Directors Meeting, June 8, 1993, The National WWII Museum Institutional Records and Archives. Boyce brought the $30 million budget recommendation to the board three months later on June 8, 1993.

10. Minutes, The National D-Day Museum Board of Directors Meeting, Apr. 14, 1993.

11. Minutes, The National D-Day Museum Board of Directors Meeting, Apr. 14, 1993.

12. "Boyce-Mansfield Report to the Board," The National D-Day Museum Board of Directors Meeting, Apr. 14, 1993.

13. Materials of The National D-Day Museum Foundation, Inc., Board of Directors Meeting, Nov. 10, 1993, The National WWII Museum Institutional Records and Archives.

14. Minutes, The National D-Day Museum Board of Directors Meeting, June 8, 1993.

15. "Business Plan for the National D-Day Museum June 1993-May 1994," Materials of The National D-Day Museum Foundation, Inc., Board of Directors Meeting, Aug. 18, 1993, The National WWII Museum Institutional Records and Archives.

5. THE TASTE OF VICTORY TURNS SOUR, 1994–1998

1. Minutes of The National D-Day Museum Foundation, Inc., Board of Directors Meeting, Dec. 14, 1993, The National WWII Museum Institutional Records and Archives.

2. "D-Day Museum Planned for New Orleans," (Lafayette, LA) *Daily Advertiser,* Apr. 15, 1994.

3. "D-Day Film Captures '44 Drama," (New Orleans, LA) *Times-Picayune,* May 22, 1994.

4. The building was known as the Roosevelt Hotel from the 1920s to the 1960s, after which it was sold and renamed the Fairmont Hotel. In 2007, it was sold again and returned to its previous name, which it retains today.

5. There was still no firm cost for the Museum. Consultants had estimated $30 million, our architect pegged it that year in a local newspaper as $22 million, and the board and consultants had estimated between $15 million and $30 million on several occasions from 1993 to 1995. Without an agreed-upon scope, construction drawings, and exhibit costs, any guess was as good or as bad as any other, but no one seemed to be concerned about solid estimates at that point. We all knew it would change.

6. Ambrose, *D-Day: June 6, 1944,* 26.

7. Raleigh Trevelyan, "Telling It Like It Was," review of *D-Day: June 6, 1944: The Climactic Battle of World War II,* by Stephen E. Ambrose, *New York Times,* May 29, 1994.

8. Lynne Jensen and Susan Larson, "Historian Stephen Ambrose Joins Notables at Normandy," (New Orleans, LA) *Times-Picayune,* June 3, 1994. Minutes of The National D-Day Museum Foundation, Inc. Board Meeting, June 22, 1994, The National WWII Museum Institutional Records and Archives. The briefing of these government officials gave Steve the opportunity to plead his case for more federal support for the Museum. Clinton gave Steve the impression that the government would contribute $15 million, but that funding never materialized.

9. Ambrose, *D-Day June 6, 1944,* 188–89.

10. Ann Devroy, "Clinton Honors D-Day Sacrifices," *Washington Post,* June 7, 1994.

11. William J. Clinton, "A Tribute to Those Who Fell at Normandy," transcript of speech delivered at Normandy, June 6, 1994, *US Department of State Dispatch,* vol. 5, issue 22.

12. Gen. Claude M. Kicklighter, Department of Defense Executive Director of the D-Day Commemoration event, secured VIP tickets as part of the official US D-Day delegation for all 500-plus

of our Museum tour participants, allowing us all to be guests at the international ceremonies held at the American Cemetery the morning of June 6.

13. Transcript, The National D-Day Museum Board of Directors Meeting, June 22, 1994.

14. Transcript, The National D-Day Museum Board of Directors Meeting, June 22, 1994.

15. Minutes of The National D-Day Museum Foundation, Inc., Board of Directors Meeting, Nov. 16, 1994, The National WWII Museum Institutional Records and Archives.

16. Minutes of The National D-Day Museum Foundation, Inc., Board of Directors Meeting, Mar. 21, 1995, The National WWII Museum Institutional Records and Archives.

17. Minutes, The National D-Day Museum Board of Directors Meeting, Mar. 21, 1995.

18. Unlike the state of Louisiana, the federal government was less concerned about whether the building or renovations could be completed, only that we had to spend the funds on legitimate capital costs for the Museum. The state required evidence of other funds or pledges to complete the Museum.

19. Minutes of The National D-Day Museum Foundation, Inc., Board of Directors Meeting, Feb. 14, 1996, The National WWII Museum Institutional Records and Archives. Minutes of the National D-Day Museum Foundation, Inc., Board of Directors Meeting, Apr. 26, 1996, The National WWII Museum Institutional Records and Archives.

20. Minutes, The National D-Day Museum Board of Directors Meeting, Apr. 26, 1996.

21. Maj. Gen. James Livingston, interview with the author, Oct. 25, 2022, The National WWII Museum Institutional Records and Archives.

22. Minutes of The National D-Day Museum Foundation, Inc., Board of Directors Meeting, Jan. 28, 1997, The National WWII Museum Institutional Records and Archives.

23. Minutes of The National D-Day Museum Foundation, Inc., Board of Directors Meeting, Nov. 28, 1996, The National WWII Museum Institutional Records and Archives.

24. Minutes, The National D-Day Museum Board of Directors Meeting, Jan. 28, 1997.

25. Minutes of The National D-Day Museum Foundation, Inc., Board of Directors Meeting, Dec. 2, 1997, The National WWII Museum Records and Archives.

26. Minutes, The National D-Day Museum Board of Directors Meeting, Jan. 28, 1997.

27. Frank Donze, "Plans for D-Day Museum Pushing Forward," (New Orleans, LA) *Times-Picayune,* May 6, 1997.

28. Minutes of The National D-Day Museum Foundation, Inc., Board of Directors Meeting, June 28, 1997, The National WWII Museum Institutional Records and Archives.

29. Materials, The National D-Day Museum Board of Directors Meeting, Dec. 2, 1997.

30. Bill Detweiler, interview with the author, Dec. 15, 2018, The National WWII Museum Institutional Records and Archives. Bill Detweiler, then the Board Secretary, later said that he was so discouraged that he had come to the Executive Committee meeting with his letter of resignation. But Livingston persuaded him to hold off submitting it, as they had just talked to me, and he thought I would accept the Chairmanship in September. That was not exactly correct, but that is what the General told him, and it was enough to keep a valuable board member in place.

31. Minutes of The National D-Day Museum Foundation, Inc., Board of Directors Meeting, Apr. 15, 1998, The National WWII Museum Institutional Records and Archives.

32. Minutes, The National D-Day Museum Board of Directors Meeting, Apr. 15, 1998.

33. Minutes, The National D-Day Museum Board of Directors Meeting, Apr. 15, 1998.

34. Minutes of The National D-Day Museum Foundation, Inc., Executive Committee Meeting, June 5, 1998, The National WWII Museum Institutional Records and Archives.

35. Minutes, The National D-Day Museum Executive Committee Meeting, June 5, 1998.

36. Materials of The National D-Day Museum Foundation, Inc., Board of Directors Meeting, Aug. 3, 1998, The National WWII Museum Institutional Records and Archives. June meeting notes were included in the August meeting materials.

37. James Varney, "Saving the D-Day Museum—'I Never Gave Up On It'" (New Orleans, LA) *Times-Picayune,* Aug. 1, 1998.

38. Minutes, The National D-Day Museum Board of Directors Meeting, Aug. 3, 1998.

39. Minutes, The National D-Day Museum Board of Directors Meeting, Aug. 3, 1998.

40. Varney, "Saving the D-Day Museum.'"

41. Stephen E. Ambrose, "Writer Pleas for Local D-Day Museum," (New Orleans, LA) *Times-Picayune,* Aug. 7, 1998.

6. ROAD TO VICTORY

1. Donze, "Plans For D-Day Museum Pushing Forward."

2. Minutes of The National D-Day Foundation, Inc., Board of Directors Meeting, Sept. 9, 1998, The National WWII Museum Institutional Records and Archives.

3. "D-day Plus 20 years, Sixth of a Series: Conversation with Eisenhower as He Looks Back to Invasion: 1944," (Victoria, British Columbia) *Daily Colonist,* June 13, 1964.

4. Minutes, The National D-Day Museum Board of Directors Meeting, Sept. 9, 1998.

5. Materials, The National D-Day Museum Board of Directors Meeting, Sept. 9, 1998.

6. Minutes, The National D-Day Museum Board of Directors Meeting, Sept. 9, 1998.

7. Minutes of The National D-Day Museum Foundation, Inc., Board of Directors Meeting, Oct. 21, 1998, The National WWII Museum Institutional Records and Archives. The capital appropriation was later raised to $3.8 million and then subsequently to $4.2 million.

8. J. E. Bourgoyne, "Ambrose Better," (New Orleans, LA) *Times-Picayune,* Nov. 18, 1998.

9. "Capital Campaign & Financial Projections 1998–2000," Materials of The National D-Day Museum Foundation, Inc., Board of Directors Meeting, Dec. 7, 1998, The National WWII Museum Institutional Records and Archives.

10. Stephen E. Ambrose, *Citizen Soldiers: The U.S. Army from the Normandy Beaches to the Bulge to the Surrender of Germany, June 7, 1944–May 7, 1945* (New York: Simon & Schuster, 1998), 487.

11. Minutes of The National D-Day Foundation, Inc., Board of Directors Meeting, Aug. 18, 1999, The National WWII Museum Institutional Records and Archives. The board authorized the final contract with some upgrades supplemented by private funds at $4.235 million. At the August meeting it was agreed the contract would be for $1,435,000 (plus $120,000 for reimbursable expenses). At the October meeting, it was said that the contract would be for $1,8 million.

12. Minutes of The National D-Day Museum Foundation, Inc., Board of Directors Meeting, Nov. 19, 1998, The National WWII Museum Institutional Records and Archives.

13. "Business Plan for the National D-Day Museum, July 1, 1999–June 30, 2000," Materials of The National D-Day Museum Foundation, Inc., Executive Committee Meeting, July 22, 1999, The National WWII Museum Institutional Records and Archives.

14. "Business Plan for the National D-Day Museum, July 1, 1999–June 30, 2000," The National D-Day Museum Board of Directors Meeting, Aug. 18, 1999.

15. Materials of The National D-Day Museum Foundation, Inc., Board of Directors Meeting, Nov. 2, 1999, The National WWII Museum Institutional Records and Archives.

16. Tom Brokaw, interview with the author, June 1, 2022, The National WWII Museum Institutional Records and Archives. Paraphrase of interview.

17. Brokaw, interview, June 1, 2022.

7. THE MARCH TO THE GRAND OPENING

1. Ambrose, *Citizen Soldiers,* 473.

2. Minutes of The National D-Day Museum Foundation, Inc., Board of Directors Meeting, Jan. 25, 2000, The National WWII Museum Institutional Records and Archives.

3. Gen. David Mize, email message to the author, Jan. 8, 2023.

4. Materials of The National D-Day Museum Foundation, Inc., Executive Committee Meeting, Jan. 11, 2000, The National WWII Museum Institutional Records and Archives. Materials of The National D-Day Museum Foundation, Inc., Executive Committee Meeting, Feb. 28, 2000, The National WWII Museum Institutional Records and Archives. Cohen's letter conveying official designation of the event was sent to the author on Feb. 15, 2000. The liaison group was the task force under General Mize that had been agreed upon when Cohen met with Mize. William Cohen, letter to the author, Feb. 15, 2000.

5. Mize, email, Jan. 8, 2023.

6. Minutes of The National D-Day Foundation, Inc., Museum Board of Directors Meeting, May 16, 2000, The National WWII Museum Institutional Records and Archives.

7. Minutes, The National D-Day Museum Executive Committee Meeting, Feb. 28, 2000.

8. Minutes, The National D-Day Museum Executive Committee Meeting, Feb. 28, 2000.

9. "Media Update May 11, 2000," The National D-Day Museum Board of Directors Meeting, May 16, 2000, The National WWII Museum Institutional Records and Archives.

10. Minutes, The National D-Day Museum Board of Directors Meeting, Nov. 2, 1999. Minutes of The National D-Day Museum Foundation, Inc., Board of Directors Meeting, Apr. 21, 1999, The National WWII Museum Institutional Records and Archives.

11. Elizabeth Mullener, "Countdown to Day—Museum on Course for Gala June 6 Opening," (New Orleans, LA) *Times-Picayune,* Apr. 9, 2000.

12. Stephen Ambrose, letter to Associated General Contractors, Dec. 20, 2000, provided by Pat Gootee.

13. "*The National WWII Museum," Grand Opening,* (Storyville, 2000), DVD.

14. "*The National WWII Museum," Grand Opening.*

15. "*The National WWII Museum," Grand Opening.*

16. "Conversations with Veterans of D-Day," C-SPAN video, 2:27:00, June 5, 2000, https://www.c-span.org.

17. "Conversations with Veterans of D-Day."

18. *"The National WWII Museum," Grand Opening.*

19. Paul Purpura, "Historian Ambrose is Decorated-Museum Founder Gets Medal for Public Service," (New Orleans, LA) *Times-Picayune,* June 6, 2000.

20. A stretch of Howard Avenue from Lee Circle to Convention Center Boulevard would be renamed Andrew Higgins Boulevard shortly after the grand opening in 2000.

21. *"The National WWII Museum," Grand Opening.*

22. "*The National WWII Museum," Grand Opening.*

23. *"The National WWII Museum," Grand Opening.*

24. Minutes of The National D-Day Museum Foundation, Inc., Board of Directors Meeting, June 21, 2000, The National WWII Museum Institutional Records and Archives.

25. "Opening of the D-Day Museum," C-SPAN, video, 2:43:30, June 6, 2000.

26. "Opening of D-Day Museum."

27. "Opening of D-Day Museum."

28. "Opening of D-Day Museum."

29. "Opening of D-Day Museum."

30. "Opening of D-Day Museum."

31. "Opening of D-Day Museum."

32. "Opening of D-Day Museum."

33. John Vachon, *Mother of three soldiers. Plaquemines Parish, Louisiana,* 1943, photograph, Library of Congress, loc.gov.

34. "The National D-Day Museum, New Orleans: Building America's National WWII Museum," capital campaign brochure, 2003, The National WWII Museum Institutional Records and Archives.

35. Elizabeth Mullener. "Crowds Keep Coming to The D-Day Museum." (New Orleans, LA) *Times-Picayune,* July 17, 2000. Minutes of the National D-Day Museum Foundation, Inc., Executive Committee Meeting, Jan. 16, 2001, The National WWII Museum Institutional Records and Archives.

36. Minutes of the National D-Day Museum Foundation, Inc., Executive Committee Meeting, June 20, 2000, The National WWII Museum Institutional Records and Archives.

37. Gordon H. Mueller, "African American Role Is Included," (New Orleans, LA) *Times-Picayune,* June 25, 2000.

38. Minutes, National D-Day Museum Executive Committee Meeting, Feb. 28, 2000.

39. Mueller, "African American Role Is Included."

40. Elizabeth Mullener, "Event to Honor Black Veterans—Scholars to Explore Men's Dual Fight," (New Orleans, LA) *Times-Picayune,* Jan. 15, 2001.

41. Paul Purpura, "Recognition, Overdue—Hearts Beating Proudly, the Forgotten Vets Parade," (New Orleans, LA) *Times-Picayune,* Feb. 4, 2001.

42. Minutes of the National D-Day Museum Foundation, Inc., Board of Directors Meeting, Sept. 20, 2000, The National WWII Museum Institutional Records and Archives.

43. Minutes, the National D-Day Museum Board of Directors Meeting, May 16, 2000. Paraphrase of Masey's presentation to the Board of Directors.

44. *Invasion in the Pacific Exhibit, Grand Opening* (Storyville, 2001), DVD.

45. *Invasion in the Pacific Exhibit Grand Opening.*

8. BECOMING THE NATIONAL WWII MUSEUM

1. Boysie Bollinger, interview with the author, Oct. 3, 2022, The National WWII Museum Institutional Records and Archives.

2. Minutes of the National D-Day Museum Foundation, Inc., Executive Committee Meeting, Oct. 31, 2000, The National WWII Museum Institutional Records and Archives.

3. Department of Defense Appropriations Act, 2001, Publ. L. No. 106–259, Stat. 114 (2000).

4. Materials of the National D-Day Museum Foundation, Inc., Executive Committee Meeting, Dec. 6, 2002, The National WWII Museum Institutional Records and Archives. This figure is the combined price of two of the properties. The Museum entered a lease agreement for the third.

5. Bollinger, interview, Oct. 3, 2023.

6. "Report of the Committee on the Future Governance for the National D-Day Museum," Materials of the National D-Day Museum Foundation, Inc., Board of Directors Meeting, May 16, 2002, The National WWII Museum Institutional Records and Archives.

7. "Education Master Plan, *Proposed,*" Materials of the National D-Day Museum Foundation, Inc., Board of Trustees Meeting, Dec. 4–5, 2003, The National WWII Museum Institutional Records and Archives.

8. Elizabeth Mullener, "New Study Center to Focus on the American Spirit—D-day Museum buys 3 Buildings," (New Orleans, LA) *Times-Picayune,* Oct. 11, 2001.

9. Department of Defense and Emergency Supplemental for Recovery from and Response to Terrorist Attacks on The United States Act, 2002, Pub. L. No. 107–117, Stat 115 (2002).

10. Mullener, "New Study Center to Focus on the American Spirit."

11. Mullener, "New Study Center to Focus on the American Spirit."

12. Minutes of the National D-Day Museum Foundation, Inc., Executive Committee Meeting, Oct. 30, 2002, The National WWII Museum Institutional Records and Archives.

13. Minutes of the National D-Day Museum Foundation, Inc., Board of Directors Meeting, Feb. 21, 2002, The National WWII Museum Institutional Records and Archives.

14. "LORD Cultural Resources Planning and Management, Inc., Proposal for Master Planning Services," Feb. 22, 2002, The National WWII Museum Institutional Records and Archives.

15. A charette is defined as "a meeting in which all stakeholders in a project attempt to resolve conflicts and map solutions."

16. Fred Barnes, "Stephen Ambrose, Copycat," *The Weekly Standard,* Jan. 4, 2002.

17. David D. Fitzpatrick, "As Historian's Fame Grows, So Do Questions on Methods," *New York Times,* Jan. 11, 2001.

18. Stephen E. Ambrose, "Accusations of Plagiarism Deserve an Honest Reply," (Biloxi, MS) *Sun Herald,* May 3, 2002. Ambrose originally wrote this article for the *Times-Picayune* on May 2, 2002, and it was reprinted in the *Sun Herald.*

19. Minutes of the National D-Day Museum Foundation, Inc., Executive Committee Meeting, Apr. 30, 2002, The National WWII Museum Institutional Records and Archives.

20. Minutes, the National D-Day Museum Board of Directors Meeting, May 16, 2002.

21. John Pope, "Senator Enthralls Museum Audience," (New Orleans, LA) *Times Picayune,* July 13, 2002.

22. "The National D-Day Museum Concept Plan," Feb. 2003, The National WWII Museum Institutional Records and Archives. The invitees to the Conceptual Planning Charette in May 2002 included the following: Dr. Allan Millett, Mason Professor of Military History, Ohio State University; Brig-Gen (Ret.) Robert A. Cocroft, President and CEO, Wisconsin Veterans War Memorial; Dr. Terrence M. Cole, Professor of History, University of Alaska–Fairbanks; Jennifer Lawson, Producer, Magic Box Media, Inc.; Donald. L. Miller, John Henry MacCracken Professor of History, Lafayette College; Marc Pachter, Director, National Portrait Gallery, Acting Director, National Museum of American History, Smithsonian Institution; Van Romans, Executive Director, Walt Disney Imagineering; Dr. Gregory J. W. Urwin, Professor of History, Temple University; Dr. John F. Votaw, Executive Director, The First Division Museum at Cantigny; Dr. Richard J. Zeitlin, Director, Wisconsin Veterans Museum; Cindy McCurdy and Samuel J. Wegner, National D-Day Museum staff.

23. "Stephen Ambrose Memorial Service," C-SPAN, video, 1:44:06, Oct. 19, 2002. The following narrative is derived from quotations or paraphrasing of remarks from the televised C-SPAN: Stephen E. Ambrose's Memorial Service, Oct. 19, 2002.

24. Stephen E. Ambrose, *Comrades: Brothers, Fathers, Heroes, Sons, Pals* (New York: Simon & Schuster, 1999). On p. 106, Steve writes on the "Friendship of Lewis and Clark" and on 96, on the chapter on our friendship, he writes "our relationship has been a joy and a privilege, indeed, an ecstasy." The remarks above are a paraphrase of remarks from both the Memorial Service video and the passages in *Comrades.*

25. Gordon H. "Nick" Mueller and Kali Martin Schick, *Building The National WWII Museum* (Baton Rouge: Louisiana State University Press, 2023), 43.

26. Bollinger, interview, Oct. 3, 2023.

27. Elizabeth Mullener, "Battlefield Promotion," (New Orleans, LA) *Times-Picayune,* Mar. 14, 2004.

28. Mullener, "Battlefield Promotion."

29. Department of Defense Appropriation Act, 2004, Publ. L. No. 108-87, Stat. 117 (2003).

30. "Congress Honors National D-Day Museum," (Baton Rouge, LA) *The Advocate,* Sept. 26, 2003.

31. Bruce Alpert, "WWII Vets in Congress to be Honored—Event Begins D-Day Museum Fund Raising," (New Orleans, LA) *Times-Picayune,* Feb. 4, 2004.

32. Alpert, "WWII Vets in Congress to be Honored."

33. Roxanne Roberts, OUT & ABOUT, *Washington Post,* Feb. 9, 2004.

34. Minutes, The National D-Day Museum Board of Trustees Meeting, Dec. 4–5, 2003, The National WWII Museum Institutional Records and Archives.

35. Minutes of the National D-Day Museum Foundation, Inc., Executive Committee Meeting Apr. 23, 2003, The National WWII Museum Institutional Records and Archives.

36. Minutes of The National D-Day Museum Foundation, Inc., Special Board of Trustees Meeting, Mar. 8, 2005, The National WWII Museum Institutional Records and Archives.

37. Minutes, The National D-Day Museum Special Board of Trustees Meeting, Mar. 8, 2005.

38. Elizabeth Mullener. "Gift Paves Way for War-Themed Parade Ground—D-Day Donor Honors Uncle, His Hero," (New Orleans, LA) *Times-Picayune,* June 1, 2005.

9. HURRICANE KATRINA

1. National Weather Service, "Hurricane Katrina—August 2005," 2022, https://www.weather.gov.

2. National Weather Service, "Hurricane Katrina—August 2005."

3. Roberta Berthelot, "The Army Response to Hurricane Katrina." US Army Military History Institute / Army Heritage Education Center, Sept. 10, 2010, www.army.mil.gov.

4. Doug MacCash, "D-Day Museum Became Sanctuary for Facility Official," (New Orleans, LA) *Times-Picayune,* Sept. 15, 2005.

5. Materials of the National D-Day Museum Foundation, Inc., Board of Trustees Emergency Meeting, Nov. 10, 2005, The National WWII Museum Institutional Records and Archives. The figures presented at this board meeting were estimations of the Museum's financial state shortly after Hurricane Katrina.

6. Minutes, the National D-Day Museum Emergency Board of Trustees Meeting, Nov. 10, 2005.

7. Minutes, the National D-Day Museum Emergency Board of Trustees Meeting Nov. 10, 2005.

8. Brokaw, interview, June 1, 2022.

9. Minutes of the National D-Day Museum Foundation, Inc., Executive Committee Meeting, Oct. 12, 2005, The National WWII Museum Institutional Records and Archives. Present were Boysie Bollinger, Tim Favrot, Louise Freeman, Nick Mueller, Bobby Savoie, and David Voelker; joining via

phone were Harold Bouillion, Maj. Gen. Jim Livingston, Phil Satre, and Gov. Pete Wilson. Six staff members were there, including Vice President and Chief Operating Officer Sam Wegner.

10. Minutes, the National D-Day Museum Emergency Board Meeting, Nov. 10, 2005.

11. Minutes, the National D-Day Museum Executive Committee Meeting, Oct. 12, 2005.

12. "Tourism Status Report," the National D-Day Museum Emergency Board of Trustees Meeting, Nov. 10, 2005.

13. "Tourism Status Report," the National D-Day Museum Emergency Board of Trustees Meeting, Nov. 10, 2005.

14. Minutes, the National D-Day Museum Emergency Board of Trustees Meeting, Nov. 10, 2005. Paraphrase of Voelker's comments.

15. Materials, the National D-Day Museum Emergency Board of Trustees Meeting, Nov. 10, 2005. The direct-mail program generated this number in gross revenue between July 1 and October 27, 2005.

16. Talking Points, the National D-Day Museum Emergency Board of Trustees Meeting, Nov. 10, 2005.

17. John Porretto, "National D-Day Museum Reopens." (New Orleans, LA) *Times-Picayune,* Dec. 4, 2005.

18. Materials, the National D-Day Museum Emergency Board of Trustees Meeting, Nov. 10, 2005.

19. Minutes, the National D-Day Museum Emergency Board of Trustees Meeting, Nov. 10, 2005.

20. Materials of The National WWII Museum Foundation, Inc., Board of Trustees Meeting, Jan. 22, 2010, The National WWII Museum Institutional Records and Archives. Figures from this board meeting suggest the Museum received about 240,000 visitors total in the 12 months before Hurricane Katrina.

21. Minutes of The National WWII Museum Foundation, Inc., Board of Trustees Meeting, Jan. 13–14, 2006, The National WWII Museum Institutional Records and Archives.

22. Talking Points, The National WWII Museum Board of Trustees Meeting, Jan. 13–14, 2006. Minutes of The National WWII Museum Foundation, Inc., Executive Committee Meeting, Mar. 17, 2006, The National WWII Museum Institutional Records and Archives.

23. Boysie Bollinger, interview with the author, July 21, 2023, The National WWII Museum Institutional Records and Archives.

24. Minutes, The National WWII Museum Board of Trustees Meeting, January 13–14, 2006.

25. Bruce Eggler, "D-Day Victory—Museum Poised to Open Center," (New Orleans, LA) *Times Picayune,* Apr. 20, 2006.

26. Minutes of The National WWII Museum Foundation, Inc., Board of Trustees Meeting, June 2–3, 2006, The National WWII Museum Institutional Records and Archives.

27. Materials, The National WWII Museum Board of Trustees Meeting, June 2–3, 2006. At the June 2006 Board of Trustees Meeting, the board approved the following revisions to the Master Plan as recommended by the Recovery Task Force: "1. Lower the Theater to the ground level. 2. Lower the US Pavilion train station to the ground level and incorporate with ticketing functions to increase building efficiency. 3. Reduce volume in the Campaign Gallery." At the same meeting, the board also approved feasibility studies for a hotel and conference center, effectively combining the CSAS and hotel projects into one.

28. Gordon H. "Nick" Mueller, *Everything We Have, D-Day, 6.6.44* (London: Andre Deutsch Limited, 2019), 30.

29. Minutes of The National WWII Museum Foundation, Inc., Executive Committee Meeting, Oct. 18, 2006, The National WWII Museum Institutional Records and Archives.

30. Materials of The National WWII Museum Foundation, Inc., Board of Trustees Meeting, Jan. 26, 2007, The National WWII Museum Institutional Records and Archives. The inaugural roster of Presidential Counselors included the following: Rick Atkinson, Dr. Guenter Bischof, Lonnie Bunch, Dr. Conrad Crane, William J. Davis, Dr. Michael Divine, Dr. Paul Herbert, Daniel Hold, Dr. Cynthia Koch, Geoffrey Megargee, Dr. Donald Miller, Dr. Allan R. Millett, Dr. Mark P. Parillo, Dr. Julian M. Pleasants, Dr. Maggie Rivas-Rodriguez, Edward C. Tracy, Dr. Gerhard Weinberg, and Dr. Richard Zeitlin.

31. "Artifact Spotlight—German Heavy Water Barrel," 2012, The National WWII Museum Blog, Aug. 13, 2012, https://www.nww2m.com/2012/08/artifact-spotlight-german-heavy-water-barrel/.

32. "Local Outreach and Distance Learning Initiatives," Materials of The National WWII Museum Foundation, Inc., Board of Trustees Meeting, June 5–6, 2007, The National WWII Museum Institutional Records and Archives.

33. Materials, The National WWII Museum Board of Trustees Meeting, June 5–6, 2007.

34. Dwight Eisenhower to Milton Eisenhower, Sept. 1, 1939, letter, Eisenhower Library, Abilene, Texas.

35. The state of Louisiana increased the original appropriation from $23 million to $26 million.

36. Materials of The National WWII Museum Foundation, Inc., Board of Trustees Meeting, June 6, 2008, The National WWII Museum Institutional Records and Archives.

37. Minutes of The National WWII Museum Foundation, Inc., Board of Trustees Meeting, June 5, 2009, The National WWII Museum Institutional Records and Archives.

38. Phil Satre, email message to Jason Van, Apr. 3, 2024.

39. Mary Foster, "WWII Museum Adds Theater, Restaurant and 'Canteen,' 1st Ld-Writethru, LA," *Associated Press News Service,* Nov. 6, 2009.

40. Copy of Stephenie Ambrose-Tubbs's remarks, courtesy of Stephenie Ambrose-Tubbs.

41. "Guardsmen Honored at National WWII Museum—Grand Opening of 'Experience the Victory,'" (Crowley LA) *Post-Signal,* Nov. 9, 2009.

10. SURGING FORWARD

1. Materials of The National WWII Museum Foundation, Inc., Board of Trustees Meeting, Dec. 5–6, 2008, The National WWII Museum Institutional Records and Archives.

2. Mary Landrieu, interview with the author, Mar. 23, 2023, The National WWII Museum Institutional Records and Archives.

3. Department of Defense Appropriations Act, 2010, Publ. L. No. 111–118, Stat. 123 (2009).

4. *My Gal Sal,* National Museum of the United States Air Force, www.nationalmuseum.af.mil.

5. "The National WWII Museum Named Travelers' Choice 2013 Winner by TripAdvisor," New Orleans & Company, last updated Nov. 1, 2022, https://www.neworleans.com/articles/post/the-national-wwii-museum-named-travelers-choice-2013-winner-by-tripadvisor/.

6. Minutes of The National WWII Museum Foundation, Inc., Board of Trustees Meeting, June 9, 2012, The National WWII Museum Institutional Records and Archives.

7. This committee was a precursor to multiple future committees and task forces, such as the Hotel Task Force and the Space and Use Subcommittee, both also chaired by John Koerner. The

Space and Use Subcommittee was part of a larger structure of committees chaired by influential board members Boysie Bollinger, John Koerner, and John Georges, further discussed in chapter 11. All these committees worked to advance the hotel and conference center project, among other projects, and eventually recommended the final design of today's Higgins Hotel & Conference Center.

8. Materials, The National WWII Museum Board of Trustees Meeting, June 9, 2012. This number includes funds for the following buildings and exhibits: Campaigns of Courage, Hall of Democracy, *The Arsenal of Democracy,* Liberation Pavilion, as well as the Col. Battle Barksdale Parade Ground, the Bollinger Canopy of Peace, the Horatio Alger Association American Spirit bridge, DARS funds, the L. W. "Pete" Kent Train Car Experience, and other resources and services.

9. Minutes of The National WWII Museum Foundation, Inc., Executive Committee Meeting, May 17, 2011, The National WWII Museum Institutional Records and Archives.

10. Materials of The National WWII Museum Foundation, Inc., Board of Trustees Meeting, Dec. 10, 2011, The National WWII Museum Institutional Records and Archives.

11. Materials, The National WWII Museum Board of Trustees Meeting, Dec. 10, 2011. Strategic Planning & Revisioning Task Force Members were the following: Trustees: Herschel Abbott Jr., Chair, Robert Edsel, Paul Hilliard, Dennis Muilenburg, Dr. Nick Mueller, Rich Pattarozzi, Phil Satre, David Voelker, Gov. Pete Wilson; Museum & Education Professional: Ford Bell, American Association of Museums, Claudine Brown, Smithsonian Institution, Michael Edson, Smithsonian Institution, Gary Johnson, Chicago History Museum, Dr. Donald L. Miller, Lafayette College, Marc Pachter, Smithsonian Institution, Van Romans, Fort Worth Museum of Science & History; Consultants: Patrick Gallagher, Todd Kinser, Petr Spurney.

12. Minutes, The National WWII Museum Board of Trustees Meeting, Dec. 10, 2011. Resolution: Whereas the Museum has conducted audience research in 2008 and 2009 that identifies 34 million Americans interested in the Museum's mission, and whereas these audiences expressed a strong desire for access to digital content and online learning experiences, and whereas the Museum's strategic vision strives to provide access to worldwide audiences, and whereas the Strategic Planning & Revisioning Task Force strongly supports the concept of the Digital Archive Research Services (DARS), and whereas the Education and Collections Committee and the Executive Committee strongly support of the full implementation of the Museum's digitization project and urge the Board of Trustees to make it a strategic priority to secure the necessary funding, and the Board directs staff to look for ways to fund and budget the DARS program. MOTION to accept the Resolution made by Hayes, seconded by Bouillion, unanimously approved.

13. Mueller and Schick. *Building The National WWII Museum,* 45.

14. There are several historians who present contested memories of the "good war" from different perspectives. A few of these are the following: Keith Lowe, *Savage Continent: Europe in the Aftermath of WWII;* Kenneth Rose, *Myth and the Greatest Generation: A Social History of Americans in WWII;* Michael C. C. Adams, *The Best War Ever: America and WWII;* Elizabeth D. Samet, *Looking for the Good War: American Amnesia and the Violent Pursuit of Happiness;* John Bodnar, *The "Good War" in American Memory.*

15. Stephan Jaeger, *The Second World War in the Twenty-First Century Museum: From Narrative, Memory, and Experience to Experientiality* (Berlin: De Gruyter, 2021), 103.

16. Gerhard L. Weinberg, *Visions of Victory: The Hopes of Eight World War II Leaders* (Cambridge, England: Cambridge University Press, 2005).

17. John Steinbeck, *Once There Was a War* (London: Penguin Books, 2001), 126.

18. The following subsection references artifacts, installations, scripts, and oral histories found in The Duchossois Family *Road to Berlin: European Theater Galleries.* The information found in the exhibit was a product of historical research from Gallagher & Associates, historian consultant Donald L. Miller, and Museum historians and curators.

19. Donald L. Miller, *The Story of World War II* (New York: Touchstone, 2001), 279.

20. John "J J" Witmeyer interview, OH.2861, The National WWII Museum.

21. Donald L. Miller, interview with the author, Sept. 14, 2023, The National WWII Museum Institutional Records and Archives.

22. Phone conversation between Maj. Gen. John C. Raaen Jr. and the author, Dec. 25, 2023.

23. Miller, *The Story of World War II,* 359.

24. Craig Nelson, *Pearl Harbor: From Infamy to Greatness* (Oxford, England: Weidenfeld and Nicolson, 2018), 333.

25. Franklin D. Roosevelt *Speech by Franklin D. Roosevelt, New York Transcript.* 1941. Pdf. https://www.loc.gov/item/afcca1000483/.

26. The following subsection references artifacts, installations, scripts, and oral histories found in Richard C. Adkerson & Freeport-McMoRan Foundation *Road to Tokyo: Pacific Theater Galleries.* The information found in the gallery was a product of historical research from Gallagher & Associates, historian consultant Richard B. Frank, and Museum historians and curators.

27. Richard Greer interview, OH.0944, The National WWII Museum.

28. Richard Frank, *Downfall: The End of the Imperial Japanese Empire* (London: Penguin Publishing Group, 2001), 118.

29. Gen. Douglas MacArthur, read aboard the USS *Missouri* (BB-63), Tokyo Bay, inscribed on Sept. 2, 1945.

30. "The GI." In *"Yank," The GI Story of the War,* by the staff of Yank, *Army Weekly,* ed. Debs Meyers, Johnathan Kilbourn, and Richard Harrity (New York: Duell, Sloan and Pearce, 1947), 11, as cited in Miller, *The Story of World War II,* 16.

31. Miller, *The Story of World War II,* 16.

32. Stephen E. Ambrose, *To America: Personal Reflections of an Historian* (New York: Simon & Schuster, 2002), 120.

33. Ambrose, *To America,* 94.

34. The following subsection references artifacts, installations, scripts, and oral histories found in *The Arsenal of Democracy: The Herman and George R. Brown Salute to the Home Front.* The information found in the gallery was a product of historical research from Gallagher & Associates, historian consultant Lynne Olson, and Museum historians and curators.

35. Franklin D. Roosevelt, "Fireside Chat on National Defense," Dec. 29, 1940, National Archives.

36. Roosevelt, "Fireside Chat."

37. Roosevelt, "Fireside Chat."

38. Roosevelt, "Fireside Chat."

39. "Executive Order 9066: Resulting in Japanese American Incarceration (1943)," National Archives, last modified Jan. 24, 2022, www.archives.gov/.

40. Norman Mineta interview, OH.4520, The National WWII Museum.

41. "About the Founder," The National WWII Museum, New Orleans, http://enroll.nationalww2museum.org/about-the-museum/about-the-founder.html.

11. PUSHING THE BOUNDARIES OF THE MUSEUM

1. "Eisenhower's Recording," Monuments Men and Women Foundation, https://www.monumentsmenandwomenfnd.org/discoveries-and-restitutions/eisenhower-s-recording.

2. Minutes of The National WWII Museum Foundation, Inc., Board of Trustees Meeting, June 5, 2010. The National WWII Museum Institutional Records and Archives.

3. Minutes of The National WWII Museum Foundation, Inc., Board of Trustees Meeting, June 3, 2011, The National WWII Museum Institutional Records and Archives.

4. Minutes, The National WWII Museum Board of Trustees Meeting, June 9, 2012.

5. Materials, The National WWII Museum Board of Trustees Meeting, Dec. 5–8, 2008.

6. Materials of The National WWII Museum Foundation, Inc., Board of Trustees Meeting, Jan. 22, 2010, The National WWII Museum Institutional Records and Archives.

7. Minutes of The National WWII Museum Foundation, Inc., Annual Meeting of the Board of Trustees, June 13, 2013, The National WWII Museum Institutional Records and Archives.

8. Minutes of The National WWII Museum Foundation, Inc., Board of Trustees Meeting, May 16, 2014, The National WWII Museum Institutional Records and Archives.

9. *2016 Annual Report,* The National WWII Museum, 32.

10. Minutes of The National WWII Museum Foundation, Inc., Semi-Annual Board of Trustees Meeting, June 12, 2015, The National WWII Museum Institutional Records and Archives.

11. Materials of The National WWII Museum Foundation, Inc., Annual Board of Trustees Meeting, June 11, 2015, The National WWII Museum Institutional Records and Archives.

12. Minutes of The National WWII Museum, Inc., Semi-Annual Board of Trustees Meeting, June 9, 2017, The National WWII Museum Institutional Records and Archives.

13. Materials of The National WWII Museum, Inc., Board of Trustees Meeting, Dec. 3, 2010, The National WWII Museum Institutional Records and Archives.

14. Grego Trumel, letter to the author, Oct. 1, 2015.

15. John Pope, "World War II Museum Director to Get France's Highest Honor—Hanks, Brokaw Also Will Be Named Chevaliers of the Legion of Honor," (New Orleans) *Times-Picayune,* May 13, 2016.

16. Also in attendance were Mike and Jan Marrington, Malcolm and Pia Ehrhardt, Norma Grace, Bob Sternhell, and Donald and Rose Miller.

17. Gordon H. "Nick" Mueller, Legion of Honor acceptance speech, The Grand Chancellery, Paris, May 20, 2016.

18. Minutes of The National WWII Museum Foundation, Inc., Annual Board of Trustees Meeting, June 9, 2016, The National WWII Museum Institutional Records and Archives.

19. Minutes of The National WWII Museum Foundation, Inc., Semi-Annual Board of Trustees Meeting, June 10, 2016. The National WWII Museum Institutional Records and Archives.

20. Materials, The National WWII Museum Semi-Annual Board of Trustees Meeting, June 10, 2016. The members of the committee were the following: Ian Buruma, Dr. James Sparrow, Dr. Jeremi Suri, Gen. Montgomery Meigs, Sarah Ogilvie, Renata Stih, Dr. Frieder Schnock, Dr. Mark Stoler, Kurt Haunfelner, Dr. John Morrow, Dr. Mark P. Lagon, Marc Pachter, Phil Hettema, and Patrick Gallagher.

21. Minutes of The National WWII Museum Foundation, Inc., Semi-Annual Board of Trustees Meeting, Jan. 26, 2017, The National WWII Museum Institutional Records and Archives.

22. Minutes of The National WWII Museum Foundation, Inc., Semi-Annual Board of Trustees Meeting, Jan. 25, 2017, The National WWII Museum Institutional Records and Archives. The following paragraphs utilize remarks and reports made at this meeting.

23. Hotel revenue was intended to increase the Museum's endowment. The endowment directly supports the Museum's educational and social aspects of the mission through the funding of student scholarships, special exhibitions, and fellowships.

24. "Remembering WWII Veteran Ralph Crump," The National WWII Museum, Mar. 31, 2020, https://www.nationalww2museum.org.

25. The National WWII Museum, New Orleans, "Gary Sinise Foundation and The National WWII Museum Partner to Honor the Greatest Generation," press release, June 24, 2015.

26. The National WWII Museum, "Gary Sinise Foundation and the National WWII Museum," 2015.

27. *2017 Annual Report,* The National WWII Museum.

28. Minutes of The National WWII Museum Foundation, Inc., Executive Committee Meeting, Nov. 15, 2017, The National WWII Museum Institutional Records and Archives.

29. "Capital Campaign Progress Report (2002–Present) Goal—$400 Million," Materials of The National WWII Museum Foundation Inc., Board of Trustees Meeting, June 9, 2017, The National WWII Museum Institutional Records and Archives.

30. "Donor Spotlight: Pam and Mark Rubin," The National WWII Museum, https://www.nationalww2museum.org.

31. Chad Calder, "'Immersive' Theater to Crown WW2 Museum's New Liberation Pavilion," (New Orleans) *Times Picayune,* Feb. 15, 2022.

32. *Annual Report 2021,* The National WWII Museum, 17. In 2021 alone, the Museum published 289 historical articles on its website, along with 116 virtual presentations and 253,678 hours of WWII content on YouTube.

33. *Annual Report 2021,* 28.

12. LIBERATION

1. William Faulkner, *Requiem for a Nun* (New York: Random House, 1951), 73.

2. The National WWII Museum, "Building the National WWII Museum: From Conception to Capstone," YouTube video, 3:57:28, Nov. 30, 2023.

3. The National WWII Museum, "Building the National WWII Museum."

4. These comments would be Marc's final remarks on the Museum as he sadly passed away just weeks later.

5. "World War II Museum Liberation Pavilion Grand Opening," C-SPAN video, Nov. 3, 2023.

6. "World War II Museum Liberation Pavilion Grand Opening."

7. "World War II Museum Liberation Pavilion Grand Opening."

8. The following subsections reference artifacts, installations, scripts, and oral histories found in the Liberation Pavilion. Much of the language in these subsections is taken from the planning documents, scripts, and text panels of the Liberation Pavilion that were developed over many years. These texts were authored by many from the Museum's staff, including Dr. Rob Citino, Dr. Stephanie Hinnershitz, Dr. Michael S. Bell, the author, and many others, together with Donna Lawrence Productions script writers. They were reviewed with commentary by Stephen Watson and Patrick Gallagher.

9. Funding came from the Trott Family Philanthropies. David Trott, who also supported the Museum in building the Horatio Alger Association American Spirit Bridge, was the major donor for the first floor of the Liberation Pavilion.

10. "The Holocaust," The National WWII Museum, https://www.nationalww2museum.org/war/articles/holocaust.

11. Part of German theologian Martin Niemöller's famous poem is displayed at the entry into the Anne Frank exhibit.

12. Edited first-person accounts and quotes from the Liberation Theater, sourced from the Museum's oral history and the USC Shoah Foundation collections.

13. The four chaplains were Father John Washington, a Catholic priest, Rabbi Alexander Goode, Rev. George Fox, a Methodist minister, and Rev. Clark Poling, Reformed Church in America pastor.

14. The Goldring Family Foundation and the Woldenberg Foundation provided $7 million to build the second floor of the pavilion.

15. Adam Kirsch, "What's Really at Stake in America's History Wars?" *Wall Street Journal*, Feb. 12–13, 2022.

16. Kirsch, "What's Really at Stake."

17. Ohchr—Universal Declaration of Human Rights, ohchr.org.

18. The following quotations in this and the following subsection are extracts from the scripts of the media piece in the Fight for Freedom and Freedom Theater exhibits.

19. The Priddy Foundation gave the Museum a generous gift to support the creation of the third floor and the Freedom Theater.

20. Mark Yost, "Liberation Pavilion Review: The American Pursuit of Peace," *Wall Street Journal*, Nov. 15, 2023.

21. "Road to Victory Celebration," video, Nov. 2, 2023, 2:00:03, The National WWII Museum Institutional Records and Archives.

22. "Road to Victory Celebration,"

23. "Road to Victory Celebration."

24. "Road to Victory Celebration."

25. "Road to Victory Celebration."

REFLECTIONS

1. These words, which the author has used more than once to describe this great global conflict, are etched on the monument honoring Steve Ambrose and me in Founders Plaza.

2. Ronald Reagan, "Jan. 5, 1967: Inaugural Address (Public Ceremony)," Ronald Reagan Presidential Library & Museum.

BIBLIOGRAPHY

All primary sources, including board documents, speeches, oral histories, and correspondence, are located at The National WWII Museum Institutional Records and Archives unless otherwise stated in the endnotes.

PRIMARY SOURCE DOCUMENTS

Articles of Incorporation of the National D-Day Museum Foundation, Inc.

Board of Directors Meeting Minutes, The National D-Day Museum Foundation.

Board of Trustees Meeting Minutes, The National WWII Museum, Inc.

Business Plan for The National D-Day Museum, July 1, 1999–June 30, 2000.

Department of Defense Appropriations Act, 1992.

Department of Defense Appropriations Act, 2001.

Department of Defense Appropriations Act, 2004.

Department of Defense Appropriations Act, 2010.

Department of Defense and Emergency Supplemental for Recovery from and Response to Terrorist Attacks on the United States Act, 2000.

Eisenhower Center for American Studies Board Meeting Minutes.

Executive Committee Meeting Minutes, The National D-Day Museum Foundation.

Executive Committee Meeting Minutes, The National WWII Museum, Inc.

LORD Cultural Resources Planning and Management, Proposal for Master Planning Services.

The National WWII Museum *Annual Report,* 2016.

The National WWII Museum *Annual Report,* 2017.

The National WWII Museum *Annual Report,* 2021.

Presidential Executive Order 9066.

SPEECHES

Ambrose-Tubbs, Stephenie. Stephen Ambrose memorial speech, 2002.
Bel Edwards, Gov. John. Grand Opening for the Liberation Pavilion speech, 2023.
Bollinger, Boysie. Road to Victory Celebration speech, 2023.
Citino, Rob. Grand Opening for the Liberation Pavilion speech, 2023.
Clinton, William J. "A Tribute to Those Who Fell at Normandy," 1994.
Eisenhower, Dwight D. Monuments Men Commendation speech, 1948.
Hanks, Tom. Grand Opening for the Liberation Pavilion speech, 2023.
Reagan, Ronald. "Inaugural Address" speech, 1967.
Roosevelt, Franklin D. "Day of Infamy" speech, 1941.
———. "Fireside Chat on National Defense," 1940.
———. State of the Union Address, 1941.
Mueller, Nick. Legion of Honor acceptance speech, 2017.
———. Road to Victory Celebration speech, 2023.
Watson, Stephen J. Road to Victory Celebration speech, 2023.

CORRESPONDENCE

Ambrose, Stephen. Letter to Associated General Contractors.
Eisenhower, Dwight D. Letter to Milton Eisenhower, 1939.
Foss, Joe. Letter to Stephen Ambrose.
Gootee, Elaine T. Letter to Stephen Ambrose.
Guggenheim, Charles. Letter to Jack Masey, 1993.
Livingston, Maj. Gen. James E. Letter to Stephen Ambrose.
Jones, Kathi. Letter to Board Members of the D-Day Museum, 1991.
Mize, Gen. David. Email to Nick Mueller, 2023.
O'Brien, Gregory. Letters to the Board of Directors, 1993.
Satre, Phil. Email to Jason Van, 2024.
Raaen, Maj. Gen. John C., Jr. Conversation with Nick Mueller, 2023.
Trumel, Grego. Letter to Nick Mueller, 2015.

ARCHIVES

Library of Congress
The National WWII Museum Institutional Records and Archives.
The Stephen and Hugh Ambrose Collection.
The Stephen and Moira Ambrose Collection.
The UNO Eisenhower Center Collection, Peter Kalikow World War II Era Collections.
The USC Shoah Foundation Collection.

INSTITUTIONAL ORAL HISTORIES

The following oral histories can be found within The National WWII Museum Institutional Records and Archives.

Ronnie Aboud
Gaston Andre
Günter Bischof
Boysie Bollinger
Ann Allston Boyce
Tom Brokaw
Paul Cambon
Jay Dardenne
Jimmy Duckworth
Joyce Dunn
Bill Detweiler
Richard B. Frank
Pat Gootee
Robert Hayes
Bob Howson
John Kelly
Sen. Mary Landrieu
Anne Skorecki Levy
Maj. Gen. James Livingston
Rep. Robert Livingston
Pio Lyons
Donald L. Miller
Gregory O'Brien
Karen Reisch
Phil Satre
Lee Schlesinger
Frank Stewart
Bart Voorsanger
Stephen J. Watson
Liz Williams
Gov. Pete Wilson
Robert Wolf

VETERAN ORAL HISTORIES

Hal Baumgarten
Walt Ehlers
Richard Greer
Norman Mineta
Allen Stephens
J J Whitmeyer

SECONDARY SOURCES

Ambrose, Stephen E. *Citizen Soldiers: U.S. Army from the Normandy Beaches to the Bulge, to the Surrender of Germany, June 7, 1944 to May 7, 1945*. New York: Pocket Books, 1999.

———. *Comrades: Brothers, Fathers, Heroes, Sons, Pals.* New York: Simon & Schuster, 2000.

———. *D-Day; June 6, 1944: The Climactic Battle of WWII.* Simon & Schuster, 2009.

———. *Eisenhower Volume I: Soldier, General of the Army, President-Elect, 1890–1952.* Simon & Schuster, 1982.

———. *Eisenhower Volume II: The President.* Simon & Schuster, 1983.

———. *The Wisdom of Dwight D. Eisenhower: Quotations from Ike's Speeches & Writings, 1939–1969.* New Orleans: Eisenhower Center for American Studies, 1990.

———. *To America: Personal Reflections of an Historian.* London, England: Simon & Schuster International, 2004.

Bacque, James. *Crimes and Mercies: The Fate of German Civilians under Allied Occupation, 1944–1950.* Talonbooks, 2013.

———. *Other Losses: An Investigation into the Mass Deaths of German Prisoners at the Hands of the French and Americans after World War II.* 2nd ed. H B Fenn, 2008.

Bischof, Guenter, Stephen E. Ambrose, and University of New Orleans. *The Crusade.* New Orleans: Eisenhower Center for American Studies, 1990.

Churchill, Winston. *The End of the Beginning: War Speeches,* London: Cassell and Company, 1943.

Faulkner, William. *Requiem for a Nun.* New York: Random House, 1951.

Frank, Richard B. *Downfall: The End of the Imperial Japanese Empire.* London, England: Penguin, 2001.

Holmes, Oliver Wendell. *The Autocrat of the Breakfast Table: Every Man His Own Boswell* (New York: F. M. Lupton, 1858), 278.

Jaeger, Stephan. *The Second World War in the Twenty-First-Century Museum: From Narrative, Memory, and Experience to Experientiality.* Berlin, Germany: De Gruyter, 2022.

Meyers, Debs, Jonathan Kilbourne, and Richard Harrity. *Yank: The GI Story of the War.* New York: Duell, Sloan & Pearce, 1947.

Miller, Donald L. The *Story of World War II.* New York: Simon & Schuster, 2002.

Mueller, Gordon H. "Nick." *"Everything We Have," D-Day, 6.6.44.* London, England: Andre Deutsch, 2018.

Mueller, Gordon H. "Nick," and Kali Martin Schick. *Building The National WWII Museum.* Baton Rouge: Louisiana State University Press, 2023.

Nelson, Craig. *Pearl Harbor: From Infamy to Greatness.* Oxford, England: Weidenfeld & Nicolson, 2018.

Steinbeck, John. *Once There Was a War.* London, England: Penguin, 2001.

Toll, Ian W. *Twilight of the Gods: War in the Western Pacific, 1944–1945.* New York: Norton, 2021.

Weinberg, Gerhard L. *Visions of Victory: The Hopes of Eight World War II Leaders,* Cambridge, England: Cambridge University Press, 2005.

Wilt, Alan F., and Stephen E. Ambrose. "D-Day June 6, 1944: The Climactic Battle of World War II." *American Historical Review* 100, no. 3 (1995): 872

NEWSPAPERS

The Advocate (Baton Rouge, LA)
Associated Press News Service
Crowley Post-Signal
Daily Advertiser (Lafayette, LA)
Daily Colonist (Victoria, British Columbia)
New York Times
Sun Herald (Biloxi, MS)
Times-Picayune (New Orleans, LA)
Wall Street Journal
Washington Examiner
Washington Post

MEDIA RELEASES

"Building the National WWII Museum: From Conception to Capstone," YouTube
"Conversations with Veterans of D-Day" C-SPAN.
"Gary Sinise Foundation and The National WWII Museum Partner to Honor the Greatest Generation," press release, June 24, 2015.
"Invasion in the Pacific Exhibit" Grand Opening, DVD.
"The National D-Day Museum Grand Opening," DVD.
"Opening of the D-Day Museum," C-SPAN.
"Road to Victory Celebration," The National WWII Museum.
"Stephen Ambrose's Last Book," CBS News.
"Stephen Ambrose Memorial Service," C-SPAN,
"World War II Museum Liberation Pavilion Grand Opening" C-SPAN.

WEBSITES

https://www.army.mil/article/45029/the_army_response_to_hurricane_katrina
https://www.garysinisefoundation.org/
https://www.nationalmuseum.af.mil/Visit/Museum-Exhibits/Fact-Sheets/Display/Article/196693/my-gal-sal/
www.nationalww2museum.org
www.nww2m.com
https://www.neworleans.com/articles/post/the-national-wwii-museum-named-travelers-choice-2013-winner-by-tripadvisor/
https://postalmuseum.si.edu/collections/object-spotlight/railway-mail-crane
https://www.ohchr.org/en/ohchr_homepage
https://www.weather.gov/mob/katrina
https://winstonchurchill.org/resources/speeches/1940-the-finest-hour/their-finest-hour/

INDEX